Understanding
Psychological Science

Understanding
Psychological Science

JANET L. JONES

Fort Lewis College

HarperCollins*CollegePublishers*

ACQUISITIONS EDITOR: Catherine Woods
PROJECT COORDINATION: Ruttle, Shaw & Wetherill, Inc.
TEXT DESIGNER: Nancy Sabato
COVER DESIGNER: Kay Petronio
PHOTO RESEARCHER: Sandy Schneider
ELECTRONIC PRODUCTION MANAGER: Valerie A. Sawyer
DESKTOP ADMINISTRATOR: Hilda Koparanian
MANUFACTURING MANAGER: Helene G. Landers
ELECTRONIC PAGE MAKEUP: RR Donnelley Barbados
PRINTER AND BINDER: RR Donnelley & Sons Company
COVER PRINTER: RR Donnelley & Sons Company

PHOTO CREDITS: Chapter 1: Janet L. Jones; Chapter 2: William Thompson/The Picture Cube; Chapter 3: AP/Wide World Photos; Chapter 4: The Dian Fossey Gorilla Fund; Chapter 5: Jean-Claude Lejeune/Stock, Boston; Chapter 6: Jon Feingersh/The Stock Market; Chapter 7: Courtesy of AT&T Archives; Chapter 8: Courtesy of Wilson Bryan Key; Chapter 9: John Henley/The Stock Market; Chapter 10: © 1992, Newsweek, Inc. All rights reserved. Reprinted by permission; and, Chapter 11: Copyright 1965 by Stanley Milgram. From the film *Obedience*, distributed by Penn State Audio-Visual Services.

For permission to use copyrighted material, grateful acknowledgment is made to the copyright holders on pp. 341–342, which are hereby made part of this copyright page.

Understanding Psychological Science

Library of Congress Cataloging-in-Publication Data

Jones, Janet L.
    Understanding psychological science / Janet L. Jones.
        p. cm.
    Includes bibliographical references.
    ISBN 0-06-501459-6
    1. Psychology—Research—Methodology.   I. Title.
BF76.5.J66 1995
150'.72—dc20   94-8456
                                                          CIP

95 96 97 9 8 7 6 5 4 3 2

Brief Contents

Detailed Contents

CHAPTER 4: NONEXPERIMENTAL RESEARCH • 75

CHAPTER 5: CORRELATIONAL RESEARCH • 103

CHAPTER 8: DESIGN VALIDITY • 181

Preface

This book has been written with one central goal in mind: to write a clear explanation of research methods that will spark the interest of typical college sophomores without sacrificing rigor. A detailed analysis of classroom successes and failures uncovered three requirements that would have to be fulfilled in order to achieve that goal. First, students enjoy and remember research examples that they find intriguing. Second, students want a book written in language that they can read and understand. Third, students want to know why they should bother learning about research methods in the first place.

The numerous examples used throughout this book are real research studies collected from a wide spectrum of psychological science. By selecting a broad assortment of examples, I hope to give readers an idea of the versatility of standard research methods. In addition, the examples allow readers to apply abstract principles in a variety of concrete ways, and they appeal to the specific psychological interests of a large number of people. Most of these examples ignited a natural curiosity in students who read early drafts of this book.

The book is also written in a style that students can understand. Research methodology is difficult enough without adding a litany of polysyllabic words into the bargain. Therefore, I have used plain language and a personal, conversational style in each chapter. Of 92 students who submitted written comments concerning draft versions of this book, 81 reported that one of its greatest strengths is its appealing and readable language.

Finally, the book emphasizes a reason for understanding scientific research that is often ignored in standard methods courses. People today need to understand research methods not because they will become scientists themselves, but because they are bombarded with research reports each time they turn on the television or pick up a newspaper. We live in an age when each of us must know a few basic facts about scientific research to make sense of our lives and our culture. In my own courses, this emphasis on each student's role as a responsible consumer of research really hits home. Accordingly, the book points out the need for critical evaluation of scientific research, then shows students how to develop the required skills.

I am indebted to many colleagues, mentors, and students for their help with this project. Hal Mansfield and Roger Peters of Fort Lewis College, and Elizabeth Bjork of UCLA, all encouraged me to write the book. Catherine Woods of Harper-Collins gave me the opportunity to try, then supported my efforts firmly.   Colleagues from many departments at Fort Lewis College generated the sense of camaraderie that bolstered my spirits during the arduous process of textbook creation.

Thirteen technical reviewers provided outstanding critiques of the first draft, generously pointing out errors and ambiguities in my work: L. E. Banderet, Northeastern University; Elizabeth L. Bjork, University of California, Los Angeles; Kelly A. Brennan, University of Texas, Austin; Beverly R. Chew, Fort Lewis College; Susan E. Dutch, Westfield State College; William F. Ford, Bucks County Community College; Hal Mansfield, Fort Lewis College; Carol S. Perrino, Morgan State University; Patricia L. Phillips, Illinois State University; Dale E. Schwartzenstruber, Ohio Wesleyan University; Paul E. Spector, University of South Florida; Valerie Stratton, Pennsylvania State University, Altoona Campus; and Bradley M. Waite, Central Connecticut State University. In addition, Gerry Jones and Leslie Jones critiqued the book from an amateur perspective, catching anomalies that we specialists had missed. Several scientists whose research is presented in the book (Paul Ekman, Madeline Heilman, Robert Levenson, and Harold Stevenson) dug through old data files to locate statistical values that allowed me to achieve a degree of research realism that is seldom seen in methods texts. Marcie Draheim, an undergraduate at Fort Lewis College, read rough drafts of each chapter so that a student's opinion would inform even the earliest stages of writing. I appreciate her honesty in pointing out passages that would put students to sleep and criticizing the boring examples that my middle-aged brain found fascinating. Another student, Jennifer Liese-Miller, helped to create the book's indexes and worked on portions of the Instructor's Manual and Testbank. All of these people have helped me to improve the book, but remaining errors are mine alone.

A special note of thanks goes to the professors who were most instrumental in contributing to my own knowledge of research methods. Bill Banks, of Pomona College, introduced me to the fun of science through his energetic devotion to lab experiments. He also gave me the chance to learn about research by employing me to help his students design independent projects and to critique several hundred of their research reports over the years. Elizabeth Bjork, of UCLA, invited me to join the cooperative effort of "Psych 42," an exemplary research methods course that she coordinates. My skills at teaching research methods were sharp-ened through experiences with the many professors, graduate teaching assistants, and students connected with that course. Tom Wickens, of UCLA, showed me how to apply the abstract principles of research to advanced projects of my own de-sign and offered his unflagging intellectual support. In addition, his sharp eye to-ward precise wording compelled me to pay close attention to language—a lesson of which I was reminded repeatedly while writing this book.

Most helpful of all has been the inspiration and encouragement I receive every day from my father and my husband. My father has been urging me to write a book for nearly 35 years now, with the absolute confidence in a daughter's abilities that only a father can maintain. My husband has provided me with every opportunity to write without distraction, even when it meant personal hardship for him. Both of them take as much pride in my accomplishments as in their own, so I only hope that this project will live up to their expectations. With deepest gratitude, I dedicate this book to them.

Janet L. Jones

Understanding
Psychological Science

1

Science

A snapshot of the author's research methods class of April 1994.

Welcome to your first course in research methods. You're not alone: Psychology majors at most schools are required to complete this rite of passage as a prerequisite for upper-division courses, and many students report that they enrolled in research methods strictly because it was required. However, by the end of the term, those same students often admit with surprise that they actually enjoyed the course and learned something that they consider valuable for everyday living. Here's hoping that your experience will be as successful as theirs!

SCIENCE AS DISCOVERY

Research methods are really just ways of discovering and evaluating new information. You are probably most familiar with **library research,** in which known, published information is found in library sources like books and magazines. **Scientific research,** on the other hand, is used when we need to gather new information, to discover facts that are not yet known. The skills you learn in this course can be applied to both scientific and library research.

Often, library and scientific research are combined to help us understand the deeper layers of events going on around us. You may recall, for example, the 1992 riots that occurred in Los Angeles after four police officers were found not guilty of using excessive force while attempting to arrest a black citizen named Rodney King. Many people had seen videotaped portions of the beating on national television and therefore questioned the verdict. The subsequent riots were considered by some reporters to be "the worst in the United States [in] this century" (Anderson, 1992, p. 10). By the time peace was restored to Los Angeles, more than 50 people had been killed, about 2,400 had been injured, and more than 16,000 had been arrested. Angry citizens started thousands of fires in their own neighborhoods and stole merchandise from local shops, with damages reaching an estimated $785 million (Bowles, 1992).

Now here is an incident that any psychologist worthy of the name would find interesting. What went wrong? What are the forces that pushed these people to such destructive criminal behavior? Most Americans assumed that the riots were caused directly by outrage at the King verdict. Undoubtedly, many rioters were angry at the acquittal of a group of police officers who had beaten an American citizen.

However, the true causes of the Los Angeles riots of 1992 may have been more complex than many of us first believed (Whitman, 1993). For example, the looting began in liquor stores, where free-flowing liquor may have loosened up long-simmering racial hostilities. The rioting began and continued for several hours before the occurrence of any protest signs or chants concerning Rodney King. Latinos played a stronger role in the riots than did blacks, and the greatest damage was done to stores owned by Korean merchants. Black police officers were treated more harshly than whites during the chaos. None of these facts fit with the simple conclusion that the riots were perpetuated solely by indignant citizens protesting the Rodney King verdict.

If you wanted to understand what really happened during the Los Angeles riots, both library research and scientific research would have been needed. Library research would have provided important background information in the form of theories concerning mob behavior, criminal activity, and racial hostility. Published accounts of previous public disturbances would have allowed comparisons that might provoke new insights about the event. Even the speculations and opinions offered in newspaper stories published during the riots would help you to form ideas.

To identify the underlying psychological and social causes of such widespread destruction, scientific research also would have been needed. Let's consider a few relevant questions that might be answered by scientific research, based on information gained through library research:

1. What role do liquor stores play in undermining civil obedience? This question may sound trivial until you learn that the neighborhood of South Central Los Angeles alone contained 728 liquor stores in 1992, with a greater number of those stores selling hard liquor than is found in 13 entire states combined (Whitman, 1993). The local liquor store in poor neighborhoods doubles as a bank and grocery store for many citizens, so it is a central meeting place that is visited frequently.

2. In what ways do television and news media influence the opinions of the general public? A 20-second portion of the videotape showing King's beating was broadcast repeatedly over national television for months preceding the police officers' trial. After seeing such brief news clips so frequently, are most people able to view remaining evidence objectively when making a decision?

3. Why did the police abandon the streets when the riots began, despite their pledges to "serve and protect" the innocent people on those streets? For the first 3 hours of the riots, Los Angeles police ignored numerous 911 calls for help and failed to take any crowd-control measures that might have curtailed the ensuing mayhem (Whitman, 1993). Does this sort of desertion encourage rioters to step up their destructive activities?

4. Are racial hostilities exaggerated by minor degrees of success among residents of disadvantaged neighborhoods? The Los Angeles riots began in a relatively successful area of the black community, not in the slums and ghettoes of the inner city. In addition, Koreans owned many of the liquor stores that served black and Latino neighborhoods, a form of success that may have increased animosity among the three cultures (Whitman, 1993).

The scientific research needed to answer these questions might involve asking the rioters themselves why they behaved as they did. It might include designing an experiment that would show the conditions under which racial hostilities are curbed or enhanced. It might require studying the influence of brief visual news clips on public understanding of complex events. I'm sure you can think of many other possibilities. The point is that both library research and scientific research are needed to understand and verify the causes of human behavior.

SCIENCE AS EVALUATION

Scientific research, as we have seen, helps us to discover new information. Although this feature of science is very important, the need to design and conduct research studies for discovery is usually limited to people in scientific occupations. However, learning about scientific research has an added advantage that fits everyone's needs: It teaches you how to evaluate the research you read and hear about every day. In today's world, critical evaluation is vital.

It's hard enough to find, read, and understand new information—but now we have to evaluate it, too? If you doubt that psychological research is being sold to an uninformed public, just take a look at today's paper. We are flooded with new reports of psychological science coming in from all directions. Some of these reports are socially important and scientifically valid; others are not. Unfortunately, many people can't tell the difference because they've had no training in research methods. The process of critical evaluation helps us to sift through all this information, so that we may make intelligent decisions on a solid base of knowledge. Let's look more closely at the reasons for critical evaluation in today's world.

The Information Explosion

The amount of new knowledge available to the average person has increased rapidly in recent years. For example, the number of new books published in the United States increased by 24% each year from 1980 to 1987. During that same period, the number of new books imported from other countries into the United States rose by 34% (U.S. Bureau of the Census, 1990). In 1992, 11,339 newspapers were published regularly, and 11,143 magazines were issued (U.S. Bureau of the Census, 1992). That alone represents a lot of information vying for our attention . . . and we haven't even considered the scientific literature yet.

About 40,000 scientific journals are published worldwide every year, each containing enough articles to produce a total of 1,000,000 new scientific reports annually (Henderson, 1990). This is the equivalent of nearly 3000 new articles per day! Figure 1.1 gives you some idea of the ultimate effect of today's information explosion, which Naisbitt (1984) considered one of the ten most important trends of the 20th century. The sheer number of magazines, books, newspapers, news programs, feature films, and television documentaries available to us nowadays means that we must select information wisely.

Accuracy

You've probably already learned, somewhere along the way, that it's dangerous to believe everything you hear or read, regardless of the source. The fact that

Figure 1.1
Buried Under Information

Oprah Winfrey or Connie Chung or even the President of the United States says that something is true doesn't mean that you should believe it. Similarly, the fact that a nonfiction book has been published by a best-selling author does not guarantee that every word in that book is true. Even textbooks can be wrong.

There are several reasons for the fact that inaccurate information sometimes turns up:

1. *Humans make mistakes.* It isn't that Oprah or Connie try to mislead us with false information. To the contrary, most reputable providers of knowledge take great pains to be accurate. Occasionally, no matter how hard we try, we are not successful.

2. *The media misinterprets scientific conclusions.* Unfortunately, few magazine writers and news reporters have been trained in the methods of scientific research. However, this does not stop them from acquiring copies of scientific articles from their local libraries and attempting to simplify that research for us in a brief article. We'll see several examples of media misinterpretation throughout this book.

3. *Most well-trained researchers write for specialized, professional audiences.* That's why our first experiences with scientific journal articles are usually so miserable. The articles seem full of jargon and are difficult to understand. Very few scientists take the responsibility of presenting their own research to the public. Instead, they rely on writers and reporters who have no scientific training.

4. *Some research studies are flawed.* Scientists are human, so they make mistakes, too. Sometimes the explanation of a study is clear and accurate, but the re-

search itself contains flaws. When you start designing and conducting your own research projects as part of this course, you'll find that it's a complicated task with plenty of room for error.

5. *Knowledge changes.* Until the 1400s, experts and common folk alike believed with certainty that the earth was flat (Loye, 1983). Even a technically flawless piece of research, conducted by an infallible human and explained with shining clarity by both specialist and generalist, is still subject to change.

Critical Evaluation in Daily Life

Psychologists and other scientists must remain skeptical about new information in order to critique existing research and develop new ideas for future studies. You will learn the value of adopting this attitude as well in order to conduct successful research studies that are based on a thorough understanding of the published literature in your area of interest. What I'm saying is simply that every good researcher must develop excellent skills in critical evaluation.

But let's face the fact that some of you, perhaps many of you, don't plan to become researchers. After all, 85% of psychology majors never become psychologists (Keith-Spiegel, 1990). Instead, they use the skills that psychology has taught them to succeed in the occupational world of their choice, whether it's medicine, law, business, carpentry, child-raising, or truck-driving. The need to develop a critical style of evaluating new knowledge is equally important for all of us, regardless of our future aspirations. To provide only a few examples, intelligent people evaluate information critically when they vote, buy groceries, care for elderly parents, and select an employer. Along with your college education comes the responsibility to learn, to lead, to question, and to think—and the skills of critical evaluation that you learn through this course will help you to succeed in those tasks.

THE BREADTH OF RESEARCH METHODS

Many students enter this course with the misconception that research methods are pertinent only to the field of psychology. Some would narrow the field even further, including only those topics that fall within "experimental" psychology. In fact, the methods of research presented in this book are not limited to any one area or discipline. Rather, they are valuable across all areas of psychology and outside the discipline of psychology as well.

Research Within Psychology

Psychology is extremely broad, with topics of study ranging from amnesia to racism to virtual reality. Yet even with that kind of breadth, a common core of research designs is used to discover new information. Let's consider a few examples of research within psychology, so that you can see how research methods are used.

Neuroscience. The 1990s have been dubbed "The Decade of the Brain" by the National Institute of Mental Health, and for good reason. Some of the most fascinating research today explores chemicals called neurotransmitters that are produced naturally by the human brain (e.g., Ornstein & Swencionis, 1990). Through the use of standard research methods, psychologists have discovered how and why these neurotransmitters cause us to become addicted to drugs, to experience certain emotions, and to relieve pain naturally. Furthermore, researchers are uncovering new facts suggesting that illnesses such as Parkinson's disease, schizophrenia, and Alzheimer's disease may be closely linked to imbalances in natural neurotransmitters. By using new drugs that alter such imbalances, physicians can reduce the immense suffering that these patients would otherwise face.

Human Development. Did you know that nearly one quarter of the infants born in large cities suffer from prenatal exposure to dangerous drugs (APS Steering Committee, 1992)? The number of pregnant women who cannot control their desires for cocaine and crack has increased so much that 10% of all the babies born in Dallas and San Francisco were exposed to cocaine within 48 hours before delivery (Revkin, 1989). We have no way of knowing how much more cocaine the fetuses endured over the earlier months of pregnancy.

These "crack babies" require intensive hospital care for weeks, sometimes months, after birth. After leaving the hospital, they continue to show serious sensory and learning deficits that will plague them throughout their lives. Some researchers (e.g., Howard, as cited by Revkin, 1989) believe that these children, as they grow up, will hinder all students in the American school system. Our next generation of Americans is at serious risk, and psychological research is vital if these problems are to be solved.

Psychotherapy. Agoraphobia is a mental disorder in which people are afraid to leave familiar surroundings or enter open spaces. The very idea of leaving the house to go shopping, for example, terrifies some agoraphobics. It is the most common and most disabling of all phobias (Atkinson, Atkinson, Smith, & Bem, 1990) but can be treated effectively through the use of systematic desensitization. This treatment changes irrational behavior by exposing the agoraphobic to fearful situations little by little. After learning to relax just outside the home, the agoraphobic progresses to the nearest corner, then to the local post office, and finally to new, open spaces far from home. The treatment is very gradual and may take weeks or months to complete.

The use of systematic desensitization to treat agoraphobia shows how the results of scientific research can be applied to a practical problem. The treatment was based on fundamental principles of learning that had been discovered through basic research studies of laboratory rats (M. C. Jones, 1924). It has now been used to help thousands of people with various types of phobias.

Memory. In state-dependent learning, human memory is thought to be more effective if both event and remembrance occur in the same physical place or mental state. For example, through simple experiments, Godden and Baddeley (1975) found that if you learn a list of words while underwater, your later memory of them will be more accurate if you are also tested underwater. Of course, most of us don't study at the bottom of a pond, but an important event to remember (like a car accident) might well occur while we were intoxicated. The research on state-dependent learning suggests that we would be more likely to recall the details of the accident if we were intoxicated once again during retrieval. In fact, experiments by Goodwin, Powell, Bremer, Hoine, and Stern (1969) have shown that this is true.

Motivation. You probably recall from an introductory psychology course that primary motives in human behavior include hunger, thirst, and sex. As the number of admitted homosexuals grows in the United States, psychologists have taken increased interest in the topic of homosexuality. One researcher (LeVay, 1991) found that the brain structures governing motivation in homosexual men were smaller than those in heterosexual men. This is a good example of research that immmediately hit the media presses and suffered some misinterpretation along the way: In less than a year, LeVay's study made the front page of *The New York Times*, was the featured cover story in *Newsweek*, and was discussed by LeVay himself and several critics on *Donahue*. As we shall see in Chapter 10, LeVay's research was reported to the public in ways that were often misleading.

Language. We'd probably all agree that few behaviors are more human than language. The reading disorder known as dyslexia has been studied in depth recently. Dyslexics usually have good vision, adequate education, average or above-average intelligence, and normal skills in most tasks (Ellis, 1984). However, the act of reading is a tremendous stumbling block for them.

One type of research that has produced new knowledge about dyslexia is the case study, which we will consider in Chapter 4. In rare instances, people whose brains have been injured by some type of accident develop reading problems called "acquired dyslexia" (Morton & Patterson, 1980). Some of these patients look at the word "lightning" and pronounce it as "ligg-tuh-ning." Others see the same word, "lightning," and read it aloud as "thunder." Both types of patients are convinced that they are indeed reading the words accurately, just as they would have before their brain injuries occurred. Such case studies have led psychologists to believe that harm to certain pathways in the brain may cause acquired dyslexia. This research may lead to future applications that can help the 4% to 6% of school children who suffer from developmental dyslexia today (Rayner & Pollatsek, 1989).

This list of examples is not complete, of course, for there are many other areas of psychology that we have ignored. Psychologists also use research methods to study motion and depth perception in sports like football, to develop computer simulations of human problem-solving, to learn why certain animals mate with the same partner for life, and to find out which forms of psychotherapy are most effective for treating mental illnesses. The research methods you will learn in this course can be applied to a wide variety of topics within psychology.

Research in Other Disciplines

Many of the scientific research methods used within psychology are also used in other disciplines. Therefore, methods learned in this course will still be of use when you need to understand and evaluate research concerning nonpsychological topics.

For instance, someday you may need to know about the influences of second-hand cigarette smoke on your children's lungs. Or perhaps you'll want to explore the effects of acid rain or oil well development on the pristine forests and meadows near your back yard. Maybe you'll be curious about why breast cancer is so common among American women but quite rare among Chinese women. There's no way of knowing when you might suddenly be faced with the need for more information about a particular topic. If you have the skills to gather and evaluate that information, whether through library or scientific research, you'll be better prepared.

Richard Keith Coleman, who was put to death in 1992, certainly might have benefited if the people enforcing his death penalty had known more about science. He was convicted of rape and murder partly on the basis of DNA evidence that the National Academy of Science later refuted. Unfortunately, when appealing the death penalty decision, Coleman agreed to take a lie detector test and failed it. The governor of Virginia admitted that he might have prevented Coleman's trip to the electric chair if Coleman had passed the lie detector test. Apparently, the governor had not evaluated his information on lie-detection: Numerous studies show that lie detector tests have only a miserable 66% chance of showing that an innocent person is indeed innocent (Kleinmuntz & Szucko, 1984). Coleman may have been one of the remaining 34% who were actually innocent even though the lie detector test found them guilty.

There's also no telling where a particular finding will lead. Watson and Crick's famous discovery in 1953 of the structure of DNA has led to current research conducted through the Human Genome Project (Shapiro, 1991). Through this project, biologists and medical researchers are discovering which genes carry certain diseases from parent to child. Equipped with that knowledge, physicians may alter certain genes to relieve symptoms in adults or cure illnesses even before a baby is born. Because of this biogenetic research, even the taste of tomatoes can now be improved by altering their genes (Locke, 1992).

Anastasi (1972) has argued that psychology is the perfect entrance to other fields of science. Many people who are afraid to jump into nuclear physics or organic chemistry will happily accept the study of human behavior as a way of learning about science. Although the specific forms of research used in psychology are not identical to those used in other disciplines such as physics or biology, the underlying principles are the same. In short, what you are learning this term is versatile, valuable knowledge that will serve you well in the future regardless of your ultimate direction.

WAYS OF KNOWING

Science is only one way of discovering and evaluating knowledge. In this section, we will consider several ways of knowing. Although we will treat them as if they are completely separate, in reality, different methods of knowing are often combined with each other. The methods include knowing by tenacity, by authority, by emotion, by common sense, by intuition, by logic, by sense experience, and finally, knowing by science.

Tenacity

The word tenacity simply means "stubbornness," and the method of **tenacity** follows that definition. Most people dislike change. Therefore, we may hold stubbornly to an idea or tradition that has never been evaluated. As that same idea is presented again and again, people who rely on tenacity grasp it ever more tightly. Knowing by tenacity is one of the most common and dangerous ways of accepting new information.

Try watching television commercials for examples of tenacity. You'll see advertisers and political campaigners repeat the same slogan so often that many people begin to accept it as truth. Most families also maintain certain traditions by way of tenacity. The proverbial story of the roast beef is a classic example: A young man observed his wife cooking beef and asked why she had sliced off one end of the roast before placing it in the oven. She replied coyly that this was a family secret, handed down through several generations, and designed to make the roast especially tender and tasty. She had observed her mother and grandmother follow the process time and again. However, her husband (a scientist, no doubt) wanted to know exactly why this process tenderized the meat. When the young woman finally telephoned her aged grandmother with this question, Grandma howled with laughter and replied, "My only roasting pan was too small to hold an entire roast!" Your family's traditions probably aren't so silly, but I'll bet you can think of one or two that are based on tenacity.

Authority

When people accept the word of a famous or respected figure without skepticism, as many people regularly do, they are gaining knowledge by **authority.** If you believe that salt will increase your blood pressure because Dan Rather said so, or because your physician said so, or because your mother said so, you are relying on authority. The main disadvantage of using this method of knowledge is that the authority could be wrong. And, in fact, although hundreds of books, talk show hosts, news reporters, medical doctors, and parents have assured us that salt really does increase blood pressure, critical evaluators know that this "fact" is not entirely true. If you check the research studies done on the effects of sodium, you'll find that only about half of the people with high blood pressure in America are affected by salt (Collins, 1988). More importantly, subjects who have normal blood pressure show no effect of salt intake (Schein, 1987). One of the most comprehensive sodium studies, conducted in 32 countries around the world, demonstrated that the link between salt and blood pressure is very weak (Intersalt Cooperative Research Group, 1988).

Another problem with knowing by authority is the tendency to attribute authority to celebrities who are famous, regardless of what they are famous for. The testimonial advertisement is a good example: Television presents Cher telling us which artificial sweetener is best, and it presents Madonna warning us of the dangers of AIDS. In fact, although Cher and Madonna are compelling authorities on the topic of musical entertainment, they are completely unqualified to educate the public on these other topics. It's important, then, to recognize the difference between celebrities and authorities.

Despite its problems, knowing by authority does have certain advantages. Often, true authority figures are correct, and we are safe in listening carefully to the information they provide. By doing so, we obtain knowledge that we otherwise might have neither the time nor the training to acquire. The key is to evaluate such knowledge skeptically, rather than accepting it on blind faith.

Emotion

We all harbor emotions or feelings that may cause us to believe more in one idea than in another. Lewis (1990) has categorized common emotional ties in a hierarchy: Most of us are very closely bound to our families, then to our friends and coworkers, beyond them to our local neighborhoods, and finally, to our nations.

Methods of gaining knowledge by **emotion** are linked to such hierarchies. New knowledge that upsets our feelings toward our country will probably be accepted more quickly and easily than new knowledge that upsets our feelings toward family members. Likewise, information concerning other countries (or other races, for that matter) is often accepted without critical evaluation, whereas information about our own country (or our own race) is considered more carefully before it is believed. Lewis explains that knowledge based on emotion is "the kind of knowledge that people care deeply about, that they can build a way of life and especially a community on, that they are prepared to defend, even to defend with their lives" (1990, p. 93).

Common Sense

Many of us have had the experience of explaining proudly to a friend how we arrived at a profound new belief or creative insight. Sometimes, the friend blinks back at us with a slightly puzzled expression, and says, "Well, yeah, but that's just common sense." **Common sense** is defined in the dictionary as "sound practical judgment that is independent of specialized knowledge" (Random House, 1987, p. 413).

Usually this sound practical judgment is based on individual experiences and perceptions, though, and is therefore not really "common" at all. Here lies the problem. Because knowledge by common sense is based on only one person's experiences, it is limited to that person's biases. Knowing to watch for rattlesnakes while on an early morning walk might be common sense to me, because I grew up in the Arizona desert where rattlers thrive. However, this same piece of knowledge may not be "common sense" to you.

Intuition

Knowledge that seems to enter our consciousness without much voluntary effort is known as knowledge gained by **intuition.** There are many stories of inventors, scholars, and artists who solved difficult problems unconsciously in their sleep or dreams. Of course, intuition must be preceded by solid preparation and hard work—we can't simply sit in the sun and wait for ideas to emerge out of blank air. As Pasteur said, "chance only favours the mind which is prepared" (as quoted by Vallery-Radot, 1928, p. 79).

Intuitive methods of knowing occasionally lead to creative solutions. Elias Howe, for example, worked and worked on the crooked seams produced by his latest invention, the sewing machine. After dreaming of warriors racing fiercely toward him carrying spears with holes drilled at their ends, Howe awoke and realized that the solution was a sewing machine needle with its hole located at the end instead of at the top (Madigan & Elwood, 1983). By following the solution presented in his dream, Howe's sewing machine became a success.

As Lewis (1990) notes, many people think of intuition as nonsense. You might imagine that many of those people are scientists, but in fact, most good scientists understand the value of creative insight and are willing to consider it even at the risk of being teased by their colleagues. Intuition, like other methods of knowing, is a good way to generate new ideas, but it is important that those ideas be tested before they are accepted.

Sense Experience

"I won't believe it till I see it with my own eyes." Now there's a person who insists on gaining knowledge by **sense experience.** The controversy over knowing by seeing, hearing, smelling, tasting, and touching has a long history, dating back at least to Aristotle and Plato around 350 B.C. While Plato preferred to sit in his armchair and theorize about the true nature of the world, Aristotle was out in the field, collecting specimens and observing them closely.

Observation by sense experience is also known as **empiricism:** gathering knowledge by observing occurrences and organisms in the real world. It's best to conduct your own observations, but scholars commonly accept observations made by others as long as they could have made the observations themselves with equal accuracy. Knowledge gathered by observing real events or by relying on other people's observations of those events is called **empirical evidence.** It's often the cornerstone of solid argument.

The proper use of empirical evidence is valuable in many arenas, especially in convincing other people of controversial claims. For instance, let's suppose that you claim that Bo Jackson was the greatest athlete of the 1980s. To persuade others that this is true, you need some type of evidence that will support your belief.

If you argue that Jackson was the best because a respected sportscaster like Frank Gifford said so, then you are relying on authority for evidence. If you argue that Jackson was best because he's your brother and you're proud of him, then you are relying on emotion. On the other hand, if you rely on empirical evidence, you will argue that Bo Jackson was best because he hit 22 home runs in his first year as a rookie for the Kansas City Royals and later achieved a .235 batting average with 53 runs batted in. In spring training, Jackson hit a 510-foot home run like it was nothing. In addition, he gained 533 yards on 78 football carries for the Los Angeles Raiders in his first six games alone. Oh, and by the way, Jackson runs the 40-yard dash in 4.175 seconds (Wiley, 1987). Now *that's* empirical evidence!

Logic

Aristotle did not limit himself entirely to empirical observation. In fact, drawing on several of Plato's ideas, he wrote one of the most respected Greek works on knowing by **logic.** The use of logical reasoning to gather and evaluate new knowledge is also known as **rationalism.** Since Aristotle's and Plato's time, rationalism has waxed and waned in popularity, reaching its pinnacle with Descartes in 1637.

Often, logical reasoning takes the form of a **syllogism,** which is a series of premises that lead to a conclusion. Consider the following syllogisms:

1. Premise: *All humans are mortal;*
   Premise: *I am a human;*
   Conclusion: *Therefore, I must be mortal.*
2. Premise: *No women can count;*
   Premise: *I am a woman;*
   Conclusion: *Therefore, I cannot count.*

You've probably already discovered the problem with knowledge by logic. If all the premises are true, the conclusion will also be true, as in Syllogism 1. However, just one incorrect premise makes the conclusion false, as in Syllogism 2. The logic in Syllogism 2 is flawless, but the fact that the first premise is wrong ensures that the conclusion will also be wrong.

Science

Finally, it is possible to gather and evaluate new knowledge through the process of **science.** The scientific method of knowing is a combination of observation by sense experience plus reasoning by logic (Whitehead, 1925). In other words, scientists start to evaluate new ideas by observing events directly. These observations are considered to be **objective,** or unbiased, because they can be verified by others. Anyone should be able to verify a scientist's observations by observing similar events and obtaining similar results. If such **replication** does not produce similar results, then the new idea is not accepted. After observations have been made and replicated, so that we believe the premises are true, then scientists use logical reasoning to explain the events they have observed. There are three building blocks in the method of science, then: empirical observation, replication by other scientists, and logical explanation.

From these building blocks comes the notion of **experimentation,** which is a powerful technique of testing two or more competing ideas and observing the results to see which idea is correct. It requires generating alternate **hypotheses,** or educated guesses, about what results would be expected to occur under certain conditions. Different hypotheses are generated, then a test is conducted. The results of that test either support or refute the various hypotheses. Later in this chapter, we'll consider a real example of this process of solving scientific mysteries.

THE ENTERPRISE OF SCIENCE

Science is a progressive enterprise. By that, I mean that it moves along gradually, building our knowledge brick by brick as new studies are completed. Often, science is engaged in a kind of improvised dance: two steps forward and one step back, in an ever-changing rhythm and pattern. It may have to backtrack because a thought-provoking new study later produced unexpected results during replication, because a particular topic has been saturated with enough experimentation for the present time, or because progress in logical reasoning is stifled by a lack of knowledge from empirical observation.

Every now and then in this slow scientific dance, a radical change occurs, which then molds the dance steps into a new rhythm and pattern. Kuhn (1962) calls these radical changes **paradigm shifts,** indicating that a specific approach to discovery (or "paradigm") has changed its direction. Some psychologists think of the change from behaviorism to cognitivism around 1960 as an example of a paradigm shift that led to a revolution of new discoveries about the human mind (Baars, 1986). The point at which a traditional approach changes is determined not only by the amount and type of scientific knowledge that has been gathered about a certain topic, but also by political and cultural events in the civilization surrounding the scientist. In other words, we develop new ways of thinking about old topics, and our new ways of thinking match the spirit of current culture.

Pure and Applied Science

Scientific research is often divided into two general categories: basic or pure science, and applied science. **Pure science** is conducted to add to the body of knowledge about a topic. Whether that body of knowledge is actually used to solve real-world problems or to develop new technology is considered irrelevant. In other words, pure science seeks to discover new facts solely for the sake of knowing them, and not because they are needed in some practical application.

Applied science, on the other hand, uses the knowledge gained through pure science and goes on to apply it in ways that will benefit people directly by solving problems that they experience. Sometimes applied science solves human problems through the development of **technology,** or technical inventions that serve people in their homes and workplaces.

All this gets a bit heady, I know. Perhaps an example will help. In the field of psycholinguistics, pure science is used to find out how humans perceive spoken language. The goal of this endeavor is strictly to build a body of knowledge that can explain the intricacies of human speech perception. How the knowledge may ultimately be used is beyond the scope of pure science. However, applied researchers have used that pure knowledge to enhance the conduction of speech over telephone wires. In other words, you can thank psycholinguists (as well as your local phone company) for the fact that your telephone transmits speech clearly even in overseas communication.

Applied science can also be defined as the discovery of new knowledge in applied settings such as schools or factories. **Evaluation research** is a special brand of this type of applied science. Here, social programs that are already being used are evaluated by researchers to find out whether they are effective. For instance, we use evaluation research to determine whether our prison programs are working, to find out whether a new method of interviewing business recruits is producing the kind of employees we want, or to evaluate the strengths and weaknesses of the quarter system used in some colleges and universities.

The Benefits of Pure Science

Many researchers are disappointed that tax-paying citizens seldom understand the value of pure science. Americans, especially, tend to be oriented toward immediate practical applications rather than toward knowledge for its own sake. As future designers, or at least consumers, of research, it is important that you become aware of the need for pure science.

What the average American taxpayer doesn't realize is that the knowledge acquired through pure science is often put to practical use in later years. However, at the time the research was done, no one was aware of its potential practical value. The technology needed to use that knowledge may not have existed, the practical problem that it later solved may not have cropped up, the person who saw how to use the knowledge may not have been alive at the time, or the political climate of the culture may have discouraged applied research on certain topics. So, although much pure science may seem useless in practical terms at the time it is conducted, we never know how valuable it may become in the future.

An excellent model of pure science's unexpected rewards is found in research conducted through the National Aeronautics and Space Administration (NASA). During the 1960s, billions of tax dollars were spent on sending someone to the moon. Some taxpayers resented the fact that so much money was being spent in pursuit of a goal they viewed as unimportant. "Who cares if we get to the moon?" was one sentiment. "Who cares if we know how gravity works or if we can build a rocket that flies around in space?" However, if those taxpayers had been able to predict the future, they might have been more willing to pay for that research. The pure science that took us to the moon also, and unexpectedly, allowed the development of technologies such as

- microwave ovens,
- contact lenses,
- television transmission by satellite,
- laser beams used for surgery,
- effective seat belts in automobiles,
- pressure suits that maintain blood circulation in injured people,
- surgical implants that allow deaf people to hear,
- weather prediction, and
- pacemakers (Levy, 1965).

Who knows what rewards are still in store?

Physical and Social Sciences

Observation, replication, and explanation are the fundamentals of all science, both pure and applied, both physical and social. Traditionally, **physical sciences** include disciplines such as biology, physics, and geology—disciplines based on exploring aspects of the universe that are primarily determined by natural physical forces. **Social sciences,** such as sociology and anthropology, explore aspects of civilization that are primarily determined by social forces. Sometimes, people refer to physical sciences as "hard" and to social sciences as "soft."

Traditionally, psychology has been considered a social science. However, as psychologists carry out more and more neurological research on various features of the human brain, this categorization has become imprecise. My own opinion is that psychology straddles the distinction between physical and social sciences. Human behavior is certainly affected by both physical and social forces.

The notion that physical science is inherently more difficult than social science must also be laid to rest. The two are different, but it seems ridiculous to suppose that the discovery of the inner workings of the human mind is any easier than the discovery of black holes in physics or plate tectonics in geology. In fact, Fischbach (1992) describes the human brain as "the most complex structure in the known universe" (p. 48).

Criticisms of Science

We're going to be focusing on scientific methods of research throughout this book, so it might be easy to get the idea that science is the only method worthy of use in gaining new knowledge. Some people suppose that scientists are almost super-human, dressed in their white lab coats with cold pure objectivity oozing from their pores. Smith (1990) believes that this myth has caused many disciplines in the humanities (e.g., English, history, philosophy) to attempt to become more scientific. Along with several other scholars today, Smith argues that 20th century reliance on science has gone too far. Other criticisms are perhaps less broad, but even more severe, and they come from within the scientific community. Let's consider the more common complaints (Passmore, 1978):

1. *Science is limited.* It cannot answer the questions that are of greatest importance to humanity: Why does the universe exist? If God made the universe, who made God? Why am I here? While this criticism is true, it is also true that every other method of knowing is limited. Certain questions may be better answered by religion or intuition than by science, but this does not negate the effectiveness of science in answering other types of questions.

2. *Science is not objective.* Traditionally, one of the mainstays of science has been its objectivity. Where religion is subjective and intuition is inconsistent, science is supposed to determine for us The Absolute Truth untainted by human weaknesses.

   In fact, however, scientists are not immune to the filtering of "objective" events through their subjective perceptions. We are human; we make mistakes; we are influenced by past experiences and cultural upbringing; we sometimes see in our research whatever it is we expected to see. Thus, on an individual level, science is no more objective than other ways of knowing. However, on a collective level, science is quite objective. One scientist may interpret data according to personal expectations or mental set; however, when 50 scientists work on the same topic and replicate each other's results, each individual's personal biases are lost in the larger view.

3. *Science discourages creativity and individuality.* The argument here is that science, by its emphasis on generalizations, prevents the use of creative thought and unique imagination. In psychology, especially, our results are determined by generalizing across all the individual differences that occur between subjects who participate in our research studies. We usually ignore the fact that one subject's memory, for example, may be amazingly better than every other subject's memory. Instead, we are interested in whether the group scores for memory differ according to some circumstance that the researcher has introduced. Science does not always require this group viewpoint, however; some psychologists do study individual differences.

   It is also true that science cannot be as purely creative as art can; we are always held back by the data of real events. However, any good scientist will tell you of the power of creative insight in research and theory. Those scientists who do not apply such creativity to their work usually remain second-rate. As Passmore (1978) has said, anyone who doubts that creativity exists in scientific theories has never studied theoretical physics or Darwinian evolution.

4. *Science fosters bad attitudes.* Science has been blamed for promoting arrogance, for encouraging its followers to ignore the complexities of real life, for encouraging humans to destroy nature, and for inspiring contempt for research that has immediate practical value. Well, that's a hefty accusation. There is no doubt that some scientists have developed bad attitudes such as these . . . just as some physicians defraud your insurance companies and some employers practice open forms of sexual discrimi-

nation. No occupation on earth is free of a few members who make a bad name for everyone else.

By virtue of their knowledge, however, the majority of scientists are even more likely than nonscientists to show true appreciation for nature and to take delight in the complex sophistication of a simple flower petal or a human blush. Although contempt for applied research was popular at one time, it has been diminished by the urgency of today's practical problems and the increased funding that applied research now receives. Accusations of arrogance may be justified among the most prestigious departments of science, but they are the minority.

These are some of the main criticisms that have been leveled at science. While it is crucial for you to appreciate the value of science as one method of knowing, it is equally important to understand its limitations. Science is subject to error, as are all human pursuits. However, even with its flaws, science remains one of the best methods we have of discovering and evaluating new knowledge. Despite its imperfections, science has saved millions of lives and eases countless others.

THE CIRCLE OF SCIENTIFIC RESEARCH

The general process of scientific research can most easily be viewed as a circular process (E. L. Bjork, personal communication, 1986). In this circle, information produced by one research study is used in the next study, and so on.

The circle of research starts with a **theory,** a series of basic principles that provide an explanation of various types of behavior. That theory, if it's a good one, will generate expectations about the kind of behavior that should occur under certain circumstances. You probably remember that such expectations are called hypotheses. Once we form a hypothesis, we have to devise some way of testing it. As soon as we have a specific test in mind, we can state specific **predictions** about the exact results that are expected to occur. Once our predictions are in place, we conduct the test. The performance of subjects is measured, and we collect those numbers carefully. We then analyze these data using statistical tests. (Aha! So *that's* why you had to take statistics.) After the data have been analyzed, we interpret their meaning and come to some conclusion. Here the circle begins again: Our conclusions are used to support or refute the theory, and the process is repeated by looking at a slightly different angle of the original research question.

An Example: Helping People in Emergencies

The trouble with this explanation of the research circle is that it's all abstract. Maybe a real example would help. Here's how Latané and Darley (1968, 1970) used the circle of research to evaluate social responsibility among humans.

Kitty Genovese was murdered after midnight in 1964 while 38 of the neighbors in her New York City apartment building watched. The public was shocked by this tragedy, with nearly everyone wondering why none of those 38 people had called the police or tried to help Genovese as she struggled for more than 30 minutes to get away from her murderer. Was it apathy? Fear of getting involved? Ignorance?

Latané and Darley developed a theory now known as diffusion of responsibility. According to this theory, responsibility is spread (or "diffused") among people whenever each of them has the potential to help. This theory suggests that humans will fail to accept individual responsibility when they know that other people in the area could be held equally responsible. The more people among which this potential responsibility is spread, the less likely that any one of them will actually accept the responsibility. Applying this theory to the Genovese murder leads to the surprising hypothesis that Genovese would have been more likely to receive help had there been *fewer* people watching her die.

Latané and Darley, then, entered the circle of research with the theory of diffusion of responsibility. From that starting point, their general hypothesis was formed: Most people will not accept individual responsibility when there are other people available to take it.

To test this hypothesis, Latané and Darley devised a situation in which subjects were faced with an unexpected emergency. To set up the study as a true experiment, Latané and Darley had to include an independent variable that they would manipulate and a dependent variable that they would measure. Their independent variable was the number of other people whom the subjects thought were aware of the emergency (none, two, or five). Their dependent variable was whether subjects would report the emergency or not. In general, then, the **independent variable** is some aspect of the situation that the researcher changes systematically in an effort to alter subjects' behavior. The **dependent variable** is the type of subject performance that the researcher measures. In other words, Latané and Darley wanted to see whether the number of people who were aware of an emergency would alter a subject's willingness to report it. These two terms, independent variable and dependent variable, will be fundamental to nearly everything you learn about research methods, so be sure you understand them. Remember, the independent variable is manipulated; the dependent variable is measured.

In fact, the experiment wasn't quite this simple. After all, researchers have no control over real emergencies! Therefore, Latané and Darley set up a fake situation, in which subjects were told that they would use an intercom system to prevent embarrassment while discussing personal issues with other subjects. The subjects were given information that placed them in one of three conditions:

1. They were told that they alone would be speaking with one other subject and that no one else would be able to hear their conversation; or
2. They were told that they were participating in a group of three people, with each person speaking through an intercom in a different room, and that no one other than the group of three would be able to hear their conversation; or
3. They were told that they were participating in a group of six people, each in a separate room, and that only those six people would be able to hear the conversation.

In fact, the voices of all people except the subject were tape-recorded before the experiment began. In every condition, one of the voices imitated the sound of a person having an epileptic seizure. This fake seizure was the unexpected emergency that Latané and Darley rigged up.

At this point, having devised a test of the research question, the scientists were able to state specific predictions. Can you guess what their predictions were? According to the theory of diffusion of responsibility, which group of subjects should be most likely to report the seizure? Think about it for a moment before we go on.

Latané and Darley predicted that subjects who thought that no one else could hear the seizure would report it quite often. On the other hand, they predicted that subjects who thought that two other people were participating in the conversation would report it less often than the first group. The subjects least likely to report the seizure were those who thought that five other people were participating in the conversation.

To this point, we've traveled around the circle of research from theory to hypothesis, to prediction, to test. Be sure you understand each step so far. After conducting the experiment, Latané and Darley statistically analyzed the data they had collected. In this case, data analysis was a simple matter of counting up the numbers of subjects who reported the seizure, and then converting those numbers to reflect a percentage of total subjects in each condition.

The results showed that 85% of the subjects who thought they were alone reported the seizure. The percentage dropped to 62% for subjects who thought they were members of a three-person group. Only a dismal 31% of subjects in the six-person group, reported the seizure!

Latané and Darley interpreted these results as supporting their predictions. In other words, the obtained results matched the predicted results. This, in turn, allowed them to conclude that their theory was correct. On the whole, people really do neglect their individual responsibilities when other people are involved in the same situation. Applied to real life, no one helped Kitty Genovese because each individual thought that someone else would take the responsibility.

The circle of research continued in two ways. First, many other researchers joined Latané and Darley's scientific effort after reading about their experiment in journal articles. These later studies explored various details of the topic, which came to be known as bystander intervention. Second, Latané broadened his view to take in many aspects of social influence that cause people to behave differently when they are in the company of others. He revised the original theory of diffusion of responsibility to take into account this broader set of behaviors and has now published a more general theory of social impact (Latané, 1981).

TYPES OF RESEARCH: A FRAMEWORK

Research in human memory has shown that if you want to learn something new, it helps to begin with a general framework. I like to think of this framework as a big wooden lattice, the kind you might use in a garden to guide and support the growth of heavy vines and large bushes. When we begin to learn, just as when we begin to plant, the lattice is bare. But planning the design of a garden, and planning the structure of your knowledge, is a good way to make sure your garden and your mind are growing in the directions you intended. So let's label a few points on the lattice, for support during future learning.

In the most general view, scientific research comes in three varieties: nonexperimental, experimental, and quasi-experimental. Nail those labels onto your lattice, leaving plenty of space between each one for future growth.

1. **Nonexperimental research** is used to describe behavior and does not use independent variables. Surveys, case studies, field observations, correlations, and archival studies are all types of nonexperimental research. Because there is no independent variable to cause a change in performance, research instruments like surveys cannot determine cause. If you and I survey 1000 college students about their drinking behavior, our results may describe when, where, and how much drinking occurs, but they will not explain why it occurs. We will consider nonexperimental research in detail in Chapter 4.

2. **Experimental research** allows scientists to determine the cause of behavior by exploring the effects of at least one independent variable while other variables are held constant. Latané and Darley wanted to know whether the number of people observing an emergency (the independent variable) would affect the likelihood of subjects reporting that emergency (the dependent variable). Because Latané and Darley controlled everything that could make subjects report emergencies, with the exception of the number of bystanders, they could conclude that emergency reports were altered because of the number of bystanders. The fact that experiments allow us to determine why a certain result occurred makes them the most powerful of all types of scientific research. Chapters 6 and 9 will explain simple and complex experiments.

3. **Quasi-experimental research** resembles experimental research in every way except that the independent variable is not under the scientist's control. Experimental research requires great control over the independent variable: A truly independent variable is something that the scientist can manipulate, like the number of bystanders in a simulated laboratory emergency. However, some variables are not truly independent because they cannot be controlled. For example, a subject's height cannot be manipulated by an experimenter; it is not under the experimenter's control. The best researcher in the world can't possibly make you short or tall! When we need to study variables that are not truly independent, we often use quasi-experimental research, which is explained fully in Chapter 10.

We'll be discussing each of these three types of research in detail throughout the remainder of this book. For now, it is important that you feel confident in your knowledge of these most basic principles, because we will build on them during the term.

SUMMARY OF MAIN POINTS
• •

- In today's world of information and technology, everyone needs to know the basic principles of scientific research, regardless of whether they plan to become scientists.

- Scientific research differs most strongly from library research in its ability to discover unknown information and to test the accuracy of existing ideas.

- Critical evaluation of information allows us to select important material from the vast explosion of information facing us and to verify its accuracy.

- A common set of scientific research methods can be applied to a wide range of research topics, both within psychology and outside of it.

- Ways of knowing include tenacity, authority, emotion, common sense, intuition, sense experience, logic, and science. Each one has advantages and disadvantages that must be considered. The ability to identify and use various ways of knowing is vital to a full development of critical evaluation skills.

- The scientific way of knowing combines replicated empirical observations with logical reasoning.

- Pure science provides basic knowledge that can be used in applied research or technology. Although pure science may not benefit society immediately, it often produces surprising rewards in the future.

- Science, like all other ways of knowing, is not perfect. However, despite its flaws, science remains a powerful method of discovering and evaluating new information.

- Scientific research proceeds in a progressive, circular fashion. We generate hypotheses from theories, test specific predictions empirically, analyze the resulting data, interpret results in light of our original predictions, and use our conclusions to support or revise the theory.

- There are three general types of scientific research methods: (1) nonexperimental research describes behavior; (2) experimental research uses independent variables to explain behavior; and (3) quasi-experimental research investigates variables that cannot be manipulated.

CHAPTER EXERCISES
• •

1. Use your own words to define each of these key terms:

library research	experimentation
scientific research	hypothesis
tenacity	paradigm shift
authority	pure science
emotion	applied science

common sense   technology
intuition   evaluation research
sense experience   physical sciences
empiricism   social sciences
empirical evidence   theory
logic   prediction
rationalism   independent variable
syllogism   dependent variable
science   nonexperimental research
objective   experimental research
replication   quasi-experimental research

2. In what ways will the study of research methods help you? Consider academic, personal, and occupational benefits.

3. For each of the eight ways of knowing explained in this chapter, write a brief personal experience in which you relied on that way of knowing.

4. In what ways might today's popular culture influence the type of scientific research that is done? Try to include specific examples.

5. Ask five people to describe their idea of "a scientist" to you. What are the general features of their descriptions? In what ways do their descriptions differ from the implied definition of a scientist given in this chapter?

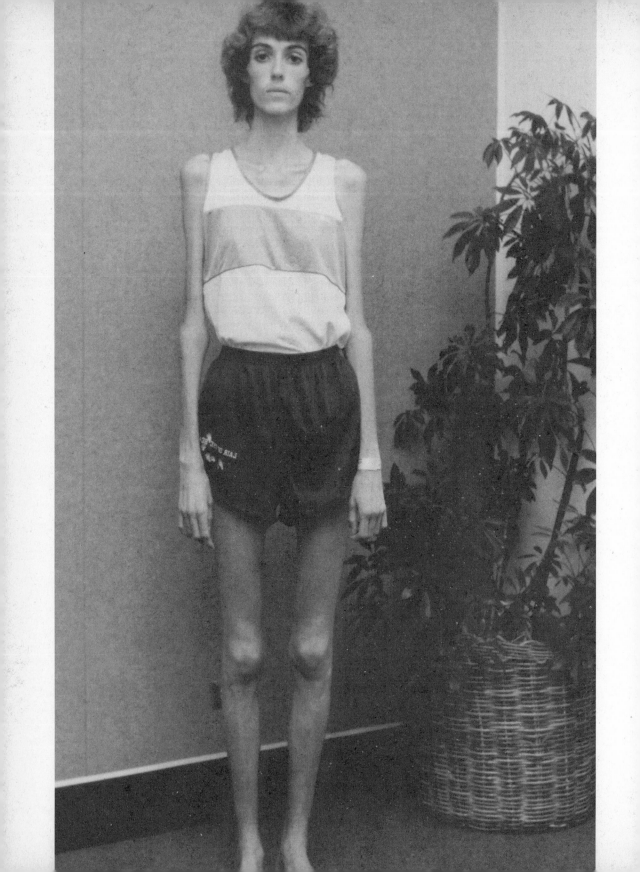

Library Research

2

The effects of severe anorexia nervosa.

Whether you are designing a study of your own or evaluating scientific research done by others, the first step is taken at your college library. To avoid repeating discoveries that have already been made, you will want to know what research has been done on your topic before you plan a new study. The task will involve finding research reports on a particular topic, reading and understanding them, evaluating their strengths and weaknesses, and thinking of ways in which they could be extended or altered in future scientific research.

CONDUCTING A LITERATURE REVIEW

Scientists often talk of the **literature** in a particular area, meaning the body of published knowledge about a certain topic. The psychological literature is enormous because of the breadth of human behavior and all its related applications. Even the best psychologists in the world cannot be familiar with all of this information; instead, we each know limited portions of the psychological literature. For example, one psychologist may be well versed in the literature on alcoholism; another may be an expert on attention.

Within each topic area, you'll find a specialized vocabulary that is difficult to grasp at first. Often these vocabularies differ so strongly between areas that psychologists with different interests are barely able to converse intelligently with each other about their specializations. For instance, clinical psychologists, whose work involves the diagnosis and treatment of serious mental disorders, often have little in common with cognitive psychologists, who study normal mental processes like remembering and thinking in healthy human subjects. The corresponding difference in the vocabularies of these two literatures is apparent at a glance, and within each body of knowledge are a number of sub-areas that have yielded their own smaller literatures. Memory, for example, is one of many sub-areas within cognitive psychology. Within memory, there are still smaller islands of literature, such as face recognition, story recall, constructive memory, autobiographical memory, semantic memory, flashbulb memory, and . . . well, the list goes on and on.

All of this complexity can be overwhelming at first. Conducting a **literature review,** or getting to know the vocabulary and research of a particular topic, is difficult and time-consuming. It is important to take one small step at a time—you won't be able to understand everything on your topic within one month or even one school term, but what portions you do learn will be useful right away. Eventually, you will get to know the literature of any topic you select.

GENERAL SEARCH STRATEGIES

Before we discuss literature reviews in detail, it may help to consider a few general strategies. The type of published knowledge that you are probably most familiar with comes from the **popular press.** This includes books, magazines, and newspapers that are readily available to anyone through bookstores, drug stores, and even grocery stores. Scientists sometimes look down on popular information because it is often inaccurate or incomplete. However, there is nothing wrong with using the popular press to gain new ideas or learn of information that you, as a critical thinker, will later verify through more rigorous library research.

In disciplines like psychology, such verification is usually done through the scientific literature, which includes specialized books, journals, and newsletters. These sources are considered to be more trustworthy than the popular press because they are written and reviewed by experts. In addition, scientific articles are based on phenomena that can be observed publicly and replicated.

Popular Press and Scientific Literature

To see the difference between a popular magazine article and a scientific journal article, let's consider the process of publication briefly. In most cases, the article you read in *Sports Illustrated* or *Glamour* has been written by a professional author. This author did not conduct any of the scientific research reported in the article and is usually not familiar with the complexities of science. Instead, the author, who probably wasn't trained in the methods of scientific research, went to the library and read about various studies that have been conducted by others on a certain topic (perhaps anorexia for *Glamour* or coaching for *Sports Illustrated*). Occasionally, conscientious authors also interview the scientists who conducted relevant research. Upon reading the author's manuscript, a magazine editor decides whether to publish it. That publication decision is usually made by one person who knows even less about the particular topic than does the professional author.

Now let's consider the publication of an article in a scientific journal. The article on anorexia that you might read in the *Journal of Clinical Psychology* was written by a scientist—the same scientist who actually designed and implemented the research that is being reported. This scientist probably spent several years learning the literature and conducting numerous studies in this area before publishing the article. Compare that with the professional author who published the *Glamour* article on anorexia after spending a few weeks doing library research. Upon receiving the scientist's manuscript, a journal editor sends copies of it to three or four **referees,** or reviewers, who are expert scientists working in the same research area as the author of the manuscript. Most reviewers spend many hours going over the new manuscript with a fine-toothed comb. They each send detailed letters of criticism to the editor, along with their individual votes as to whether the manuscript should be published or not. In this case, then, the publication decision is made by a group of experts, not by one magazine editor who knows very little about anorexia. (Although most scientific journals carried by libraries are refereed, some are not. Accordingly, nonrefereed journals are less prestigious and less likely to be accurate.)

Another advantage of scientific journal articles is that they are always accompanied by a fully documented list of sources, so that any reader can check the author's claims before believing them. In contrast, the authors of popular articles seldom cite their sources in full.

Given this comparison, it shouldn't be surprising to you that knowledge made available through the scientific literature is considered more reliable than knowledge made available through the popular press. Reading popular books and magazines is vital if you want to keep up with the most current events and acquire a lot of general ideas. However, if you intend to act on that information, be sure to verify it first through more trustworthy sources.

FINDING THE INFORMATION YOU NEED

Most people I know walk into a library and do one of three things:

1. Stand just inside the door and look confused.
2. Wander over to the reference librarian and mumble something like, "I have to write a paper."
3. Walk directly to the catalogs and indexes to begin a relevant search.

Let's try to make sure that you fall into the third category. It's important to know how to use your library efficiently. Each hour you spend now learning library techniques in psychology will be rewarded with many hours of free time later.

Finding Books

When you start to learn the literature of a particular topic, it helps to look at books. The reason for this is that books are usually written at a more general level than journal articles are. Often, just one or two chapters in a book can introduce you to vocabulary and concepts that will be used in more technical articles. After reading some of the general material in relevant books, you will be ready to proceed to specialized sources.

In general, when you begin to search for specific books in the library, it is best to use the card catalog. Most libraries have now converted their card catalogs to computer, so that you can find books by topic, author name, or title quickly and easily. If you don't know the names of any authors or book titles in your area of interest, simply enter the name of the topic (such as "anorexia" or "coaching") and go from there. It is vital that you know how to use the computerized card catalog in your library. Most of them are very simple to learn with only a few words of help from your librarian or a classmate.

Certain types of books may be especially useful in your literature review. These include textbooks, popular books, anthologies, edited books, and monographs. To make our discussion more concrete, let's suppose that we are interested in finding out about the mental disorder called *anorexia nervosa*.

Textbooks. To begin with, you may not even know what *anorexia nervosa* is. One of the first places to look when beginning the study of a particular area is in introductory textbooks. Almost all of you have completed a course in Introductory Psychology by now, and the vast majority of you will have been assigned a textbook for that course. Unfortunately, most of you probably made the mistake of selling these textbooks at the end of the term, as if all the information they contained was memorized and digested and will be available to you at any time by retrieval from your perfectly functioning memory banks.

Textbooks are among the most valuable tools you have, yet they are one of the most commonly neglected sources of information. If there is any way that you can afford to keep your textbooks, especially the introductory ones, do so. You'll refer to them again and again throughout your college career and thereafter when you need quick, general information on some topic and references to lead you to more information.

For example, a quick glance at the index of one introductory psychology text shows that anorexia nervosa is discussed on page 255. There, the disorder is defined: "An illness in which a normal-weight person (usually an adolescent female) diets to become significantly . . . underweight yet, still feeling fat, continues to starve" (Myers, 1990, p. 255). In addition, the text provides an example (a 5'3" teenager who dieted to 80 pounds and still feels fat) and a brief cultural explanation of the disease. Finally, the text also contains the full reference to a scientific article about anorexia. All of this basic knowledge will help tremendously with our search. It took me about three minutes to retrieve this information from an introductory text that I keep at home.

If you do not have any textbooks relevant to your topic, try to find some at your library or college bookstore. Once you do find a suitable text, use the book's index to locate your topic, read what the book has to say about it, and don't forget to jot down references that sound promising. The references section at the back of the book will contain an entire listing of every study that was discussed, and this information will save you many hours of searching later.

Popular Books. You are already aware of the pitfalls of using popular literature for a scientific search. However, as I mentioned earlier, the popular press contains general explanations of a huge variety of interesting topics. Don't deny yourself that information just because it might be inaccurate. Remember, all printed information (scientific or not) has the capacity to be wrong. Use popular books freely to generate topic ideas, but remember to check the accuracy of what you read.

A popular book informed me of several interesting facts about anorexia nervosa that will need to be checked. In discussing the possibility that cultural expectations lead some women to starve themselves, Tavris (1992) pointed out the effects of social role models, television characters, and magazine advertisements as our society's expectations have changed over the years. For example, she noted that Miss Sweden of 1951 weighed 151 pounds and stood 5'7" tall, whereas Miss Sweden of 1983 weighed 109 pounds and stood 5'9" tall. Sixty-nine percent of the female characters in television programs during the late 1980s were considered very thin, but only 18% of the male characters in those shows were very thin. A total of 63 advertisements for diet foods were found in 48 popular women's magazines, but only 1 was found in the same number of men's magazines.

Tavris' (1992) book is an unusual mix of popular press and psychological literature because she happens to be a well-known psychologist in addition to being a professional author. Fortunately, therefore, she provides full references for the information presented in the book, so that we can go back to the original sources easily to verify her statements.

Anthologies and Edited Books. Instead of being written entirely by one author (or a few authors working together), some books contain selections from many different authors. When the collection is made up of previously published articles, the book is called an **anthology.** When an editor asks several authors to write individual articles on a given topic for a new book, the resulting collection is called an **edited book.** Anthologies and edited books can provide specialized or general information from a variety of standpoints, because each article is written by a different author but on the same general topic. The only thing you need to watch out for is bias in the selection of articles included. Remember that one or two editors decided which articles they wanted to include and, more notably, which articles they wanted to exclude. You may be seeing only one side of the picture through their biased view.

Monographs. Any book containing specialized information on a narrow topic is considered a **monograph.** Your library probably contains many monographs, all of which can be located through the computerized card catalog by title, author's name, or topic. Often, monographs are written by respected scientists who have conducted some of the research that is reported in the book. They are fairly reliable sources of information for that reason, but remember—no source is foolproof! Think about what you read, then check facts by considering more than one source.

Using Newsletters

Most scientific associations publish newsletters regularly and send them to members. For example, the American Psychological Association (APA) publishes a monthly newsletter called *The APA Monitor,* and the American Psychological Society (APS) publishes a newsletter called *The APS Observer.* These newsletters contain short reviews of topic areas, brief articles about people who are doing interesting research, announcements of meetings and conventions, employment advertisements, and requests for scientists to conduct studies or submit manuscripts on particular topics. Scanning the newsletters is a good way to find out what's happening in current American psychology.

A few newsletters can be acquired through the library, but more often, they are sent to individuals who are members of professional associations. Some associations allow students to join at a discounted price. In Table 2.1, addresses of the two largest psychological associations (APA and APS) are provided so that you can write to them for information on joining as a student affiliate. *The APA Monitor* and *The APS Observer* are mailed directly to members and student affiliates. You may also be interested in writing to Psi Chi, the national honor society for students in psychology.

Using Encyclopedias, Dictionaries, and Reviews

There are several encyclopedias and dictionaries that explain basic psychological concepts. When you enter a new area of interest, these sources can help you to understand the vocabulary used in the specialized journals. In addition, they often explain theories and concepts in a brief and general manner, just to give you a

Table 2.1 ASSOCIATIONS THAT
ENCOURAGE STUDENT MEMBERSHIP
....

American Psychological Association
1200 17th Street, N.W.
Washington, DC 20036

American Psychological Society
1010 Vermont Avenue, N. W.
Suite 1100
Washington, DC 20005-4907

Psi Chi National Office
407 East Street, Suite B
Chattanooga, TN 37403

quick overview of the topic. Table 2.2 lists some of the encyclopedias and dictionaries available at most college libraries.

Aside from encyclopedias and dictionaries, the *Annual Review of Psychology* is a helpful book. Each year, the editors of *Annual Review* ask the top scientists in the most popular fields of psychology to write an article reviewing the literature in that field. These articles are then bound together in one volume. The first *Annual Review in Psychology* was published in 1950, and most college libraries have all the yearly editions. If you browsed through the *Annual Review* for any particular year, you'd find several useful items:

1. The table of contents represents the 15 or 20 hottest topics of that year within psychology. A history of what's "in" and what's "out" can be gathered quickly by scanning the contents of successive editions.
2. Each article presents a scholarly review of the scientific literature that was current at the time the *Annual Review* was published. Note that this review is scholarly, which means it may be rather difficult to read unless you have already studied some basic information on the topic.
3. Each article is followed by a reference section that lists all the research studies that were considered most important within a particular topic. These references provide starting material for your own search.

Using Indexes

Indexes are large sets of books that list most of the journal and magazine articles that have been published in a given discipline. They are the equivalent of a card catalog for publications that are issued repeatedly at regular intervals, or **periodicals.** The most common index that lists popular magazine articles is the *Reader's Guide to Periodical Literature.* The *Reader's Guide* for 1994, for example, lists articles by topic that were published in popular magazines during that year. We could look up "anorexia," for instance, and find the references for several popular articles on that topic.

Indexes are organized in several different ways, sometimes by author, sometimes by topic, sometimes by journal or magazine name, and sometimes by article title. Many indexes cross-reference their contents according to all of these

Table 2.2 SOME ENCYCLOPEDIAS
AND DICTIONARIES IN PSYCHOLOGY

Dictionary of Animal Behavior and Learning
Dictionary of Behavioral Science
Dictionary of Developmental and Educational Psychology
Dictionary of Personality and Social Psychology
Dictionary of Physiological and Clinical Psychology
Dictionary of Psychology
Encyclopedia Dictionary of Psychology
Encyclopedia of Depression
Encyclopedia of Psychoanalysis
Encyclopedia of Psychology
Encyclopedia of Suicide
International Dictionary of Psychology
International Encyclopedia of Psychiatry,
　Psychoanalysis, and Neurology
International Handbook of Psychology
Oxford Companion to the Mind

categories. If you know which indexes list the psychological literature and how to use them, a world of knowledge will be open to you. The most popular index within psychology is called *Psychological Abstracts*, fondly dubbed *"Psych Abs"* by many researchers.

The reason that we need indexes listing the journal articles in psychology is that the number of published articles is huge. *Psych Abs* contains listings of every article published in more than 1300 psychological journals from 45 different countries, and it doesn't even cover every psychological journal that is available. In 1990 alone, more than 32,000 of the journal articles published in psychology were listed in *Psych Abs*. Even if you narrowed your search to only one year's worth of information, imagine locating one of those 32,000 articles without any kind of index to help you!

Using Psychological Abstracts. Your first glance at the *Psych Abs* section in your library may be hazardous: You'll see volume after volume of books, taking up one or two entire tables in the library. Don't despair—we'll learn how to use *Psych Abs* one simple step at a time.

If you take a look at Figure 2.1, you'll see that Psych Abs is separated into four sections: the Thesaurus, the Subject Index, the Author Index, and the Abstracts themselves. There are several ways of using these books, but we'll concentrate on the simplest one. A warning first: Reading passively about how to use an index can get very boring and doesn't really teach you to use the actual books once you have your hands on them. Therefore, I recommend that you take this textbook to your library, sit down in front of *Psych Abs* for half an hour or so, and follow the steps using the actual index.

Step 1: The Thesaurus. To start, select a topic that interests you. I'm going to continue with the topic of anorexia as an example, and you may want to follow along with that at first. However, after going through the process once with me, choose your own topic and try again.

Figure 2.1
The Four Categories of Psychological Abstracts

The first problem we run into is that we don't know what term *Psych Abs* uses for anorexia. It might be that they list articles on this topic under the name of the disorder *(anorexia nervosa)*, but maybe not. There are certainly a variety of other terms that could be used, such as *starvation, body weight, thinness,* and who knows what else. Just because we thought of the term *anorexia* first doesn't mean that *Psych Abs* uses that term.

To find out which term *Psych Abs* does use, open the Thesaurus, a paperback book that will be located near the most recent *Psych Abs* volumes. Using the "Relationship Section," look up the term *anorexia*. If *anorexia* is listed in *Psych Abs*, it will appear in alphabetical order within the "Relationship Section." In the Thesaurus, you will see that *anorexia* alone is not listed, but *anorexia nervosa* is. This means that *Psych Abs* does not use the term *anorexia*. Instead, it uses the full name of the mental disorder, *anorexia nervosa*. The portion of the *Psych Abs* Thesaurus showing *anorexia nervosa* is reproduced in Table 2.3.

Before we continue using the Thesaurus listing for *anorexia nervosa*, let's see what would have happened if we had looked up some other term. The term *thinness* is not listed in the Thesaurus at all. Some beginners assume that this means there is no information on thinness in the psychological literature, but that's not true. Instead, the fact that the Thesaurus doesn't include the term *thinness* merely means that *Psych Abs* doesn't use that word as a category. The term *underweight* is listed in the Thesaurus (and reproduced for you here in Table 2.4), indicating that this term is used throughout the index.

Notice that both entries in the Thesaurus *(anorexia nervosa* and *underweight)* head a list of other terms that *Psych Abs* uses. Thus, when we find the term *underweight,* broader (B), narrower (N), and related (R) terms are also listed. By considering the specific nature of what you want to know, you'll be able to select the best term for your search. In this case, we are not interested in people who are underweight because they have hyperactive thyroid glands; we want to know more about people who are underweight because they have a mental disorder called

Table 2.3 "ANOREXIA NERVOSA" IN THE
PSYCHOLOGICAL ABSTRACTS THESAURUS

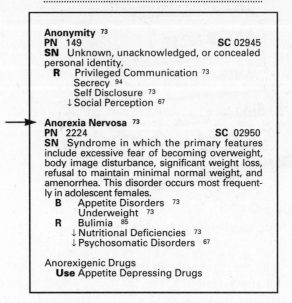

Anonymity [73]
PN 149   SC 02945
SN Unknown, unacknowledged, or concealed
personal identity.
    R   Privileged Communication [73]
        Secrecy [94]
        Self Disclosure [73]
        ↓ Social Perception [67]

Anorexia Nervosa [73]
PN 2224   SC 02950
SN Syndrome in which the primary features
include excessive fear of becoming overweight,
body image disturbance, significant weight loss,
refusal to maintain minimal normal weight, and
amenorrhea. This disorder occurs most frequently in adolescent females.
    B   Appetite Disorders [73]
        Underweight [73]
    R   Bulimia [85]
        ↓ Nutritional Deficiencies [73]
        ↓ Psychosomatic Disorders [67]

Anorexigenic Drugs
  Use Appetite Depressing Drugs

anorexia nervosa. Because the Thesaurus lists the term *anorexia nervosa*, we know it is used in the Subject Index.

All of this attention to terms may seem unnecessary to you now. However, one of the most common complaints that professors hear from students is, "Our library doesn't have *anything* on topic x." Usually, even small libraries have plenty of information on topic x, but the student has been searching under some term that is not used by the index at hand. The next time you hear someone say that *Psych Abs* has no information on *children*, for example, you'll know that they've probably been searching under a term like *kids*. Take this opportunity to verify for yourself that *Psych Abs* uses the term *children* instead of *kids*.

Step 2: The Subject Index. Once you know that a term is used by *Psych Abs*, it's time to look up that term in the Subject Index. *Psych Abs* is categorized by subject for each year's worth of articles that are listed. Thus, you must decide first which year you wish to search. The best decision is usually a recent year, unless you know that your topic was very popular a few years ago and is now less common. Let's take 1990 for our example on anorexia.

Your library should have two hardback volumes called Subject Indexes for the year 1990. One contains subjects in alphabetical order from A through L; the other contains subjects starting with M through Z. According to the Thesaurus, the term we want is *anorexia nervosa*, so we look under the A's in the first 1990 Subject Index. From pages 140 to 142 of that index, all the 1990 entries for *anorexia nervosa* are listed. A simple count will tell you that 122 articles on the topic of anorexia were listed in *Psych Abs* in 1990 alone.

Scan the list of 1990 articles on anorexia, looking for the aspect of the topic that interests you most. Perhaps we want to find out how to treat anorexia, so we

Table 2.4 "UNDERWEIGHT" IN THE
PSYCHOLOGICAL ABSTRACTS THESAURUS

Underweight 73
PN 38   **SC** 54770
   B   Body Weight 67
       Symptoms 67
   N   Anorexia Nervosa 73
   R   ↓ Appetite Disorders 73
       Diets 76
       Hyperthyroidism 73
       ↓ Nutritional Deficiencies 73

Undifferentiated Schizophrenia 73
PN 59   **SC** 54780
   B   Schizophrenia 67

Unemployment 67
PN 910   **SC** 54790
   B   Employment Status 82
       Social Issues 91
   R   Employment History 78
       Job Search 85
       Job Security 78
       ↓ Personnel 67
       Personnel/ Termination 73
       Reemployment 91
       Retirement 73

look under "treatment" on page 142 and find three articles devoted to the treatment of anorexics. These three entries are reproduced in Table 2.5.

After deciding which entry sounds most relevant to your interests, write down the abstract number of that listing. The article on treating patients with eating disorders sounds fairly general. A general article would be good for someone who wasn't entirely familiar with the literature on anorexia, so let's find out more about that article. Jot down the abstract number, 17813, and remember to record the year of the volume, 1990. Recording the year is important because there are many other abstracts numbered 17813, each one for a different year. The number we wrote down refers to the 17,813th article that *Psych Abs* listed in the year 1990.

Step 3: The Abstracts. An **abstract** is a short summary of a longer article. It contains only the major points of that article, but this provides a quick method of determining whether the entire study is worth reading. The Abstracts for 1990 are contained in four large hardback volumes, categorized by number. Find the one volume of 1990 Abstracts that contains the number 17813.

When you've got that volume, search it by number, not by alphabetical order as we did in the Subject Index and Thesaurus. You'll see the abstract numbers listed on the top outer corner of each page in the Abstracts. On page 1766 of the third volume of Abstracts for the year 1990, you'll find abstract number 17813. Don't take my word for it—verify this yourself!

Table 2.6 shows the abstract as it appears in the 1990 volumes of *Psych Abs*. You now have the author's name, the title of the article, the name of the journal in which that article is printed, and even the year, volume number, and page number of that article. In short, you have everything you need to get the article from your library's periodicals section or through interlibrary loan.

Table 2.5
USING THE *PSYCHOLOGICAL ABSTRACTS SUBJECT INDEX*

Anorexia Nervosa   **Volume 77**
                              SUBJECT INDEX

screening & inpatient chemical abuse rehabilitation, 24 yr old female with concomitant anorexia & bulimia nervosa, 15618

self & other body size perceptual cue utilization, anorexic vs bulimic vs obese adult females, implications for Brunswikian lens model for body image research, conference presentation, 5191

self preoccupation & food cues & perceptions of women's body size, female college students at risk for anorexia nervosa, 28733

self reported defense styles, female adolescents with restrictive vs bulimic anorexia vs normal weight bulimia, 20248

separation individuation difficulties, cognitive behavioral indicators of anorexia nervosa & bulimia, female college students, 12687

serum amylase levels, detection of binging & purging behavior, underweight vs recovered anorexic vs normal weight bulimic females, conference presentation, 1867

sex & race & marital status & religious characteristics, patients with anorexia nervosa or bulimia, 15163

social historical & feminist vs psychobiological & family system & multidimensional psychiatric approach to anorexia nervosa & bulimia, 5205

social historical perspective of females & hysteria & anorexia nervosa, 12333

sorbitol abuse, 17-35 yr old females with anorexia nervosa &/or bulimia, 10165

specificity of Eating Disorders Inventory scales, female anorexic vs general psychiatric vs bulimic patients, England, 29850

spinal trabecular bone density, 20-40 yr old females with past or current history of anorexia nervosa, 1872

spinal trabecular bone density, 20-40 yr old females with past or current history of anorexia nervosa, erratum, 15092

symbiosis & separation imagery in Rorschach profiles, borderline vs nonborderline females with bulimia or anorexia, 12706

TAT measured perception of role in life as active vs passive &/or in control vs controlled & early memories, anorexic vs bulimic anorexic females, 25965

treatment & recovery, males & females with anorexia nervosa, Netherlands, 17787

treatment, patients with eating disorders, 17813

treatment, White female 75 yr old with anorexia nervosa, case report, 31468

Type A behavior, heart rate & BP & EKG changes in response to stress, adults with anorexia nervosa, 15038

undiagnosed schizophrenia & anorexia nervosa, female 14 yr old, case report, implications for ego development, 4593

urinary MHPG excretion, bulimic vs anorexic vs normal 17–39 yr olds, 28784

ventricular size & clinical characteristics & vigilance task performance, patients with anorexia nervosa vs bulimia, 23083

zinc status, 14-25 yr olds with anorexia nervosa or bulimia, 15097

Table 2.6 FINDING THE ABSTRACT

17812. **Wasyliw, Orest E. & Cavanaugh, James L.** (Rush U, Rush Medical Coll, Chicago, IL) **Simulation of brain damage: Assessment and decision rules.** *Bulletin of the American Academy of Psychiatry & the Law*, 1989, Vol 17(4), 373-386. —Reviews principles and procedures related to the evaluation of fabrication or exaggeration of the effects of brain damage. Using the personal injury case as a general model, the author lists 4 requirements for proving a case with brain damage claims and discusses 3 types of cognitive deficits. Possible outcome states in forensic evaluation are outlined, and the presence of inconsistency as the hallmark criterion for evaluating malingering is discussed. Psychometric assessment of malingering is described within the categories of general fabrication and exaggeration of psychiatric symptoms, neuropsychological malingering, assessment of memory vs amnesia, and minimization.

17813. **Yates, Alayne.** (U Arizona Coll of Medicine, Tucson) **Current perspectives on the eating disorders: II. Treatment, outcome, and research directions.** *Journal of the American Academy of Child & Adolescent Psychiatry*, 1990(Jan), Vol 29(1), 1-9. —Most eating disordered patients are difficult to treat and present with an already chronic illness. Treatment of anorexia often involves correcting starvation and promoting weight gain, behavior modification, and individual, family, and group therapy. Cyproheptadine, an antiserotonin and antihistamine agent, appears to be the most promising medication for anorexics, but no medication is efffective in all patients and none should be used without other forms of therapy. Treatment of bulimics may involve exposure plus prevention therapy, cognitive-behavioral treatment, active symptom management, long-term exploratory therapy, or antidepressant medication. The prognosis in anorexia is worse than that of bulimia, and anorexics appear more resistant than bulimics to outpatient intervention.

Best of all, you have found an abstract that can be read quickly before you get the actual article. This abstract can be read in a minute or two, whereas the entire article might take several hours to read. After reading the abstract, decide whether the article is likely to capture your interest. If so, write down (or photocopy) the relevant information. If not, go back to the Subject Index and select one of the remaining 121 articles from 1990 that may be of greater interest. If all 122 of them fail, remember that you have only searched one year's worth of *Psych Abs* so far.

This is a simplified explanation of using *Psych Abs*. Perhaps the most likely source of confusion is the fact that some *Psych Abs* volumes are hardback, whereas others are softback. The softback volumes are the newest issues your library has. They are softback because they have not yet been bound into the wide hardback volumes that we used in the example. You'll quickly learn how to use both, but at the beginning just concentrate on the hardback volumes.

There are many other ways to use *Psych Abs* that we haven't covered. For example, you can search for articles by author's name, and in 1992, *Psych Abs* began listing books and book chapters as well as journal articles. Entries in *Psych Abs* dated after 1974 are now available on computer in some libraries, which speeds the search process considerably. You'll pick up these methods in time.

Using Other Indexes. We've only discussed the most popular psychological index here, but there are others. *Social Sciences Citation Index (SSCI)* lists journal articles within the social sciences and tells us which other authors have cited those articles as background information. This allows us to backtrack through the research on a particular topic, seeing the exact progression of ideas from one author to the next. *SSCI* also indicates the number of times a specific article is cited by other authors, so that we can see the relative influence of various articles and authors on the field as a whole. *Science Citation Index* and *Index to Scientific Reviews* operate on much the same principles as *SSCI* does, but they contain a broader variety of topics. *Child Development Abstracts* is an example of a narrower listing that is similar in format to *Psych Abs.*

Psychology itself is so broad that indexes from other disciplines are needed sometimes. Topics that cross into the biological side of psychology (e.g., biopsychology, behavioral medicine, neuroscience) are often listed in *Index Medicus*, a common indexing system used to categorize the medical literature. The *Education Index* may be helpful if you are concerned with topics surrounding educational or developmental psychology, such as teaching gifted children or noticing attentional deficit disorder in the classroom.

Electronic indexes are also available. Many libraries have acquired compact discs (CDs) that contain all those listings that used to be found in huge sets of books. As mentioned earlier, *Psych Abs* is now completely electronic in some libraries, so that you can find abstracts quickly on computer rather than slowly through book volumes. The name of the computerized version of *Psych Abs* is *PsycLIT*. Another relevant index on computer is *ERIC*, which is an electronic listing of articles in educational psychology.

Finally, *Current Contents: Social & Behavioral Sciences* is a monthly listing of the tables of contents of 6500 journals within the social and behavioral sciences. By looking through *Current Contents*, you will become aware of new articles concerning your topic of interest. A computerized index that performs the same service as *Current Contents* is called *Uncover*. Check with your librarian to see which of these indexes is available to you.

Getting the Journal Article

Library indexes merely tell us which journal contains a particular article that we want. We still have to find a copy of that journal and obtain the article from it. Once you have jotted down the reference information for a series of articles that sound promising, go to the Periodicals section of your library.

Every library has a listing of periodicals to which it subscribes, so that we can determine whether the library we are visiting has the particular journal or magazine we want. Suppose you are looking for an article on anorexia in the *Journal of Clinical Psychology*. Check first (on the periodicals listing) to make sure that your library carries that journal. If it does, you can find the journal right away in the Periodicals section of your library.

Using Interlibrary Loan. With the costs of journal subscriptions rising as quickly as the budgets of many libraries are dropping, your library may not subscribe to the journal you want. **Interlibrary loan** is a technique that allows libraries to share books and periodical articles with each other. Although your library may not carry *The Journal of Clinical Psychology*, some other library undoubtedly does. Using interlibrary loan, you may request that another library send the book or journal article you want to your own library. You may then borrow the book or acquire a copy of the article from your library.

The cost of interlibrary loan is usually minimal. At my college library, it costs about the same amount to acquire an interlibrary copy of a periodical article as it does to locate and photocopy an article that the library owns. Books are also available through interlibrary loan, usually with no borrowing charge at all.

Interlibrary loan is a wonderful addition to library services, but it has one drawback: It takes time to get the publication from another library. A few of my interlibrary requests arrive within two or three days; others take two or three weeks. Therefore, it is wise to begin conducting your literature review early so that there is enough time for interlibrary loan to come to your aid. This is especially true if you use a small library that does not carry many journals.

A final technique that some people use is traveling to other libraries near their community. Although most nonacademic libraries don't carry scientific journals or monographs, they will have an array of popular books and magazines that you may find useful. For academic sources that you need in a hurry, you might consider traveling to another college or university within driving distance of your own. Many neighboring libraries share computerized card catalogs to some extent, so it should be possible to determine whether your neighboring library has the publication you want before you drive there to get it.

USING YOUR OWN LIBRARY

Every library is different, so it is vital to get to know the services and physical layout of your own library. Many colleges offer short courses in "library survival." If this is available at your school, make use of it today! Spending the time now will mean that you won't have to waste hours learning how to use the library on the day before a major paper or research proposal is due. Furthermore, it will help you to develop skills that you will need for a lifetime.

If your college does not offer a formal course in library skills, go to the librarian and ask for help. Earn your librarian's respect by explaining that you want to know exactly how the library works, what indexes it owns, what hours it is open, whether interlibrary loan is an option, and how to find the sources you are likely to need. A librarian with some spare time might give you an individual tour or, at the least, invite you to join a group orientation at some later date. Every library in this country offers some method of introducing people to its services. Don't be shy about asking.

In addition to taking a tour of your library, several other suggestions will help you to get the most out of a literature search. First, get to know your reference librarians. They can provide all sorts of welcome information when you need to find something obscure. Second, remember that your professors are experts in various areas of psychology. Get to know each psychology professor's area of expertise, then ask the relevant person for tips on useful sources. Third, allow plenty of time for a literature search. The most common mistake students make in library research is underestimating how long it will take to find the sources they need.

SELECTING SOURCES

One problem that many students fear in a library search is that there won't be enough information on their topic of interest. Indeed, this can be troublesome, especially when your topic is very new, very old, or very obscure.

A different problem is even more common than sparse sources, though. Many students conduct a thorough literature review, only to be faced with hundreds of potential articles and books that are relevant to the topic. You should be able to see how easily this problem could occur, given the 122 scientific articles on anorexia nervosa that had been published in only one year, according to only one index. It's impossible to read that many articles in a short period of time.

Perhaps a few suggestions will help you to select the best sources:

1. Scribble down every source that seems relevant during the early stages of your search. In other words, save the selection process for later rather than trying to find and select at the same time. This will ensure that your search is thorough, and it will show you how many sources you can afford to discard from the original list.

2. Read a general chapter on the topic before conducting a full search. This chapter should introduce you to the basic concepts and vocabulary within your topic of interest. You'll need to plan ahead to allow enough time for this, of course.

3. After you've become familiar with the general aspects of your topic, try to narrow the scope of your research question. What exactly are you trying to find out? Do you want to know how common anorexia is in the United States? Do you want to compare the incidence of anorexia in America with the incidence of anorexia in other countries? Are you most interested in teenage or adult anorexics, female or male anorexics? Do you want to focus on how anorexics are best treated, or on why anorexics develop their disorders? Perhaps you want the answers to all these questions—if so, write them down and select sources one by one, corresponding to each question. What you don't want to do is carry out the entire search and selection process with the idea in mind that you simply want to know "something about anorexia."

4. Before you gather actual articles, read their abstracts in *Psych Abs*. Does it sound like the article will answer your specific research question(s)? Is the article published in a journal that is available to you? Is it published in a journal that can be acquired easily through interlibrary loan? Do you have enough time for interlibrary loan?
5. Once you've narrowed the list of sources this far, get the articles from the periodicals section of your library. Glance over each page and ask yourself these questions: Will you be able to understand this article? Is it written at a level that is too advanced for your current state of knowledge?

These five suggestions should help you to select the best sources from your original list. Sometimes you will need to go through the selection process several times. For example, you might start by selecting the best five articles on your list. After reading those five articles, you may realize that two of them just aren't what you expected. At that point, you may have to go back to your original list of sources and select the next best three or five articles.

The question of how many sources are needed is difficult because the answer depends on several unknown factors. If you are conducting a full-fledged literature review, one that might be published in a journal, you will probably need to be familiar with hundreds of sources. If you are writing a 6–8-page essay using empirical evidence, you may get by with only 5 good sources or you may need 15. If you are designing a simple research study of your own, and searching for sources that will provide introductory background material on the topic, you may need anywhere between 2 and 10 sources.

The number of sources you need also depends on the quality and relevance of the references you find. If you locate two background studies that lead perfectly into your hypothesis, that may be enough. On the other hand, if you must generate your hypothesis piece by tiny piece because each reference provides background on only a small portion of your idea, 10 sources may be required. Your professor can provide the best advice, depending on what sort of work is expected and what sources you find.

HOW TO READ A JOURNAL ARTICLE

Obviously, after selecting the journal articles that seem most relevant to your research question, you're going to have to read them. You may wonder why it's necessary to devote an entire section of this book to reading a journal article. After all, college students already know how to read, so what's so special about reading journals? The best answer I can give is a demonstration: Go and look carefully at the average journal. (The *Journal of Experimental Psychology: General* is a common journal that most college libraries carry, if you don't know where to start.) Try reading the first few sentences of the first article in an issue of that journal. Tough, right? Well, maybe that was just the first article. Flip farther back in the journal and try again. Hmmm . . . maybe it's just that you picked up an especially difficult journal. Try another one. Not much better, I'll bet!

Scientific journal articles are difficult. Anyone who tries to convince you otherwise is doing you a disservice. It takes time and practice to learn to read journal articles and to understand what they are saying. It also helps to have a few pointers at the beginning:

1. Understand why you are reading a journal article.
2. Use abstracts wisely.
3. Allow enough time.
4. Know the APA format of content organization.
5. Talk about your reading.
6. Search for weaknesses.
7. Search for limitations.
8. Search for applications.

These pointers are provided with the assumption that you have already read and mastered general discussions of your topic, such as book chapters or encyclopedia entries. The journal article should not be your first stop on the way to new knowledge. Let's consider each of the eight suggestions for reading a journal article in some detail.

Understand the Purpose

If the purpose of any task is not clear, motivation to complete it often suffers. There are several reasons to read journal articles. First, if you are designing and conducting original research, you will want to verify that your hypothesis has not already been tested adequately by someone else. You will need to become familiar with the literature so that you can apply common theories to your research. You will need to learn the typical methods that are used when testing hypotheses within your topic so that your results will be comparable to those of other scientists.

Second, if you are writing reports on research that has been done as a class exercise in this course, you may need to find background information for the introductory sections of your report. You will want to know exactly which predictions are most likely to be correct, based on theories or related research that has already been done.

Third, you will be expected to know how to find and read journal articles when you move beyond the Research Methods course to that promised land of upper-division learning. Most upper-division courses are devoted to one fairly specialized area of psychology, and to grasp that area in depth, students must understand the research it produces.

A fourth reason to read journal articles is to evaluate the new information you hear on television and read about in magazines. If a loved one contracts some disease, you'll want to find out as much as possible about that disease in order to help in a meaningful way. With a little practice at finding and reading journal articles, you'll be able to evaluate new ideas and gain new knowledge in small amounts of time.

Use Abstracts Wisely

Most journal articles begin with a one-paragraph summary that explains the research to be reported. Reading that abstract carefully will prepare a mental framework for your comprehension of the entire article.

Allow Enough Time

It can take hours to read a scientific research report once, especially when you're just learning the process. Plan enough time so that you're not trying to grasp new concepts in a hurry. In addition, recognize that to really understand the article, you may have to read it several times.

Know the APA Format

Appendix A explains how to write research reports in the format recommended by the American Psychological Association (APA). Most articles published in psychological journals are written in APA style, which includes an organizational format that helps readers to locate certain types of information. The information you need from a journal article will usually appear in one of four sections: Introduction, Method, Results, or Discussion.

If you want to know about background material, relevant theories, or hypotheses and predictions, concentrate on the Introduction. The Method section contains specific details about how the experiment was actually conducted. Numbers corresponding to summaries of the data gathered are presented in the Results section. To determine how the authors interpreted their results, what conclusions they came to, and how this work could be applied or used in a wider sense, focus on the Discussion. Read with a specific purpose in mind—if your main interest lies in a cultural explanation of anorexia, you probably need to focus most on the Introduction and Discussion sections of the research reports.

Talk About Your Reading

Sometimes it's hard to know whether you've really understood an article or not. One way to find out is to talk with professors, classmates, family, or friends about the article. In the course of explaining it to them, new questions will come up and new information may be provided. Offer the same "listening service" to your classmates in return for their time spent helping you.

Search for Weaknesses

Don't assume that a piece of research is flawless just because it has been published. As you begin to design studies, you'll find that all kinds of unexpected problems can occur despite the most careful planning. In addition, certain problems can be difficult to uncover by referees and may get past the review process and into the journal. Much research is built on mistakes of the past. Later chapters in this book will teach you how to search for scientific mistakes.

Search for Limitations

Some research studies are technically flawless but limited in scope. For example, anorexia has been studied most often in teenage girls, partly because it occurs most often in that population. However, some adult women do suffer from anorexia nervosa, as do a few teenage boys, and it might be interesting to find out how their problems differ from those of the female adolescent group. As you read, ask yourself who the study applies to and whether that group excludes anyone of scientific interest.

Search for Applications

Remember that most of pure science is caught up in the race for new knowledge without regard for practical application. When you read a journal article, consider the potential use in society of the study's results. Try to think of a particular situation, perhaps relevant to your own life, in which a new finding could be used. Thinking about a study's practical applications will help you to understand and remember it.

THE VALUE OF LIBRARY SKILLS

By now, it should be obvious that good library skills are mandatory to design, conduct, evaluate, and explain your own scientific research. But good library skills certainly don't end there. The time you spend learning how your library works will be repaid every time you write a paper or research a speech for any college course. It will be repaid after college, too, when your boss asks for information on a new topic, when you need to check a claim that you don't trust, or when you choose to read a book for sheer pleasure. Don't be left standing at the doorway, looking confused.

SCIENCE ON THE CUTTING EDGE

You've heard of "life in the fast lane." Well, the analogy in science is what we call "research on the cutting edge." This phrase refers to the very latest, most recent scientific discoveries, often discoveries that haven't even been published yet. New knowledge discovered through scientific research changes with time, and often those changes occur quickly. Because of this, scientists try to keep up with the most current studies. Relying only on published literature can impair this goal because of the **publication lag,** or time from completed research to published article, in scientific journals.

Designing the proper test of a complicated hypothesis may take months. Testing subjects and collecting data add more time to the process. Then, after the results of a research study are obtained, the scientist must spend several weeks writing a clear report. After that, it often takes two or three months for referees to review each manuscript and make a decision about whether it should be published. Almost all manuscripts are sent back to the author for revisions, even if the editor and referees decide to publish the article. Meanwhile, the clock is ticking ... other scientists are designing and conducting various studies on the same topic, and the knowledge base is changing slightly. Finally, after writing, reviewing, and revising, the article has to be printed in a journal, and this printing process is lengthy. All in all, publication lag can mean that the article you read in today's journal describes a research study that was conducted a couple of years ago.

To avoid the problems of publication lag, most scientists learn about the work of other researchers by talking with those researchers instead of waiting until the written report is published. There are several practices used to maintain open conversation between scientists: Lab groups, electronic mail, and professional conventions are among the most common.

Lab Groups

Professors at most large universities and many small colleges conduct regular meetings made up of a group of students and other professors who are interested in a certain topic. The members of these lab groups read and discuss articles in the literature, brainstorm with each other to generate new ideas, help others to design solid studies, offer advice on everything from pure science to applied technology to the best gourmet coffee, and, in general, provide a sounding board for new ideas.

Electronic Mail

E-mail, as it is known by users, is simply a form of communication between people over their computers. Instead of sending letters to each other through the postal service, messages are typed into one computer and sent electronically to another computer. Computer networks are now so widespread that it is possible, even easy, to send messages from computers in the United States to computers in other countries all over the world. E-mail is much faster than standard mail but cheaper than telephone, so it provides a practical form of communication.

Computer communication allows scientists whose research interests are similar to work together even though their locations are far apart. We call these groups of scientists working together by computer **virtual communities.** They do not constitute real communities because they are not grouped together in the same location, but their communication by computer allows them to participate in something very much like a physical community.

Professional Conventions

In addition to providing newsletters, most professional associations hold conventions each year in different locations. We learn about the latest research at these conventions by listening to formal presentations and by conversing informally with friends who have also traveled to the meeting.

Student organizations, such as Psi Chi, also hold annual conventions specifically for undergraduates. In addition, many colleges and universities sponsor regional conventions so that undergraduate students may present their own research and hear about the work of other students.

At any scientific convention, you can expect to hear keynote addresses by well-known scientists, open discussions of popular topics by several experts on a panel, and presentations of research papers. In addition, most conventions include **poster sessions,** in which the bare highlights of many research studies are presented on posters, with the researchers standing nearby hoping to talk with you about their work. This is a great way to meet and talk with other people who share your interests.

SUMMARY OF MAIN POINTS

- The first step in scientific research is to conduct a literature review at the library. This step ensures that someone else has not already tested your hypothesis, and it provides valuable information concerning the design and predictions of your research study.

- Popular magazines and books provide new ideas concerning current events, but they require careful verification. Journal articles are more reputable but can be difficult to read.

- Journal articles should never be the first stop on your way to new knowledge. Begin instead with textbook passages, book chapters, and psychological encyclopedias or dictionaries.

- Scientific journal articles are cataloged in indexes such as *Psychological Abstracts, Index Medicus,* and *Social Sciences Citation Index.* Popular magazine articles are cataloged in indexes such as *Reader's Guide to Periodical Literature.*

- After compiling a list of available information on a topic, select sources by narrowing your research question, reading abstracts, and assessing the difficulty of writing style used in the article.

- Be patient with yourself in learning to read journal articles. To make the task easier, be sure you understand the purpose of reading such tedious material, use abstracts to prepare a mental framework, allow plenty of time, make use of the APA organizational format, and talk with others about your reading. To develop new ideas from journal articles, search for the weaknesses, limitations, and practical applications of each research study you read.

- Scientists keep up with the latest developments in their areas of expertise by participating in lab groups, communicating through electronic mail, and attending professional conventions.

CHAPTER EXERCISES
. . . .

1. Use your own words to define each of these key terms:

literature	periodicals
literature review	abstract
popular press	interlibrary loan
referees	publication lag
anthology	E-mail
edited book	virtual communities
monograph	poster sessions
indexes	

2. Take a tour of your college library. Write a brief description of the psychological sources that are available to you there. For example, which encyclopedias and dictionaries are available? Which print indexes are available? Which electronic indexes are available? Try to be thorough in making a list of the general sources that you can use in the future.

3. Using *Psychological Abstracts*, find one article on the topic of athletic coaching techniques, one article written by a professor in the psychology department at your college, and one article published in the current year. Write down the reference material for each of these articles.

4. Find a journal article at your college library on any psychological topic you choose. Be sure it is a research report rather than a descriptive article. Read the article, then answer the following questions:

   In one sentence, what was the main point of the study?
   What was the researcher's hypothesis?
   Did the reported results support that hypothesis?
   What conclusions did the researcher come to in light of the results?

5. Using *Reader's Guide to Periodical Literature*, find a popular magazine article on the same topic you selected for exercise 4. Read the magazine article, then compare its style, content, and documentation with that found in the journal article.

Using Statistics

3

A 1987 train collision that killed 16 people and injured 170, after the engineer and brakeman had been smoking marijuana.

This may come as a surprise, but statistics are very much like hammers. Just as a hammer is a tool, used to achieve some goal greater than the mere activity of pounding nails, statistics are tools used to help us answer the questions of scientific research. Also, like hammers, statistics must be used with skill, and this skill can be developed with practice. If you don't know how to build a table, then it won't help to own even the best hammer in the world. Likewise, if you don't know how to construct a research study properly, even the finest statistical analysis will be useless.

PUTTING YOUR KNOWLEDGE TO USE

Quite a few students dislike the study of statistics. This is partly because developing any skill in isolation is usually less enjoyable than using that skill to complete a higher goal. If your stats course was anything like mine, you probably spent a lot of time plugging numbers into formulas and wondering why it was important to consider how often a coin would turn up heads or tails given 100 flips. Real research seemed a long way off from that! Going back to our analogy, hammering nails straight into two-by-fours all day long isn't much fun either, if you're not building anything.

In true research, statistics are put to use for a greater purpose. Before we begin to use them, it is vital that you understand the basic concepts of central tendency, variability, sampling, and significance. Although these abstract concepts might be familiar to you, their concrete application to hands-on research may have been ignored. To fill that gap, this chapter is devoted to statistical application and should not be considered a mere review. Specific statistical tests are discussed in later chapters, corresponding to their use as tools in answering the questions set forth by certain research designs. Our emphasis throughout this book is on the proper use and interpretation of statistics, not on calculation. We want to build meaningful research studies, not just hammer nails.

SCALES OF MEASUREMENT

Many psychological research studies involve setting up some task and inviting human or animal subjects to perform it while the experimenter records various measures. Maybe children run on treadmills while you measure their heart rates. Perhaps adults look at pictures of faces and then try to recognize the faces at a later time, while you record the total number of faces that each subject remembered. Schizophrenics might be given medically approved drugs, while you record the number of hallucinations they report before and after taking the drug. Regardless of the particular situation, all of this measuring is going to produce a large set of numbers.

After testing subjects, you will be faced with that jumble of numbers, which we call **raw data.** Now what? You're going to have to make some sense of the numbers before you can figure out what they mean. Making sense of a large set of numbers is exactly what statistics allows us to do. But to decide which statistics to use on raw data, you need to classify the type of data you have. The importance of this decision is apparent in Table C.1 (on page 312), which shows which statistical tests should be used for different scales of measurement. There are four general scales of measurement used in gathering data: nominal, ordinal, interval, or ratio.

Nominal Data

Nominal data are numbers produced by a scale that represents named categories with no inherent numerical value, like Democrat/Republican, Yes/No, or Breakfast/Lunch. When I say nominal data have no "inherent numerical value," I mean that any numbers assigned to those named categories are purely arbitrary. There is nothing about the category itself that suggests a certain value. For example, the categories of Democrat and Republican have no numbers associated with them. To say a Democrat is equal to 43 and a Republican is equal to 17 is merely to assign arbitrary symbols that refer to each category. We could just as well have called them "x" and "y" or "blue triangle" and "green diamond."

Often, nominal data are assigned arbitrary numbers like 1 and 2. The reason for this is that it makes statistical analysis by computer easier. The computer can not perform arithmetic calculations on words like "Democrat" or "Republican," but it can calculate ones and twos. (Of course, it can also calculate 17s and 43s, so it would make no difference to the computer if we decided to use those numbers.) Therefore, we simply assign each category an arbitrary number when using nominal data. It is then up to us to remember which category each number stands for.

Ordinal Data

Just as the word *nominal* stems from the word *name,* the term *ordinal* stems from the word *order.* Consequently, **ordinal** data are numbers that come from a scale in which categories can be assigned a clear order. Restaurants and hotels are commonly assigned a star rating: If you're staying at a five-star hotel and eating at three-star restaurants, you're living very well. On the other hand, a one-star restaurant isn't considered special—it just serves food. And a one-star hotel will provide a bed, but don't expect to find an 18-hole golf course on the grounds!

Ordinal data are based on ranked preferences, and that implies that one category is better than another. In this way, ordinal data differ from nominal data. For example, the answer "yes" is not inherently better than the answer "no" on a survey that uses a nominal scale of measurement. However, on an ordinal scale, the three-star restaurant is considered to be better than the two-star restaurant, and the two-star restaurant is better than the one-star.

Although ordinal data reflect an ordering of preferences from lowest to highest, they do not imply that one category differs by an equal amount from other categories. In other words, a four-star hotel is worse than a five-star hotel, but it is not clear exactly how much worse it is. When you're just spending the night, the difference between a three- and a five-star hotel is probably much less noticeable than the difference between a one- and a three-star hotel. Although the two intervals seem to be numerically equal, they are not truly equal.

Interval Data

Interval data are measured in units that differ from each other by an equal amount. A classic example of interval data is the Fahrenheit temperature scale. The difference between 4° and 5° is exactly the same as the difference between 1° and 2°. In each case, the temperature differs by 1°, and that degree represents an equal amount no matter where it falls along the scale.

The reason that Fahrenheit temperature is such a good example of interval data is that it goes below its zero point. Zero does not represent the absence of temperature—it merely represents another interval along the scale. On an interval scale, temperatures can drop below zero without altering the fact that each degree represents an equal amount of change in temperature.

Ratio Data

In some scales of measurement, zero does represent a meaningful absence of whatever is being measured. For example, if we were measuring heart rate, and a zero score was obtained, that would indicate an absence of heartbeat . . . and that absence would certainly be meaningful! In this case, the interval between heart rates of 75 and 65 is vastly different from the interval between heart rates of 0 and −10, even though both intervals can be represented in theory by the same numerical value (10). In fact, though, it makes no sense to think of the units of heart rate as ranging below zero. When you are working with data that represent equal amounts of change at each value but can not drop below zero, you have **ratio** data.

Table 3.1 will help you to remember the four scales of measurement. They will be important as we consider the use of statistics in research, because the particular statistical tool we choose will depend critically on the type of data we wish to analyze. It's worth taking a little extra time now to be sure you understand Table 3.1.

DESCRIPTIVE STATISTICS

Sometimes the tools of statistics are used simply to describe a set of numbers. These are **descriptive statistics,** or numerical values that describe key characteristics of the larger data set. Descriptive statistics are numbers like means and standard deviations that tell other researchers what our entire data set is like, so that they don't have to inspect each piece of raw data individually.

For example, if a set of raw data consists of 100 numbers, and I tell you that their mean is 5 and their standard deviation is 0, I have accurately described

Table 3.1 SCALES OF MEASUREMENT
....

Data	Brief Definition	Example
Nominal	The number is an arbitrary name for a category that has no numerical value.	Yes/No
Ordinal	The number signifies a rank ordering that does not imply equal amounts between categories.	Star ratings for restaurants
Interval	The number represents a numerical value with equal amounts between units above and below the zero point.	Fahrenheit temperature
Ratio	The number represents a numerical value with equal amounts between units, but the values can not drop below zero.	Heart rate

every number in the set with only two descriptive statistics. You may recall that standard deviation is a measure of variability, so $SD = 0$ means that the numbers in the set do not vary from each other at all. With that information plus the fact that the mean is 5, you can determine that all 100 numbers must have the value of the number 5. The only problem with this example is that it's artificial: A set of raw data collected from a psychological research study would not have a standard deviation of zero, because human and animal performance differs from one individual to the next.

The most common descriptive statistics represent frequency, central tendency, and variability. Let's see how these statistics are used to describe data from the four scales of measurement.

Frequency

To describe nominal data, we typically use a measure of **frequency,** which simply shows us how often a particular answer occurred in a given category. To calculate frequency, just count up the number of times that the same response occurred.

Let's suppose that you sent out a survey asking high school students whether they use illegal drugs. You've written the question so that subjects must answer either "yes" or "no." In order to describe the incidence of drug abuse among high school students, you need to determine the frequency of "yes" responses. After counting responses, you might find that 443 out of 1,000 subjects answered "yes" to your question. Frequencies are often converted into percentages (simply by dividing 443 by 1,000 in this case). The reason is that percentages provide more information than simple frequency counts do. To say that 443 students use drugs doesn't mean much without explaining how many students were asked. Was it 443 out of 443 students (100%) who use drugs? Or was it 443 out of 1,000 (44%)? The percentage tells us what we need to know in only one number, whereas the frequency count requires at least two numbers to be meaningful.

Incidentally, by conducting a series of such surveys, Johnston, O'Malley, and Bachman (1989) found out that 39% of American high school seniors in 1989 admitted using illegal drugs during the previous year. This was lower than the 54% of American high school seniors who admitted using illegal drugs in 1978, but it still places the United States as the country with the highest rate of drug abuse among all industrialized nations in the world. This meaningful knowledge was provided by a simple frequency count on nominal data.

The fact that nominal data require frequency counts is easy to understand, but many students attempt without thinking to calculate a mean instead. Calculating a mean on yes/no responses is like trying to pound nails with a saw. It's vital to learn to use the right tool for the right job.

Central Tendency

The descriptive statistic called **central tendency** describes the center point of a set of raw data. The most common descriptions of central tendency are means, medians, and modes. It's acceptable to use the term **average** to refer generally to all three measures of central tendency, but researchers reserve the terms *mean*, *median*, and *mode* for more specific purposes. In other words, if you report an "average," most researchers will immediately wonder what kind of average it was: mean, median, or mode?

A **mean** represents the central point of a data set when all its values are added, then divided by the number of values in the set. Means are the most popular measures of central tendency because they have the advantage of being sensitive to each score in the data set. However, this same sensitivity can also be a disadvantage because the mean can be affected too easily by a few extreme values. Just one or two extreme scores in a data set can make the mean fail to represent the general picture.

The median solves this problem by ignoring extreme scores. The **median** is the number that falls in the center of a list of data when scores have been placed in order by value. For example, the set of data including 3, 7, 9, 13, and 14 has a median of 9. Note that even if the values of the lowest and highest numbers changed drastically (e.g., –302, 7, 9, 13, and 1047), the median would still be 9. However, the means of these two data sets would have been 9.2 and 154.8, respectively. You can see that the mean is influenced strongly by extreme scores, but the median is not.

Table 3.2 VARIATION AMONG AVERAGES

Raw data	
2	
3	
3	Mode = 3
5	Median = 7
7	Mean = 15
9	
13	
16	
78	

The **mode** is the simplest measure of central tendency. It is the number that appears most frequently in a group of scores. In the data set 3, 3, 3, 9, 11, 12, and 13, the mode would be 3. Modes tell us what the most frequent score is, but they don't tell us how often it occurred. They ignore other values in the data set that may be important to consider. Like all statistics, the use of the mode depends on the research question you want to answer. A mode would not be very effective if we wanted to know the extent of drug abuse among high school students in the United States. However, it might be useful if we wanted to find out how much money high school students typically pay for a bag of marijuana or a gram of cocaine. We would simply ask each subject to report the going price, then calculate a mode to show which price occurred most often.

Table 3.2 illustrates the dramatic variations in the three averages we've discussed when applied to the same data set. Verify for yourself that I have calculated the mode, median, and mean of this data set accurately. These descriptive statistics are quite different from each other, even though the data set remained the same. That's why it is important to know which type of average to use for a given situation.

Choosing the Best Measure of Central Tendency

Means are the most popular measures of central tendency in psychological research because they are sensitive to all numbers in the data set. They may be used on interval or ratio data sets whose numbers fall along a normal distribution. On a **normal distribution,** all scores fall across the entire range of measurement in a balanced manner, with most of the scores clustering around the center and only a few reaching the extremes. This pattern, as shown in Figure 3.1A, is what we'd expect under normal circumstances.

If, for example, you stood at center court and tossed a basketball at a hoop 100 times, you'd miss by a general margin most of the time. Occasionally, however, you might make the basket; sometimes, you'd miss by a mile. If we measured the distance between your ball and the basket each time the ball's arc reached the point at which it should have fallen through the basket, most of your

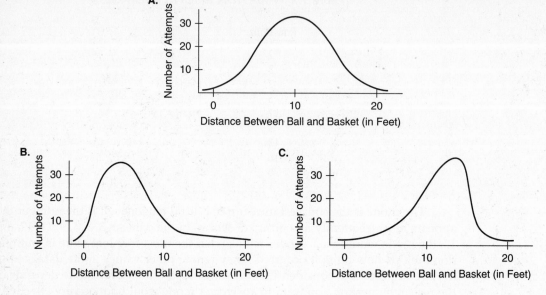

Figure 3.1
Distributions of Data
A, Normal distribution; B, positive skew; C, negative skew.

scores would cluster around the center of the distribution. Only a few especially good and especially bad scores would occur at the outer ends of the distribution, just as they do in Figure 3.1A.

Occasionally, the mean is not appropriate even for data that were measured on an interval or ratio scale. Instead, the median should be used for data that contain several unusually high or low scores, because the median is not as strongly affected by extreme scores as the mean is. In addition, the median should be used when numbers in the data set do not fall on a normal distribution. Distributions of scores that are not normal are usually skewed: They contain a large number of scores at one extreme or the other. Figures 3.1B and 3.1C illustrate two types of skewed distributions, **positive skew** and **negative skew,** depending on which extreme the majority of scores fall into.

In the positively skewed distribution, shown in Figure 3.1B, most of the player's throws came within only a few feet of the basket. However, the negatively skewed distribution shown in Figure 3.1C indicates that most of the player's throws missed the basket by a wide margin.

If you smoked marijuana just before throwing the basketball at the hoop, would your scores be positively or negatively skewed? Think about the question as you check out Figure 3.1. It may help to know that marijuana does impair normal abilities of perception and coordination (Committee of the Institute of Medicine, 1982). If you answered that basketball scores from a stoned player would be negatively skewed, you're right: you'd miss the hoop by a long way most of the time. Michael Jordan, however, would probably produce a positively skewed distribution of scores (minus the marijuana, of course). In both of these instances, the median should be used as a measure of central tendency.

Either means or medians may be used on interval or ratio data, depending on the distribution and variability of scores, but we have already seen that they are not appropriate for nominal data. The reason for this will be clear if you think about the types of research questions that can be answered with the various scales of measurement. If the "yes" and "no" responses in your drug abuse survey had been coded into ones and twos, it would be possible, but completely meaningless, to calculate a mean. You could say that the mean response to the question of whether high school students are using drugs was 1.25, but what would that really mean? Not much.

Typically, the mode is used on nominal or ordinal data, though theoretically it can be used with other scales of measurement as well. Its main advantage is that it can describe the central tendency of nominal data, whereas means and medians can not. However, this advantage is often overridden by the fact that simple frequency counts provide more information about nominal data sets, yet are just as easy to calculate as modes. For example, Johnston et al. (1989) could have reported the mode of high school drug abuse: That is, the central tendency among students in 1989 was *not* to use illegal drugs. But that mode is not as descriptive as the exact frequency, which shows that 63% of the students did not use illegal drugs. This statistic tells us both the central tendency and the extent of use. Even under the best of circumstances, then, the mode is not a popular measure of central tendency.

Finally, either the mode or median may be used to describe the central tendency of a data set measured on an ordinal scale. The mean should not be used on ordinal data because the computation of a mean is based on the assumption that intervals between categorical units (such as two-star and three-star) are equal in amount. However, we know from the definition of ordinal data that this equality does not exist.

For example, a hotel manager may decide to conduct a survey of the hotel's guests. Each guest might be asked to rate the hotel on the traditional five-star scale. Upon analyzing these ordinal data, a mode might show that the maximum response frequency occurred for the four-star category. A median might tell us that the midway point in the ordered data occurred in the four-star category. Either way, the hotel manager would probably be pleased and might use the results to ask the owner for a pay raise! However, calculating a mean on these ordinal data would be misleading: It might indicate that guests rated the hotel at 4.5, but there really is no 0.5 within the scale of measurement. Our hotel manager might want to believe that the 0.5 indicates an overall rating near the perfect five-star category, but because the intervals between categories are not equal, that isn't really true.

Variability

By itself, the descriptive statistic of central tendency is not enough to describe a set of numbers thoroughly. In addition to knowing where their center point is, we also need to know the amount of **variability** among them, or how much each number varies from the center point. As we've seen, if variability was equal to zero, each number would be exactly the same as the value of the mean for the entire data set. There are three basic measures of variability: range, variance, and standard deviation.

The **range** of a set of numbers refers to the difference between the smallest and largest values in the set. For example, we might state range when describing the age of subjects who participated in a research study. For our sample of high school seniors, we would expect a range of about 4 years, from 14 to 18 years of age. If the range was 20 years, we would be startled because it is very unusual to find middle-aged adults or young children enrolled in high school.

Range, like other descriptive statistics, gives us an idea of what the data set looks like without our having to inspect it closely. Because our ultimate purpose in determining range is to describe variability, it is important to recognize that smaller ranges (like 4 years) represent less variation than do larger ranges (like 20 years).

A more exact measure of variability is found in the **variance,** which tells us how much each score varies, or differs, from the mean score. In general, a large variance is obtained when the scores in a data set vary a lot. A small variance is obtained when the scores are similar to each other. Variance is used in many statistical formulas, but in terms of understanding your research results, it is less useful than the standard deviation.

The **standard deviation** also measures how much each score differs from the mean, but it does so in units of measurement that match our data. In other words, the value of a given variance tells us only whether there's a lot or a little variability in a set of raw data. The standard deviation tells us exactly how much each score deviates from the mean, on average, in numbers that correspond directly to the numbers in our data set.

Perhaps a brief example will help to clarify this. We already considered a sample set of 100 numbers whose mean was 5 and standard deviation was 0. In this case, because there was no variability at all, we knew that each of the numbers had to be equal to 5. Now, let's suppose that we had another set of 100 numbers with the same mean ($M = 5$) but a standard deviation of 1. This means that each individual score varies, *on average,* one point from the mean. If the standard deviation was 2, the scores would vary, again on average, by two points from the mean.

A general rule of thumb concerning variability is that about 65% of all the numbers in a normal data set fall within one standard deviation above or below the mean. About 95% of the numbers fall within two standard deviations above or below the mean. This leaves only 5% of the values in a data set falling into the extreme portions of a normal distribution.

INFERENTIAL STATISTICS

In addition to their use as descriptive statistics, central tendency and variability are also vital to an understanding of inferential statistics. Descriptive statistics *describe* a set of numbers; **inferential statistics** are used to *infer* something, or make a decision, about the meaning of that set of numbers. Some examples of inferential statistics are values like t (in t-tests) and F (in analyses of variance). Inferential statistics allow us to determine the likelihood that differences obtained in the subject sample that we tested really represent differences in the entire population of potential subjects. We can consider this idea in more detail by reviewing the concepts of sampling, hypothesis testing, probability, and statistical significance.

Sampling

We've already seen that a stoned basketball player, puffing on a joint in the gym, is likely to show poor motor coordination. Let's suppose now that we want to know just how long the negative effects of marijuana last on tasks of human performance. Do physical abilities return to normal within 1 hour after smoking marijuana? Within 6 hours? 12? Think about how you might design a research study that would answer this question, then we'll see what other researchers have done.

To test the hypothesis that marijuana's negative effects on coordination are long-lived, one of the first things we would have to do is select a subject sample. The **sample** is a small group of people who will actually participate in the research study. Undoubtedly, there are many more marijuana smokers in the world than just the handful we select for our sample. This larger group of marijuana smokers would be known as the **population,** the full set of every potential subject who falls into our category of interest.

This business of population and sample is important because the purpose of inferential statistics is to allow us to infer something about the entire population from a test of only a small sample of that population. If it were possible to test every existing marijuana smoker in the world, we wouldn't need inferential statistics at all. There would be no reason to make an inference from a sample if we could test the entire population.

In most cases, though, the notion of testing an entire population is ridiculous. After all, life is short! Therefore, we test only a small sample of people, even though we want to make generalizations about the entire group. If all marijuana smokers in my sample showed negative effects 12 hours after smoking, I would want to say that marijuana produces this effect in most humans, not just in the 10 or 20 humans that I happened to select. Inferential statistics tell scientists whether that generalization is likely to be accurate or not.

Hypothesis Testing

A basic feature of science is to use research designs and statistical analyses to test hypotheses. However, we do make a distinction between a research hypothesis and a statistical hypothesis. A **statistical hypothesis** states the possible outcomes of a research study in terms of obtained numerical results. The research hypothesis, as introduced in Chapter 1, states a general relationship that we expect to find, based on past research and logical reasoning. In the marijuana example, perhaps we have discovered police reports showing that drivers in car wrecks often insist that they had not smoked marijuana for several hours even though their urine tested positive for THC (tetrahydrocannabinol—the active ingredient in marijuana). This background information might guide us toward the general research hypothesis that marijuana has long-lasting effects.

An Example: Marijuana and Airplane Crashes

Yesavage, Leirer, Denari, and Hollister (1985) were intrigued by a report that the co-pilots of Central Airlines Flight 27 had smoked marijuana 24 hours before their plane crashed, killing them, in 1983. Yesavage et al. designed a research study in which 10 experienced pilots were required to perform landings on a flight simulator, both before and after they had smoked marijuana. Thus, the manipulated independent variable was time of marijuana use (either before or after flight simulation), and the measured dependent variables reflected landing performance.

Measuring landing performance both before and after smoking marijuana allowed the researchers to make a comparison. In terms of a statistical hypothesis, or statement of alternate outcomes, two possibilities existed:

1. Landing performance would be the same before smoking as it was 24 hours after smoking. This would be the **null hypothesis,** which states that there will be no difference in results between the two conditions.
2. Landing performance would be better before smoking than it would be 24 hours after smoking. This would be the **alternate hypothesis,** which states that there will be some difference between the conditions. Often, the direction of the possible outcome is specified, as it is here, but that is not mandatory for a statistical hypothesis.

Null and alternate hypotheses are statistical terms that are used in hypothesis testing. In essence, whenever we use inferential statistics, we are comparing the likelihood that the null hypothesis is correct to the likelihood that the alternate hypothesis is correct. You may have noticed that the alternate (statistical) hypothesis is closely related to the research hypothesis.

To continue with our story, Yesavage et al. trained their 10 pilots on the flight simulator for 8 hours before the day of the experiment. At 8:00 a.m. on the day of the experiment, each pilot was asked to land the simulated plane, just as if an examination by the Federal Aviation Administration (FAA) were being conducted for licensing. To assess landing performance, the experimenters measured various aspects of a simulated airplane landing. These included measurements such as the distance from the center of the runway upon landing and deviations from the most accurate flight path into the descent.

After landings were completed in the "before smoking" condition, the pilots smoked 19 mg of THC in the form of a joint. Yesavage et al. report that 19 mg of THC is the "equivalent of a strong social dose" (1985, p. 1326). Thus, it was not an abnormally high amount of marijuana to have inhaled. Subjects were tested in the "after-smoking" condition the next morning at 8:00 a.m., after 24 marijuana-free hours had passed.

Now, here's where the concepts of central tendency and variability begin to play a role in inferential statistics. Let's look at three of the dependent variables used in the Yesavage et al. study: distance from runway center on landing, lateral

Table 3.3 SIMULATED LANDING PERFORMANCE BY PILOTS

| | Marijuana Condition | | | |
| | Before smoking | | After smoking | |
Landing Performance	M	SD	M	SD
Distance off-center in feet	12	6.5	24	8.2
Lateral deviation from path in feet	19	6.4	34	11.2
Vertical deviation from path in feet	26	13.0	40	18.4

From "Carry-over Effects of Marijuana Intoxication on Aircraft Pilot Performance: A Preliminary Report" by J. A. Yesavage, V. O. Leirer, M. Denari, and L. E. Hollister, 1985, *American Journal of Psychiatry, 142*, p. 1328. Copyright 1985 by American Psychiatric Association. Adapted by permission.

deviation from an ideal flight path, and vertical deviation from an ideal flight path. Descriptive statistics concerning these variables are presented in Table 3.3. Take a look at the table and try to understand what the descriptive statistics mean before reading my explanation. Consider only the first dependent variable for now (distance from center upon landing).

The data from two conditions ("before smoking" and "after smoking") have been summarized by means and standard deviations in Table 3.3. First, we must understand the dependent variable: A perfect landing would occur 0 feet from center; that is, the plane would land exactly in the center of the runway. However, this kind of precision is difficult to achieve with an airplane. According to Table 3.3, before smoking marijuana, the subjects' mean distance from center upon landing was 12 feet. Because these were experienced, licensed pilots who were instructed to take the task as seriously as they would for an FAA examination, we may assume that such deviation from center is fairly normal. The standard deviation for that condition is 6.5, indicating that the average variation from the mean distance of 12 feet was $6\frac{1}{2}$ feet. In other words, some subjects may have landed the plane exactly 12 feet off center, but (on average) many landed the plane 6.5 feet closer or farther away than that.

Now let's think about the "after smoking" condition. According to Table 3.3, 24 hours after smoking, the subjects' mean distance from center upon landing was 24 feet. The mean had doubled by comparison to the "before smoking" condition. In other words, subjects were now landing twice as far from center as before. Yesavage et al. report that 24-foot landing errors are "extremely serious" and "can easily lead to crashes" (1985, p. 1328). What about the standard deviation? It's 8.2 feet, which indicates that more variability occurred among "after smoking" landings than among "before smoking" landings. However, the increase in variability is nowhere near as large as the increase in mean distance from center across the two conditions.

Verify for yourself that the other two dependent variables shown in Table 3.3 also indicate worse performance in the "after smoking" condition than in the "before smoking" condition. This is true even though the flight landing test occurred a full 24 hours after a strong, but not abnormal, dose of marijuana had been inhaled.

Statistical Significance

So far, we've ignored a major problem in this picture. We've established that the means between two conditions differ: To consider distance from center alone, the "before smoking" mean is 12 feet, whereas the "after smoking" mean is 24 feet. Clearly, 12 and 24 are different from each other. But is this difference consistent enough that we would be willing to generalize from that sample of 10 pilots to the entire population of marijuana-smoking airline pilots? In other words, is this difference reliable or not? This is the crucial question that inferential statistics can answer.

If you look carefully at the formulas used to calculate inferential statistics, like t in a t-test, you'll see that they take into account both the central tendency and the variability of each set of scores to be compared. It is not enough to consider central tendency alone. Let's see how variability also affects statistical significance by looking at some imaginary data sets.

In Table 3.4A, you'll see ten numbers whose mean is 12 and ten numbers whose mean is 24. Look at them briefly and think about what each set's standard deviation must be. Obviously, it's zero: The numbers within each set do not vary from each other at all. Suppose that these twenty imaginary numbers had actually been collected as distance-from-center scores produced by 10 pilots. This would be an extremely consistent difference between conditions, wouldn't it? Every subject would have done twice as badly after smoking marijuana than before smoking it. Such results would be very compelling in convincing us that the negative effects of marijuana really do last for 24 hours. Note that this consistency is reflected in very low standard deviations: the lower the standard deviation, the smaller the amount of variability among scores.

Now look at Table 3.4B. Here are two groups of ten numbers with the same means as before, but their standard deviations have increased, indicating that the difference between before- and after-smoking conditions is not perfectly consistent. Some subjects show a strong effect of the marijuana; others show a weaker effect. This is a more realistic pattern of data than the set shown in Table 3.4A. Although some variation exists, there is still some consistency to the effect. All of the subjects performed more accurately before smoking than they did after smoking, but to differing degrees.

Finally, let's consider Table 3.4C. Here, the example is taken to its opposite extreme. Suppose we have two groups of ten numbers, again with means of 12 and 24 feet, but this time the means are affected by some very extreme scores. Accordingly, the standard deviations are huge, indicating a large amount of variability in the data. Lots of variability concerns good researchers—it means that the difference between conditions in central tendency may only be caused by a set of extreme scores. Surely we wouldn't want to issue a general edict to everyone (*"Marijuana impairs performance for 24 hours after smoking!"*) on the basis of scores from some highly unusual subjects.

The important similarity to notice between sections A, B, and C of Table 3.4 is that, in every case, the means remain at 12 and 24 feet. However, the standard deviations differ dramatically. Because inferential statistics take into account both

Table 3.4 HYPOTHETICAL DISTANCE OFF
CENTER DATA (IN FEET) SHOWING EFFECT OF VARIABILITY

A.

Distance Off Center Before Marijuana	Distance Off Center After Marijuana
12	24
12	24
12	24
12	24
12	24
12	24
12	24
12	24
12	24
12	24
$M = 12$	$M = 24$
$SD = 0$	$SD = 0$

B.

Distance Off Center Before Marijuana	Distance Off Center After Marijuana
11	23
12	24
11	25
13	23
10	20
15	20
9	28
11	23
13	25
11	25
$M = 12$	$M = 24$
$SD = 2$	$SD = 2$

C.

Distance Off Center Before Marijuana	Distance Off Center After Marijuana
1	83
25	16
17	27
6	4
30	7
2	60
1	10
11	20
18	5
10	9
$M = 12$	$M = 24$
$SD = 10$	$SD = 27$

central tendency and variability, we would expect to see a corresponding difference in statistical significance.*

Indeed, we do. When a *t*-test was conducted on the unrealistically consistent data set shown in Table 3.4A, the difference was found to be statistically significant. This means that we can confidently generalize from the results of the sample to the entire population. We would expect that any pilot (not just the ones in our sample) who smoked marijuana 24 hours before flying would be *likely* to experience negative effects during the flight. Later, we'll see why it's impossible to be absolutely certain that every pilot would experience negative effects.

When a *t*-test was used to analyze the more realistic data in Table 3.4B, the difference was also statistically significant. The inferential statistic, *t*, is telling us that the mild amount of variability in these data is not large enough to override the strong difference in central tendency. Once again, because the difference is statistically significant, we can confidently generalize from the sample to the population.

Finally, the third set of data (in Table 3.4C) produced a *t* value that was not statistically significant. This should come as no surprise. After all, we know that the variability was huge in that sample because so many subjects produced extreme scores. Because the difference between means is not statistically significant (according to our inferential statistics), we cannot generalize from the sample to the population. In other words, even though the means are identical in all three examples, the data from Table 3.4C do not allow us to say that marijuana smoking hampers flying ability 24 hours after inhalation in the entire population of marijuana-smoking pilots.

The main point of working through these hypothetical data carefully is to show you why inferential statistics are necessary. Too many people make the mistake of assuming that any large difference between means must be a significant difference. In fact, looking only at the difference between two means, without taking variability into account, does not allow us to determine whether the results are significant or not.

Now, one more thing. Go back to Table 3.3, which shows the data that were collected by Yesavage et al. These descriptive statistics are real—they are the actual numbers that Yesavage et al. obtained when they tested their 10 pilots. Since Table 3.3 lists means and standard deviations for three different dependent variables, there are three different comparisons to be made. Look again at the standard deviations. Wouldn't you agree that the largest amount of variability occurs within the two conditions in which vertical deviation from the ideal flight path was measured? What does this variability mean? Is the difference between those two conditions (*M* = 26 feet and *M* = 40 feet) likely to be statistically significant? It will really help if you try to answer this question before reading further.

If you said no, you were right. Although the absolute difference between 26 and 40 (40 − 26 = 14) is greater than the absolute difference between 12 and 24

---

*Actually, statistical significance depends not only on the standard deviation of each set of ten scores, but also on the standard deviation of difference scores between the two conditions. I have simplified for the sake of clarity.

(24 − 12 = 12), *t*-tests showed that the smaller difference is significant, whereas the larger difference is not. By now, you should understand why: Although the means differ in each case, the variability among sample subjects in their vertical deviation from the ideal flight path was too large to signify a consistent difference in the population as a whole.

The first two differences shown in Table 3.3 were statistically significant. In other words, by considering both central tendency and variability of the data, our inferential statistics show that 24 feet is significantly farther than 12 feet from the runway center, and 34 feet is significantly farther than 19 feet from the ideal lateral path to landing. The data in these conditions are consistent enough that we would expect to see the same general pattern in most marijuana-smoking airplane pilots.

Probability

It would be nice if statistical significance was as definite as I've made it sound in the previous section. However, life is never quite that simple. The fact is that inferential statistics cannot tell us with absolute certainty whether sample results will really hold true for the population. In other words, they do not provide definite answers like "yes" or "no." Instead, inferential statistics use the notion of **probability,** which is the likelihood (not the certainty) that a particular statistical hypothesis is true. They can tell us that a pattern of results will probably hold true for the population as a whole, but they can never determine definitely that those sample results will hold true for the population. The only way to determine with absolute certainty whether sample results can be generalized to a population is to test the entire population, which is usually impossible.

Let's think about this for a moment in terms of null and alternate statistical hypotheses. Recall that the null hypothesis always says that there is no difference in mean scores between conditions. When we obtain sample data that do appear to differ between conditions, the null hypothesis is in danger of being false. Inferential statistics help us to decide whether to reject that null hypothesis or accept it. Rejecting the null hypothesis is equivalent to saying that there really is a difference in mean scores between conditions in the population and that therefore the null hypothesis must be false. Accepting the null hypothesis is like saying that it is true; if we tested the entire population, there really would be no difference in mean scores between conditions.

Inferential statistics provides us with an exact measure of the likelihood that our decision to reject the null hypothesis will be wrong. We call this value p for probability. (Sometimes, this probability is measured by a value called **alpha,** represented by α. For our purposes, either term is acceptable.) The value of p is not just any probability; it's the probability that a Type I error has occurred.

A **Type I error** is the mistake we make when we reject the null hypothesis even though it was really true. Yes, I know—you heard that mumbo-jumbo in Stats 101 and didn't understand it back then either. Maybe an example will help. Let's say we compare two means (12 and 24 were nice numbers, for example) and decide that the difference between them is statistically significant and therefore does hold true for the population as a whole. We reject the null hypothesis that says there won't be a difference between the two means in the population. But because inferential statistics are not capable of producing definite answers, there is some possibility that this rejection was a mistake. Maybe if we went out and tested the entire population, we'd find that there was in fact no difference in the means between conditions. This would show that the null hypothesis, which we rejected, was actually correct. We should not have rejected it. In this case, we would have made a Type I error.

The value p measures the probability that we made this error. If $p = .50$, this means there is a 50% chance that the decision we made (to reject the null hypothesis) was wrong. This is an enormous chance of error! Surely, we wouldn't want to stake our scientific reputations on decisions that have only a 50/50 chance of being correct. By common convention, behavioral scientists have selected the value of $p = .05$ as the maximum error they will allow. This means that any statistical decision with a probability of Type I error greater than 5% is not to be trusted.

Sometimes this concept is difficult to grasp at first, so let me say it again in another way. We are willing to accept a 5% chance of being wrong in rejecting the null hypothesis, but we are not willing to accept any greater chance of Type I error. Therefore, whenever the value of p exceeds .05 (or 5%), we do not reject the null hypothesis. Instead, we accept it and conclude that the apparent difference obtained in our sample data is not reliable enough to warrant a generalization across the entire population. We report that the effect (in this case, a difference between means) is not significant.

On the other hand, whenever the value of p is less than .05 (or 5%), we do reject the null hypothesis. We conclude that the sample difference is reliable enough to warrant a generalization across the entire population. There is always a chance that our decision will be wrong. When our inferential statistics tell us that $p = .05$, we have a 5% chance of being wrong. If $p = .01$, our chance of being wrong is reduced to only 1%. Thus, the value of p is a direct measurement of the likelihood that our decision to reject the null hypothesis was the wrong decision.

Yesavage et al. (1985) made their decision that certain differences between "before smoking" and "after smoking" conditions were significant by looking at the value of their inferential statistic, t, and the probability of error, p. To be considered statistically significant, the value of p must have been smaller than .05 for the first two dependent variables listed in Table 3.3. The third dependent variable produced data that were not statistically significant; in that case, p must have been larger than .05.

Don't despair if all this seems rather confusing. It's tough to learn the proper use and interpretation of statistics just from reading about it. You need to have a set of data along with a real decision to make. Undoubtedly, your research methods professor will soon provide that opportunity, and your skill in statistical interpretation will develop with concrete practice.

Finding the Value of p

You've seen that the important decision of whether a difference between means is statistically significant, and therefore can be trusted in generalizing to a population, depends strongly on the value of p. How can this value be determined? In other words, exactly what process should be followed in order to decide whether a difference is statistically significant or not?

There are two common methods that may be used to determine significance once you have calculated the inferential statistic of your choice, such as t or F. First, you may have calculated the statistic by hand from a formula found in a textbook. This is probably the method many of you learned in your basic statistics course. In this case, the easiest way to determine significance is to compare the obtained value of the statistic you calculated with the critical value shown on a statistical table. Common statistical tables are published at the back of this book, in Appendix C, for your reference.*

Yesavage et al. computed the value of the inferential statistic called t to assess the difference between the two means concerned with distance from center upon landing ("before smoking" $M = 12$ feet; "after smoking" $M = 24$ feet). If you had their raw data and calculated a t-test according to the formula in any statistics book, you, like they, would have obtained the value of $t = -3.52$. To assess the significance of this inferential statistic, you would need to consult the statistical table of critical values for a t-test. Table C.5 is on page 316 of Appendix C in the back of this book. Take a look at it before we continue.

The critical value table asks you for two pieces of information: the number of degrees of freedom (df) in your data set and the probability of error (p) that you are willing to accept. Degrees of freedom are related to the number of subjects in your sample or the number of categories in your research design; the more subjects or categories, the greater the degrees of freedom. It is simple to calculate degrees of freedom: You'll find the formulas listed at the bottom of each critical value table in Appendix C of this book. Take a look at the bottom of page 316 to verify that the formula for degrees of freedom for a dependent t-test is $N - 1$. In the Yesavage et al. experiment, the number of subjects (N) was equal to 10, which leaves 9 degrees of freedom ($10 - 1 = 9$). Determining the probability level you are willing to accept is also simple: By convention, psychologists are willing to accept no more than a 5% chance of error, so $p = .05$.

To use the critical table, simply find the row corresponding to 9 degrees of freedom and the column corresponding to a .05 probability of Type I error. The critical value that is shown in that row and column is 2.262. Compare your obtained value of t (-3.52) to the critical value, and pay no attention to whether the t value is positive or negative. *Whenever the absolute value that you obtained is larger than the critical value in the book, the difference you are assessing is statistically significant.*

In this instance, therefore, the effect is significant because the absolute value of our obtained $t = -3.52$ is larger than the critical value listed on the table, 2.262. If the obtained t value had been smaller than the critical value, the difference between means would not be considered statistically significant.

---

*Appendix C contains critical value tables for two-tailed tests only. Most careful researchers prefer two-tailed tests, even for alternate statistical hypotheses that specify direction, because they are less likely to result in Type I error.

I mentioned earlier that there are two methods for determining significance. The second one is easier: Most scientists now use computer programs to calculate the values of inferential statistics like t. In addition to computing obtained values, which you could compare to critical values on published statistical tables, these computer programs sometimes provide the exact value of p. Therefore, it is possible that you will have access to a computer program that provides both the obtained value of a statistic and the probability of Type I error that is associated with it. In this case, you would simply assess the value of p. If it is larger than .05, the difference between means is not significant; if it is smaller than .05, the difference is significant.

Increasing Statistical Power

When scientists design a study, their research hypotheses indicate that some difference between conditions will occur. This is because inferential statistics are capable of telling us the likelihood that we are making a Type I error, but they cannot determine as precisely the likelihood of a Type II error. To refresh your memory, a **Type II error** occurs whenever we decide to accept the null hypothesis even though, in reality, the null hypothesis was false.

Yesavage et al.'s third dependent variable, vertical deviation from the ideal landing path, provides an example. Because the data were highly variable, the difference between vertical deviation in the before-smoking condition ($M = 26$ feet) and vertical deviation in the after-smoking condition ($M = 40$ feet) was not significant. This means that Yesavage et al. accepted the null hypothesis that there was no difference between those conditions in the general population. If, in fact, there had been a difference in the population, Yesavage et al. would have made a Type II error: accepting the null hypothesis when in fact it was false.

Inferential statistics can measure the probability that a Type I error has been made. As you know, using a probability level of .05, there is a 5% chance, at most, of rejecting the null hypothesis by mistake (Type I error). However, we do not know exactly how much chance there is of accepting the null hypothesis by mistake (Type II error). Therefore, when researchers are faced with results that indicate no effect, they cannot determine the likelihood that there really is no effect in the population.

To avoid this problem, researchers design their studies so that a difference between conditions can be predicted. We then try to enhance the **power** of the statistical test, which is its ability to detect a significant difference if the difference really exists. Basically, there are two ways to increase statistical power. Before reading further, think about what they might be based on what you have already learned from this chapter.

1. Statistical power can be increased by reducing the variability among scores. We've seen in several examples that data sets containing lots of variation are not likely to produce statistically significant results. Therefore, anything we can do to reduce that variability and make the data more consistent will boost our chances of finding significance.

2. Statistical power can be increased by increasing the number of subjects in the study. As you know, the number of subjects is directly related to the degrees of freedom, and we have seen that degrees of freedom are crucial in determining statistical significance. Take another look at Table C.5 in Appendix C (page 316). We used 9 degrees of freedom to assess the significance of Yesavage et al.'s effect because they had 10 subjects in their experiment. What would have happened if we had used 10 degrees of freedom, or 12 or 40? In each case, note that the critical value decreases. In fact, you can run your finger down any column in that table, and as the degrees of freedom increase, the critical value decreases. Because it is easier for your obtained value to exceed lower critical values, you are more likely to find significance using larger numbers of subjects.

It is important that you understand the basic concepts behind statistical power because we will be considering them repeatedly in different contexts throughout this book. Over time, you will learn to design research studies that provide the best chance of finding an effect if it is there.

Effect Size

The fact that statistical significance can be boosted by testing large numbers of subjects leads to a paradox in psychological research: On the one hand, we need enough subjects to provide a representative sample of the population. On the other hand, statistical significance would be artificial if it were achieved merely by testing hundreds of subjects. We solve this paradox by assessing the size of an effect in addition to its significance.

Because statistical significance is based largely on data variability and sample size, any consistent difference between large subject groups will be significant even if it is small. Suppose, for example, that we obtained a consistent average difference of six inches in runway landing position between pilots who smoked marijuana 24 hours earlier and pilots who did not. If we tested a large enough sample of subjects, this difference would be statistically significant but too small to worry about.

Beginning scientists often assume that the size of an effect can be known merely by looking at the value of its inferential statistic. This assumption is not true. For example, a large t value like 4.77 does not necessarily reflect a larger effect than a small t value like 1.22. Instead, the difference may only tell us that more subjects were tested to produce the first value than the second. Likewise, an effect that is statistically significant at a low p value like .01 is not necessarily larger than an effect with a higher p value like .05.

To measure an effect accurately, we use simple formulas that provide a percentage value for effect size. Yesavage et al.'s t value of −3.52, for example, produces an effect size of .58. This means that 58% of the variation in subjects' runway positions on landing can be accounted for by the marijuana they smoked. The remaining 42% of the variation in their landing positions must have been caused by individual differences in skill, fluctuations in measurement and flight simulation equipment, and other uncontrolled variables. An effect size of .58 for a *t*-test is very large. Thus, we can conclude that the harmful effect of marijuana on pilots' performance even 24 hours later is consistent enough to be statistically significant and large enough to be of practical importance.

The basic information that you will need in order to assess effect size in the research that you conduct or evaluate is presented in Table C.7 on page 318. Each of the formulas presented there is discussed in relevant chapters of this book, and all of them are simple to calculate. Effect size may seem a bit mysterious to you right now, but by the time you finish this book, it should be easy to understand.

PARAMETRIC AND NONPARAMETRIC STATISTICS

We have discussed in some detail the basic distinction between descriptive and inferential statistics. Now, we must review briefly the difference between parametric and nonparametric statistics.

Parametric statistics are inferential tests that are designed for data sets that meet certain requirements. There are several requirements, but the most important of them is that the data fall along a normal distribution. Many data sets meet this requirement; therefore, parametric statistics are used more commonly than nonparametric statistics. Examples of parametric tests include the *t*-test, analysis of variance (ANOVA), correlation, and regression.

Some data sets, however, contain scores that do not fall along a normal distribution. Instead, these scores may be negatively or positively skewed. In this case, parametric statistics are not appropriate. **Nonparametric statistics** are inferential tests that are designed for data sets that cannot be represented along a normal distribution. Examples of nonparametric tests include the Mann-Whitney U, Wilcoxon, and Kruskal-Wallis tests.

Because parametric tests are more commonly used in beginning research, we will concentrate on them and have little to say about nonparametric statistics in this book. You should be aware, though, that in some cases, the data you collect will force you to use nonparametric statistics. The basic concepts behind nonparametric statistics are the same as those behind parametric statistics; it is primarily the calculation formulas that change.

STATISTICS IN SCIENTIFIC CONTEXT

Please remember that the purpose of this chapter has been to show how the basic concepts of statistics are put to use. Throughout this book, we'll use the information from this chapter as a foundation on which to build greater skill in applying the tools of statistics to the design and evaluation of scientific research. Our approach will be to use and interpret statistics in the context of certain research designs. Later chapters, each devoted to a specific type of research, will provide this opportunity.

SUMMARY OF MAIN POINTS

- Statistics are used in scientific research to describe data sets concisely and to determine whether research results are likely to hold true in the general population.

- To use statistics properly, data must be classified according to nominal, ordinal, interval, or ratio scales of measurement.

- Descriptive statistics can characterize entire data sets with only two or three numbers. They include measures of frequency, central tendency, and variability. Different descriptive statistics are selected depending on the scale of measurement used to gather data and the research question to be answered.

- Inferential statistics allow us to infer whether the results of a sample are likely to hold true in the population at large.

- Null and alternate hypotheses are types of statistical hypotheses that state potential research outcomes. Research hypotheses state general expectations depending on theory and past studies, and they usually resemble alternate statistical hypotheses in content.

- Statistical significance in hypothesis testing depends on the central tendency and variability of the data being analyzed. Highly variable data are not likely to yield significant differences even if measures of central tendency are very different from each other.

- Probability levels represent the likelihood that the null hypothesis was rejected in error and, in behavioral science, are limited to .05.

- The power of a statistical test may be increased by reducing variability or by increasing the number of subjects who participate in the research.

- A statistically significant effect is consistent enough to be generalized to a population, but it may be small or large in size. Both significance and size should be assessed.

CHAPTER EXERCISES

1. Use your own words to define these key terms:

raw data	range
nominal	variance
ordinal	standard deviation
interval	inferential statistics
ratio	sample
descriptive statistics	population
frequency	statistical hypothesis

central tendency	null hypothesis
average	alternate hypothesis
mean	probability
median	alpha
mode	Type I error
normal distribution	Type II error
positive skew	power
negative skew	parametric statistics
variability	nonparametric statistics

2. Briefly describe one example for each of the four scales of measurement. Use examples that are different from those presented in this chapter.

3. Assess the significance of the following obtained values of t by referring to the critical value Table C.5. In each case, the number in parentheses refers to the degrees of freedom. Use the conventional limit of probability for Type I error.
   a) $t(18) = 2.55$
   b) $t(8) = 14.73$
   c) $t(30) = -2.041$

4. Using a computer or calculator, determine the mean and standard deviation of each column of numbers below. Which of the two comparisons is more likely to be significant? Why?

Data Set		Data Set 2	
A	B	A	B
14	15	13	16
13	15	11	15
11	12	11	4
14	16	13	12
13	16	46	10
11	16	15	29
12	14	12	13
16	16	12	1
13	14	16	43
11	13	27	6

5. Behavioral scientists accept a probability of Type I error at a value no greater than .05. Compare the use of a probability level set at .05 in standard research on human memory with the use of the same probability level used in the detection of cancerous tumors by X-ray. Should the probability limits for Type I error be set at a higher or lower value for cancer detection? Why?

Nonexperimental Research

4

Dian Fossey observing mountain gorillas in central Africa.

In Chapter 1, we began constructing a framework of research designs in the form of a garden trellis. Now that we've covered the preliminaries of library research and statistics, it's time to start filling in the bare spots on that trellis. So far, it only contains the three basic types of research: nonexperimental, experimental, and quasi-experimental. In this chapter, we will consider nonexperimental research in more detail.

Nonexperimental research describes human behavior, but it does not allow scientists to determine what caused that behavior. In general, nonexperimental research uses no independent variables. In other words, the researcher does not attempt to manipulate a particular variable in hopes of changing a subject's performance. Thus, all forms of nonexperimental research may be defined by two characteristics:

1. They describe behavior but do not specify its cause.
2. They do not use independent variables.

There are five major types of nonexperimental research: case studies, archival research, natural observation, surveys, and correlational research. The last of these, correlational research, is discussed in Chapter 5. This chapter examines each of the other four types.

THE CASE STUDY

The simplest type of nonexperimental research is the **case study,** a detailed look at one individual who usually shows some rare form of behavior. You may be familiar with the case study of a woman called Sybil Dorsett, who developed 14 female and 2 male personalities throughout an abusive childhood. Her story was first published in the psychiatric literature as a formal case study, then became a best-selling book (Schreiber, 1973) and a television movie.

Case studies are used in the earliest stages of exploring a new topic. Multiple personality disorder is fairly well known nowadays, but it was quite novel at the time Sybil was discovered. Often, the observation of one individual like Sybil leads to a host of new questions that can be studied in different ways.

Case studies are also popular in exploring extremely rare behaviors because it is difficult to gather a sample of subjects with similar psychological patterns. For example, the studies of acquired dyslexia that we considered briefly in Chapter 1 are conducted on a case-by-case basis because so few people exhibit the same patterns of reading difficulty after brain injury. For that matter, just finding a group of subjects who all had experienced injury to the same part of the brain would be a very challenging task. That's why the case study is such a valuable part of our arsenal of research designs. Psychologists would be missing a crucial piece of the puzzle without knowledge of such rare cases.

Despite these advantages, case studies are criticized frequently. For example, Freud's (1917/1952) theory of normal personality was formed after he studied only a few individuals who had experienced bizarre feelings and beliefs. Many scientists have argued that case studies of five or six rare individuals do not form an adequate basis for a theory of personality that is supposed to apply to all of us (Schultz & Schultz, 1987). What do you think? Why would it be dangerous to rely on small numbers of abnormal case studies when building a theory of normal behavior?

Here are some of the reasons that professional critics have offered:

1. *Lack of generalization.* You know from Chapter 3 that the purpose of inferential statistics is to tell us whether it is safe to generalize from the results of a subject sample to the members of an untested population. However, with a case study, there is no sample and there can be no statistical analysis. Only one person has been observed, and that person's actions might be completely unique.

2. *Existence of unknown variables.* You'll soon see that this is a problem common to all types of nonexperimental research. When we merely observe without taking some control of a subject's situation, the subject may be influenced by all sorts of variables. For example, Schreiber (1973) reports that Sybil was physically abused by her mother: Isn't it possible, then, that her multiple personalities were caused by physical injury to the brain? There is no evidence that such brain damage did occur, but it could have.

3. *Subjects sometimes lie.* People have all kinds of motives for lying. An adult patient with acquired dyslexia might be embarrassed to admit having reading problems that most third-grade children have overcome. A person suffering from histrionic personality disorder may embellish stories of sexual experiences in an attempt to get attention. A mass murderer might lie to psychologists to get milder punishment through an insanity plea. It is risky to base any generalization on one story that may not be true.

4. *Interpretation may not be objective.* Researchers who conduct detailed investigations of the inner lives of individuals are likely to become emotionally attached to their subjects. Sybil's psychoanalyst, Cornelia Wilbur, became a personal friend during the 2,354 office sessions that Sybil required for treatment (Schreiber, 1973). A relationship between researcher and subject spanning that much time would undermine the objectivity that a researcher might normally bring to the interpretation of a subject's responses.

These four problems surrounding the use of case studies should be considered whenever you conduct a case study yourself or evaluate one in either the popular or scientific literature. Case studies are valuable in exploring rare behaviors and generating new ideas, but they do not allow us to draw general conclusions about the behaviors we have observed.

ARCHIVAL RESEARCH

People who analyze and interpret existing data are conducting **archival research.** The term comes from the word *archives*, which refers to written records. Public documents such as birth and death records, marriage licenses, divorce decrees, and census information are commonly used in archival research. By studying existing data, social scientists are able to uncover important historical and social trends within and between various cultures. A simple example of such trends might be the fact that about 50% of American marriages ended in divorce during the late 1980s, whereas the divorce rate reached only 23% in 1950 (U.S. Bureau of the Census, 1989).

Perhaps you've already thought of one advantage of archival research—someone else has collected the data! All you have to do is find, analyze, and interpret them. (Don't be fooled, however: Archival data analysis still requires time and effort.) Another advantage of archival research is its relevance to the real world. Information that is likely to be collected from large portions of the population usually has immediate practical value.

However, like case studies, the interpretation of archival data can be hampered by several problems:

1. *Data may be biased.* Usually, archival records are maintained by people who are not trained in scientific research. Often, they collect data in a haphazard manner, with little regard for research design. Babies born in extreme poverty at home may never receive a birth certificate; couples divorced outside of the country are not listed in American archives; many people do not tell the truth when asked to write down their annual incomes. With these biased data, the researcher's interpretation of trends concerning birth rate, divorce rate, and average income may be flawed.

   In addition, archival data often come from biased sources such as newspapers. Organizations like Accuracy In Media (AIM) have pointed out that the political bias of many newspapers sometimes causes their information to be slanted in deceptive directions. For example, if your archival research involves counting the number of times a particular presidential candidate was photographed in a major newspaper, you may be counting the newspaper's selection bias more than the candidate's public appearances.

2. *Statistics can be misleading.* This is especially true when statistics are computed from archival data. Even unbiased data might still be taken from a sample that does not adequately represent the population. A classic example of this occurred in a famous archival study conducted during the mid-1980s regarding marriage statistics. Although the study was seriously flawed, the massive publicity it received "set off a profound crisis of confidence among America's growing ranks of single women" (Salholz, 1986, p. 55). The study and its flaws are presented in Box 4.1.

3. *Unknown variables may exist.* A third problem with interpreting archival research is, once again, the problem of unknown variables. A marriage certificate simply says that a couple has been married—it doesn't tell us why they got married, or whether either partner had been married before, or any number of other important details. When we interpret these archival data, we may be tempted to ignore some of those variables. The price is high: We may end up with an interpretation that fits the existing data but is entirely wrong.

Box 4.1 THE GREAT AMERICAN MARRIAGE CRUNCH

Some of you may have read about the shortage of unmarried men during the 1980s, when it was argued that single college-educated women had only a 20% chance of finding a husband by age 30. Worse yet, these women's chances dropped to 5% at age 35, and down to a dismal 1% at age 40. As a point of comparison, *Newsweek* even claimed that single women over the age of 40 "were more likely to be killed by a terrorist" than to marry (Salholz, 1986, p. 55).

The archival research leading to these conclusions was conducted by Bennett, Bloom, and Craig, three research scientists employed by Harvard and Yale Universities. The actual statistics were provided to the press before they had been published. Questions about the validity of their conclusions led Bennett et al. to cancel their plans for scientific publication, but not before every major American newspaper, television news show, magazine, and television or radio talk show had publicized the results. The news reporter who published the first story from Bennett without checking it said, "We usually just take anything from good schools. If it's a study from Yale, we just put it in the paper" (Petersen, as quoted by Faludi, 1991, p. 9).

It turned out that Bennett et al.'s conclusions were completely false because of misleading data and inappropriate statistical analyses. First, they based their estimates of the numbers of men and women in the United States on a small sample of subjects that did not accurately represent the population. As Faludi has pointed out, a quick glance at the U.S. Census Bureau's population records would have shown that there were more than enough single men in America to accommodate marriages. Second, Bennett et al.'s conclusions were based on the assumption that women marry men who are 2 to 3 years older than they are. This assumption was simply not valid for the 1980s: At that time, many women married men the same age or younger or much older than they were. Third, Bennett et al. used a statistical analysis that was new and untested for this type of application. The scientist who developed that statistical model agreed that using it to compute chances of marriage was risky.

When another researcher (Moorman, 1986) corrected these problems and analyzed the archival data again, she found that college-educated women of age 30 had a 58% to 66% chance of marriage. By age 35, their chances had dropped to 32% to 41%, and at age 40, their chances were 17% to 23%. These statistics are quite different from those presented by Bennett and his colleagues. Unlike Bennett et al.'s mistakes, which made front-page headlines and received massive popular attention, Moorman's corrected archival research was buried in fine print on the inside pages of only a few newspapers. The average reader would never have known that the results obtained by Bennett et al. had even been questioned.

To make matters worse, the statement that a middle-aged woman's chances of marrying were even lower than her chances of being murdered by a terrorist was completely unfounded. During a personal interview with a member of *Newsweek,* Faludi learned that this spice for the story was based on a joke: "One of the bureau reporters was going around saying it as a joke—like, 'Yeah, a woman's more likely to get bumped off by a terrorist'—and next thing we knew, one of the writers in New York took it seriously and it ended up in print" (as quoted by Faludi, 1991, p. 100).

Many conclusions that are drawn from archival data are weak because of these potential problems. Such conclusions are published regularly in the popular press, however, with no warning of their weakness. Archival research can provide important information, but it must be interpreted carefully.

NATURAL OBSERVATION

Some of you may have seen the popular movie *Gorillas in the Mist* a few years back. The movie presented the story of Dian Fossey (1983), a scientist who spent 13 years observing the behavior of rare mountain gorillas in Africa. The type of research that she conducted is known as **natural observation:** that is, simply observing human or animal behavior in natural settings. It is commonly used in anthropology, sociology, and biology as well as in psychology. Sometimes the term **field observation** is used, but it means the same thing as natural observation.

There are two types of natural observation. **Participant observation** occurs when the researcher becomes a member of the group that is being studied, usually without the knowledge of other members of the group. **Nonparticipant observation** occurs when the researcher observes from the sidelines, but is not a member of the group being studied. Most of the time, it is easy to distinguish which type of observation was used in a given study.

Which type of natural observation did Fossey use? Without knowing much about her research, you should be able to deduce that she must have used nonparticipant observation. After all, she could hardly have transformed herself into a gorilla! However, it is also true that Fossey imitated various forms of gorilla behavior to gain the trust of these huge animals. Eventually, they reached out to touch her and allowed her to hold and play with young gorillas of their clan. In this way, Fossey was able to observe certain gorilla behaviors that had never been recorded before. Although you and I would classify Fossey's work as nonparticipant observation, the subjects of her study might have held a different opinion.

Natural observation usually provides new knowledge that represents real life accurately. The artificial flavor of the experimental laboratory is nowhere to be seen here. Participant observation has the advantage that subjects maintain their typical behavior because they do not know that they are being observed. However, we have to consider the ethics of observing and recording people's behaviors without their awareness. Many people might question the ethics of observing homosexual behavior in the restroom of a gay bar, for example, as was done by Humphreys (1970).* A second problem with participant observation is that the researcher may lose objectivity after becoming a full-fledged member of the group being studied.

Nonparticipant observation reduces this loss of objectivity. The researcher observes from the sidelines and is able to remain fairly unbiased about the behaviors under study. However, nonparticipant observation isn't perfect, either. People tend to change their behavior when they know that a stranger is watching

---

*Humphreys participated as a lookout.

them and writing down everything they do. Even animals are affected by overt observation—just try following your pets around with a camera for a while, and see how their normal behavior changes.

One solution to this problem is for the nonparticipant researcher to remain hidden. This method is often used when developmental psychologists observe childhood behaviors. A one-way mirror is installed along one wall of a playroom, so that the children see only their own reflections in the mirror, whereas the observers on the other side can see through the mirror into the playroom. The children do not know that they are being observed in their natural setting.

Maintaining Reliability in Natural Observation

Reliability is a vital ingredient of good research, whether the research is nonexperimental, experimental, or quasi-experimental. We must be certain that our measurement of behavior is **reliable,** or consistent; that a particular behavior will be recorded in the same way each time it is observed. In natural observation, reliable measurement is often challenged by all the unexpected problems that occur outside of a controlled laboratory setting.

One of the many gorilla behaviors that Fossey (1983) studied was chest beating. To come to an understanding of the meaning of chest beating in gorilla culture, Fossey had to record similar actions consistently each time they occurred. For the measurement of chest beating in gorillas, you might be tempted to begin by recording the frequency and intensity of chest beats in one gorilla. Each time this gorilla beats its chest, you write down the number of beats that you heard and the general strength of each series of beats.

This plan sounds simple, but in reality there are a lot of things that can go wrong. First, chest beating sometimes occurs very rapidly—you may not be able to count fast enough to keep up with the number of chest beats that actually occurred. Second, one series of chest beats may vary in intensity, starting softly and becoming progressively louder. Third, the data collection is subject to personal perception: what sounds like a thunderingly loud and scary chest beat to me may be merely a patter to Fossey. Some reliable method of recording these chest beats must be worked out before the natural observation begins.

What we really need here are **operational definitions,** ways of defining fuzzy concepts precisely so that they can be measured in a reliable manner. For example, if you and I were going to conduct a study of gorillas, we might agree that "loud" chest beating refers to any chest beat that can be picked up by a tape recorder back at our camp. Like most operational definitions, this one isn't perfect: The distance between gorilla and camp will partly determine whether the tape recorder captures the chest beating. It is still useful, however, because it allows us to record most "loud" chest beats precisely and with little doubt as to what constitutes "loudness."

Researchers in all areas must develop operational definitions of the concepts they are studying. A sociologist who is compiling statistics on homeless people will need to operationally define "homeless," just as an anthropologist exploring ancient cultures must operationally define "primitive." Operational definitions sharpen the accuracy of scientific observation and, when stated in published reports, they allow critical readers to assess deeply the strengths and limitations of a research study.

To measure chest beating reliably, then, operational definitions must first be determined. After this step is completed, we might devise a rating sheet for each category of chest beating. For example, we could use an ordinal scale of measurement, assigning only one star to a chest beat that lasts less than 5 seconds and cannot be picked up back at camp, but assigning three stars to any chest beat that lasts more than 15 seconds and is captured on our tape recorder.

With a precise rating sheet, records of observed chest beating will be more reliable than if you had sauntered into the jungle with a blank piece of paper and no plan in mind. Furthermore, when the time comes that you need multiple observers so that several gorillas can be watched simultaneously, the rating sheet will help to produce consistent ratings across different observers. In Chapter 5, we will discuss how to assess the amount of consistency across multiple observers in situations like this. For now, when you conduct a natural observation or read about one in the literature, remember to consider the precision of rating sheets and operational definitions that were used. More importantly, keep in mind that all good research requires consistent measurement and precise operational definitions.

Incidentally, through natural observation, Fossey learned that chest beating is a ritual demonstration among male gorillas that is used to ward off physical aggression and maintain peaceful coexistence. This knowledge led comparative psychologists to a new understanding of the methods that gorillas and other animals use to avoid fights that would reduce the size of their endangered populations.

SURVEY RESEARCH

Survey research, which is the practice of administering questionnaires to many subjects to determine their opinions and beliefs, is the most common type of research conducted today (Judd, Smith, & Kidder, 1991). It is used for political prediction, consumer marketing, business management, fashion merchandising, musical composition, . . . well, the list could continue indefinitely. You have probably participated in survey research as a subject at one time or another, either by personal interview in a shopping mall, by telephone interview, or by writing down answers to a questionnaire that came in the mail.

People who don't know much about research methods often think of surveys as easy. Indeed, they do look easy, as if we merely scribble down a few questions one afternoon and send out a thousand copies that night, then wait for all those responses to arrive. Nothing could be farther from the truth. Although it is easy to design a bad survey, designing a good one requires time, effort, and knowledge. Graduate programs in psychology typically offer entire courses, sometimes a full year in length, devoted solely to survey research.

The myth that survey research is easy is not only false, it's dangerous. It encourages unqualified people to design and administer surveys, and it inspires authors of popular magazine and newspaper articles to interpret survey results carelessly. Examples of flawed surveys are easy to find: they were designed poorly, administered poorly, and interpreted poorly, but publicized only too well. One of the most famous is the Hite survey on sexuality.

An Example: Female Sexuality

Hite (1987) surveyed 4,500 women and found that 84% of them were not satisfied with their intimate relationships with men. In addition, 78% of them reported that they were treated as equals only occasionally by their male partners, and 96% believed that they gave more emotional support to men than they received. These results were snatched up immediately for a cover story in *Time* magazine (Wallis, 1987) and made headlines all across the United States.

As Hite's book describing the survey results became a best-seller, scientific researchers began to protest. Hite had used two methods of distributing her survey, and both were problematic. First, she mailed the survey to members of various women's organizations, primarily political groups, professional groups, counseling clinics, and women's rights organizations. Second, through talk show interviews and her previous books, Hite publicized an address to which any woman could write requesting a copy of the survey.

Can you spot the flaw here? Women who are active members of political and professional organizations may not represent average American women. In addition, subjects who take the time to write a letter requesting a survey probably have unusually strong opinions that they wish to express. In short, the women who filled out Hite's survey do not represent the general population of American women.

But wait, there's more. Only 4.5% of these biased women in Hite's sample actually bothered to complete the survey! In other words, 95% of them never responded to Hite; after receiving the survey, they did not mail it back to her. This is not surprising because the survey contained 127 questions, each encouraging a lengthy essay answer. In addition, many of the questions asked about extremely personal sexual practices. Only a special type of woman would have answered this sort of questionnaire. We now have a set of results based on only 4.5% of a biased set of women in the United States, yet Hite generalized those results to all American women.

To their credit, the *Washington Post* and *ABC News* were concerned enough about Hite's methodology to conduct a telephone survey of a more representative female sample (Squires, 1987). They found that only 7% of American women were dissatisfied with their intimate relationships, as opposed to Hite's figure of 84%. In addition, only 15% of the *Post-ABC* subjects reported sporadic equality, whereas 81% of them reported receiving equal treatment most of the time. Finally, in comparison to Hite's report that 96% of American women gave more emotional support than they received, only 41% of married women in the *Post-ABC* poll agreed.

Although differences between telephone and mail surveys may account for a portion of such discrepancies, the *Post-ABC* poll indicated that Hite's sampling techniques and low response rate had indeed produced misleading results. Hite, however, is correct in pointing out that telephone administration of the survey may have caused some women to alter their natural responses to important questions. The study of sexuality and equality among American women in contemporary culture deserves far more rigorous study than either Hite or the *Washington Post-ABC News* team provided.

The Hite study has become a classic example of how to do bad survey research. Now, let's consider the steps that are necessary in designing and conducting good surveys. Suppose that you are the manager of a small but growing business company. Recently, some of your better employees have expressed dissatisfaction with their jobs. This concerns you because you know from experience that job dissatisfaction among employees has all sorts of negative effects on small businesses.

Knowing the Literature

Learning the literature is our first step in undertaking any research study. There's no sense spending a lot of time and effort conducting scientific research to find out what others already know.

Upon reading the literature in organizational psychology, you might learn that job satisfaction depends on many different aspects of employment. Two-factor theory (Herzberg, 1966) proposes that satisfaction depends on one set of factors such as achievement, recognition, and responsibility, whereas dissatisfaction depends on a different set of factors, including company policy, administration, supervision, and physical working conditions. Facet satisfaction theory (Lawler, 1973) argues that internal factors are most important, such as the way in which an employee perceives the job. Past studies show that benefits, such as health insurance and paid vacations, do not have a strong effect on job satisfaction (Landy, 1985). It is clear from reviewing the literature that job dissatisfaction can stem from a large number of different factors and that the extent to which any one factor affects an employee will depend on that employee's perception of the situation. As a manager, you need to identify and solve the problem—but solutions will depend on the exact type of dissatisfaction that your employees are experiencing.

Framing a Research Question

Think about what a likely research question might be in an instance such as this. Will it help for you to find out what sorts of activities each employee performs every day? Perhaps. Will it help to determine the average amount of pay received by employees in similar jobs all across your state? Maybe. But what you really need to know before anything else is why your employees are dissatisfied. It might be that their salaries and activities are perfectly acceptable, but that some other aspect of their jobs is bothersome. It might be that their perception of the job does not match reality. Thus, your research question is, "Why are my employees dissatisfied?" After this question has been answered, others will advance or recede in importance accordingly.

The importance of selecting and framing a specific research question may seem obvious, but in fact it is the most common error made by beginning researchers. Too often, people hammer out a survey without a clear, precise understanding of exactly what it is they want to learn from the survey results. The more concretely you define your research question, the better your survey will be.

Writing Survey Questions

The cardinal rule of writing survey questions is to use plain, simple language. Many adult survey respondents are confused by even simple questions. Occasionally, this is because the subjects are poorly educated or nervous about completing the survey. However, more often the confusion is caused by survey questions that really are ambiguous. Questions that seem perfectly clear to you may be interpreted in a number of different ways by other people. For example, which of these two questions would you find easiest to answer?

1. *Do you like your job?*
2. *Do you experience satisfaction in accomplishing the daily activities involved with your employment?*

Because of its plain wording, question 1 would be preferred on a survey.

In addition to being clear and simple, survey questions should never convey your personal opinions. It is easy to slant a question according to your own beliefs without realizing that you are doing so. Consider the simple difference between using the frame, "do you. . . ?" and "don't you. . . ?" in the following example:

1. *Do you believe that the sole purpose of having a job is to earn money?*
2. *Don't you believe that the sole purpose of having a job is to earn money?*

If you were trying to please the experimenter, as most subjects do, how would you answer each question? Most people would agree that the wording of Question 2 encourages agreement in the form of a "yes" response. The same query, asked in a slightly different way in Question 1, is not biased toward a positive answer.

A third rule is to avoid **double-barreled questions.** These are questions that ask for two opinions but force subjects into one response. Whenever a question contains conjunction words like *and* or *or*, check to make sure that it is not double-barreled. Of course, questions that contain no conjunctions may also be double-barreled, as in the following example:

1. *Do you like your supervisor enough that you talk with her often?*

If you do like your supervisor and talk with her often, it will be easy to answer "yes" to this question. Likewise, if you don't like your supervisor and seldom talk with her, it will be easy to answer "no." However, what answer is appropriate if you like your supervisor very much, but seldom get the opportunity to talk with her? Double-barreled questions force the subject to respond with an answer that may not be entirely true.

Table 4.1 SURVEY QUESTIONS AND MODES OF RESPONSE

1. *Open-ended*
Why do you come to work every day? _____

_____

2. *Restricted*
Do you like your job? Yes _____ No _____

3. *Partially open-ended*
Which of the following job factors do you find dissatisfying?
    Relationship with supervisor _____
    Relationship with co-workers _____
    Annual salary   _____
    Insurance benefits   _____
    Availability of incentives   _____
    Daily work duties
    Other _____

_____

4. *Likert rating scale*
I am very satisfied with my job.

1	2	3	4	5
strongly disagree	disagree	neutral	agree	strongly agree

Designing Modes of Response

Designing possible modes of response is just as important as writing questions. A question like *Do you like your job?* could be followed by a number of different response modes, each illustrated in Table 4.1. Let's consider each of them in turn.

1. Questions can be **open-ended.** This means that no particular means of response is suggested. The question is followed by some blank space in which subjects are to write an answer. Remember that the amount of blank space following a question tells subjects how much information to provide. An open-ended question followed by a half-inch blank would likely be answered with one short word, such as "yes" or "no." However, an open-ended question followed by 10 blank lines of space encourages the subject to write several sentences of explanation.
2. **Restricted** questions are followed by a selection of possible answers. Subjects choose the one answer that represents their beliefs and circle it or place a checkmark next to it.
3. It is possible to compromise between open-ended and restricted questions by using the **partially open-ended** question. In this case, a selection of possible answers is provided along with the choice called "other." If none of the listed answers is appropriate, the subject may mark "other," then write a short explanation.

4. Rating scales are popular in survey research because they allow for precise statistical analysis. It's easy to set up an ordinal or interval level rating scale following a question, and that simple scale will often provide more information and give subjects a wider array of response than restricted modes allow.

One common mode of response is the **Likert rating scale,** named after a researcher who developed the scale in 1932. The Likert scale presents a statement rather than a question, then subjects rate their level of agreement with the statement by circling one of the numbers along the scale. Although the Likert rating scale shown in Table 4.1 contains only five rating intervals, they may contain more than that. If you want to provide subjects the opportunity to respond in a neutral manner, use an odd number of intervals, such as five, seven, or nine, so that there is a clear neutral point. On the other hand, if you prefer to force subjects' responses to lean in one direction or the other, use an even number of intervals.

What are the advantages and disadvantages of these four types of responses? In other words, which ones should you use in a survey on job satisfaction? The open-ended question allows an infinite variety of responses, but is difficult to analyze statistically. The restricted question allows some statistical analysis, but limits the subjects to a subset of answers that may not reflect their true experiences. The Likert rating scale offers a special advantage because it is considered an interval, rather than ordinal, scale of measurement by common convention. Because interval data may be analyzed by a wide variety of statistical tests, survey researchers often prefer the Likert scale.

The four modes of response listed here and illustrated in Table 4.1 are only a small set of the possibilities that you could use in a survey. Furthermore, they are not limited to surveys, but may be used in experimental and quasi-experimental research as well. One good way to learn about other useful methods of response is to review the literature of your selected topic area to find out which response methods are common among researchers in that field. This practice will not only give you new ideas, but will also allow you to gather data that may be compared directly to previous results.

Arranging the Questions

The final aspect of writing the survey that we need to consider is the placement of questions. Most amateur survey writers assume that any haphazard arrangement of questions will do, but that's not so. Dillman (1978) has presented several tips for the arrangement of questions on a survey:

1. Present related questions in subsets of their own, so that the general concept being explored is obvious. This helps your subjects to focus on one issue at a time, and thinking of related items in one general context may enhance their memories so that you obtain more accurate data.

2. If your survey includes questions about sensitive topics (such as sexual experiences or drug use), place those questions near the end of each con-

tent-related section. People are more likely to answer sensitive questions after they have committed themselves to filling out the survey by answering a series of less objectionable questions. After all, how would you react if the very first question on a survey asked about your sexual preferences?

3. To avoid losing subjects' interest in your topic, place demographic questions at the end of the survey. **Demographic questions** ask for basic information such as age, sex, race, education level, and annual income. These factors will be important when it comes time to interpret the results of your survey, but they are perceived as boring if presented too soon.

Visual Appeal of the Survey

After spending all this time writing, revising, and polishing the language and placement of your questions, don't neglect the visual appeal of the survey. Photocopies should be dark, clean, and easily legible. If your machine is producing a smear across each page, or if the copies are too light or too dark, take the time to find a better copy machine that can provide top-quality duplication. In addition, arrange the questions on each page in a visually appealing manner. Allow plenty of space on each page, and resist the temptation to change pages in the middle of a question.

Why is it so important to pay close attention to the visual appeal of your survey? One reason is to show subjects that you are professional, competent, and proud of your work. Subjects who perceive you in this way will be reassured about the confidentiality and interpretation of their data and, therefore, will probably be more honest and careful in making their responses. A second reason for producing an attractive survey is to encourage your subjects to respond. Filling out questionnaires takes time and is usually not much fun, so many subjects will abandon the project at the first opportunity. If a page is photocopied poorly, so that even a few phrases are difficult to read, many subjects will throw the survey over their shoulders into the wastebasket and return to more satisfying activities.

Selecting a Subject Sample

Now that you have written a legible survey that contains plain, unbiased questions concerning a specific issue, it's time to administer that survey to a group of subjects. Recall from Chapter 3 that we usually have to select a small sample of subjects from a larger population because it's so difficult to survey the entire population.

The purpose of inferential statistics is to determine whether the results obtained from a small sample are likely to hold true in an entire population. Therefore, it is important that our sample truly represents the population. We've already seen examples of research that was flawed by unrepresentative samples, such as the Hite sexuality survey and the Bennett et al. study of marriage.

The best way to get a sample of subjects that truly represents the population is to select them randomly. The term "random" does not mean "chaotic" or "accidental" in research contexts. Instead, **random sampling** occurs when every member of a population has an equal chance of being selected as a member of the sample.

Defining the Population and Sample. You may have noticed by now that the definitions of "population" and "sample" change as the research question changes. In other words, if you are only interested in job satisfaction among female parachute jumping instructors born in the northwestern United States, your population will be small. There just aren't many such people around. However, if your research question focuses on job satisfaction among employed humans around the world, your population will be very large.

We have been considering an example in which a manager would like to know why the employees in one small business organization are dissatisfied with their jobs. Given this research question, would a subject sample be necessary? Why or why not? Think about it before reading further.

If you answered "probably not," you're right. If the organization contains a total of 50 employees, for instance, it would be possible to survey the entire population instead of selecting a small sample. Of course, this "population" would be limited because it only consists of employees from one small organization. However, if we do not wish to generalize the results collected from the 50 employees in this organization to other employees in other organizations, then there would be no need to select a random sample or use inferential statistics.

If we did try to infer something about all employees based on this set of 50, we would be using that subject set as a sample. Would it be a random or a nonrandom sample? Nonrandom is correct, because only the members of one organization had a chance of being selected for the sample.

Most of the time, it is necessary to select a random sample of subjects from a population. There are several ways to do this: you can use simple random sampling, stratified random sampling, or proportionate random sampling.

Simple Random Sampling. Even when the definition of random sampling is clear in your mind, it is easy to become confused about whether a sample of subjects is truly random. Perhaps an example will help. Imagine that you sample 50 people out of a group of 500 in a movie theater, to learn their opinions of the new movie they just saw. If you interviewed only the first 50 people who entered the theater, would the sample be random? No, because the remaining 450 people would not have had an equal chance of being selected.

The danger of using such a nonrandom sample is that it does not represent the population: People who enter a theater first are often the kind of people who are seldom late, who plan ahead, who buy their tickets early, and who don't eat popcorn. We can also be fairly certain that they saw the beginning of the movie. The opinions of these people may be very different from the opinions of people who rush in 5 minutes after the movie started with an overflowing bucket of popcorn clutched in their hurried hands.

To give every member of the population a true chance at being selected for the sample, **simple random sampling** allows us to choose people without a systematic pattern. Because our brains hold information in an organized and structured fashion, it is difficult for humans to do much of anything in a truly random manner. Therefore, the best way to achieve simple random sampling is to use a random number table generated by a computer, like Table C.2 on page 313.

It's easy to use the random number table. Just imagine that all the members of your population are assigned arbitrary numbers. In the movie theater example, you might go by seat numbers, or you could simply assign numbers in order from 1 to 500 as people enter the theater. After assigning numbers to each member of the population, go to the random number table. The first entry of that table is 12. Thus, the first subject selected for the sample would be population member number 12. The second subject would be population member 39, and the third would be population member 53. This process continues until you reach the desired sample size.

Stratified Random Sampling. Sometimes a population is composed of groups of people that differ from one another in important ways. For example, suppose that the population of 500 people in the movie theater is composed of both children and adults. The opinions of children may be based on different criteria and expressed in different ways than the opinions of adults. It might be risky to ignore this distinction by using simple random sampling.

Stratified random sampling allows us to take into account different groups of people within a population. We divide the population into its naturally occurring segments, such as children and adults, then randomly select a certain number of subjects from each of the segments. This process ensures that your sample will represent each segment of the population of interest.

Here's how we would actually use stratified random sampling in practice. Suppose that we notice that the population of 500 people watching the movie is composed of about 250 adults and 250 children. Rather than selecting 50 subjects without regard for their age, we would select 25 children and 25 adults to make our sample of 50 subjects. We would still use the random number table, but this time it would have to be used twice in succession: once to select the child subjects and once to select the adult subjects. All of these people saw the movie and have an opinion about it, but now the opinions of children and adults are equally represented.

Proportionate Random Sampling. It was certainly handy that our movie population of children and adults was evenly divided in half, wasn't it? That's not very likely to happen in real life, though. If the movie was *Aladdin,* the theater would probably be filled with more children than adults. On the other hand, if the movie was *Schindler's List,* the theater would probably contain far more adults than children. It wouldn't be fair to select equal numbers of child and adult subjects for a sample if the numbers of children and adults in the population were not equal.

To get around this problem, researchers use **proportionate random sampling.** Suppose that the movie audience contains 450 adults and only 50 children. By basic division, we can determine that 450 (out of 500) adults represents 90% of the total population. (For those of you who have forgotten simple arithmetic, 450 divided by 500 equals .90.) Likewise, 50 (out of 500) children represents 10% of the total population. If our sample is to contain 50 subjects, we now need 10% of the sample to be children and 90% of the sample to be adults. We need 5 children and 45 adults in our sample, then. This would provide an accurate and proportionate representation of the population, but all subjects would still be selected randomly using the random number table.

These three types of random sampling are commonly used in psychological research. Each provides a safe method of selecting subjects that truly represent the population. Occasionally, we are forced to use a less desirable form of subject selection known as **convenience sampling.** This term refers to a sample of subjects who were selected in a nonrandom manner based on availability and willingness to participate. In general, convenience sampling should be avoided.

Although we have discussed the selection of subject samples in the context of survey research, it is important to remember that the same sorts of random sampling are used in other types of good research. Random sampling is not limited to survey research by any means!

The Realities of Random Sampling

In everyday practice, most samples are not as random as we would prefer. Sometimes, randomly selected subjects refuse to participate in our studies. After all, we can use the most rigorous methods of random sampling to select subjects, but human subjects always have the right to say "no" if they don't want to participate. This is why it's important to determine the **response rate** of survey research. The fact that 1,000 subjects were selected randomly from a large population sounds impressive until we learn that only 45 of those 1,000 subjects bothered to complete the questionnaire. This is exactly the kind of "minor detail" that routinely gets left out of newspaper and magazine reports of survey research. Response rate can impact random sampling very seriously and, in turn, the interpretation of results may be inaccurate.

A second problem with random sampling is that we often ask subjects to volunteer for research. Clearly, people who volunteer for research differ in important ways from people who do not volunteer. Even when subject participation is required (a common practice in introductory psychology courses, for example), students are usually given the option of choosing the one study, out of ten or twenty possibilities, that they prefer. Subjects who choose brief, fun experiments differ substantially from subjects who choose long, difficult experiments. Many researchers complain that student subjects who sign up for experiments early in the term produce significantly different results from subjects who wait until the last week of classes.

A third problem occurs when the population itself is more limited than we would like. For example, a common complaint within social and cognitive psychology centers around the use of first-year college students as subjects. The use of such a narrow population has limited the generality of our results. Because many studies of human behavior use college students as subjects, this complaint has broad implications. Perhaps the "general" explanations of behavior that we have discovered are not really so general after all.

Don't be discouraged by the imperfections of real-life research as opposed to textbook research. In practice, psychologists strive to achieve the most random sample possible, with the understanding that we will not always succeed completely. When good researchers do not achieve a sufficiently random sample and high response rate, they admit that their conclusions are weakened accordingly. Many a careful scientist has shelved years of work rather than risk publishing a seriously flawed study.

Administering the Survey

The most popular methods of administering surveys to subjects are by mail, by telephone, or by face-to-face interview. Each alternative has its strengths and weaknesses.

Mail Surveys. It is convenient and fairly cheap to send a survey to subjects through the mail. We simply send out the survey, along with a stamped return envelope, and wait for responses to arrive. The trouble with surveying by mail is that the responses often don't arrive. Mail surveys typically produce low response rates even when reminders are sent to subjects who have not responded. Another potential problem with mail surveys is that the subject can not ask about ambiguous questions or explain why a particular response was chosen. Although a few subjects will jot notes in the margins of your questionnaire, explaining their answers or pointing out confusing questions, most will not.

Telephone Surveys. Telephoning subjects and reading the survey to them one question at a time allows people to ask for clarification or to explain their responses in full. If the telephoning is local, this type of survey also has the advantage of being inexpensive.

However, there are many disadvantages to administering surveys by telephone. It is time-consuming for the researcher to read questions to and record answers from each subject in the study. It is often difficult for subjects to hold long lists of possible response choices in memory, without being able to read the survey at the same time. Some bias in results may be introduced by the way the researcher treats subjects or responds to their answers. For example, the simple distinction between a preoccupied "uh-huh" and an enthusiastic "oh, yes!" can alter subjects' responses dramatically. This experimenter bias (which is covered in detail in Chapter 7) occurs whenever a researcher's actions or appearance lead subjects to behave in a different way than they normally would. This bias is usually unintentional, but it still has serious negative consequences.

Although mail can be opened and answered at a time that is convenient to the subject, the telephone often rings at inconvenient times. You may have called just when a subject's dog ran out the door into a busy street or while the subject was in the middle of a family meal. Telephone interviewers often do not pay proper attention to clear pronunciation, so that subjects must strain to comprehend their speech. Furthermore, many subjects are becoming suspicious of telephone interviews because of their increasing use by salespeople and con artists.

Finally, in certain areas of the United States, telephone surveying and soliciting have become so rampant (e.g., six to eight calls per day) that people get very angry at being interrupted constantly in the privacy of their own homes.

Face-to-Face Interviews. The best aspect of face-to-face interviews is that they allow you to gather complete information regarding each subject's response to your questions. If a shrug or a scowl or a smile occurs while the subject is responding, you can ask then and there for more information. The ability to view subjects while they answer questions gives researchers greater insight into the opinions and beliefs of each subject.

The main disadvantages of the face-to-face interview are time and experimenter bias. Sitting down with each and every subject, and talking with that person at length about certain topics, is time-consuming and tiring. In addition, if experimenter bias was a problem over the phone, think how much worse it would be in the face-to-face interview. Verbal responses and tone of voice can bring out a researcher's personal biases, but if we add to that the effects of facial expression, attractiveness, height, weight, and clothing, serious problems begin to arise. All of these factors affect the subjects' responses to your survey.

In summary, mail surveys are easy and cheap, but yield poor response rates. Telephone surveys are plagued by problems, but do allow researchers and subjects to clarify their questions and answers. Face-to-face interviews take a lot of time and suffer from experimenter bias, but provide the researcher with greater latitude in interpreting subject responses.

The choice of an administration method depends not only on practical constraints but also on the research question at hand. If you are studying very personal, sensitive issues such as sexuality, drinking behavior, or drug abuse, subjects might withhold responses because of embarrassment in a face-to-face interview. On the other hand, topics that are potentially boring in written form (such as detergent preferences) might be livened up by an animated interviewer. The specific research question that you have decided to investigate will direct you toward an appropriate method of survey administration.

Advantages and Disadvantages of Survey Research

By now, I hope you can see that there's more to survey research than meets the eye. If you're going to conduct a survey, you now have the basic information needed to make a good start. In return for careful construction, a well-designed survey will produce results that can be analyzed statistically to allow valid inferences from sample to population. In addition, surveys are inexpensive, and they provide a quick method of determining people's attitudes toward an unlimited variety of topics.

On the down side, surveys often suffer from biased subject samples, low response rates, and poor construction. In addition, subjects do lie occasionally, especially when asked about sensitive issues, so many researchers are leery of self-report measures. The next time you read about the results of a survey in your newspaper or magazine, watch closely for these common flaws.

NONEXPERIMENTAL DATA ANALYSIS

Nonexperimental research allows scientists a great deal of freedom in studying various topics. This breadth means that it is impossible to set forth only one or two methods of data analysis that would be appropriate for nonexperimental research. However, a few common statistics can be identified.

Descriptive Statistics

Descriptive statistics such as means, standard deviations, and frequencies are almost always useful in archival research, natural observations, and survey research. Bennett et al. needed to summarize the frequencies of single men and women in the United States, Fossey had to calculate the number of times that gorillas beat their chests, and a job satisfaction survey would be useless if we didn't at least tally up the number of employees who were satisfied and compare it to the number who were dissatisfied. These are just a few examples of how descriptive statistics are used in nonexperimental research.

We might find, in a job satisfaction survey of one small company, that 60% of the dissatisfied employees reported being unhappy because of a lack of available incentives, 18% because of poor relationships with co-workers, 15% because of low salary, and only 7% because of inadequate insurance benefits. These frequencies, converted to percentages, would fit with past research, which really does show that few employees are concerned with benefits, whereas many would like more incentives and rewards offered for good work (Landy, 1985). (And the kind of treatment shown in Figure 4.1 isn't what they have in mind!) Such results would also provide the company manager with a clear direction for change: Leave health insurance and salaries as they are, but start a reward and recognition program for outstanding workers.

Inferential Statistics: Chi-Square

Nonexperimental research is extremely versatile in terms of the data it produces and the research questions it answers. For that reason, the statistical analysis of nonexperimental research draws from a wide variety of possibilities. One survey alone, for example, might include the use of correlational statistics, t-tests, analyses of variance (ANOVAs), and chi-square tests. You may remember that Table C.1 (on page 312) shows how each of these inferential statistics corresponds to a particular type of research design and scale of measurement. Because correlations, t-tests, and ANOVAs are discussed fully in later chapters, I have elected to focus only on the chi-square test here.

Chi-Square Analysis. An inferential statistic that is quite common in survey research is known as **chi-square** (abbreviated with the Greek symbol χ, and pronounced "ky" as in "sky"). Chi-square is used on nominal data whenever you

"Keep up the good work, whatever it is, whoever you are."

Figure 4.1
Source: Drawing by Stevenson; © 1988 The New Yorker Magazine, Inc.

want to know whether there is a relationship between two sets of frequencies. To take an easy example, let's suppose that you asked 140 employees whether they were satisfied with their jobs. After tallying up the data, you find that 70 employees reported liking their jobs and 70 reported disliking their jobs. The idea that an even half of the employees are satisfied with their work could be misleading, though. Perhaps some other results of interest are lurking below the surface of that finding.

Tallying up the response to demographic questions might help you to find out what's going on. Perhaps men report being satisfied more often than women do, or maybe laborers like their jobs more than managers like theirs. Assuming you were wise enough to design a survey that requested demographic information concerning age, let's see whether age is related to job satisfaction.

The first thing to do is construct a **contingency table,** which shows the frequencies for each of the two factors under consideration. One factor of interest is job satisfaction, and the other factor of interest is age. (We must operationally define "old" and "young"; I have considered the ages of 25 to 35 years as young and the ages of 55 to 65 years as old.) By combining these two factors, we make a table

A.

	Satisfied Employees	Dissatisfied Employees	
Young Employees	30	50	80
Old Employees	40	20	60
	70	70	

B.

	Satisfied Employees	Dissatisfied Employees	
Young Employees	21%	36%	57%
Old Employees	29%	14%	43%
	50%	50%	

Figure 4.2
Contingency Tables for Chi-square Analysis
A, Frequencies; B, Percentages.

with four empty cells in it. We now count up the numbers of subjects who meet the requirements of each cell. This means that we need four frequency counts:

1. The number of satisfied workers who are between the ages of 25 and 35 years,
2. The number of satisfied workers who are between the ages of 55 and 65 years,
3. The number of dissatisfied workers who are between 25 and 35 years, and
4. The number of dissatisfied workers who are between 55 and 65 years.

In Figure 4.2A, four hypothetical numbers are entered into the contingency table, each corresponding to one of the categories specified above. Marginal sums are also presented, showing that of all 140 subjects, half are satisfied and half are not; 80 are young and 60 are old. Although this example requires a contingency table with four cells, other research questions might produce larger or smaller tables.

The first thing to do with any set of frequencies like these is to think carefully about the pattern they describe. In a chi-square contingency table, this process can be eased by converting frequencies to percentages, as has been done in Figure 4.2B. Look carefully at these percentages and imagine how you would describe the pattern they represent to a friend who knew nothing about statistics. I would probably say that the majority of young employees seem dissatisfied with their jobs, whereas most of the old employees like their work.

To determine whether this relationship can be generalized beyond our sample of 140 employees to the general population, we must calculate the statistic of chi-square by hand or by computer. A basic statistics textbook will show you how to do the calculation if you have forgotten. Basically, it is a simple matter of comparing the observed frequencies in the contingency table to the frequencies that would be expected under the null hypothesis. For any statistical test to provide valid results, a minimum number of subjects must be represented in the sample. For the chi-square test on a four-cell contingency table like this one, the minimum number of subjects is equivalent to 10 expected frequencies per cell (Hays, 1981).

The value of chi-square for this contingency table would be 11.66. As always, to determine whether this obtained value represents a significant relationship, we compare it to the critical value of chi-square shown in Table C.3 (on page 314). The chi-square table is used in the same way that any other table of critical values would be used. Before reading further, use Table C.3 to decide whether our chi-square test indicates significance, reviewing page 67 if necessary.

You should have come to the conclusion that our obtained value of chi-square does represent a significant relationship. The obtained value ($\chi^2 = 11.66$ with 1 degree of freedom) was larger than the critical value (3.84), indicating statistical significance. Now comes the hard part: What does that significance mean?

In this example, the significant value of chi-square means that there is a relationship between employee age and job satisfaction within the sample of subjects who were tested. In addition, it means that this relationship has a 95% chance of being true in the population as a whole. In general, we can now say that older employees are usually more satisfied with their work than younger employees are.

Assessing Effect Size for Chi-Square. In addition to finding out whether the relationship between age and job satisfaction is significant, we need to know its size. If the relationship is strong, scientists and managers alike will need to consider age carefully when exploring job satisfaction.

To calculate the effect size of a chi-square statistic, use the formula from Table C.7 (page 318):

$$\phi^2 = \chi^2/N$$

The symbol ϕ stands for "phi" (pronounced like "fi" in the word "fine"). **Phi-squared** measures effect size for a two-by-two contingency table like the one in Figure 4.2.* You can see that the formula for phi-squared is very simple: We just divide our obtained χ^2 value by the total number of subjects in the study. Here's how that is done:

$$\phi^2 = 11.66/140 = .08$$

The value of phi-squared (.08), in this example, means that 8% of the variation in job satisfaction is related to a subject's age. The remaining 92% variation

---

*Chi-square contingency tables that are more complex require a different formula. Also, in the formula presented here, phi has been squared so that it can be related to r^2 and interpreted as the proportion of variance.

must be related to other factors, such as the particular occupation a subject holds, sloppiness in completing the survey, and individual differences.

An effect that accounts for only 8% of the variation in data must sound very small to you. However, according to guidelines set by Cohen (1977) and presented in Table C.7, a phi-squared of .08 is considered a medium effect. Although Cohen's guidelines must be used with caution, they do give us some idea of how one effect compares to others in the behavioral sciences.

Many psychological effects are small or medium in size because psychologists often study subtle human behaviors that are linked to a complex blend of multiple causes. As Cohen argues, effects that are very large can be seen so easily by the naked eye that they do not encourage scientific research. For example, if many older people praised their jobs effusively while most young employees complained vehemently about theirs, effect size would be huge. In such obvious situations, there is little need to conduct research or run statistical analyses.

Interpreting Results Carefully

It is crucial, in all types of research, to interpret results with care. This is especially important in nonexperimental research, which can describe behavior but cannot explain it. Often, the correct interpretation is hidden by a number of incorrect ones that appear at first glance to be perfectly plausible. Indeed, much of science progresses by comparing alternate interpretations to determine which one is most likely to be correct.

Landy (1985) presents a good example of alternate interpretations in his consideration of the relationship between age and job satisfaction. In keeping with our hypothetical example, many researchers really have found that older employees like their jobs more than young employees do. Weaver (1980) found that this pattern held up in surveys conducted annually for several years. There are several ways to interpret this finding:

1. Older people are likely to hold higher-level and more prestigious jobs than younger people hold. If the job itself is better, then it's no wonder that the person holding that job would be more satisfied than someone with a low-level position.
2. Older people may be more skilled and better able to perform their jobs than younger people are. This would explain why the older people are more satisfied.
3. People's expectations may lessen over time so that the same mediocre job seems fine to an older person but boring to a younger person. This explanation would be supported by the fact that young adults often expect far more in salary, responsibility, prestige, and leisure time than real entry-level jobs provide.
4. Perhaps dissatisfied employees eventually quit working. This would mean that the older subjects in the sample seem more satisfied with their jobs only because they are the ones who didn't quit. The others, who did quit because of dissatisfaction, could not participate in the survey.

5. Maybe dissatisfied workers die at an earlier age than satisfied workers do. If so, older people who held jobs they disliked would have died by the time the surveys were conducted, and their dissatisfaction would not have been reported.

Here are five different interpretations, then, of the same simple result. You may be able to think of additional ones yourself. Each interpretation is plausible—it could be correct—but we would have to conduct further research to determine which one is most likely to be true. Remember this the next time you hear a news reporter interpret a research finding in a 20-second sound bite.

SUMMARY OF MAIN POINTS

- Nonexperimental research describes behavior but does not determine what caused it to occur. Independent variables are not used in nonexperimental research.

- Case studies are helpful in exploring new topics and rare behaviors, but they suffer from low generalizability, uncontrolled variables, dishonest subjects, and subjective interpretation.

- Archival research allows us to spot trends in existing data but, like all research, it must be evaluated thoughtfully. Common flaws include biased data, misleading statistics, and uncontrolled variables.

- Because it occurs outside the laboratory, natural observation can provide important knowledge about real-life behavior. Ethics, objectivity, and the possibility that observation changes natural behavior must be taken into account.

- Surveys must be designed and administered carefully, with special attention to placement and wording of questions, modes of response, visual appeal, and methods of survey administration.

- Reliable measurement, precise operational definitions, and random sampling of subjects are key characteristics of all types of scientific research.

- Data gathered from nonexperimental research designs may be analyzed in many ways. This chapter works through the use and interpretation of the chi-square analysis, but other statistical tests might also be used to assess data from nonexperimental studies.

CHAPTER EXERCISES

1. Use your own words to define these key terms:

case study	partially open-ended questions
archival research	Likert rating scales
natural observation	demographic questions

field observation	restricted questions
participant observation	random sampling
nonparticipant	simple random sampling
observation	stratified random sampling
reliable	proportionate random sampling
operational definitions	convenience sampling
survey research	response rate
double-barreled	chi-square
questions	contingency table
open-ended questions	phi-squared

2. Supply an operational definition for each of the following concepts:
   a) a good professor   e) a nice house
   b) a late paper   f) beauty
   c) a hot date   g) success
   d) a bad cold   h) intelligence

3. Develop a survey on a topic of your own choosing. Keep the survey short and simple, with about five questions, but aim for as much precision and professionalism as you can muster. Be prepared to defend your choice of response mode, placement of questions, and selection of questions.

4. Imagine that you have a large glass jar filled with pennies, nickels, dimes, and quarters. Explain how you would select a subset of these coins from the jar by using:
   a) simple random sampling
   b) stratified random sampling
   c) proportionate random sampling
   d) convenience sampling

5. Telephone interviews are sometimes conducted by computer nowadays. The computer asks all questions and records all answers from the subjects. What are the advantages and disadvantages of using a computer to conduct telephone interviews?

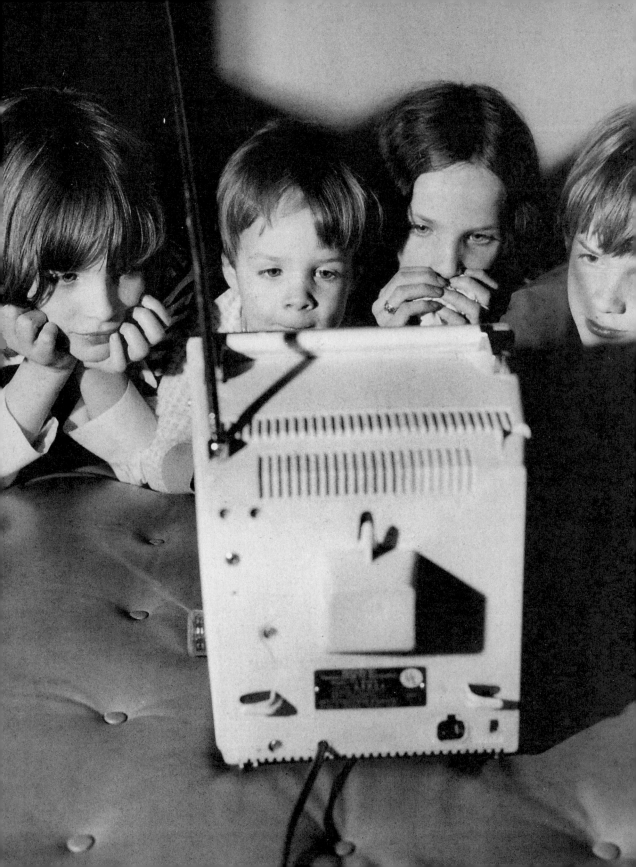

Correlational Research

In what ways does television affect young children?

If you read magazines or newspapers at all, you have seen many reports of correlational research. In fact, most Americans learn about the results of correlational studies through the popular media. Unfortunately, this research is often misinterpreted, even in reputable magazines, newspapers, and television shows. To uncover these popular misinterpretations, you need to understand the basic techniques of correlational research.

RELATING DEPENDENT VARIABLES

In its simplest terms, **correlation** is a method of determining whether two sets of measurements, or dependent variables, are related to each other. Height and weight are variables that are "co-related" in this way; the taller people are, the more they tend to weigh. Another way of defining correlational research, then, would be to say that it allows scientists to search for relationships between the dependent variables that we measure.

Correlational research is considered to be one type of nonexperimental research because it does not include independent variables. For example, researchers can measure height and weight, but we cannot manipulate them. Under natural conditions, even the best scientist cannot change your height or alter your weight!

Like other types of nonexperimental research, correlations describe behavior. They do not determine what caused that behavior to occur. We'll see later that this distinction between description and causality is one that many reporters fail to understand.

CONDUCTING A CORRELATIONAL STUDY

In conducting any type of scientific research, there are several first steps that are vital. Try to recall them now in your mind. Does your list agree with mine?

1. Review the literature concerning your topic.
2. Shape your research question precisely.
3. Select a random sample of subjects who represent their population.

Let's suppose that you select as a topic of interest the effects of our national pastime, watching television. Since about 1960, when the television became a common object in most American homes, psychologists have studied the effects of watching TV on a variety of human behaviors.

One area of research that has received tremendous attention concerns the effects of television on human aggression. Television presents a great deal of violence to its viewers. If you doubt this claim, consider a few facts marshalled by Myers (1990):

1. Television programs shown during prime time present an average of five violent acts per hour (Gerbner, Gross, Signorielli, & Morgan, 1986).

2. Saturday morning cartoons for children show an average of twenty violent acts per hour (Gerbner et al., 1986).
3. By age 18, the average American who has cable TV or a videocassette recorder in the home will have observed 32,000 successful murders and 40,000 attempted murders on television (Radecki, 1989).
4. Television police shows typically depict officers firing their guns at least once in almost every episode. By contrast, the average police officer in the city of Chicago fires a gun on the job only one time in every 27 years (Radecki, 1989).

Many people have wondered whether this sort of unrealistic television violence affects viewers in a negative way. Perhaps increased violence on television is linked to the increase in real murder, rape, and other violent crimes that occur in today's society.

The ideal way to determine whether TV violence causes increased aggression would be to conduct an experiment. However, this would require researchers to manipulate the amount of violent television that subjects watched each day. Can you think of any problems with this requirement? One might be that it is difficult to ensure that subjects will really follow our viewing instructions on a daily basis. But another, more severe problem has to do with ethics. As scientists, we cannot require people to engage in some activity that we suspect will harm them. Therefore, the ideal experiment on television and aggression is difficult to conduct within practical and ethical constraints.

Here's where correlation steps in. Although we cannot require subjects to watch violent television against their will, we can measure the amount of violent television they happen to watch of their own volition. We are now measuring instead of manipulating. Rather than telling subjects how much television to watch, we merely record the amount they select. This change from an experiment to a correlational study means that we will not be able to determine whether violent television causes aggressive behavior. However, we will find out whether the two variables are related to each other in some way.

A correlational study must involve at least two measurements. In our example, one measurement must assess the amount of violent television viewed by a given subject. The other measurement must assess the amount of aggression exhibited by the same person. If these two dependent variables are related to each other in many subjects, we will suspect that there is some link between watching violent television and acting aggressively. Further research will then be needed to test our suspicions more rigorously.

Of course, operational definitions of "aggressive behavior" and "violent television" must be clarified before conducting the study. After all, television programs that seem violent to me may not seem so violent to you. The term *aggression* is equally cloudy.

The best way to select appropriate operational definitions is to review the literature thoroughly so that you get to know which operational definitions have been used in the past. Sometimes it is best to use the same definitions so that your results can be compared directly with the results obtained by past researchers. On the other hand, we create new operational definitions when the old ones omit aspects of behavior that we believe may be important. For example, if all previous researchers had focused only on physical aggression, it would be important to conduct a study looking at verbal aggression, too.

An Example: Television and Aggression

Perhaps it will help to consider a real correlational study of violent television and aggressive behavior. We'll begin with a simple example, then build on it as we move through this chapter. To probe the relationship between television and aggression, Eron, Huesmann, Lefkowitz, and Walder (1972) first tested 211 9-year-old boys. Several measurements were taken, but for the sake of simplicity, we will consider only two of them.

The first dependent variable was the amount of violent television that each boy liked to watch. Eron et al. determined these scores by asking each child's mother to name the child's three favorite television programs. Independent raters were then asked to classify these programs as violent or nonviolent. A rating scale was used; subjects for whom none of the favorite programs were violent received a 1, whereas subjects for whom all three of the favorite programs were violent received a 4. Thus, in this study, the operational definition of violent television was the number of each child's favorite programs that were considered violent by independent raters. Instead of defining "violence" in absolute terms, Eron et al. required agreement between raters as to which television programs were violent and which were not.

The second dependent variable was the amount of aggression displayed among these same boys. Aggressive behavior was assessed by asking the subjects' school peers to answer questions about their classmates. Examples of these questions included:

1. "Who pushes and shoves other people?"
2. "Who starts a fight over nothing?"
3. "Who says mean things?" (Eron et al., 1972, p. 254).

Aggression scores were calculated on the basis of these peer ratings. Higher scores were given to those subjects who were named by many of their peers in answers to many of the questions.

With these two measurements in hand, the researchers were ready to analyze their data. They found that the amount of violent television preferred at age 9 was positively correlated to aggressiveness at age 9. These results will become easier to understand as you read the next section.

UNDERSTANDING SCATTERPLOTS

After collecting the two measurements for each subject in the sample, analysis begins by looking closely at the data. Correlation is usually illustrated by constructing a **scatterplot**, or **scattergram**, which is a figure showing the relationship between two dependent variables. Figure 5.1 presents a scatterplot showing measurements of aggression and television viewing for each subject, as might have been obtained by Eron and his colleagues.

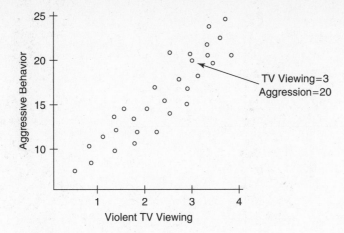

Figure 5.1
Scatterplot for Television Viewing and Aggression

By inspecting Figure 5.1, you can see that the two measurements for each subject are represented on the scatterplot by one dot. The **abscissa,** or horizontal axis, shows the amount of violent television a subject watched, and the **ordinate,** or vertical axis, shows the amount of aggressive behavior that subject displayed. (Incidentally, the placement of the two variables on the abscissa and ordinate can be reversed without altering the outcome in any way.) Dots in the far upper right corner of Figure 5.1 represent subjects who watch a lot of violent television and often act aggressively. To provide a more exact case, the data point marked by an arrow in Figure 5.1 represents a subject who received a viewing score of 3 and an aggression score of 20. Every dot provides similar information about some subject in the sample, so that the entire scatterplot represents all the data collected from all the subjects in the study.

Before we get too involved with the statistical analysis of correlational research, let's look at the overall patterns that two variables may produce. Remember, statistics are merely tools that allow us to assess the significance and size of relationships that we have seen . . . but first, we must step back and see them! We call this process "eyeballing the data," a somewhat comical phrase that is nevertheless used regularly by even the most sophisticated scientists of the 20th century. In general, there are four basic patterns that you might see in a scatterplot: a positive correlation, a negative correlation, no correlation, or a curvilinear relationship. Let's think about positive correlation first.

Positive Correlation

Scientists who looked at the scatterplot in Figure 5.2A would guess that a positive correlation probably exists between the two variables of interest. How would

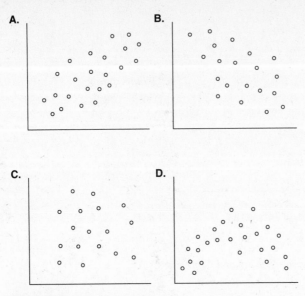

Figure 5.2
Possible Patterns of Correlation
A, Positive; B, Negative; C, None; D, Curvilinear.

they know? Whenever you see a scatterplot in which the majority of data points fall along an upward angle (from lower left to upper right), a positive correlation probably exists. If you consider individual data points in such a scatterplot, the reason for this guess will become clear. When the correlation is positive, a data point that represents a low score on one variable (television viewing, in this instance) also represents a low score on the other variable (aggression). Likewise, any data point that represents a high score on one variable also indicates a high score on the other variable. Look carefully at the data points in Figure 5.2A, so that you can see these facts for yourself.

Once you understand the upward angle of the points in the scatterplot, it's easier to grasp the general definition of a **positive correlation.** Whenever two variables are positively correlated, any increase in one variable is accompanied by an increase in the other variable. Another way of saying this is, "the more of x, the more of y." It is this increase-increase relationship that causes the dots in a scatterplot to fall into a pattern along an upward angle.

What does this pattern of data mean? We can't make a full interpretation until we have assessed the statistical significance and size of the correlation, but from eyeballing the data, it looks like aggression and television viewing are related to each other. The scatterplot in Figure 5.2A suggests that people who watch a lot of violent television are likely to behave aggressively. This pattern of positive correlation fits perfectly with Eron et al.'s results, in which young boys who preferred violent television were also likely to act aggressively.

Negative Correlation

Figure 5.2B shows what a negative correlation would look like. The data points on this scatterplot fall along a downward angle (from upper left to lower right), suggesting that subjects with very high aggression scores are likely to have very low viewing scores. A **negative correlation** occurs whenever an increase in one variable (such as violent television viewing) is accompanied by a decrease in the other variable (aggressive behavior). In this case, we could say, "the more of x, the less of y." The increase-decrease relationship between the two variables causes the dots to fall into the pattern of a downward angle. Sometimes a negative correlation is called an **inverse relationship.** Either term is acceptable.

Although we can't be certain of the interpretation until a statistical analysis has been conducted, the scatterplot in Figure 5.2B suggests that people who like violent television do not tend to be aggressive. On the other hand, those who seldom watch violent television are likely to behave aggressively. As you know, this pattern of negative correlation does not match real research results concerning television and aggression.

No Correlation

A third possible outcome of correlational research is that there might be no relationship at all between two variables of interest. In our example, this would mean that watching violent television is not linked in any way with behaving aggressively.

The pattern that occurs with no correlation is as easy to see as the upward and downward angles of positive and negative correlations. If there is no relationship between variables, the data points in a scatterplot will fall randomly throughout the graph. Figure 5.2C shows how this would look.

Curvilinear Relationship

Finally, a scatterplot may indicate a **curvilinear relationship** between two variables. In this instance, the data points appear to form a curve rather than a straight line. Figure 5.2D illustrates the pattern of dots that might be seen in a curvilinear relationship. As we will see in a later section of this chapter, correlational statistics can only measure straight-line relationships. For that reason, curvilinear patterns require special attention when results are interpreted.

STATISTICAL ANALYSIS: CORRELATION

After constructing a scatterplot and eyeballing the data, we can begin to see whether a statistically significant relationship exists between two dependent variables. Just because a correlation appears to show a positive or negative pattern on a scatterplot does not mean that it is necessarily significant. To assess the significance of a correlation, we must use statistical tests. Some of you may remember from basic statistics that the value computed to assess the significance of a correlation based on interval or ratio level data is called r. This value, r, represents the Pearson product-moment correlation and can be calculated by hand or by computer. Sometimes r is called the **correlation coefficient.** It varies from −1.0 to +1.0, so the strength of any correlation can be represented by either a positive or a negative value.

As you might expect, a value of r between 0 and −1.0 would occur for negative correlations, and a value of r between 0 and +1.0 would occur for positive correlations. The stronger the negative correlation, the closer r will be to −1.0. Likewise, the stronger the positive correlation, the closer r will be to +1.0. (In practice, the plus sign is seldom used to signify a positive correlation, but the minus sign must be used for negative correlations.) When there is no correlation at all, the value of r will remain near zero.

What does r represent? As with most inferential statistics, r assesses a pattern of data by taking into account the variability of the two sets of scores as well as the central tendency of their relationship. It helps us to infer whether the relationship between any two variables is consistent enough to occur not only in the subject sample, but also in the population from which the subjects were drawn.

Central Tendency

Scatterplots allow us to represent geometrically the central tendency of a relationship and the variability among two sets of scores. You already know that every pair of scores for each subject is represented as a data point on the scatterplot. Once data points are positioned on the graph, a **line of best fit** (also called a **regression line**) can be determined by hand calculation or computer. This straight line travels through an area that is nearest the majority of data points, and it signifies the central tendency of their relationship. In other words, this single line "fits" the data points most closely.

Figure 5.3 shows a scatterplot with a line of best fit drawn through the central angled area in which most of the data points fall. By now, you should be able to glance quickly at Figure 5.3 and tell whether it shows a positive or negative correlation. Which is it? If you said "positive," you were right.

Variability

The way the dots are scattered around the line of best fit must also be taken into account. This scatter represents the amount of variability in the scores. Variability can be seen by looking at the distance between each data point and the line of best fit. Data points that are clustered near the line represent little variability. In other words, these data are close to the central tendency and do not vary much. The greater the distance between a data point and the line of best fit, the greater the difference between that score and the average score. In other words, variability increases as the distance between data points and their line of best fit increases.

The amount of scatter in a set of correlational data is signified by the absolute value of r. When r is equal to +1.0, every data point falls on the perfectly straight line of an upward sloping angle, indicating that there is no variability

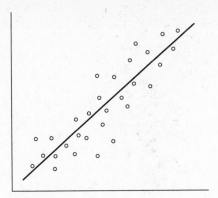

Figure 5.3
Line of Best Fit

among scores. This would be called a perfect positive correlation, as shown in Figure 5.4A.

A negative correlation may also be perfect ($r = -1.0$), as shown in Figure 5.4B. In this case, each data point falls directly on the downward slope of the line of best fit. As before, variability is represented by the distance between the data points and their line of best fit. Data points that fall directly on the line of best fit signify a complete lack of variability.

Perfect correlations, whether positive ($r = +1.0$) or negative ($r = -1.0$), are nearly impossible to achieve in psychological research. Human behavior is never perfectly consistent, and the relationship between various factors that affect our behavior is not simple. Therefore, positive correlations obtained in psychological research achieve some value of r that is less than +1.0. As the value of r gets closer to +1.0, the relationship between the two variables becomes stronger. Similarly, perfect negative correlations of −1.0 are almost never obtained. Instead, r ranges between 0 and −1.0 for a negative correlation, with the relationship becoming stronger as r nears −1.0. Most correlational research in the social sciences produces correlation coefficients ranging from .30 to .70, whether positive or negative (Freedman, Pisani, & Purves, 1980).

To summarize, you should now understand that the correlation coefficient r is based on two aspects of the data: central tendency, which is represented by the line of best fit on a scatterplot, and variability, which is represented by the clustering of data points around the line of best fit. If perfect correlations are represented by a series of data points that are located right on the line of best fit, then imperfect correlations must produce data points located farther from the line. Data points that are located farther from the line represent greater variability, suggesting that the obtained relationship will not be significant. The reason for this is that inconsistent, or highly variable, data cannot be trusted in inferring behavior from a sample to a population. Thus, when you see a scatterplot with dots that are clustered very near the line of best fit, you will know that the relationship between variables is consistent, strong, and likely to be significant. Accordingly, the absolute value of r will be large. Likewise, when dots are scattered around at some

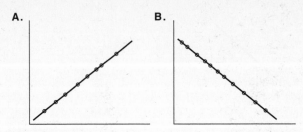

Figure 5.4
Perfect Correlations
A, Positive; B, Negative.

distance from the line of best fit, the data are inconsistent and unlikely to be significant. In this case, you would expect the absolute value of r to be small.

Did you ever imagine there was so much to see in a simple graph? We've covered some challenging material in the last few paragraphs. If you still feel a bit confused about the line of best fit and the use of data points to estimate variability, you may want to read those paragraphs once again.

Assessing Significance

Once the value of r has been calculated, it's easy to determine whether the relationship between variables is statistically significant. We simply compare the obtained value of r with the critical value on a statistical table. Table C.4, showing critical values for r, is found on page 315.

By now, you should be able to assess the significance of an obtained statistic, like r, without help. Give it a try, using an obtained value of $r = -.25$ derived from a sample of $N = 75$ subjects. Table C.4 contains all the information you need to decide whether this correlation coefficient is statistically significant.

The correct decision is based on a critical value of .232, corresponding to the usual probability level of .05 and 73 degrees of freedom. By convention, psychologists round down when the exact value for degrees of freedom does not appear on the table. Therefore, even though our degrees of freedom were 73, which is not listed on Table C.4, we use the row on the table that corresponds to $df = 70$. When the negative sign is ignored, our obtained value of $r = -.25$ is larger than the critical value of .23, so the correlation is significant.

Determining Effect Size

You should remember from Chapter 3 that an effect may be small even though it is consistent enough to be statistically significant. To calculate the size of a correlational effect, we use a statistic called the **coefficient of determination**. As shown in Table C.7 (on page 318), this value is obtained by squaring r, and it tells us how much of the variation in one set of scores can be accounted for by the variation in another set of scores.

As an example, let's use Eron et al.'s (1972) value of r for the correlation between violent television and aggressive behavior at age 9. Their obtained value of r was .21, which was statistically significant with a probability of Type I error less than 1% ($p < .01$). If we square this value (.21 times .21), we find that the coefficient of determination is .044. According to Cohen's guidelines in Table C.7, this effect is about halfway between small and medium in size. There are two ways to think about the meaning of the number. First, 4% of the variation in scores of aggression may be accounted for by the amount of violent television the subjects watch. Second, 4% of the variation in television preferences may be accounted for by the aggressiveness of each subject. Either way, the remaining 96% of the variation must be caused by individual differences, error in measurement, or other factors that we have not measured.

COMMON ERRORS IN INTERPRETING CORRELATIONS

A correlation shows only that two variables are related to each other in some way. We'll find in this section that their correlation could be completely accidental, it could be produced artificially by an uncontrolled variable, or it could be caused by either of the two variables that were measured. These possibilities are often ignored when newspaper reporters, magazine writers, television newscasters, and talk show hosts attempt to publicize scientific research. Once you become aware of these types of misinterpretation, you'll see them frequently in your local paper and on the evening news.

People seem to be convinced that a correlation must mean something more than a mere relationship between variables. The five most common flaws in interpreting correlational research are assuming causation, assuming direction, ignoring third variables, restricting the range of data, and ignoring curvilinear relationships. Let's consider each of these in turn. Along the way, I'll introduce some techniques, such as cross-lagged and partial correlation, that help us to interpret correlations accurately.

Assuming Causation

Correlation does not imply causation. In other words, the fact that two variables are related to each other does not mean that one factor must cause scores of the other factor to change. In fact, many pairs of variables are correlated significantly yet bear no meaningful working relationship to each other. Such correlations are known as **spurious relationships,** with the word *spurious* meaning "false" or "counterfeit." One example of a spurious relationship is found in the fact that the United States population has increased while the number of front-wheel-drive cars has also increased over the last 25 years. Although this positive correlation might well be statistically significant, in no way does it suggest that the relationship between automobiles and population is causal. Certainly we would not want to argue that the population increase causes people to operate front-wheel-drive cars. And it's even more ridiculous to suppose that front-wheel drive causes people to have babies!

Sometimes, a spurious relationship is not purely accidental but, rather, is caused by some third variable that has not been investigated. We shall return to this possibility in the section entitled "Ignoring Third Variables."

In general, it is never safe to assume that there is a causal relationship between two variables that are correlated. To return to Eron et al.'s (1972) study, it seems unlikely that the relationship between watching violent TV programs and acting aggressively is purely accidental. But we can not be sure from correlational research alone. By itself, even a significant and strong correlation fails to show cause.

Assuming Direction

Even if two variables are causally related, the direction of causality is difficult to establish from correlational research. My students enjoy a silly example of the direction mistake. Sometimes a ridiculous example is useful because it's easy to remember and apply to more difficult situations. Suppose that the local fire department conducts a study to determine how many new fire trucks they will need to purchase in the next decade. They learn that there is a positive correlation between the size of a fire and the number of fire trucks seen at that fire: the larger the fire, the more trucks.

A thoughtful person, well trained in the methods of critical research evaluation, would accept that fact and halt any further interpretation. However, the average news reporter might find the fact fairly boring and, in an effort to print the most sensational story, might leap to an unwarranted conclusion. Picture the headlines: *Research Proves That Fires Are Caused by Fire Trucks!* The imaginary reporter goes on to explain that fire trucks are almost never seen in areas where there are no fires. However, each time a fire occurs, there seems to be at least one fire truck in the vicinity. And at large fires, there are lots of fire trucks. Hence, it must be these fire trucks that are causing the fires.

As I said, it's a ridiculous example. But keeping it in mind the next time you read or hear a popular report of correlational research may help you to discover less obvious errors of interpretation.

Now that you've got the general idea, let's try to apply the notion of directionality to Eron et al.'s (1972) research. Even if we knew that aggression and violent television are related to each other in a causal fashion, we still would not know which variable causes the other to change. Maybe watching violent television programs causes children to act more aggressively than they otherwise would. However, it is equally plausible that children who are aggressive by nature prefer to watch violent television programs. It is impossible to determine from a simple correlation which of these two alternate interpretations is true.

A **cross-lagged correlation**, however, would help us to explore the direction of causality. This technique includes a time lag between measurement of one variable and measurement of the other. In fact, Eron et al. (1972) reported a cross-lagged correlation after testing, 10 years later, the same boys who had participated in the first stage of their study. Using similar peer ratings of aggression for these subjects at age 19, Eron et al. (1972) found that the amount of violent television the boys watched at age 9 was correlated positively with the amount of aggressive behavior they displayed at age 19. Their correlation coefficient (r = .31) was statistically significant ($p < .01$). What's the coefficient of determination in this case, and what does it mean? You'll learn more if you try to answer these questions before reading further. The coefficient of determination ($r^2 = .31 \times .31 = .096$) indicates that the correlation accounted for about 10% of the variance in television and aggression scores. That's certainly a more respectable percentage than the first stage of the study produced.

How does the cross-lagged correlation help us to establish direction? Well, think about it: TV viewing was measured at age 9, but aggression was measured at age 19. If we theorize that the relationship may be causal, then the 10-year time lag suggests that behavior at age 9 was more likely to have caused behavior at age 19 than the other way around.

A strong dose of caution is required when interpreting the results of cross-lagged correlations. They merely provide clues to the direction of an effect that *might* be causal. They do not allow us to determine whether the effect truly *is* causal. Furthermore, the clues they provide to direction are never ironclad: It is possible that Eron et al.'s subjects were as aggressive before watching violent television at age 9 as they were 10 years later at age 19.

Ignoring Third Variables

As you know, a spurious relationship can be purely accidental, or it can result from some third variable that influences both of the measured variables. There are several potential third variables lurking in the background of the correlation between violent TV and aggression. Think about what they might be: A **third variable** has to be something that was not measured in the correlational study but could be responsible for the observed correlation between the variables that were studied. This third variable must have the capacity, theoretically, to produce both behaviors that were measured. In Eron et al.'s study, then, we need to think of some factor that could produce a preference for violent TV and an increase in aggression. Can you think of some variable that meets both of these requirements?

Actually, there are many possible third variables, but a prime example would be parental punishment. Many psychological studies have shown that physical punishment can cause a child to behave aggressively (e.g., George & Main, 1979; Singer, 1984). At the same time, children who are accustomed to observing and enduring physical punishment in their homes might prefer violent television programs.

To determine whether a third variable is truly responsible for a spurious relationship, **partial correlation** can be used. This technique involves measuring all three variables (e.g., television, aggression, and punishment), then statistically removing the effect of the third variable from the correlation of the other two variables. If the third variable, parental punishment, was responsible for the observed correlation between TV and aggression, then that correlation should disappear when the effect of punishment is removed.

In fact, Eron et al. (1972) conducted a partial correlation to investigate the influence of parental punishment on their subjects. The correlation persisted between television at age 9 and aggression at age 19 despite removal of the punish-

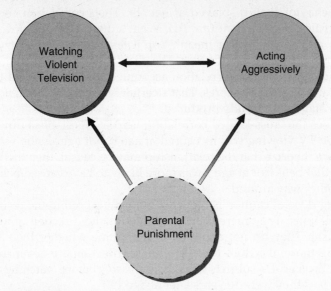

Figure 5.5
Identifying a Third Variable

ment effect. Therefore, Eron et al. concluded that the observed correlation was not produced by this third variable. (Of course, it still could have been produced by some other third variable that was not measured.)

Because the third variable problem is so common, let me present just one more example of it. In men, there is a significant positive correlation between incidence of marriage and loss of hair. In other words, men who get married are likely to lose their hair. Now, before all you men out there vow never to approach the altar, think about the issue of causality. Clearly, marriage does not cause baldness. At the same time, we know that baldness is not likely to encourage marriage, right? The relationship must be spurious.

Is there a third variable that could be responsible for this spurious relationship between marriage and baldness? Yes, it's age. As men grow older, they are more likely to get married. In addition, older men are more likely to become bald. Thus, the third variable of age produces the spurious correlation between marriage and baldness. Although the correlation is spurious, it may still be statistically significant and large in size.

Figure 5.5 provides a diagram that may help you to identify third variables. When you analyze a correlation in search of a third variable, it helps to draw such a diagram. The two circles on top represent the two variables that were studied in the research and were found to be correlated. The bottom circle represents a third variable, which must be capable of causing both measurements that occurred. Please take note of the crucial fact that such "causation" is purely theoretical: Just because a third variable is *capable* of causing certain behaviors, we can not be certain that it did in fact cause those behaviors.

Restricting the Range of Data

A fourth error in interpreting correlational research can occur when data are not gathered from the full range of possibilities. An attempt to correlate height with weight, for example, will fail if all of your subjects are in the height range from 5'6" to 5'9". There is a significant correlation between height and weight, but it can not be observed within such a restricted range.

Likewise, a correlational study of television viewing will produce misleading results if the only people tested are those who watch very little or very much television. Instead, it is necessary to test people throughout the entire range of television viewing behavior, from the bookworms who watch only 1 hour per week to the couch potatoes whose eyes are glued to the set for 10 hours a day.

Ignoring Curvilinear Relationships

Correlation is capable of discovering relationships between variables only if the variables are related in a linear (straight-line) manner. Thus, if one variable increases as the other increases, we have a positive linear correlation. Likewise, if one variable increases as the other decreases, we have a negative linear correlation. But what happens when one variable increases as the other increases only up to a point, and then the relationship changes direction?

As I mentioned earlier, this is a curvilinear relationship, which the correlation statistic r is not capable of assessing. The classic example of a curvilinear relationship has to do with motivation, or arousal. The word *arousal* in this sense means heightened physical readiness or mental alertness. Most people assume that this heightened alertness is positively correlated with performance. Think about what that means: As we become more aroused, our performance gets better. In fact, if we look only at the restricted range of low to medium arousal levels, this positive linear correlation is exactly what psychologists obtain.

If we ignored the possibility of a curvilinear relationship, we would interpret this finding in the simplest way: Motivation by arousal enhances job performance. We might be asked to provide this advice to business managers, sports coaches, and school teachers so that they could improve the performance of their employees, athletes, and students. However, in this instance, that advice would ignore an important part of the total picture.

Figure 5.6 shows that when the entire range of arousal levels is studied, we find that the correlation between arousal and performance is not linear. In fact, when motivation by arousal becomes very strong, performance declines. The curvilinear relationship indicates that, up to a certain point, arousal helps us to perform well. However, as good coaches and managers know, when this kind of motivation becomes so strong that it is perceived as intense pressure to perform, many fine athletes and employees begin to fall apart. At that point, arousal is having a negative effect on their performance. Incidentally, this relationship is known as the Yerkes-Dodson Law, named after the two researchers who first studied it in 1908.

Because r only measures linear relationships, a statistical analysis of these data would suggest that there is no relationship between the two variables ($r \approx 0$).

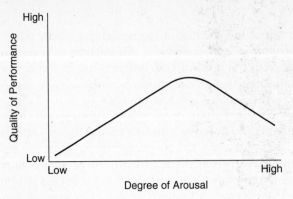

Figure 5.6
A Curvilinear Relationship
Source: Based loosely on Yerkes and Dodson, 1908.

On the contrary, there *is* a strong relationship, but it does not proceed in a simple linear manner. Since *r* cannot detect curvilinear relationships, the best way to see one is to construct a scatterplot of the data.

Revisiting Television and Aggression

Before we turn to other aspects of correlation, you may be curious about the conclusions from research on violent television and aggressive behavior. Since 1960, hundreds of researchers have explored the effects of watching violent TV shows. When the results of all their studies are merged, we find that the link between television and aggression is statistically significant and widely replicated, but small to medium in size.

Thus, television alone can explain only a portion of the human variation in aggression. Of course, even a small effect can have important practical consequences (Rosenthal, 1986). If you agree, for example, that the global aggression level is currently high enough, then you can see that we wouldn't want it to increase even a little bit. And when other factors are combined with television preferences, much stronger effects begin to emerge. Singer and Singer (1986) achieved a hefty correlation coefficient of .65 between aggression and a combination of poor sleep, family apathy toward cultural events, frequent punishment by parents, large amounts of television at preschool age, and excessive viewing of "realistic action-adventure" television shows.

After reviewing the research that has been done on this topic, the National Institute of Mental Health stated that "the consensus among most of the research community is that violence on television does lead to aggressive behavior" (1982, as cited by Myers, 1990, p. 446). We now know that exposure to television and film violence teaches people how to act aggressively, weakens social sanctions against aggression, and reduces an observer's sensitivity to the victims of aggression (O'Neal, 1991). Despite these facts, television networks continue to develop

Figure 5.7
Source: Chris Britt, *Durango Herald*, July 5, 1993.

shows with increasing amounts of violence and, as Figure 5.7 suggests, televised warnings are not likely to help. The TV set, which blares away for 7 hours a day in the average American home (Myers, 1990), may be more harmful than we'd like to think.

PREDICTING THE FUTURE

Correlational studies are used frequently to predict future behavior. In other words, once we know that two sets of measurements are strongly correlated, we can then use our knowledge of one measurement score to predict what the other, related score is likely to be. Let's consider prediction in more detail.

An Example: SAT Scores for College Admission

All of you are probably familiar with the use of scores on college entrance exams to predict future college performance. Nearly everyone reading this book would have been required to take an exam like the Scholastic Assessment Test (SAT) or American College Test (ACT) before entering college. Scores from such exams were sent to colleges of your choice, where they were used by admissions officers to decide whether you should be invited to attend those colleges.

SAT and ACT scores are used in this way because past research has shown a significant positive correlation between entrance exam scores and first-year college grade point average (GPA). You should understand exactly what that means by now: People who achieve high scores on the SAT tend to earn high college GPAs in the future. Because admissions officers want people who will succeed in college, they search for students who have achieved high SAT scores.

Before any correlation between variables can be used predictively, it must be statistically significant and fairly strong. Assessing the significance and size of the value of r between two variables for the use of prediction is called assessing **predictive validity.** In other words, we must make sure that it is valid to use one score to predict another before we do so.

When correlation is used to predict unknown values, we usually identify predictor and criterion variables. The **predictor variable** is the one that is known at the present time and is used to predict future behavior. SAT scores would be the predictor variable in our example because they are known before the student has even entered college, and they are used to predict future college GPAs. The **criterion variable** is the one that is being predicted. In our example, first-year college GPA is the criterion variable. It helps to find out how the correlation is being used to predict future behavior before trying to identify predictor and criterion variables. As you might imagine, the stronger the correlation between predictor and criterion variables, the more precisely we can predict future behavior.

Typical correlation coefficients for SAT scores and college GPA hover around $r = .35$ (Kaplan & Saccuzzo, 1989). If we square that value, we get a coefficient of determination of 12% ($r^2 = .12$). This coefficient of determination means that high school SAT scores account for 12% of the variation in college GPAs. It is probably safe to speculate about direction in this instance because the SAT scores were achieved long before the student even started college.

Although the correlation is consistent enough to be statistically significant, and the effect size is large enough to qualify for Cohen's (1977) medium category, a mere 12% of the variation in GPAs may not sound like much to brag about. That's why admissions officers use a variety of indicators, such as high school grades, letters of recommendation, portfolios of art work or musical ability, as well as considerations of the student's extracurricular activities, public speaking skills, job experience, and writing ability.

When these factors are combined, predictive validity is increased. For instance, high school grades are correlated with college GPA by a coefficient of approximately $r = .55$ (Kaplan & Saccuzzo, 1989). When both high school grades and SAT scores are used in combination to predict college GPA, we reach a correlation coefficient of about .62 (Kaplan & Saccuzzo, 1989). Now we're getting somewhere: Squaring that value gives us a coefficient of determination of .38. Thus, by combining high school grades and SAT scores, we can now account for 38% of the variation in future college GPA. The process of correlating several variables in this way is known as **multiple correlation,** or simply put, the correlation of more than two variables simultaneously. We already saw another example of multiple correlation in Singer and Singer's (1986) research on the combination of factors that are so strongly linked to aggression. Because human behavior is so complex, many correlations with predictive validity are multiple. In other words, one predictor variable alone is often not enough to determine future behavior in a valid manner.

One note of caution: We must remember that prediction operates by *averages*. Even with a perfect correlation of +1.0 or −1.0, we can never say with certainty that every person on the face of the earth who did well in high school and aced the SAT will also succeed in college. There are always exceptions. Correlational research, like most other forms of scientific research, concentrates on overall generalities rather than rare instances. It is important to keep this fact in mind as you learn to conduct and evaluate scientific research.

Prediction is a valuable tool in our society. Nearly every area of psychology has benefited from it. Furthermore, prediction is not restricted to psychological science. Through correlation, medical researchers can predict the length of our lives based on how many cigarettes we smoke each day; musical educators can predict which children will become fine musicians based on the accuracy of their pitch perception; molecular biologists are learning to predict who will develop Alzheimer's disease based on genetic makeup; agronomists can predict which crops will do well in certain locations by examining nutrients in the soil.

USING CORRELATION AS A STATISTIC

I have ignored, until now, the fact that the word "correlation" is ambiguous. It has two meanings: One refers to a type of research in which relationships between two or more sets of measurements are studied. The second meaning refers to a type of statistic, most often represented by the Pearson product-moment correlation r. (By the way, there are other statistics like r that also measure correlation, but they are beyond the scope of this book.)

This ambiguity in meaning can be very confusing for beginning scientists. It helps to remember that correlation can be either a type of research or a type of statistic. The next uses of correlation that we will discuss are statistical analyses that are performed in the course of conducting many types of research including, but not limited to, correlational studies.

Assessing Interrater Reliability

As a statistic, correlation may be used to assess the reliability with which various observers rate the behavior of a subject. We discussed this practice briefly in Chapter 4, in connection with Fossey's (1983) natural observation of mountain gorillas. Now that you understand the basics of correlation, it will be easier to apply that knowledge to the measurement of interrater reliability. **Interrater reliability** is simply the consistency of measurements between several observers who are rating the same behaviors.

Suppose that we have two observers recording the behavior of one subject at the same time. Under ideal circumstances, if our operational definitions are clear and our rating sheets are precise, we would hope that the two observers would produce identical ratings. However, this pie-in-the-sky ideal is not very realistic.

If the behavior being observed is at all complex (and it usually is), we would expect the ratings to differ slightly between observers.

If the two observers' ratings are fairly similar to each other, we usually trust the data. However, if the two observers' ratings differ widely, we must consider discarding the data and beginning the research study again with a more careful design. In other words, if you and Dian Fossey were crouched in the jungle recording chest beating behavior from the same gorilla, we would expect a little bit of variation between your ratings and Fossey's, but not much. Thus, it is important to determine the degree of similarity between the ratings of various observers.

The ratings of subject behavior by two observers are really just two sets of measurements that can be graphed on a scatterplot and assessed by the correlation coefficient r. If the two observers produced identical ratings, we would expect to obtain a value of $r = 1.0$, indicating that the correlation is perfect. If the two observers produced ratings that were completely different from each other, as if one observer had been watching a different subject's behavior, then we would expect to obtain a value of $r = 0$. In reality, consistent observation using precise rating scales usually produces a significant positive correlation, though not a perfect one.

Assessing Test Reliability

Sometimes we are concerned not with reliable ratings among multiple observers, but with reliable scores on multiple forms of the same test. For example, there are many different forms of the verbal SAT, but all of them are expected to test the same skills and to produce similar scores. It would certainly be unfair if two people's verbal SAT scores differed substantially just because one test form was harder than another!

To avoid this problem, we use Pearson's r to appraise the consistency in scores from different test forms. **Alternative-form reliability** is assessed by computing the correlation coefficient that represents the relationship between scores on Form A and scores on Form B of the same test. To show that a test produces consistent scores each time it is given, we measure **test-retest reliability.** In this case, the same individuals take the same test at two different times. If the test produces similar scores each time, the correlation between scores will be strong and, accordingly, the value of r will be large.

As a matter of fact, test-retest and alternative-form reliability are quite strong for the SAT test, with r around .85 to .90 (Kaplan & Saccuzzo, 1989). This means that your score on the SAT should remain fairly consistent regardless of the various test forms you might be given.

Assessing Relationships in Noncorrelational Research

Any type of research can produce two sets of scores that might be related to each other. In these instances, correlation (as a statistic) may be used to appraise the degree of that relationship, regardless of whether the original research study was nonexperimental, experimental, or quasi-experimental. For example, I mentioned briefly in Chapter 4 that correlational analysis is sometimes used in survey research.

The speed/accuracy tradeoff found in many studies of human cognition is a good example of a correlational relationship obtained through experimental research. Cognitive scientists often measure the amount of time that it takes a subject to respond to some stimulus during an experiment. By measuring response time, we are able to make inferences about the unobservable mental processes that allow human minds to operate properly every day. Sometimes, these researchers measure the subject's accuracy in responding to a stimulus, in addition to measuring speed. Here we have two sets of scores that might be related in some way. Think about what sort of relationship you might expect to see between speed and accuracy before reading further.

What usually happens is that a subject's speed can be influenced by pressure to be more accurate, and vice versa. In other words, a subject who is pushed to respond very quickly is likely to make a lot of errors. As the same subject slows down, accuracy increases. Another way of describing this relationship is to say that speed and accuracy are correlated negatively. Negatively? Think about it: With greater speed, there is less accuracy. You've probably experienced the same effect yourself when typing or playing a musical instrument. The point is that the speed/accuracy tradeoff is measured by using correlation as a statistic, even though the data of response times and mistakes can be collected using many types of research.

THE VALUE OF CORRELATIONAL RESEARCH

We have seen several drawbacks to correlational research in this chapter. For instance, correlational studies cannot determine cause, and they are vulnerable to the influence of many uncontrolled variables. These sorts of criticisms may lead you to believe that correlational studies should always be avoided in scientific research. Let me try to dispel that notion now.

Although correlational research is tricky to interpret, it is quite valuable to knowledgeable scientists. When a topic is new and unexplored, correlations provide important information. At the very least, the lack of a correlation between variables tells us that they are not related to each other. In the muddy waters of a mysterious new topic, even this simple fact can be helpful. Once we know which variables are related and which ones are not, we can design other types of research to explore more rigorously the influences of related factors on human or animal behavior.

Correlational research also helps us to investigate variables that can not be manipulated ethically. Because correlation does not require the manipulation of independent variables, it allows us to explore topics that would otherwise be off limits. Some of our most pressing national problems, such as the number of deaths caused by lung cancer or the ever-increasing rate of violent crime in our cities, have been addressed by correlational research.

SUMMARY OF MAIN POINTS

- Correlational studies represent a type of nonexperimental research in which we measure two or more variables to see whether they are related to each other.

- Correlational data should always be graphed on a scatterplot so that the general pattern of an effect may be seen. This is especially important when the pattern is curvilinear.

- A positive correlation, signified by a value of r between 0 and +1.0, indicates that scores from both variables increase together. A negative correlation, signified by an r value between 0 and −1.0, indicates that scores from one variable increase while scores from the other variable decrease.

- Both central tendency and variability can be seen in a scatterplot containing a line of best fit. As always, they are used in determining the statistical significance of an observed correlation. Data points fall near the line of best fit when the relationship is consistent enough to be significant. They appear scattered widely around the line of best fit when the relationship is highly variable and unlikely to be significant.

- The statistical significance of a correlation is determined by the correlation coefficient, r. Effect size is determined by the coefficient of determination, r^2.

- Correlations are difficult to interpret accurately. Common flaws of interpretation include assuming causation, assuming direction, ignoring third variables, restricting the data range, and ignoring curvilinear relationships.

- Cross-lagged correlations are useful in studying the most likely direction of an effect. Partial correlations help us to determine whether a third variable is influencing the relationship of interest. Multiple correlation is required for complex forms of behavior in which many variables may be operating simultaneously.

- Strong correlations allow us to predict an unknown score on one variable from a known score on another variable. When correlation is used for prediction, we identify predictor and criterion variables.

- Correlation is a type of research, but it is also a type of statistic. The correlation statistic may be used on data gathered from any type of research. It is also used to assess interrater, alternative-form, and test-retest reliability.

- Correlational research is valuable as an ethical means of exploring new topics. After related variables have been discovered, more rigorous forms of research are needed to pinpoint cause and effect.

CHAPTER EXERCISES

1. Use your own words to define these key terms:

    correlation   coefficient of determination

    scatterplot   scattergram

abscissa	cross-lagged correlation
ordinate	third variable
positive correlation	partial correlation
negative correlation	predictive validity
inverse relationship	predictor variable
curvilinear relationship	criterion variable
correlation coefficient	multiple correlation
line of best fit	interrater reliability
regression line	alternative-form reliability
spurious relationship	test-retest reliability

2. Identify potential third variables in the following spurious relationships:
   a) People who drink a lot of coffee show an increased risk of heart attack.
   b) Before a vaccine was introduced, the incidence of polio and the sales of soft drinks were correlated positively.
   c) Students who smoke cigarettes are likely to earn poor grades in school.

3. Identify the predictor and criterion variables in the following descriptions:
   a) A biologist wants to predict the number of squirrels that live in a forest by counting the trees in that forest.
   b) Personnel administrators in a police department decide which of 1,000 applicants to hire, based on scores from physical endurance tests and group interview scores.
   c) Fashion designers estimate the perfect leg length on a model: one that will sell the largest number of bathing suits.

4. The following advice was given to parents in an article written by a physician in *Woman's Day* magazine:

   > For some children, excessive television watching leads to obesity—partly because it is a sedentary activity, taking time away that could be spent running and climbing. (Stern, 1992, p. 22)

   After reading this quote carefully, try to identify problems with Stern's interpretation and explanation of the correlational research she describes.

5. Find a newspaper or magazine article that illustrates the misinterpretation of a correlation by implying causation, assuming direction, or ignoring a third variable.

6

Experimental Research

Experimenting with aerobics.

Experimental research is the second general category of research design that we will discuss. Experimental studies are more powerful than nonexperimental and quasi-experimental studies because they allow us to determine the cause of an observed behavior. A case study provides a detailed look at rare behavior, a survey describes general opinions, a correlation shows how dependent variables are linked, but only an experiment can show us what causes people and animals to behave as they do. You may recall Latané and Darley's (1968) study of bystander intervention from Chapter 1: It was an experiment in which the existence of fewer bystanders caused people to report more emergencies.

THE KEYS TO EXPERIMENTATION

There are three basic requirements that every experiment must meet: manipulation, measurement, and control (E. L. Bjork, personal communication, 1986). Keeping these requirements in mind will help you to design your own studies and to evaluate work done by other researchers. An experiment in which any one of these requirements has been ignored is seriously flawed.

Manipulation

A true experiment always includes at least one variable that is manipulated by the researcher. This variable, as you may remember from Chapter 1, is called the **independent variable.** We call it "independent" because it does not depend on the subject's behavior. Instead, the independent variable is determined and manipulated by the researcher and does not change no matter what the subject does. If a study does not have an independent variable that has been manipulated in this way, it is not an experiment.

For the next few chapters, we will limit our discussion to **simple experiments,** which are experiments that have only one independent variable. (We'll see that they're not always "simple" in the usual sense of the word, though!) Experiments that have more than one independent variable are called **complex experiments.** We will get to those in Chapter 9, after the basics of simple experiments are clear.

Measurement

A true experiment must also include at least one **dependent variable,** which, as I mentioned in Chapter 1, is the variable that is measured. The standard definition of a dependent variable is one whose value depends on the experimental manipulation, or independent variable. However, the statement that "a dependent variable depends on the independent variable" seems pretty obscure. For now, you may find it easier to think of a dependent variable as the aspect of a subject's behavior that was measured in an experiment.

Control

In order to determine cause, an independent variable must be manipulated so that we can determine its effect on some dependent variable. But there is something more that must be done: Other variables must be controlled. There are all kinds of other variables in the world, and even in the experimental laboratory, that might affect subjects' behavior. These are called **extraneous variables,** because they are "extra" factors that the researcher did not intend to study.

Extraneous variables can make trouble in one of two ways. First, they can add variability to the data by interfering randomly with subjects' behavior. For example, behavior might be altered slightly by minor annoyances such as the sound of voices in an adjacent room or by a bee that entered through an open window. These annoyances cause random variation in scores that, in turn, reduce our chances of obtaining significant effects.

The second problem arises when a special type of extraneous variable, called a **confounding variable,** is not controlled. A confounding variable is one that varies systematically, not randomly, along with the independent variable. Suppose, for example, that the pesky bee buzzes around the laboratory while one group of subjects is tested but escapes by the time a second group is tested. If there is a significant difference in results between the two groups, we have no way of knowing whether it was caused by the independent variable or by the bee. In this way, the extraneous variable prevents us from interpreting results accurately. The importance of experimental control will become especially clear as we travel through the next two chapters, which are devoted to a thorough understanding of the flaws produced by lack of control.

My students say that one of the most valuable lessons they learn in the research methods course is the ability to identify independent, dependent, and extraneous variables quickly. There is no better way to grasp the underlying design of a research study in preparation for a more complete understanding of the details. In addition, identification of variables is necessary before determining which statistical test is appropriate for data analysis. It will be impossible for you to design and analyze your own experimental studies properly without these skills. Furthermore, if you wish to evaluate critically any of the numerous research reports that arrive at your doorstep every day, identifying variables at a glance will speed the process.

SELECTING THE INDEPENDENT VARIABLE

As the designer of a research study, you will be expected to choose the independent variable that is most appropriate for your experiment. For each research question, there are a number of different independent variables that might be appropriate. Which one should you choose, and exactly how should you manipulate it?

Relevance to the Research Question

At the risk of sounding overly simplistic, your independent variable must be relevant to your research question. This may seem obvious now, but in the heat of research design, it's easy to end up with an independent variable that is precise and creative but has little to do with the research question you wanted to answer. There are two ways to avoid this pitfall: First, specify your research question clearly and keep it in mind at all times during the design process. Second, look at past studies of related research questions to see which independent variables other scientists used. In some cases, you will want to use the same variable for direct comparison; in others, you will see the need for a different variable that might change the outcome of a new study.

Selecting the Number of Levels

Once you have selected the best independent variable for your research question, it's time to decide how many levels of manipulation to use. The **levels** of an independent variable are the different values of it that will be used in your experiment. For instance, a study of the effects of the amount of aerobic exercise on mood might include two levels: 15 minutes of aerobic exercise per day, and 45 minutes of aerobic exercise per day. The difference between levels does not have to be numerical, either. For certain research questions, it would be more relevant to consider the effects of type of exercise rather than amount. In this case, we might use "type of exercise" as the independent variable, with two levels: 30 minutes of aerobic exercise per day versus 30 minutes of weight training per day. I'm sure you get the idea.

Sometimes we call these levels of the independent variable **treatments.** The term is used to signify that something is done to the subjects; some "treatment" is given. Such usage is easiest to understand in clinical studies, where subjects receive medical treatment, but the term has become common in all types of experimental research.

When specifying levels, consider the need for a **control group.** A control group is a group of subjects (and a level of the independent variable) to which no treatment is given. In the example we just discussed, adding a third level of no exercise at all would provide a control group. Thus, one group of subjects would receive a treatment of 30 minutes of aerobic exercise, one group would receive a treatment of 30 minutes of weight training, and the third (the control group) would receive no treatment at all.

Many beginning researchers assume that every experiment must have a control group. This assumption is simply not true. Although every experiment must provide some means of comparison between levels of an independent variable, it is quite possible to achieve that comparison without using a control group. Whether you need a control group depends on your research question. If you want to know whether exercise of any kind affects mood, then you'll want to include exercise (treatment) and no exercise (control) levels in your experiment.

However, if you want to know which kind of exercise affects mood, an adequate comparison could be made by specifying levels of aerobic exercise (treatment 1) and weight training (treatment 2), with no control group at all.

At the risk of overload, let me introduce a little more terminology here. The term **condition** is used when we want to refer to the groups in which subjects participate. Thus, if we have two levels (aerobic exercise and weight training) of one independent variable (type of exercise), it is appropriate to refer to the levels as conditions. Common ways of using the term are to ask, "which condition is that subject in?" or "how many conditions are there in the experiment?" When we are discussing simple experiments, like those presented in this chapter, it is acceptable to use the terms *levels, conditions,* and *groups* interchangeably. In Chapter 9, we'll see that the first two terms take on distinct meanings when complex experiments are being discussed.

Anticipating Manipulation Strength

Once you have specified at least two levels of the independent variable, think about the strength of the manipulation. Is the difference between the two levels strong enough that it will cause subjects to behave differently in the two conditions? A good researcher will try to ensure that the answer to this question is "yes," even though we can never be certain in advance about how subjects will behave.

The purpose of conducting an experiment is to find out whether some independent variable will have an effect on the subjects' behavior. If the levels are too similar to each other, the manipulation may not be strong enough to produce a difference that we can detect. For example, we would probably expect to see a difference in mood after 45 minutes of aerobic exercise as opposed to only 15 minutes of aerobic exercise. However, if the levels had specified 45 versus 40 minutes of aerobic exercise, any resulting effect on subject behavior would probably be too small to detect. At the other end of the spectrum, we must also avoid the "sledge hammer" effect: A huge difference in mood would occur if the levels specified 15 minutes versus 6 hours of continuous aerobic exercise, but that difference would carry little meaning. Obviously, a subject who is hospitalized for exhaustion will not be in a very good mood!

Between-Subjects and Within-Subjects Designs

Finally, we must decide whether to manipulate the independent variable between subjects or within subjects. When an independent variable is manipulated **between subjects,** each subject is assigned to one condition or the other, but never to both. Sometimes a between-subjects design is called an **independent groups** design, because the two groups of subjects are not related to each other in any way. They are two completely separate sets of people. When the independent variable is manipulated **within subjects,** each subject participates in every condition. This is sometimes called a **repeated measures** design because the experimenter repeats the same measure on the same subjects as they participate in each different condition. An easy way to remember this distinction is to place yourself in the position of an imaginary subject. Then ask yourself, "If I had been a subject in this study, would I have participated in only one condition or would I have participated in all conditions?"

To review, when selecting an independent variable, there are several points to consider. Is the independent variable directly relevant to the research question that you want to answer? How many levels of the independent variable are needed? Does your research question require a control group? Is your manipulation between levels strong enough to produce a detectable difference in behavior? And, finally, will the independent variable be manipulated between subjects or within subjects?

ADVANTAGES OF THE WITHIN-SUBJECTS DESIGN

The decision to manipulate the independent variable between subjects or within subjects is an important one that defines many other characteristics of the experiment being conducted. We will see that there are certain advantages and disadvantages associated with each of the two choices. Furthermore, those factors are linked closely to the statistical analysis of data obtained from an experiment.

Within-subjects experiments are preferred to between-subjects experiments for several reasons. Let's explore each of these advantages so that you can see why it's useful to try to manipulate your independent variable within subjects.

No Need for Random Assignment

As you know, in a between-subjects experiment, each subject is assigned to participate in only one condition or level of the independent variable. But how will we decide which subjects should participate in a given condition? Would it be acceptable to assign the first 20 subjects who volunteer for the experiment to one condition and the last 20 to the other condition? Think about it: Why not?

The reason, which you've probably discovered for yourself, is that this would introduce a confounding variable to the experiment. If all the eager beavers are in one condition and the late stragglers are in another, we will have no way of knowing whether obtained effects were caused by differences in the independent variable or by differences in the subjects. After conducting the experiment, we might say, "Aha! Aerobic exercise causes people to display bright, happy moods, but weight training causes people to seem tired and bored." A critical reader would pounce immediately on our bad reasoning: "No way. Subjects in the aerobic exercise condition seemed brighter and happier because they were so eager to participate. They wanted to exercise; they wanted to be subjects in an experiment. No wonder they seem bright and happy! Their moods had nothing to do with the type of exercise you required them to perform."

One proper way to assign subjects to conditions in a between-subjects experiment is to do it randomly. Random assignment ensures that unavoidable differences between individual subjects will be spread out over all conditions in the experiment, rather than consolidated in one condition. If these individual differences are spread over various conditions, we would have no reason to believe that they could affect the results of one condition in a systematic way.

Random assignment to experimental conditions can be done by using a random number table, like the one in Table C.2 on page 313. We simply assign a random number from the table to each subject, so that the first subject is number 12, the second subject is number 39, the third is 53, and so on. For an experiment with two conditions, we could then assign all odd-numbered subjects to one condition and all even-numbered subjects to the other. For example, suppose I am the first subject you test and even-numbered subjects are to be assigned to the weight training condition. You will then send me off to pump iron because 12 is an even number.

Note that random assignment to conditions is different from the random sampling of subjects from a population. In every research study that uses more than one subject and attempts to infer population behavior from a subject sample, it is vital to try to achieve *random selection of subjects*. However, *random assignment to conditions* is used only in between-subjects experiments, when each subject must be assigned to one condition or another.

If you elect to use a between-subjects design, you will have to assign subjects randomly to conditions. However, if every subject is going to participate in every condition, there is no need for random asssignment. This is one advantage of the within-subjects design. Removing the need for random assignment saves a little time and energy on the part of the researcher, but more importantly, it removes the possibility of a weakness in the experiment caused by nonrandom assignment.

Fewer Subjects

The statistical tests used most commonly in experimental research, such as *t*-tests and ANOVAs, require a minimum number of 10 scores per condition to produce trustworthy results. Note that this is a minimum—it's much better to have more than 10 scores in each condition if possible. Simple arithmetic will show that fewer subjects are needed to produce these scores in within-subjects experiments than in between-subjects experiments.

Suppose that we plan to test only the minimum of 10 subjects per condition. If the independent variable is manipulated between subjects and we have two levels, how many subjects will be needed in the experiment? We would need 10 subjects in Condition 1 and 10 in Condition 2, for a total of 20. But what if the same experiment were conducted within subjects? This time, we could achieve the same minimum number of 10 scores per condition with only 10 subjects. This reduction in the number of subjects to be tested is a major advantage of the

Table 6.1 WITHIN-GROUPS VARIABILITY AND BETWEEN-GROUPS VARIABILITY

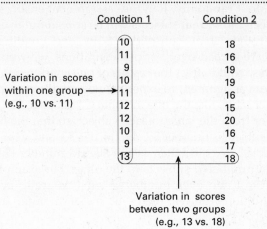

within-subjects design because it's not easy to recruit large numbers of subjects. A lot of people just have other things they'd rather do.

Greater Statistical Power

The most important advantage of the within-subjects design is that it increases the statistical power needed to detect a significant effect. This increase in power occurs because a within-subjects design reduces variability among data scores. In general, when the same subjects participate in multiple conditions, individual differences between those conditions are lessened. In turn, variability is reduced, and statistical significance becomes more likely. Let's consider this concept in more detail.

Start by taking a look at Table 6.1, which shows imaginary scores from two groups of subjects. The first thing to notice is that the numbers vary in the column marked Condition 1 (e.g., 10 versus 11). This fluctuation in scores is known as **within-groups variability,** or the variation among scores within one condition. It merely reflects the fact that each one of us is a little bit different from everyone else. You can see that individual differences also cause the scores within Condition 2 to fluctuate.

Now, concentrate for a moment on the differences between scores across the two conditions (e.g., 13 versus 18). This variation occurs because the two conditions represent a difference introduced by the manipulation of the independent variable. In fact, this kind of variation, called **between-groups variability,** is highly desired. When we manipulate an independent variable between two conditions, we hope that one column of scores (from one condition) will vary dramatically from the other column of scores (from another condition).

Statistical tests that search for a difference between groups compare the amount of variability among scores within one column to the amount of variability between the two sets of scores across columns. In other words, they compare the amount of within-groups variability to the amount of between-groups variability. Whenever the between-groups variability is greater than the within-groups variability, we are likely to have a statistically significant difference.

If this is clear, turn your attention now to the difference between the two types of designs we have been discussing. The between-subjects design produces data in two columns, and those two sets of data come from two different groups of subjects. The within-subjects design also produces data in two columns, but those two sets of data come from the same subjects. This slight difference turns out to be critical.

When you have two groups of different subjects, as in a between-subjects design, the variability between the two groups comes partly from your manipulation of the independent variable and partly from individual differences. However, when both groups of scores are produced by the same subjects, as in a within-subjects design, any variability between the two conditions must come from your manipulation of the independent variable. It couldn't possibly be caused by individual differences, because there are no individual differences between one subject's score in Condition 1 and that same subject's score in Condition 2. After all, these two scores came from the same person. This reduction in individual differences causes the within-subjects design to have greater statistical power than the between-subjects design.

If you didn't understand every word of the last few paragraphs, don't panic. Many people have trouble catching on to this at first. It will help to re-read the section carefully, jot down any questions you have, and then see your professor for help. It is important that you grasp these basic concepts, however, because we will be building on them in future explanations of more complicated research.

Within-subjects designs are not perfect. In fact, we'll see in the next chapter that they can introduce potential problems requiring careful control. To avoid those problems, we sometimes choose to use a between-subjects design. However, in general, within-subjects designs are preferred because they remove the chance of nonrandom assignment and require fewer subjects, yet provide greater statistical power than do between-subjects designs.

SELECTING THE DEPENDENT VARIABLE

Selecting the best dependent variable is a task that deserves every bit as much attention as we have given to the choice of independent variables. There are literally hundreds of possible dependent variables that a researcher could use in an experiment. We might measure response time, heart rate, accuracy, self-reports of personal experiences, recall ability, vocabulary skills, motor coordination, respiration rate, body temperature, facial expression, time spent depressed or elated, type of speech errors produced . . . the number of possibilities seems infinite.

As with selecting a good independent variable, knowing the past literature surrounding your topic is vital. If you wish to compare your results directly to the results of other researchers, you need to use the same dependent variable they used. On the other hand, if a crucial aspect of the topic is ignored by a popular dependent variable, then it may be time for you to introduce a new measurement. In addition, as with choosing the independent variable, make sure that your dependent variable is directly relevant to your research question.

Beyond thorough knowledge of the background literature and relevance to the research question, selecting the best dependent variable requires consideration of five other criteria: reliability, validity, reactivity, availability, and statistical analysis.

Reliability

A **reliable** measure is one that yields the same result each time you apply it. A yardstick is a good example of a reliable measure: Every time I hold it up to the same table, it will measure the same number of inches in height or width of that table. If I measured the table once and obtained a height of 19 inches, but then measured it again and obtained a height of 23 inches, my measuring device would not be reliable. Using a yardstick that yielded such vastly different measurements would produce unreliable, or inconsistent, results. (Tiny variations in measurement, like 19 inches as opposed to $19^1/_{16}$ inches, are usually the result of human error, not of an inherent lack of reliability within the measuring device.)

Of course, you critical readers are correct to point out that psychologists don't use yardsticks to measure dependent variables very often. But the principle is the same regardless of the particular measure chosen. When we measure response time, we want to be sure that any changes in that measure are linked to the subject's behavior and not to a faulty clock. Likewise, when we administer a test (perhaps the SAT or a Rorschach inkblot or the Peabody vocabulary test), we want to know that any changes in scores on that test are due to the subject and not to the test. If you achieve a score of 530 on the mathematical section of the SAT one time, then 6 weeks later your score leaps to 630, the reason had better be linked to something about you, not to something about the test. If the test is reliable, large changes in scores will be caused by subject behaviors such as studying hard, recuperating from a serious illness, or overcoming severe test anxiety.

Fortunately, we don't have to guess at reliability. As we discussed in Chapter 5, it can be measured directly by using correlation. If you decide to use a standard test to measure subjects' behavior, the *Mental Measurements Yearbook* (Kramer & Conoley, 1992) provides a listing of available tests along with correlational assessments of their reliability. If you design your own measure, consider assessing its reliability first through the use of correlation coefficients.

Validity

Let me begin this section with a caution: The term *validity* is applied to several distinct aspects of research methods, which often confuses beginning scientists. The kind of validity we are discussing here refers strictly to dependent variables. Later, in Chapter 8, we will turn our attention to the validity of entire experiments, which is a rather different concept.

A dependent variable is **valid** if it really measures what you intended it to measure. Thus, our yardstick is a valid measure of height or length or width, but it is not a valid measure of weight or intelligence or mood. Much of the current controversy concerning the use of IQ tests has to do with their validity—do they really measure native intelligence, or do they measure cultural upbringing and school experience?

The validity of a dependent variable can be considered in several different ways. For certain research questions, some considerations will be more important than others, but you should be familiar with all possibilities:

1. **Face validity.** A dependent variable is face valid if it seems to measure what it's supposed to measure. This is a vague criterion, I know, but it can be useful. For example, the idea of using a yardstick to measure intelligence can be rejected immediately because it's not face valid. A yardstick does have face validity for measuring length, though.

2. **Construct validity.** A **theoretical construct** is an abstract concept that plays a central role in a theory but may not exist in real life. For example, theoretical physicists use the construct of the atom: No one has ever seen or touched a real atom, so we can't be sure they exist, but they do play a central role in theories that attempt to explain our universe.

   Androgyny is a construct used in psychological theory—it refers to the concept that people may have both masculine and feminine traits regardless of whether they are male or female. This construct was first suggested by Bem (1974), who developed a paper-and-pencil test to measure the abstract concept of androgyny. To assess the construct validity of the test, she correlated test scores with other assessments (e.g., self-reports) of the extent to which women sometimes behave in masculine ways and men in feminine ways. Strong correlation coefficients validated the use of her test to measure the new construct called androgyny.

3. **Concurrent validity.** Whenever a new dependent variable is introduced, we want to be sure that it produces the same consistent results that a standard measure of the same behavior produces. We can use correlation to compare scores produced by the two measures to assess concurrent validity. The standard American ruler and the European metric ruler are concurrently valid because they both produce equivalent measurements.

4. **Predictive validity.** Any measured scores that are used to predict performance on some other dependent variable must have predictive validity. You probably remember from Chapter 5 that predictive validity can be assessed through the use of the correlation coefficient. To provide a simple reminder, if we plan to use height to predict a person's weight, we must know first through correlation that height is related closely to weight. If it is, then height may be used as a valid predictor of weight.

Reactivity

Even the most reliable and valid dependent variable may still be flawed by reactivity. **Reactivity** occurs whenever subjects "react" to the dependent variable so that it is measuring unusual reactions instead of natural, everyday behavior.

You may have experienced reactivity at a physician's office when your blood pressure was taken. Some people become concerned at the very mention of blood pressure measurement. This concern causes physiological arousal in the form of faster heart rate and rapid, shallow breathing. As the nurse brings the dreaded cuff closer and closer to the vulnerable upper arm, these patients become increasingly nervous. By the time the measurement is taken, their blood pressure is quite high. Under normal circumstances, their pressure would be lower, but the act of measurement causes a reaction that changes the value of the dependent variable quite dramatically.

Availability

Perhaps the easiest criterion to achieve in choosing a good dependent variable, and also the easiest one to forget, is availability. Beginning researchers sometimes design elaborate experiments before they realize that the equipment they need is not available. Within the area of cognitive science, for example, the use of brain imaging techniques (such as positron emission tomography [PET] scans) has become popular. However, even today, only a handful of major universities have easy access to the equipment needed to measure brain activity through a PET scan. Chances are good that yours isn't one of them.

That example brings up an important point concerning technology. Some research ideas are impossible to execute because the technology needed to implement them does not exist. Even the earliest prototypes of computerized axial tomography (CAT), PET, and magnetic resonance imaging (MRI) scans were not developed until the 1970s, and they were not in common use until the 1980s (Andreasen, 1988; Monen, van Zijl, Frank, Lebihan, & Becker, 1990). Before that time, researchers who wanted to study internal structures of the human brain had to dissect dead human subjects. Those who were interested in the internal functioning of the live brain had to rely on devices like the electroencephalograph (EEG), which provides few solid conclusions. Research in neuroscience and related areas of psychology really took off during the 1980s with the advent of brain scanning techniques.

Most students who conduct their own research do so under the supervision of a course professor or an academic sponsor. It's a good idea to ask your professor or sponsor to explain what equipment is available before you design your research. That way, you can keep practical considerations in mind as you plan your study.

Don't completely discard ideas that require unavailable equipment, however. Most of you will be required to enroll in upper-division laboratory courses, in which you'll be expected to design research studies with greater latitude in technical apparatus. If not, the time may come that you wish to spend a summer internship working as a research assistant at an institution that has access to sophisticated equipment. Or, perhaps you will decide to go on to graduate school, where the chances of acquiring or borrowing high-tech measuring devices are greater. Should any of these opportunities ultimately beckon to you, you'll be glad to have that file of ideas at hand. Think about the people who had excellent research ideas requiring brain scans during the 1970s: They were out of luck at the time, but within only a few years the technology they needed was available.

Analyzing the Data

Earlier in this chapter, you learned that a common error among beginning researchers is to conduct an experiment based on a particular independent variable, only to realize later that it had little to do with their research question. An equally common mistake occurs when people collect their data, then learn that it can't be analyzed. A vital rule for good research is to *plan ahead.* Time spent carefully during the planning stages of your research will be time saved during data analysis and interpretation. Don't dive into your research program without first making sure there's water in the pool.

The dependent variable that you choose will dictate which statistical test may be used to analyze the data. If you choose self-reports in which large numbers of subjects write lengthy essays about their feelings, for example, the ensuing data are going to be difficult to analyze statistically. If you elect to use nominal or ordinal scales of measurement, your choice of inferential statistics may be limited to nonparametric tests. For experimental research, interval and ratio scales of measurement are versatile in their capacity for analysis, but sometimes they're not suited to the research question that you wish to answer.

By the time you finish this book, you should have a visual overview in your mind of how various types of dependent variables can be analyzed statistically. Table C.1 (on page 312) will help you not only in selecting statistical tests but also in choosing the best dependent variable. For now, do the best you can with the knowledge you have—take time to think about statistical analysis before you collect data, and ask your professor for guidance concerning analyses that we have not yet covered in this book.

To summarize, when you choose a dependent variable, make sure that it is reliable, valid, and readily available to you. In addition, be certain that it does not cause unusual reactions from subjects and that it will yield a set of data that can be analyzed statistically.

AN EXAMPLE: EYEWITNESS TESTIMONY

Until now, we've focused on a lot of abstract principles concerning the design of experimental research. Sometimes it helps to consider examples of true research, to see exactly how these abstract principles are realized in the lab on an everyday basis. Or, as some of my students so eloquently put it, "C'mon, get real!" Let's look first at a simple between-subjects experiment with two conditions. This study was actually conducted by Loftus and Palmer in 1974.

For years, the American legal system has assumed that people who have seen a crime have accurate memories of that crime. Because of this assumption, eyewitness testimony in court receives serious consideration from jurors. If an objective eyewitness tells 12 members of a jury the sequence of events that occurred during a crime, those jurors are very likely to believe the eyewitness. Likewise, if a respected eyewitness identifies someone as a criminal, the police usually file charges against the accused individual without delay. In past years, the notion that reputable eyewitnesses might be mistaken was seldom considered.

Loftus and her colleagues implemented a program of research in which this notion would be tested. They wondered whether eyewitnesses really did have such accurate memories and, if not, how those memories might be altered by various events that occurred during and after the observed crime. Previous research (e.g., Bransford, Barclay, & Franks, 1972) had suggested that human memory is constructive so that forgotten details are supplied automatically in a way that fits with remembered information but may not be accurate. Loftus decided to follow up such early studies by applying them to the legal world of eyewitness testimony. She was not concerned that eyewitnesses were lying about what they had seen; rather, she was afraid that they might believe confidently in memories that were incorrect because of constructed details.

Loftus and Palmer (1974) used a two-group between-subjects experiment to test the hypothesis that memory could be altered by simple forms of questioning. Often, after eyewitnesses observe a crime, they are questioned by police. Was it possible that the wording of these questions could alter people's memories of an event?

One hundred subjects in this experiment watched a short film showing a traffic accident and were then questioned about what they had seen. Before being questioned individually, the subjects were assigned randomly to one of the two experimental conditions. The independent variable was the wording of one of the questions. One group of subjects was asked, "How fast were the cars going when they hit each other?" The other group of subjects was asked, "How fast were the cars going when they smashed into each other?" After seeing the film and being asked one of these two questions (along with several others), the subjects were thanked for their participation and told that the experiment was over.

Loftus and Palmer reasoned that the manipulation in the wording of that one question might cause subjects' memories of the event to change. They predicted that subjects who believed the cars had merely "hit" each other would be likely to recall the accident as a minor one in which both cars were traveling at low speeds. However, subjects who believed the cars had "smashed into" each other would probably recall a more severe accident at higher speed.

Sure enough, the results showed that subjects who were asked how fast the cars were traveling when they "smashed into" each other reported a mean speed of 10.46 miles per hour. Subjects who were asked how fast the cars were traveling when they "hit" each other reported a mean speed of 8.00 miles per hour. Statistical analysis showed that this difference was significant. The manipulation of only one word during questioning had affected subjects' estimates of traveling speed, suggesting that their memories of the accident were altered.

A further test of the predictions occurred a week later, when the subjects returned for the second half of the experiment. This time, the subjects were asked a few more questions about the accident, including "Did you see any broken glass?" The "yes" or "no" answer to this question represented the researchers'

Table 6.2 MEMORY FOR BROKEN GLASS

Response	Verb condition	
	"Smashed"	"Hit"
Yes	16	7
No	34	43

From "Reconstruction of Automobile Destruction: An Example of the Interaction Between Language and Memory" by E. F. Loftus and J. C. Palmer, 1974, *Journal of Verbal Learning and Verbal Behavior, 13*, p. 587. Copyright 1974 by Academic Press. Adapted by permission.

second dependent variable. In fact, no broken glass was present at the filmed scene of the accident.

The results of the second part of this experiment showed that subjects who were told that the cars had "smashed into" each other were significantly more likely to report broken glass than were subjects who were told that the cars had "hit" each other. You can see from Table 6.2 that only 7 out of 50 subjects in the "hit" condition reported seeing broken glass, whereas broken glass was reported by 16 out of 50 subjects in the "smashed" condition. Their reports were altered by the type of questioning they received shortly after viewing the accident.

Statistical Analysis: Independent *t*-Test

To select the right statistical test for data analysis in an experiment, we must identify the dependent variable, independent variable, and number of levels in the study. You've seen that there were really two parts of the Loftus and Palmer experiment. Both made use of one independent variable with two levels, but in the first, subjects' reports of automobile speed were measured, and in the second, subjects' reports of broken glass were measured. We'll look at each of these dependent variables in turn.

Automobile Speed. The first step in choosing an appropriate statistical test is to determine the scale of measurement that was used. What scale of measurement would you say was used in reports of automobile speed? Car speed is measured by numerical values, in equal amounts between units, but the speed of travel never drops below the value of zero. These facts should lead you to decide that a ratio scale of measurement was used. (If you selected some other scale, better review Table 3.1 on page 53.)

Table C.1 on page 312 tells you which statistical test to use depending on scale of measurement, number of independent variables, and number of levels. Verify for yourself that ratio level data from an experiment with one independent variable and two levels should be analyzed using a *t*-test. Now, there is only one further decision to be made: Should you use an independent *t*-test or a dependent *t*-test? This decision is easy. Whenever the independent variable in this type of experiment is manipulated between subjects, use the independent *t*-test. Whenever it is manipulated within subjects, use the dependent *t*-test. The terminology comes from the fact that when an independent variable is manipulated between subjects, the two sets of scores are "independent of," or unrelated to, each other. However, when the same subject produces scores in two or more conditions, those scores are related to each other. They are likely to be similar because no individual differences are interfering with them.

If you have concluded that Loftus and Palmer should have used an independent *t*-test to analyze their data concerning speed of travel, you're right. And, indeed, that's exactly what they did. Their obtained value of *t* was 2.00, with 98 degrees of freedom. If you compare that value to the critical values in Table C.5 (page 316), you'll see that Loftus and Palmer were correct in reporting that the effect was statistically significant.

Of course, statistical significance tells us that the difference in reported speeds was consistent, but a responsible researcher will also assess the size of the effect. When *t* is used, we use ω^2 to measure effect size, as you can see in Table C.7 (page 318). The symbol ω is called "omega," and omega-squared allows us to measure effect size in terms of the proportion of variance accounted for by the independent variable.

The formula for omega-squared is easy to use as long as you have the obtained value of *t* and the number of subjects tested in each condition:

$$\omega^2 = \frac{|t|^2 - 1}{|t|^2 + N_1 + N_2 - 1}$$

To refresh your memory, the vertical lines surrounding *t* in this formula mean that its absolute value, regardless of positive or negative signs, should be used when calculating omega-squared. Once omega-squared has been determined, it can be compared to Cohen's guidelines for effect size shown in Table C.7. Let's work through the simple calculation together one time:

$$\omega^2 = \frac{4 - 1}{4 + 50 + 50 - 1} = \frac{3}{103} = .03$$

The Loftus and Palmer data concerning automobile speed produced a significant, but rather small, effect. Omega-squared is equal to .03, indicating that only 3% of the variation in speed estimates was caused by the manipulation of question wording.

Reports of Broken Glass. Table C.1 (on page 312) can also be followed to determine which statistical test to use for the second dependent variable. Ask yourself:

1. What is the scale of measurement of the dependent variable?
2. How many independent variables were there?
3. How many levels occurred for each independent variable?

Once these questions have been answered, refer to Table C.1. Why not go ahead and get some practice at this right now? Don't read further until you have tried to decide which statistical test to use.

The most common mistake that students make here is to select a *t*-test because the experiment contains one independent variable with two levels. However, the question "Did you see broken glass?" yields either "yes" or "no" for an answer. That fact should have guided you to identify the scale of measurement as nominal, and nominal data are analyzed with the chi-square test.

After selecting the proper test, you can calculate the chi-square statistic by hand or by computer. The chi-square obtained by Loftus and Palmer for reports of broken glass would have been 4.58, with 1 degree of freedom, based on the data presented in Table 6.2. As always, because the obtained value is larger than the critical value in Table C.3 (page 314), we know that subjects' reports of broken glass were indeed altered by the wording of the questions they were asked.

We already discussed how to calculate effect size for chi-square in Chapter 4. If necessary, refresh your memory by looking at Table C.7 (page 318), then go ahead and calculate the size of the obtained effect. In this case, phi-squared is equal to .05, indicating that Loftus and Palmer uncovered an effect of question wording that is small to medium in size. To interpret phi-squared, we would say that the independent variable (wording of the question) caused 5% of the variation in glass reports. The remaining 95% of the variation must have been caused by individual differences and other factors.

Obviously, when you analyze data of your own, you need to know which statistical test to use. But people often forget that there are also other reasons to know how to select the proper analysis for a set of data. As a critical evaluator, sometimes you will want to verify that the research you hear about is not flawed by the use of inappropriate statistics. Remember: The fact that a study is published does not guarantee that its data were analyzed correctly. Furthermore, newspaper and magazine writers sometimes report studies that have not been published at all. The "Great American Marriage Crunch" presented in Chapter 4 is a good example of scientific research that was publicized widely without ever being reviewed by referees or published in a scientific journal.

AN EXAMPLE: HEMISPHERIC DIFFERENCES IN THE BRAIN

Differences in the functioning of the left and right hemispheres have also been presented (often inaccurately) in the popular press. In this case, the research is usually solid but very complex, too complex for most nonscientific writers to interpret properly. Because of this complexity, it is necessary for us to travel back in time to one of the earliest studies of hemispheric differences to find a simple example of the two-group, within-subjects experiment.

Today, much of the research on hemispheric differences is conducted using split-brain patients as subjects. These people have had surgery in which the two hemispheres of the brain are separated from each other. Such surgery is used to treat severe epilepsy. Before split-brain patients existed, two psychologists obtained results suggesting that the left hemisphere of normal subjects is more accurate at recognizing English words than the right hemisphere is (Mishkin & Forgays, 1952). Let's see how their experiment worked.

Mishkin and Forgays made use of an apparatus called a **tachistoscope** that was popular in psychological research at the time. The tachistoscope is simply a device that presents visual stimuli (e.g., words or pictures) for very brief durations, such as 1 millisecond (one one-thousandth of a second). Computers now do

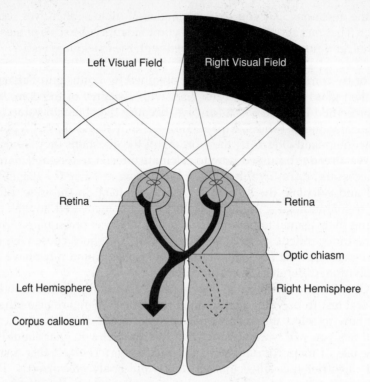

Figure 6.1
Pathways from Visual Field to Hemisphere
Source: From *Psychology of Language* by D. W. Carroll. Copyright © 1986
by Wadsworth Inc. Original source *Left Brain, Right Brain* by S. P. Springer &
G. Deutsch (Freeman, 1981). Reprinted by permission of Brooks/Cole Pub-
lishing Company.

this for us, but tachistoscopes are still used occasionally for extremely rapid presentation of stimuli such as photographs. Anyway, in the study by Mishkin and
Forgays, the tachistoscope was used to present written English words to either
the left or right hemispheres of 16 normal subjects.

Because of the way the human brain is structured, stimuli that are presented
to the right visual field are sent to the left hemisphere for processing. Likewise,
stimuli presented to the left visual field are sent to the right hemisphere for processing. The diagram in Figure 6.1 illustrates this relationship. By tracing the lines
in Figure 6.1, you can see that the image of a word appearing to the left side of
your central gaze will be sent to the right hemisphere of your brain. If the hemisphere to which stimuli are sent first cannot process that information well, it shut-
tles the information over to the other hemisphere. This shuttling process takes
time and increases the probability of error, both of which can be measured by the
psychologist.

Each subject in Mishkin and Forgays' experiment sat in front of the tachistoscope, staring at a centered fixation point, while written words were flashed

briefly to either the left or right side of the fixation point. These brief presentations lasted for only 150 milliseconds per word, which is between one- and two-tenths of a second. Such rapid presentation ensured that there was not enough time for subjects to plan and execute eye movements away from center before the stimulus word disappeared (Matlin, 1988). Meanwhile, Mishkin and Forgays recorded the subjects' accuracy at naming each briefly presented word aloud.

Can you identify the independent variable, levels, and dependent variable from the information provided in the preceding paragraph? Try it before reading further. You should have concluded that the independent variable was location of word presentation, with two levels: either left visual field or right visual field. The dependent variable was accuracy of word identification.

One remaining design feature is important to consider. Mishkin and Forgays could have presented words to only the left visual field for half of their subjects and to only the right visual field for the others. Instead, they presented words to both the right and left visual fields of every subject in their experiment. Thus, the independent variable was manipulated within subjects.

By conducting this simple experiment, Mishkin and Forgays discovered that subjects were significantly more accurate at identifying words that had been presented to their left hemispheres (via the right visual field) than they were at identifying words presented to their right hemispheres. It appeared that written language was being processed by the left hemisphere of the human brain. This finding was one of the earliest precursors to the research on hemispheric functioning that has become so popular today.

Statistical Analysis: Dependent t-Test

Analyzing ratio or interval level data from a two-group within-subjects experiment is very similar to the process used for a two-group between-subjects experiment. We still have two groups of scores, whose central tendency and variability must be assessed to decide whether any observed difference in our small sample of subjects is likely to occur in the overall population as well. The only difference is that in a within-subjects experiment, each score in one condition depends on (or is linked to) a score in the other condition. This linkage, or dependence, occurs because the same subject produced both scores, reducing the possibility that individual differences caused variation between the two sets of data.

Table C.1 (page 312) shows that the appropriate statistical test to use for an experiment like Mishkin and Forgays' is the dependent t-test. In fact, Mishkin and Forgays obtained a t value of 7.79 with 15 degrees of freedom. By now, we have covered the information you need to know to assess the significance and size of the hemispheric effect that Mishkin and Forgays obtained. You'll learn more by trying to carry out that assessment on your own before reading further. Be sure to use the formula for effect size corresponding to a dependent t-test this time.

Let's check your work. First, you should have determined from Table C.5 (page 316) that a t value of 7.79 with 15 degrees of freedom is significant ($p < .05$).

Second, you should have obtained a value of omega-squared equal to .80 for effect size.[*] Third, you should have described the effect as very large, according to Cohen's rules of thumb presented in Table C.7 (page 318). Finally, you can describe the value of omega-squared as showing that 80% of the variation in word identification was caused by the location of word presentation in either the right or left visual field.

THE MULTIPLE-GROUP EXPERIMENT

So far, we have considered simple experiments with only two levels of one independent variable. However, it is possible to include more than two levels in a simple experiment. To answer a research question, it may be necessary to manipulate the independent variable across three or four levels instead of only two. The same criteria are present in multiple-group experiments: You must select the independent and dependent variables carefully, specify levels, decide whether to manipulate the independent variable between or within subjects, and control extraneous variables. Manipulation, measurement, and control are still the three keys to good experimental research, regardless of the number of conditions we use.

In principle, you may add as many levels to one independent variable as you wish. However, in practice, the analysis and interpretation of such designs becomes more difficult as the number of conditions increases. In addition, if you use a between-subjects design, the number of subjects multiplies with each condition that is added. For these reasons, most researchers try to restrict the number of levels to the minimum needed to address the research question adequately.

AN EXAMPLE: HUMAN EMOTION

Let's go through one more sample study to be sure you understand the mechanics of a multiple-group experiment with one independent variable. This time, it might be fun to consider the research on emotion done by Ekman, Levenson, and Friesen in 1983.

Many of you may remember from your introductory psychology course that there are several theories of human emotion. The James-Lange theory says that we feel emotions whenever the autonomic nervous system becomes aroused, causing our bodies to react with rapid breathing, increased perspiration, faster heart rate, and the like (James, 1891/1952). The idea here is that this physical arousal causes us to feel emotion; as James said, "we feel sorry because we cry, angry because we strike, afraid because we tremble" (1891/1952, p. 743). However, no one would deny that humans do feel different types of emotion. In other words, the feeling of sadness is quite different from the feeling of happiness. Therefore, if the James-Lange theory is correct, then different patterns of physical arousal must be linked to each emotion.

---

[*]$\omega^2 = \dfrac{|t|^2}{|t|^2 + N - 1} = \dfrac{60.68}{60.68 + 16 - 1} = .80$

Although this hypothesis was generated by their theory, neither James nor Lange had any support for it. Furthermore, another theorist, Cannon (1927), argued that their theory was flawed. He maintained that arousal of the autonomic nervous system causes the same body changes to occur regardless of which emotion we experience. Thus, he believed that feelings of happiness, for example, are accompanied by the same patterns of physical arousal as are feelings of sadness or disgust or fear.

Ekman, Levenson, and Friesen (1983) decided to put the argument to a scientific test. Do different patterns of physical arousal really occur with certain emotions or not? To answer this research question, they designed an experiment with one independent variable (type of emotion) and six levels (anger, fear, sadness, happiness, surprise, and disgust). Type of emotion was manipulated within subjects.

You may be wondering how Ekman and his colleagues could possibly manipulate the emotions that people feel. In the experiment, 16 subjects, mostly professional actors, were asked to act out each emotion by making appropriate facial expressions (like frowning or smiling) while remembering true emotional experiences. While the subjects did this, the researchers measured their physiological arousal. Five measures of arousal were actually used in the experiment, but we shall only consider two of them: changes in heart rate and changes in body temperature.

Every subject acted out each of the six emotions six different times, for a total of 36 trials per subject in the experiment. For each trial, heart rate and body temperature were recorded. Average measurements were then calculated by computing the means of each set of six trials per emotion. This sort of averaging is used commonly as a way of minimizing tiny differences from one trial to the next.

Let's apply the manipulate/measure/control requirements to this study. What did these scientists manipulate? What did they measure? What did they have to control? Answer these questions in your own mind before going on.

The researchers manipulated the type of emotion that subjects would act out. They measured changes in subjects' heart rate and body temperature during the experience of each emotion. Averaging of measurements across trials was one type of control, but the researchers also controlled several extraneous variables. For example, the emotions of natural embarrassment and frustration were held at bay by using professional actors as subjects. Any possible effects of mimicking the six emotions in a constant order (such as always pretending to be angry first, or happy last) were controlled by "counterbalancing." This is a common control technique that you will learn in Chapter 7.

The results of this research are shown in Figure 6.2. Figure 6.2A shows how heart rate changed as subjects experienced various emotions. It's easy to see that anger and fear caused heart rate to increase by an average of eight beats per minute, whereas disgust was accompanied by a normal heart rate for most subjects. Statistical analysis of the heart rate data showed that anger, fear, and sadness each produced significantly greater change in heart rate than did happiness, surprise, or disgust.

Figure 6.2B shows how body temperature changed with various emotions. Anger had the largest effect, with an increase of about .15° Centigrade. Emotions

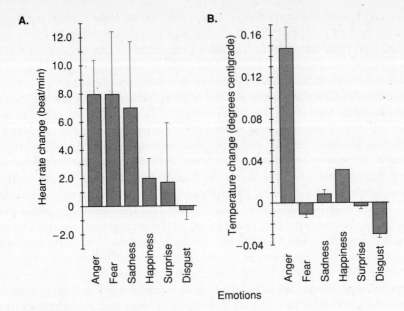

Figure 6.2
Changes in Heart Rate and Temperature with Varying Emotions
Source: From Ekman, et al., 1983.

other than anger did not seem to produce large changes in body temperature. When the temperature data were analyzed, Ekman et al. found that the increase in body temperature associated with anger was significantly greater than the temperature changes associated with any of the other five emotions.

From these results, Ekman, Levenson, and Friesen concluded that there really are physiological differences in arousal associated with various types of emotion. Cannon was wrong, then, in his assertion that all emotions are accompanied by the same patterns of physical arousal. Although these results still leave some room for alternative interpretations of human emotion, they have been cited widely as support for the James-Lange theory.

Statistical Analysis: One-Way ANOVA

As always, to select the proper statistical test for an experiment, we must answer several questions:

1. On what type of scale was the dependent variable measured—nominal, ordinal, interval, or ratio?
2. How many independent variables were used in the experiment?
3. How many levels of each independent variable were used in the experiment?

The answers to these questions tell us which statistical test Ekman et al. should have used. If you answer these questions accurately, then refer to Table C.1 on page 312, you should be able to decide which statistical test is best. Why not try that for yourself right now? Answer the three questions, then determine from Table C.1 which statistical test is appropriate.

Those of you who selected the one-way within-subjects analysis of variance (commonly called ANOVA) are correct. Changes in heart rate and temperature are measured on interval scales, which lead to the use of a one-way ANOVA when they are accompanied by one independent variable with more than two levels. By the way, a separate statistical analysis would have to be conducted for each of the two dependent variables in this experiment. In more advanced courses, you may learn to use a technique called multivariate analysis for comparing the results of multiple dependent variables with each other, but we will ignore that for now.

Assessing the Significance of F

Briefly, one-way ANOVA works by comparing the variability among scores within each condition to the variability among scores between different conditions. Whenever there is more variability between conditions than there is within each one of them, the one-way ANOVA produces a value of F that is likely to be statistically significant.

As usual, we compare the obtained value of F to a critical value to assess significance. Table C.6 on page 317 of Appendix C provides a table of critical values for F. This critical value table is a little more complex than the ones we've used so far. The biggest difference is that we now have to compute two values for degrees of freedom instead of just one.

The two values for degrees of freedom in an ANOVA are related to the comparison of within-groups variability to between-groups variability. As always, the formulas for calculating degrees of freedom can be found at the bottom of the critical value table. As shown at the bottom of Table C.6, the first value $(a - 1)$ is computed according to the number of different conditions we are comparing. Ekman et al. compared six conditions $(a = 6)$, so their degrees of freedom for between-groups variability $(a - 1)$ would be 5. The second value for degrees of freedom $(a - 1)(s - 1)$ depends on the number of subjects that were tested in each condition. Ekman et al. tested 16 subjects in each of six conditions, so $a = 6$ and $s = 16$ in their study. Calculating $(a - 1)(s - 1)$, or $(6 - 1)(16 - 1)$, leads us to 75 degrees of freedom for within-groups variability.

Once the values for both degrees of freedom have been determined, we simply follow the appropriate row and column to a critical value. If your obtained value of F is larger than that critical value, you have discovered a statistically significant effect. For changes in heart rate, Ekman et al. obtained an F value of 8.78 with 5 and 75 degrees of freedom. You can see from Table C.6 on page 317 that this effect is significant.

Determining Effect Size for *F*

Effect size can be calculated for *F* by using the same statistic, omega-squared, that is used to assess the effect size of *t*. However, to make calculation easier following an ANOVA, Table C.7 (page 318) provides a formula for omega-squared that requires the obtained value of *F* instead of *t*. Omega-squared for *F* is interpreted as proportion of variance, exactly as it is for *t*.

Let's work through an example of effect size for *F*. We know that Ekman et al. obtained an *F* value of 8.78. The formula for omega-squared, from Table C.7, is:

$$\omega^2 = \frac{(a-1)(F-1)}{(a-1)(F-1) + as}$$

As before, *a* refers to the number of conditions being compared, and *s* refers to the number of subjects in each condition. If we plug the proper numbers into the formula, we arrive at an omega-squared of .29.* This would suggest that 29% of the variance in scores is accounted for by the type of emotion that subjects were attempting to act out. Table C.7 tells us that this effect is quite large.

Post-hoc Tests

A significant *F* value in a one-way ANOVA means only that there is at least one significant difference *somewhere* among all the possible comparisons. Perhaps the heart rate change for anger is significant, or maybe it is the heart rate change for disgust or sadness that is significant. The *F* value alone does not tell us exactly which of these comparisons are significant and which are not. To answer that question, a **post-hoc test** must be conducted. It's called "post-hoc" because the meaning of this Latin phrase is "afterward," and indeed, the test is done only after a significant *F* value has been obtained.

Post-hoc tests assess the significance of each possible comparison among multiple conditions. They tell us exactly which differences are significant after the ANOVA has informed us that there's a significant difference in there someplace. When Ekman et al. conducted post-hoc tests on their data, for instance, they found that anger was the only emotion to produce a significant change in temperature. Furthermore, the three emotions of anger, fear, and sadness produced significant changes in heart rate, but happiness, disgust, and surprise did not. Without post-hoc tests, Ekman et al. would not have known exactly which of all the possible comparisons in their study were really significant.

There are several different types of post-hoc tests. You may have heard some of their names: The Tukey test, the Newman-Keuls test, and the Scheffé test are a few examples. Later, if you take an advanced statistics or research methods course, you may learn which test is best under specific circumstances. At this basic level, different professors prefer to use different post-hoc tests, depending

---

$$^*\omega^2 = \frac{(6-1)(8.78-1)}{(6-1)(8.78-1) + (6)(16)} = \frac{38.9}{134.9} = .29$$

on which is most appropriate for the data and which is most readily available to students. Your professor can show you how to calculate and interpret the particular post-hoc test that you are asked to use.

SUMMARY OF MAIN POINTS

- An experiment must include the manipulation of an independent variable, the measurement of a dependent variable, and the control of extraneous variables.

- A good independent variable is relevant to the research question, contains enough levels to afford adequate comparison, and is manipulated with enough strength to produce detectable differences.

- An independent variable may be manipulated within or between subjects. Within-subjects designs are usually preferred because they eliminate the possibility of nonrandom assignment, require fewer subjects, and provide greater statistical power.

- A good dependent variable is reliable, valid, nonreactive, available to the researcher, and generates data that can be analyzed using common statistical tests.

- Multiple-group experiments have only one independent variable but more than two levels of that independent variable.

- The F value in a one-way ANOVA shows only whether there is a significant difference somewhere among all possible comparisons. To pinpoint the source of significance, post-hoc tests must be conducted after the ANOVA has been finished.

CHAPTER EXERCISES

1. Use your own words to define these key terms:

independent variable	repeated measures
simple experiment	within-groups variability
complex experiment	between-groups variability
dependent variable	reliable
extraneous variable	valid
confounding variable	face validity
levels	construct validity
treatments	theoretical construct
control group	concurrent validity
condition	predictive validity
between subjects	reactivity
independent groups	tachistoscope
within subjects	post-hoc test

2. Review the Loftus and Palmer (1974) study of eyewitness testimony presented in this chapter. Why didn't these researchers use a within-subjects design?

3. Consider Mishkin and Forgays' (1952) experiment on hemispheric differences. Why didn't they use a between-subjects design? Which extraneous variables would have had to be controlled if they had used a between-subjects design?

4. Suppose that you own a pet store and wish to determine the best marketing strategy for selling puppies. You have two litters of blue-eyed Siberian husky pups for sale. You place one litter in a standard wire cage with food and water. You place the other litter in a standard wire cage with food, water, and toys. You then record the number of people who admire the puppies in each cage, as well as the time it takes to sell each puppy.

   Is this study a true experiment? If so, identify its independent variable(s), levels, and dependent variable(s). If not, explain how the study would have to be changed to make it a true experiment. Finally, for each dependent variable, which statistical test should be used?

5. Imagine that you developed a new device to measure rainfall very accurately. How would you assess the face validity and concurrent validity of your new invention?

Controlling Extraneous Variables

Subjects in the Hawthorne studies, c. 1925.

Designing research might sound easy on the surface. Swayed by this perception, some students express surprise at how many flawed studies are conducted. However, when they begin to design their own research, a different view emerges. The number of things that can go wrong in a simple experiment is stupefying. That's why it is so important to try to control potential variables that have not been either manipulated or measured.

In this chapter, we will look closely at common extraneous variables that can weaken the conclusions of research studies. We'll consider several specific problems such as demand characteristics, subject and experimenter bias, ceiling and floor effects, and order effects. Although these problems are not limited to experimental research, we will discuss them in that context. Along the way, we'll think about how each of these weaknesses can be controlled so that you will know how to prevent such flaws in your research.

DEMAND CHARACTERISTICS

Once upon a time, there was a horse named Clever Hans. Indeed, Hans was very clever: He was able to count, spell, add, subtract, and even tell time. Hans responded to questions by striking his hoof against the ground. Thus, if his trainer asked Hans, "What time is it?," Hans might tap the ground seven times with his hoof, indicating that it was 7:00 (Schultz & Schultz, 1987).

I can hear you scoffing already! How on earth could a horse perform such feats? Well, it turns out that Hans had a lot of unintended help from his audience. In 1904, a young experimental psychologist named Pfungst (as cited by Schultz & Schultz, 1987) designed a series of experiments that would test Hans' ability. In one early experiment, Pfungst manipulated the audience's knowledge of answers to the questions that were asked of Hans. He set up two conditions: One required Hans to respond to questions in the presence of an audience who knew the answers, and the other required Hans to respond to questions in the presence of an audience who did not know the answers. The results of the experiment showed that Hans was accurate only in the first condition. When the audience surrounding him did not know the answer to a question, Hans could not produce it.

Over time, Pfungst discovered that Hans was able to detect tiny movements that observers made while watching him. Just after a question had been asked, the audience would inadvertently look downward at Hans' hoof. This provided the signal that told Hans to begin tapping. When the horse had tapped his hoof the correct number of times, most people in the audience would look up—Hans' signal to stop tapping.

Clever Hans was doing what many human subjects do: picking up subtle cues that provide information about expected behavior. These cues are called **demand characteristics,** because they are characteristics of the situation that "demand" certain types of behavior. Subjects seldom search consciously for these cues, nor are they aware that demand characteristics influence their thoughts and actions. Still, when demand characteristics are removed, as when Clever Hans lost his knowledgeable audience, behavior can change drastically. Because psychologists are interested primarily in discovering the mechanics of normal behavior, any demand characteristics that could change normal behavior must be removed.

Controlling Demand Characteristics

Perhaps the best way to control demand characteristics is to plan carefully and conduct a **pilot study,** or trial run of the experiment, followed by thorough questioning of the practice subjects. After planning an experiment, go through the procedure in your mind or on paper, looking for any clue that might help subjects to figure out your hypothesis. These clues must then be eliminated from the experiment, if possible. The clues you miss may be noticed by practice subjects in the pilot study. After testing these subjects, ask them what they thought about each aspect of the experiment. You may be surprised to find that certain portions of the procedure led the subjects to make unusual assumptions about the purpose and hypothesis of the study. Once you are aware of such assumptions, revise the research design or procedure to avoid them before you begin conducting the real experiment. Sometimes several pilot studies must be completed before you are satisfied that all demand characteristics have been controlled.

Another method of controlling demand characteristics is **deception,** which occurs when we hide important facts from our subjects until after they have participated in the experiment. In addition to not telling the whole truth, deception can involve lying to subjects. Leading subjects to believe that you are studying a phony topic prevents them from figuring out the true purpose of the experiment.

The study of bystander intervention conducted by Latané and Darley (1968), which we considered in Chapter 1, is a good example of the use of deception. If subjects had known that the epileptic seizures they heard were fake, they would have responded in an unusual way—perhaps by laughing or ignoring the event. On the other hand, if subjects had known that Latané and Darley were recording their willingness to report a serious emergency, almost all of the subjects would have reported it. Accurate results were based on the requirement that subjects not know everything that was going on.

Although deception can be an effective method of controlling demand characteristics, it is sometimes unethical. In fact, the American Psychological Association (1992) enforces strict guidelines that must be followed when deceiving subjects. Furthermore, deception is not allowed at all unless the scientists can show that it is absolutely necessary for valuable research.

SUBJECT BIAS

Whenever subjects arrive at the experimental laboratory, they bring with them many expectations and worries. In this respect, testing human subjects is very different from studying plants, observing chemical reactions, or predicting the location of stars in the sky. **Subject bias** is a general term referring to hopes and beliefs that can cause subjects to respond to the research environment in ways that bias, or alter, the results of our studies.

The psychological scientist must always keep in mind Orne's (1962) reminder that every research study involving an experimenter and a subject is a social situation. Unfortunately, the social dynamics of an experiment are easy for researchers to ignore. We are preoccupied with setting up equipment, selecting subjects according to impersonal criteria, assigning numbers to them, gathering accurate data, and getting the job done with a minimum of time and conversation. We forget what it was like to be a subject for the very first time. Most subjects are eager to perform well, concerned about what the experiment might entail, nervous about meeting the experimenter, curious about what the experimenter is really trying to find out, and afraid that electric shock studies might still be a common form of psychological research. These feelings of eagerness, concern, nervousness, curiosity, and fear form a potent emotional brew that can alter the results of an experiment quite dramatically.

Subject bias seldom occurs intentionally. In other words, few subjects arrive at the lab door planning to sabotage our experiments. Instead, unconscious bias alters the normal behavior of subjects in subtle ways that can cause enormous changes in our results. For example, human nature leads curious, intelligent subjects to try to figure out what an experiment is all about. If demand characteristics are available to aid this natural curiosity, subjects may guess the hypothesis of an experiment and then try to provide the results they believe the experimenter wants. Two specific types of subject bias are social desirability and placebo effects.

Social Desirability Bias

Social desirability bias is the tendency for subjects to behave in ways that they believe are desired by others. Most subjects want to look good in the eyes of the experimenter. This is especially true when graduate or upper-division students test first-year undergraduates, who perceive the situation as a chance to make friends or prove their social skill.

Subjects often misunderstand the motives of the experimenter. What they view as socially desirable behavior in an experiment may be very different from what we researchers view as socially desirable behavior. As evidence of this, one of the most common questions subjects ask at the end of experiments that are designed to measure normal behavior is, "How did I do?" They want to hear that they performed "better than average" or "in an unusually creative way" or "extremely well." They don't want an answer like, "You did normally, just like everyone else." These subjects perceived the situation as something like a public achievement test in which they could show us their abilities and skills. Their efforts to perform well were motivated by their misunderstanding of the kind of behavior desired in this social setting. Subjects are often disappointed when they find out that we were simply tracking everyday, typical behavior and that, in fact, it wasn't desirable at all to include data from a subject who was trying hard to excel.

Controlling Social Desirability Bias

Social desirability bias is extremely difficult to control. No matter what experimenters do, it is natural for subjects to try to determine what behavior is desired and then to provide it. Perhaps the best way to handle this extraneous variable is to look for its effects in the data. In other words, when drawing conclusions from your results, keep in mind that the data could be contaminated by social desirability bias.

Placebo Effects

A second type of subject bias is the **placebo effect,** in which a subject's belief that some treatment will have an effect actually causes the effect to occur. This may sound a bit like voodoo magic to you, but it is a strong effect that has been seen in many different settings. In fact, some scientists believe that the placebo effect is a plausible explanation of voodoo magic: It works best on people who believe in it.

Placebo effects are common in medical research, especially when new drugs are being tested. These drug studies make use of "inert" pills, sometimes called **placebos,** which are pills that look and taste exactly like a real drug but in fact contain no active substance. Many studies have shown that subjects who think they have been given a drug will report feeling the effects of that drug, even when they have actually received only the placebo (e.g., Lowinger & Dobie, 1969). For example, people who believe they have been given aspirin are less likely to report pain, even though the actual pill they received contained no aspirin (Hardy, Wolff, & Goodell, 1952).

Similar placebo effects occur outside of the medical domain. In an interesting psychological twist, Abrams and Wilson (1983) have shown that subjects who thought they had been drinking alcohol reported feeling more sexually aroused than subjects who thought they had not been drinking alcohol. In fact, all the subjects had been given nonalcoholic beverages to drink—only their beliefs had been manipulated.

Controlling Placebo Effects

One good way to control placebo effects is to add a placebo control group to an experiment. The **placebo control group** is a group of subjects who receive what they believe is a treatment, when actually it is not. Their performance is then compared to that of subjects who truly did receive the treatment. These comparisons are used to separate the effect of true treatment from the effects of subjects' beliefs about that treatment. Sometimes the performance of the placebo control group is also compared to the performance of subjects in an **empty control group,** who knew they had received no treatment at all.

EXPERIMENTER BIAS

Orne's (1962) reminder that the experiment is a social situation should make it apparent that experimenters themselves, as well as their subjects, can bias the results of a research study without intending to do so. As we noticed in Chapter 4, researchers can bias subjects' behavior inadvertently by their own actions, expectations, or appearance. When this happens, we say that **experimenter bias** has weakened the research.

Experimenter bias can be introduced by the sex of the experimenter. This is especially troublesome in research concerning sensitive issues such as sexual preferences. Many subjects are most comfortable talking about such matters with an experimenter of the same sex. The same kind of problem can occur in less obvious contexts, too. Even the most boring topics are subject to standard male-female dynamics, especially when both subject and experimenter are young and single.

Similar bias can occur with other aspects of physical nature as well. For instance, a very attractive experimenter can bias subjects' responses, particularly in opposite-sex situations. Likewise, certain types of clothing worn by the experimenter may cause subjects to behave in unusual ways. Of course, we cannot completely control the physical appearance of experimenters. If you happen to have especially attractive facial features, you will not be expected to wear a bag over your head while testing subjects! However, it is wise to remember that the subject observes everything, searching unconsciously for clues about the experiment.

Aside from physical appearance, the actions of an experimenter can also bias subjects' behavior. It's surprisingly easy to introduce experimenter bias through your actions when testing subjects individually over several weeks. Suppose that one of the conditions of your experiment requires setting up a more sophisticated apparatus than does the other condition. When you test subjects in the condition that does not require sophisticated apparatus, you may start the experiment right on time with a friendly smile and a relaxed attitude. However, when the sophisticated equipment has to be used, you might be flustered with mechanical problems that could get the experiment off to a late start and put you in a bad mood. If this bias occurred systematically across the two conditions, a confounding variable would have been introduced. Significant data differences between the two conditions could then be caused by manipulation of the independent variable or by the confounded variation in the experimenter's treatment of subjects.

Expectancy

Because the potential for experimenter bias exists in nearly every research study, especially within psychological science, several scientists have studied it in depth. The most famous of these is Rosenthal, a psychologist who conducted a lengthy and revealing program of research concerning the expectancy effect. The **expectancy effect** is experimenter bias that has been caused by the researcher's expectations of subjects. When an experimenter expects subjects to act in a particular way, they usually do.

An Example: Expectations in the Classroom

Students sometimes complain that their teachers hold high expectations of them that seem impossible to fulfill. On the surface, it might seem that these expectations should be lowered so that students could meet them more easily. However, many students reconsider this issue after they learn about the effects of low teacher expectations on school children. Rosenthal and Jacobson (1968) were the first scientists to study such expectations systematically, and their controversial findings led to hundreds of other studies.

Rosenthal and Jacobson conducted their research by telling the teachers in an elementary school that certain students showed superior intellectual potential. The teachers believed that these students had been identified by rigorous testing, but in fact their names were drawn randomly from the school population. There was really nothing special about these particular students at all. By the end of the school year, however, Rosenthal and Jacobson found that these children's IQ scores showed significantly greater improvement than those of the other children in the school. The teachers' expectations during the course of the school year had caused the "superior" children to excel.

We know now that this expectancy effect is not limited to the classroom, but also appears in the business office, on the sports field, and in the experimental laboratory. Rosenthal has demonstrated the fact repeatedly that experimenters who expect certain kinds of results from their subjects are very likely to obtain those results.

Controlling Experimenter Bias

Experimenter bias in the laboratory is usually unintentional, and that makes it all the more difficult to control. It's difficult to treat all subjects in similar ways, to forget our expectations while testing subjects, and to reduce the effect of our own physical appearance on subjects. Two techniques that can help are automation and blind testing.

Automation reduces experimenter bias through the use of automatic devices that remove the personal touch of the researcher. In practice, automation can mean playing instructions over a tape recorder instead of reading them aloud, programming a computer to present experimental stimuli rather than presenting them by hand, or videotaping subjects' behavior rather than introducing nonparticipant observers into the situation.

Let's consider the practice of instructing subjects as an example of how automation can reduce experimenter bias. A researcher who reads instructions to subjects might introduce some undesirable variation in the data by making slight changes in readings to different subjects. We've already seen, from Loftus and Palmer (1974), that altering just one word in a question can change results significantly. Subjects are also affected by the facial expression, tone of voice, and attitude of the researcher while the instructions are being read aloud. As much as we may try to hold these extraneous variables constant across all our subjects, it is often impossible to do so. By tape-recording the instructions, wording and tone of voice are held absolutely constant and facial expression is removed.

In **double-blind testing,** neither the subject nor the experimenter knows which condition the subject is in. This reduces expectancy effects quite a lot: If the experimenter does not even know which condition a subject is in, behavioral expectations will be minimal. Conducting a double-blind experiment requires the help of an objective colleague who will keep track of condition assignment for subjects that someone else tests or a "blind" research assistant who will test subjects after you have assigned them to conditions. In addition, the stimuli and tasks used in each condition must be designed so that they do not provide information to the experimenter about which condition the subject is participating in. In drug studies, for example, although the dosage of a drug may change across conditions, the physical appearance of all capsules or injections must be identical. The point of double-blind testing is to prevent the person who actually tests subjects from knowing which condition they are in, and consequently, from knowing what sort of behavior to expect from them.

Double-blind techniques work well to control experimenter bias. Of course, it is crucial that someone keep careful records of subject participation across conditions, or else you may wind up in the not-so-humorous situation shown in Figure 7.1.

AN EXAMPLE: LIGHTING IN THE WORKPLACE

A real-life example may help to pull together the new concepts of demand characteristics, subject bias, and experimenter bias. Several well-known experiments, called the Hawthorne studies, were conducted by a team of organizational psychologists from 1924 until 1933. The research was conducted at a telephone manufacturing plant, the Hawthorne branch of the Western Electric Company in Chicago, Illinois. Its purpose was to increase the morale and productivity of Western Electric's employees, who are shown at their work tables in the photograph at the beginning of this chapter.

One of the variables the researchers considered was lighting: Perhaps brighter lighting would motivate workers to become more productive. They designed an experiment that would test this hypothesis. Sure enough, as the brightness of the lights in the factory increased, productivity began to increase also. However, the experimenters soon became suspicious of these results because it seemed that no matter what they did, productivity continued to improve. For instance, in some cases, the productivity of employees whose lighting was never changed increased almost as much as the productivity of employees whose lighting had been improved. Furthermore, even after brightness was *reduced* by 70%, the workers' productivity remained at heightened levels.

After further experimentation and thought, the researchers concluded that the Western Electric workers' morale and productivity had improved because their needs were suddenly receiving attention. It was the increase in attention, not the increase in brightness, that caused the change in behavior. This research be-

Figure 7.1
Triple-Blind Testing
Source: © 1984 by Sidney Harris, *Johns Hopkins Magazine*.

came so well known that we now use the term **Hawthorne effect** to refer to situations in which subjects' behavior is altered by the attention they receive during a research study.

The Hawthorne studies are well known in psychological research because of their impact on the treatment of employees in the American workplace. They were the first studies to show that the way in which employees perceive their work environment is as important as the actual reality of that work environment.

Recently, however, the Hawthorne studies have also been criticized in an interesting book (Gillespie, 1991) that exposes many flaws in the design and interpretation of the experiments. For example, while the researchers purposely manipulated factors such as lighting, rest breaks, and work weeks, they also left extraneous variables such as changes in the pay system uncontrolled. The Great Depression began in 1929, in the midst of the Hawthorne studies, and would have had strong effects on the workers' desires to remain productive in order to keep their jobs. Experimenter bias was an additional problem—in most cases, the Hawthorne experimenters told their subjects that productivity was being studied and sometimes even counseled the subjects about expected behavior.

Finally, social desirability bias was strong. In one series of tests, 6 young women were selected to work in a special room where they received extra rest breaks, tempting snacks, and a more beneficial pay system than other workers were allowed. Obviously, the socially desirable response to all of this attention was greater productivity, and the women responded to that expectation with enthusiasm. Gillespie's (1991) story becomes especially intriguing when he explains how the prestige of this new situation affected the 6 female subjects. These young Polish immigrants, accustomed to poor treatment, began to assert their independence to the point of eventually telling the male experimenters how the Hawthorne studies ought to have been conducted.

CEILING AND FLOOR EFFECTS

In Chapter 6, we discussed how to select the best independent and dependent variables for an experiment. Another important decision occurs when designing the task that subjects are expected to perform. If our research topic is motor coordination, bicycle riding might be an acceptable task; if it is lucid dreaming, sleep might be an acceptable task; if it is attention, studying while heavy-metal music plays loudly in the background might be an acceptable task.

Obviously, then, the task that subjects are expected to perform must be relevant to the research question at hand. In addition to that requirement, the task must provide data that vary enough to allow comparison. If a task is too easy or too difficult, the range of collected data prevents comparison between conditions.

Let's suppose that you are interested in the effects of loud music on people's ability to comprehend what they have read (a likely topic for anyone who lives in a college dorm). The task you select for subjects is to read long passages while loud music, soft music, or no music at all can be heard in the background. You then test their comprehension of those passages by asking questions. Your dependent variable is the accuracy of subjects' answers to the questions.

If your comprehension test is too easy, most subjects will be able to answer all the questions accurately. This is going to produce a pattern of results like that shown in Figure 7.2A. When a task is so easy that average responses in all conditions approach the highest possible score, you have obtained a **ceiling effect.** The term comes from the idea that your data scores are hitting the very top, or the ceiling, of the range of scores that is possible.

Now, let's suppose the opposite mistake occurs: If your comprehension test is too difficult, very few subjects will be able to answer any of the questions accurately. This will produce the reverse pattern of results, as shown in Figure 7.2B.

A.

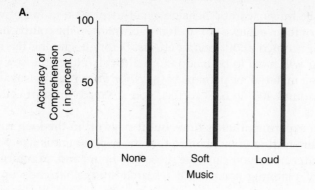

B.

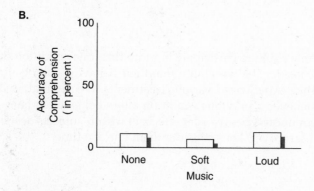

Figure 7.2
Ceiling and Floor Effects
A, Ceiling; B, Floor.

This time, the task was so difficult that no one in any condition could perform it well, and the data produced are near the floor, or lowest point, of the possible range. This is known as a **floor effect.**

The trouble with floor and ceiling effects is that they may mask a real difference among the conditions. Maybe music really does affect people's ability to comprehend what they read, but we can't see that difference when the task is too easy or too difficult across all conditions.

Controlling Ceiling and Floor Effects

How can we control ceiling and floor effects? Here, the pilot study comes in handy once again. Practice the task on a group of people who will not be participating in the real experiment. In practice, these people often end up being family members and friends of the experimenter. Once the plan for the design of your study is in place, get all the materials you need and run through the experiment with someone whose ability level is likely to be similar to that of your potential subjects.

When conducting a pilot study, we usually aim for scores near the midpoint of the possible range. This reduces the likelihood of floor and ceiling effects. Thus, if you practice the music/comprehension experiment on a group of your room-mates and most of them achieve 90% to 100% accuracy on the comprehension test, you should be concerned about ceiling effects. Before beginning the real experiment, something will have to be made more difficult: either the comprehension test or the reading material, or perhaps both. When your practice subjects achieve accuracy rates around 40% to 60% correct, you are ready to start collecting data from real subjects.

Piloting an experiment takes time, but it pays off in the long run. You can spend a few hours testing your plan, so that the experiment is likely to produce trustworthy results . . . or you can save those few hours and, in return, waste the many months of planning spent on a research study that ends up providing meaningless data.

ORDER EFFECTS

Whenever the same subjects participate in more than one condition of an experiment, we must consider the possibility that their behavior will be altered by the order in which they experienced various treatments. We say that an **order effect** has occurred whenever a previous condition alters behavior in later conditions. The three most common types of order effects in within-subjects designs are practice, fatigue, and carryover. Let's consider them one at a time.

Practice

Place yourself in the position of an imaginary subject for a moment. If you had to participate in four conditions, performing some difficult task each time, is it possible that your performance would improve with practice? Of course it might. When subjects perform increasingly well in successive conditions, we must be concerned with **practice effects.**

The purpose of an experiment is to determine the effect of the independent variable that was manipulated. If practice effects are also occurring, we can not know whether a significant difference between conditions was caused by the independent variable or by the subjects' practice. In other words, practice can be a confounding variable in any within-subjects experiment. To return to the example mentioned above, suppose that all subjects read a passage and take a comprehension test while listening to soft music first, and only then perform the same task while listening to loud music. Results might show that comprehension was more accurate in the second (loud) condition than in the first (soft) condition. But we are immediately faced with a dilemma: Is this difference in comprehension caused by the volume of the music, or is it caused by the practice that all subjects received in the first condition?

Fatigue

When I asked earlier what would happen if you had to perform a difficult task in four different conditions, you might have thought that this would be pretty tiring.

Fatigue effects are the opposite of practice effects: Subjects become tired with successive conditions, so their performance worsens over time. Once again, the trouble with fatigue effects is that we can not be sure whether any obtained difference between conditions was caused by the independent variable (as we hope) or by the fact that subjects were worn out when they finally reached the last condition.

Carryover

The dynamics of practice and fatigue effects are easy to understand, perhaps because we all have experienced them in daily living. Everyone knows what it feels like to practice some skill again and again, until ability improves. Equally universal is the feeling of becoming tired at performing some activity, until skill levels decrease.

Carryover effects may be slightly more difficult to grasp at first. Whenever the treatment that is given in one experimental condition alters behavior in later conditions, a **carryover effect** has occurred. That is, the treatment in one condition is lingering, or "carrying over" to the next condition.

An Example: Using Mental Imagery to Aid Memory

An example that may help you to understand and remember carryover effects comes from research on human memory. Over the ages, many strategies for remembering have been developed. To remember a series of names, for example, you might use the strategy of mental imagery or the strategy of rote memorization. Of course, there are many other memory strategies, but let's concentrate on just these two for now.

Rote memorization is what most people use when they want to remember something: They repeat it over and over to themselves. Mental imagery occurs when we try to visually imagine something in relation to the item to be remembered. If I were introduced to a person named Bill Banks, for example, rote memorization would lead me to repeat his name again and again to myself to remember it. A strategy of mental imagery would lead me to visualize the pages of my monthly telephone bill strewn along the banks of a river, fluttering in the breeze.* The fact that mental imagery is usually the more effective means of remembering has been demonstrated many times in research on human memory (e.g., Bower, 1972).

Carryover effects would be very likely in an experiment that assessed the effectiveness of these two memory strategies. We don't always know in advance exactly which aspect of a treatment will carry over from one condition to the next, but let's suppose that it was strategy interference. Any of you who have tried using two memory strategies in succession know that it can be difficult to switch strategies on command. The strategy used in the first condition, whether rote memorization or mental imagery, might interfere with the strategy used in the

---

*The name Bill Banks is not merely an ideal example for explaining the use of imagery; Dr. Banks is also the psychologist who first taught me research methods.

second condition. For example, the silent inner speech that had been used during rote memorization in the first condition might pop up during mental imagery despite the subjects' most valiant attempts to suppress it. Similarly, mental imagery might be difficult to ignore or suppress when subjects were using rote memorization in the second condition.

In either case, the treatment given in the first condition is carrying over into the second condition and interfering with normal behavior. In our memory example, the second condition, no matter what it is, is always affected negatively by strategy interference. However, the first condition, whether rote or imagery, is never affected by strategy interference. This introduces a confounding variable. We want to determine the effect of the independent variable, type of memory strategy, not the effect of strategy interference. If carryover were not controlled, both effects would be woven together in a way that is impossible to untangle.

Controlling Order Effects

There are two common techniques used to control the negative effects of condition order. One is quite simple: Between-subjects designs eliminate the possibility of order effects because each subject participates in only one condition. Therefore, if order effects are a serious potential problem in a design, it may be necessary to use a between-subjects manipulation instead of a within-subjects manipulation.

You should already be aware of the problem with this solution, however. Between-subjects designs require more subjects and have less statistical power than within-subjects designs. If it is possible to use a within-subjects design, that is usually the best choice.

The second technique for controlling order effects is called counterbalancing. **Counterbalancing** evens out, or "balances," order effects by distributing them across all conditions. Let's see exactly how counterbalancing works by starting with the simple practice effect.

Counterbalancing Practice and Fatigue Effects

When subjects perform a task twice, practice effects often cause performance to improve in the second condition, no matter which condition that happens to be. If all subjects participated in Condition A first, and then in Condition B, performance in Condition B would be enhanced artificially by the practice effect. The resulting data would show this artificial enhancement. Likewise, if all subjects participated in Condition B first, and then in Condition A, the data from Condition A would be enhanced artificially by the practice effect. The way to solve this problem is to counterbalance the order of participation, so that half the subjects do Condition A and then B, whereas the other half do Condition B and then A. Figure 7.3 presents a diagram of the balance that this countering of order would produce.

It's important to remember that counterbalancing does not eliminate order effects; it merely distributes them evenly across conditions. For this reason, half of the data from condition A and half of the data from condition B will be contami-

Figure 7.3
Counterbalancing Two Groups

nated by the practice effect. The other two halves will not. When the data are averaged together to produce one mean score for condition A and one mean score for condition B, the practice effect will be absorbed across conditions and only the difference caused by the independent variable will remain. The same logic is used to understand counterbalancing of fatigue effects. Be sure you understand it before we go on.

Counterbalancing Carryover Effects

When you feel comfortable with the reasoning behind the counterbalancing of practice and fatigue effects, we can move on to carryover effects. We'll apply the procedure to our earlier example of carryover in the memory strategy experiment. The technique of counterbalancing allows us to disentangle the effects of two different variables, such as type of memory strategy (the independent variable) and strategy interference (the confounding variable, or carryover effect).

The general method of counterbalancing carryover effects is the same as for practice and fatigue effects. We will require half of the subjects in a two-group within-subjects experiment to participate in the rote condition first, then in the imagery condition. Because the strategy of rote memorization carries over and interferes with imagery, these subjects will experience poorer recall in the imagery condition than we would have expected. To counterbalance this negative effect, we require the other half of the subjects to participate in the two conditions in opposite order: first the imagery condition, then the rote condition. Now, rote memorization (instead of imagery) will be hindered by that nasty carryover effect. By testing subjects in opposite orders, carryover has opposite effects, which can be balanced out later by averaging the scores within each condition.

Once again, counterbalancing does not eliminate the negative effects; carryover will continue to exist, but in measurable amounts and directions per condition. That is, through the use of counterbalancing, we can see how large the effect of strategy interference was, over and above the effect of memory strategy. We can then extract that carryover effect and ignore it momentarily, leaving the pure effect of type of memory strategy.

Table 7.1 HYPOTHETICAL MEAN RECALL
IN A MEMORY EXPERIMENT

Subject Set 1		Subject Set 2	
Rote →	Imagery	Imagery →	Rote
50%	60%	70%	40%

Perhaps some hypothetical means, applied to our example of memory strategy, will help to clarify the concept. Table 7.1 shows these hypothetical means per condition, based on our knowledge that imagery is a more effective memory strategy than rote memorization.

Look first at Subject Set 1. This set is made up of half the subjects in the entire experiment. They memorized a list of names using rote memorization first, then memorized a different, but equivalent, list of names using mental imagery. On average, rote memorization allowed them to remember correctly 50% of the names on the list. In the imagery condition, these subjects were hampered by strategy interference. Try as they might to use imagery only, rote memorization occasionally crept in. By trying to suppress the rote memorization, the subjects in Set 1 were distracted from their memory task. This distraction, or interference, hindered performance, so that the mean percentage of names recalled correctly in the imagery condition was only 60%.

Now, granted, that figure of 60% is higher than it was in the rote condition. However, we would have expected even better performance from the imagery condition under normal circumstances. Indeed, we would have expected the imagery strategy to yield recall scores nearing 70% correct, as it did for the subjects in Set 2, who could not have been affected by carryover at the time they used the imagery strategy.

Now, let's consider the hypothetical results of subjects in Set 2. These subjects participated in the same conditions as did subjects in Set 1, except that the order of participation was reversed. Imagery was used first, followed by rote memorization. On average, subjects in Set 2 recalled 70% of the names correctly when using mental imagery. In the second condition, when strategy interference hampered their performance, rote memorization produced a low score of only 40% correct.

Looking at all four means in Table 7.1, we can see that subjects in Set 1 provided us with a mean recall score for the rote condition that was pure, or uncontaminated by carryover. Likewise, the subjects in Set 2 provided us with a pure recall score for the imagery condition. Only the means from Condition 2 in each set (60% and 40%) are contaminated by the carryover effect.

If we now average across order, preserving only the differences between rote and imagery strategies, we should be left with an accurate measurement of the effect of memory strategy. Averaging mean scores from the rote conditions (50% and 40%) produces a mean of 45%. Averaging mean scores from the imagery condition (60% and 70%) produces a mean of 65%. The difference between those two means (45% and 65%) represents the effect of memory strategy.

Statistical analysis would show whether that difference was significant. If it was, we could safely conclude that mental imagery is a more effective memory strategy than rote memorization, *regardless of order effects.* The undesirable effects of one order were countered by the undesirable effects of the other order, and balance was achieved.

The procedure of counterbalancing is fairly simple when only two conditions exist. As a rule, if you want to control order effects by counterbalancing, assign one order to half your subjects and the opposite order to the other half. It is the reasoning behind counterbalancing that is difficult, and it will be helpful to try to understand it clearly before reading further. Almost all beginning research methods students become confused at their first experience with counterbalancing, so don't be concerned if you feel the need to review this section one more time.

Counterbalancing More Than Two Groups

Once you understand counterbalancing the order of two conditions, we can continue. Suppose that your experiment contains more than two conditions—perhaps you specified three levels of an independent variable, or even six, as did Ekman, Levenson, and Friesen (1983) in their study of emotion.

Now what? How can we counterbalance order across so many conditions? One solution is to use **complete counterbalancing,** in which a group of subjects completes every possible order of conditions. If we had three conditions (A, B, and C), six orders would be possible:

1. A B C
2. A C B
3. B A C
4. B C A
5. C B A
6. C A B

In complete counterbalancing, each subject would be assigned to one of these six orders. If I were assigned to Order 5, I would complete Condition C first, then Condition B, and finally Condition A. If you were assigned to Order 2, you would do Condition A first and Condition B last. And so on.

One side effect of counterbalancing order is that the number of subjects must be a multiple of the number of orders. With six orders, we could use 12 subjects (2 per order) or 18 subjects (3 per order) or 60 subjects (10 per order), but we could not use 11 or 19 or 58 subjects.

Latin Square Counterbalancing

Complete counterbalancing works perfectly well for the purpose of controlling order effects. However, as the number of conditions in an experiment increases, complete counterbalancing gets cumbersome. We have already seen that having three conditions produces 6 possible orders. Having four conditions produces 24 orders. If Ekman et al. had used complete counterbalancing to control order effects across the six conditions of their study of emotion, they would have had to contend with 720 possible orders!

Fortunately, there are two ways around this problem. One way is to present each subject with a different, random order of conditions. Thus, we might represent each condition with a small piece of paper on which a letter (e.g., A, B, . . .) would be written. These papers could be thrown into a hat or bowl, tossed, and then pulled out randomly one by one. The order of letters coming out of the hat would represent the order of conditions in which a given subject would participate. Although randomization usually controls order effects adequately, it has two drawbacks: A large number of different orders must be used, and even distribution of the carryover effect across all conditions is not guaranteed.

A better technique, called a **balanced Latin Square,** is a special type of counterbalancing that allows us to distribute order effects evenly while maintaining a small number of condition orders. In fact, the number of orders used in a balanced Latin Square is equal to the number of conditions that subjects will have to complete. Thus, whereas complete counterbalancing of six conditions would have required 720 orders in the Ekman et al. experiment, a balanced Latin Square would have required only 6 orders. That's quite an advantage, wouldn't you say?

Grab a pencil, and let's try some Latin Square schemes. Imagine that you've designed a within-subjects experiment with one independent variable and four levels. To control order effects, you plan to use the balanced Latin Square because it requires smaller multiples of subjects than using complete counterbalancing.

The first thing to do is assign letters to each experimental condition so that you don't have to write out entire names each time you want to refer to a condition. It's going to be a lot easier to work with a label like "C" than to write out "rote memorization condition" each time!

Now make a table with four columns and four rows. The four vertical columns will represent the order in which conditions will appear in your experiment, first through fourth. The four horizontal rows will represent each set of four subjects who participate in your experiment. It helps to label each position clearly so that you don't forget what it stands for. Figure 7.4A shows what the first stage of a balanced Latin Square looks like.

Now we're ready to begin filling in the empty table. It's important that each condition occurs first for an even number of subjects in the experiment, so you can simply enter the four condition labels (A, B, C, and D) in order down the length of the first column. Figure 7.4B shows what your table should look like now.

At this point, you need to enter the condition order horizontally across the first row of the table. This is the order of conditions that the first subset of subjects will complete. To determine the proper order of the first row of letters, use the following formula:

A, B, x, C, x −1, D, x −2, . . .

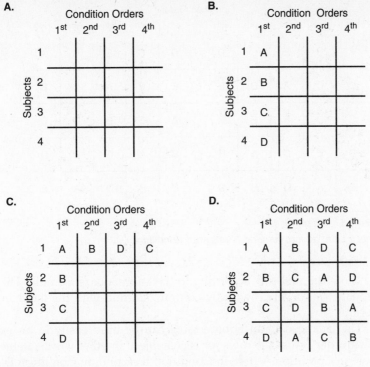

Figure 7.4
Four Steps in Constructing a Balanced Latin Square
A, Step One; B, Step Two; C, Step Three; D, Step Four.

In this formula, x refers to the last of a series of conditions. We have only four conditions, so x refers to condition D. If we had six conditions, x would refer to condition 6, or F, and x – 1 would refer to condition 5, or E.

The formula tells us that the ordering of four conditions for the first subgroup should be A, B, x, C. Since x refers to condition D, this means the order should be A, B, D, C. So we enter that order into the table. Now your table should look like the one shown in Figure 7.4C.

There's only one step left, and it's easy. To fill in the rest of the table, we enter letters in alphabetical order down each vertical column. First we go to the second column and, starting with B, fill out the remainder of the letters in order. The second column would then list conditions B, C, D, and A. Because the third column starts with D, we would construct a vertical list that included D, then A, B, and C. Your final version of the balanced Latin Square table should look like mine in Figure 7.4D. By inspecting Figure 7.4D carefully, you'll see that order effects are distributed perfectly across all conditions. Each condition now precedes and follows every other condition equally often.

Every balanced Latin Square can be constructed in this way. In each case, start by drawing an empty table, fill out the first column in alphabetical order,

Condition Order

	1st	2nd	3rd	4th	5th	6th	7th	8th	9th	10th
1	A	B	E	C	D	D	C	E	B	A
2	B	C	A	D	E	E	D	A	C	B
3	C	D	B	E	A	A	E	B	D	C
4	D	E	C	A	B	B	A	C	E	D
5	E	A	D	B	C	C	B	D	A	E

Subject

Figure 7.5
Balanced Latin Square for Odd Number of Conditions

and fill out the first row according to the Latin Square formula. Then add letters in alphabetical order column by column, starting with the letter in the top row each time.

The balanced Latin Square table can be used easily in an experiment by reading order across the rows for each subject. In other words, Subject 1 will participate in Condition A first, in Condition B second, in Condition D third, and in Condition C last. Subject 3 will receive Condition C first, but will participate in Condition A last. When you get to Subject 5, simply begin at the top row again, with order A, B, D, C.

The only drawback to the balanced Latin Square is that it must be adjusted when the order of an odd number of conditions is to be counterbalanced. Thus, if we had five conditions, two Latin Squares would have to be constructed, one being the exact reverse of the other. Each subject would then have to participate in every condition twice to achieve perfect balance of carryover effects across all conditions. Figure 7.5 shows a balanced Latin Square that was constructed for an odd number of conditions.

Counterbalancing can be difficult to master in practice, so allow yourself enough time to take it all in. Practicing the actual process of counterbalancing in simple classroom demonstrations or experiments of your own will also help. Everyone makes a few mistakes at first—you'll get it down eventually.

EXTRANEOUS VARIABLES VERSUS INDIVIDUAL DIFFERENCES

We've now covered the major types of extraneous variables that can weaken the conclusions of research studies. I think you will agree that there are a lot of potential problems to control in even the simplest experiment. Because you understand that now, it is probably safe to extend the warning that you not go too far in your search for potential extraneous variables.

One of the most serious flaws of experimental research is the confounding variable, which must be avoided at all costs. Confounding variables, which vary systematically along with the independent variable, damage the researcher's integrity and destroy the validity of the experiment. Other extraneous variables do occasionally creep in and may not be exceptionally dangerous if distributed randomly across conditions.

A common mistake that is made in beginning research is to assume that individual differences are also an extraneous variable that should be controlled. In fact, that is not true. Individual differences cannot be eliminated, but they are not considered to be extraneous variables. Moreover, the existence of individual differences in research data is to be expected, and it does not weaken the conclusions of your research.

One of the most essential facts of human life is that each person is unique. Some subjects are more intelligent than others, some subjects are friendly whereas others are rude, a few people will view the experiment as great fun but more of them will seem bored. Some subjects arrive at the lab on an empty stomach whereas others have just finished wolfing down half of a chocolate cream pie. Although most psychologists concentrate on studying natural, everyday behavior, we would never deny that each person will behave in a slightly different way than the next person does.

Individual differences can threaten an experiment only when they vary systematically across conditions. In other words, if 1 or 2 out of 20 subjects in a particular condition are hungry during an experiment, their hunger will merely add to normal within-groups variability. However, suppose that 18 or 19 subjects out of 20 in that condition are hungry, whereas the 20 subjects in another condition are not. This kind of systematic difference between conditions would be a serious problem. Fortunately, with random assignment to conditions, individual differences seldom stack up in this way.

GENERAL METHODS OF CONTROL

Throughout this chapter, we've considered several common extraneous variables and studied techniques for controlling each of them. Now it will help to step back and summarize general methods of control. This will provide you with several plans of attack to use against uncommon extraneous variables that haven't been discussed. In general, there are five ways to control an extraneous variable.

Hold It Constant

The first, and best, method of controlling an undesirable variable is to hold it constant. In other words, take control of it and don't allow it to vary at all. If you were testing subjects in a room that contained light and temperature controls, you might want to verify that the room temperature and brightness were identical every day during the testing of each subject.

The trouble with holding extraneous variables constant is that it is often impossible to do in real life. In many large institutions, the temperature controls for a building are located in some central physical plant that is not accessible to you. Similarly, you may not have control over the noise level outside your testing room or the brightness of a windowed area.

Add It to the Design

One option that may be useful when an extraneous variable cannot be held constant is to purposely manipulate it as an independent variable. This is a particularly wise strategy if you believe that the extraneous variable could have strong effects on subjects' behaviors and if those effects have not been studied in the past.

When Rosenthal decided to investigate the expectancy effect, he was making use of this strategy. Previously, expectancy had been merely a nuisance, an extraneous variable that got in the way of good research and had to be controlled somehow. But Rosenthal turned this reasoning on its head, took hold of the extraneous variable and manipulated it, transforming a nuisance into an impressive and meaningful body of new knowledge that has been applied to many practical aspects of daily life.

If you decide to add an extraneous variable to your design by manipulating it systematically, it is not necessary to abandon the independent variable you had originally selected. In Chapter 9, you'll learn how to design experiments that contain more than one independent variable, so that the effects of several factors may be explored at one time.

Counterbalance It

We considered the technique of counterbalancing in the context of controlling order effects in within-subjects designs. This is its most common use, but there are other possibilities. For example, the presentation of small numbers of word or picture stimuli is sometimes counterbalanced to avoid carryover within one condition. That is, a very powerful picture might affect subjects' responses to other pictures within a condition. To avoid this, we might counterbalance the order of pictures within that condition. Counterbalancing is a general control technique that can be applied to a variety of potential problems in addition to condition order.

Randomize It

Randomization was also discussed in the context of order effects but can be applied to many other situations. It, too, is often applied to the order of stimuli as well as the order of conditions. For example, a study of physical attractiveness might require subjects to view a series of many photographs showing people's faces. There might be 100 photographs, and it might be risky to present them to all subjects in the same order. Because 100 stimuli are too many to counterbalance, randomization would be an effective method of control. The photographs could be shuffled and presented in a new, random order for each subject.

Incidentally, the advent of computer technology for experimentation makes stimulus randomization easy. The computer can be programmed to present stimuli in a new random order for each subject, with a minimum of hassle to the experimenter. Any potential effects of stimulus order will be offset by the fact that every subject, regardless of the order of conditions, saw the stimuli in a different order.

Match It

Holding an extraneous variable completely constant is often impossible, but certain features of stimuli may be matched to reduce variation. For example, a researcher using facial photographs as stimuli might match the photos on dimensions such as color, size, or position of the face in the picture. Likewise, stimulus words are often matched across conditions in length, part of speech, frequency of usage, and number of syllables. In this way, we can determine the effects of one independent variable such as memory strategy without worrying that other factors inherent in each specific word are fouling up our results.

SUMMARY OF MAIN POINTS

• Demand characteristics occur whenever the research situation gives subjects cues about expected behavior. They can be controlled through pilot studies or deception.

• Subject bias refers to hopes and beliefs that may cause a subject to act in certain ways during a research study. Social desirability bias and placebo effects are two types of subject bias. The latter can be controlled by using placebo and empty control groups.

• Experimenter bias endangers research whenever the experimenter's actions, expectations, or appearance causes subjects to alter their normal behavior. Experimenter bias is controlled by using automation or double-blind testing. The expectancy effect is one type of experimenter bias.

• Ceiling and floor effects occur whenever the subjects' task in an experiment is too easy or too difficult, causing the scores from all conditions to be similarly high or low.

• Order effects include practice, fatigue, and carryover. They are problematic only in within-subjects designs, where all subjects complete all conditions in some order that may alter results. Order effects are usually controlled by counterbalancing the order of conditions across subjects.

- A balanced Latin Square is a special type of counterbalancing that allows researchers to distribute order effects evenly across conditions while using a minimum number of different orders.

- Confounding variables are especially important to control in every experiment. Other extraneous variables are usually less dangerous. Randomly dispersed individual differences are to be expected in every research study.

- Five general methods of control may be applied to an extraneous variable: hold it constant, add it to the design, counterbalance it, randomize it, or match it.

CHAPTER EXERCISES

1. Use your own words to define these key terms:

    demand characteristics   double-blind testing
    pilot study   Hawthorne effect
    deception   ceiling effect
    subject bias   floor effect
    social desirability bias   order effect
    placebo effect   practice effect
    placebos   fatigue effect
    placebo control group   carryover effect
    empty control group   counterbalancing
    experimenter bias   complete counterbalancing
    expectancy effect   balanced latin Square
    automation

2. Draw a diagram showing a balanced Latin Square for an experiment with one independent variable and six levels. Then specify the order in which Subjects 3, 7, and 11 would participate in all six conditions.

3. Suppose that you were the principal investigator in the Hawthorne studies. Design an experiment using a placebo control group, in which you could separate the effect of attention from the effect of increased lighting.

4. Review the description of the memory experiment provided in this chapter. Which statistical test would be used to analyze the difference between memory strategy means of 45% (rote) and 65% (imagery) after carryover was balanced out? After statistical significance was assessed, which measure of effect size would be suitable?

5. The control problems discussed in this chapter can be applied to many situations outside of the experimental laboratory. Identify the problems that have occurred in the following descriptions, then explain how you might solve them:

    a) People who take their cars to a mechanic for servicing report that the cars perform better afterward. Unknown to them, however, the mechanic never got around to working on their cars.

b) A midwestern gardener tests three fertilizers to determine which one is best for his 10 rose bushes. On May 1, he uses Loam Soil on all the bushes; on June 1, he uses Chemi-Squirt; and on July 1, he tries Home Grow. Home Grow produces the best blooms.

c) Just for fun, a father tests his daughter's extrasensory perception (ESP) by having her guess the identity of symbols (e.g., stars, triangles) drawn on cards. On each trial, he holds a card up so that the symbol on it is facing him but is invisible to her. Although the daughter cannot see the symbols on the cards, she is able to guess their identity quite accurately. Later, she admits that she was able to see the symbols reflected in her father's eyeglasses.

Break out the frosty bottle

and keep your tonics dry!

Design Validity

Is there a subliminal message in this advertisement?

Extraneous variables seem to be lurking in every corner, just waiting to complicate the answer to your research question. But there are larger problems to watch for, too: problems that are closely linked to the overall design of an experiment. Controlling all the extraneous variables in the world still won't allow us to overcome the flaws of a bad design.

In this chapter, we will consider various types of experimental designs. We'll start with some bad designs that are especially vulnerable to problems such as history, maturation, testing, instrumentation, and statistical regression. Examples of these flaws in real research are presented to help you apply the abstract principles to concrete situations. Then, we'll see how those problems can be overcome through the use of good experimental designs. By the time we finish, you'll be able to identify a design and anticipate its pitfalls quickly. Critical evaluation is much easier if you know exactly which problems to look for from the start.

THE ONE-SHOT CASE STUDY

The very worst type of "experimental" design is known as the **one-shot case study,** and it really isn't an experiment at all. In the one-shot case study, a group of subjects is selected, a treatment (or level of the independent variable) is administered to the entire group of subjects, and some aspect of their behavior is then measured by a dependent variable. A diagram of the process is shown in Figure 8.1.

The name of this design can be confusing, because a one-shot case study in the context of experimental design is not at all similar to the nonexperimental case study that was introduced in Chapter 4. There, one individual's rare behavior was studied in depth, but here, a group of subjects is typically observed. To clarify the distinction, some researchers (e.g., Bordens & Abbott, 1991) use the term **demonstration** to refer to the one-shot case study. The only problem with "demonstration" is, of course, that it has a wide variety of other meanings in common English.

You know a lot about basic research methods by now, so a good look at Figure 8.1 should alert you to a serious problem with the one-shot case study. What is it? Well, only one level of the independent variable has been included in this study, so there is no way to make a comparison. Perhaps a concrete example will help.

An Example: Smoking and Hypnosis

Let's suppose that you are interested in the use of hypnosis as a form of therapy. A search of the literature on that topic uncovers a large number of studies showing that hypnosis has been used to treat obesity, cigarette smoking, alcoholism, migraine headaches, hypertension, asthma, warts, and even cancer (Wadden & Anderton, 1982).

In a chapter about the use of hypnosis as an aid to stop smoking, Strauss and Margolis (1986) praise an "impressive" (p. 99) study in which subjects abstained

Figure 8.1
One-Shot Case Study

from smoking for 1 full year after receiving hypnotherapy. Indeed, this is a long span of abstinence, worthy of special recognition if the study were conducted properly. In the study, Kline (1970) had 60 smokers participate in a 12-hour mass hypnosis session. While in a trance, the subjects were told what sort of physiological and emotional feelings they should expect while their bodies were weaned from tobacco. As these feelings were explained, the subjects were also encouraged to experience deep relaxation. The idea was to teach subjects how to offset uncomfortable feelings with the pleasure of relaxation. Kline reported that "at the end of one year, 88% of [the subjects] had not resumed smoking" (1970, p. 274).

Many readers would be tempted to admire this study for two reasons: first, because Kline's (1970) hypnotherapy produced such a high percentage of successful ex-smokers over a full year, and second, because Strauss and Margolis (1986) hailed Kline's research as an impressive piece of work. But is the study worthy of their praise?

You should be able to see right away that it's not. Kline's (1970) research is a good example of the one-shot case study, which is probably the worst type of bad design. Only one group of subjects was tested, they all received the same treatment, and the smoking behavior of all subjects was measured 1 year after the treatment had occurred. This pattern fits perfectly into the diagram of the one-shot case study shown in Figure 8.1.

The problem with the one-shot case study is that nearly anything could have caused the subjects to stop smoking. It might be that the hypnosis was effective. However, it is equally possible that the hypnosis had nothing whatsoever to do with the change in behavior. Subjects might have quit smoking because they wanted to quit for their own personal health, because they wanted to please the experimenter, because they wanted to fit in with other members of their group, or because they were tired of spending so much money on cigarettes. I'm sure you can think of other possible reasons yourself.

To make this a legitimate experiment, Kline needed to add a group of 60 other subjects who also wanted to stop smoking and who also met for 12 hours in a group session but who did not undergo hypnosis. In other words, he needed a control group. If the control subjects also abstained from smoking for 1 year, then it couldn't be hypnosis that caused their behavior to change. On the other hand, if a significantly larger percentage of subjects from the hypnotized group were successful in their attempt to stop smoking, then we would be willing to entertain the notion that hypnosis was an effective way of helping people to kick the habit.

To fulfill the requirements of good experimental design, Kline's control group would also have had to be equivalent to his experimental group. To produce **equivalent groups,** all 120 subjects would be assigned randomly to one of the two conditions by the experimenter. Equivalence between groups ensures that subjects in one condition do not differ in systematic ways from subjects in another condition. In within-subjects designs, equivalence is achieved by using the same subjects in each condition, but in between-subjects designs, equivalence is usually achieved by assigning each subject randomly to some condition.

Because Kline did not have a comparison group, your first reaction to his "impressive" demonstration should be, "So what?" The fact that published authors, Strauss and Margolis, praised the research merely reduces our respect for their powers of critical evaluation. In fact, the 88% success rate after a full year proves absolutely nothing about the effectiveness of hypnotherapy. Because there was no comparison group, there is no way of knowing what caused the subjects to stop smoking.

Incidentally, there is at least one other problem with Kline's study that you may have noticed. As Wadden and Anderton (1982) point out, most researchers who assess the effects of hypnotherapy on smoking behavior gather their measurements simply by asking subjects whether they still smoke. Kline also followed this practice. We all know how tempting it would be to lie under these conditions. Kline should have attempted to verify each subject's year-end progress report by gathering physiological data such as the amount of nicotine-based chemicals in the blood or urine.

An Example: Subliminal Messages in Advertising

Because the results of one-shot case studies are presented so frequently in the media, we might be wise to consider another concrete example. Subliminal messages have become a popular topic of conversation in the last decade or so, especially in relation to music and advertising.

During the early 1970s, the Gilbey's gin advertisement shown at the beginning of this chapter was popular. Most people see only a glass full of ice cubes standing next to a bottle of gin. However, Key (1973) argued that this ad contains a subliminal message that is highly sexual in nature. He argues that the letters S, E, and X are visible in the second, third, and fourth ice cubes, respectively. Furthermore, he sees the faint silhouette of a face in the first and fourth ice cubes, as well as legs and erect male genitalia in the bottle's reflection on the table. Key carries the scene even further, but I'm sure you get the idea.

Key (1973) believed that the American public was being hoodwinked into buying Gilbey's gin by the subliminal sexual message concealed in the ad. To find out, he tested the effects of that message on more than 1,000 subjects by using a one-shot case study. Sixty-two percent of both male and female subjects reported that they became sexually aroused after viewing the ad (but before being told of its subliminal contents). Based on this finding, Key concluded that a subliminal message caused sexual arousal.

This conclusion is unfounded because it depends on the results of a one-shot case study. In fact, the alcohol, the notion of partying, or any number of other factors surrounding the advertisement could have caused subjects to report sexual arousal. The study itself gives us no reason to believe that sexual arousal was caused by viewing a disguised word and a couple of hidden faces unconsciously.

Of course, it is also possible that Key was correct; the point is that the faulty design prevents any definite conclusion.

The moral of the story? Don't use the one-shot case study under any circumstances, and don't trust its results. It proves nothing at all and only serves to mislead people who accept what they hear without evaluating the information critically.

THE ONE-GROUP PRETEST-POSTTEST DESIGN

With a little background knowledge, it is pretty easy to see that the one-shot case study is severely flawed. Of course, many readers and television watchers don't have as much education about research methods as you do. Sometimes they seem willing to believe almost anything, as long as it's preceded by the word "scientific" intoned by a deep, authoritative voice.

The flaws of the one-group pretest-posttest are a little more difficult to spot. Beware! This design may look admirable on the surface, but it is really just as bad as the one-shot case study. The name alone ("one-group") should sound off an alarm inside your brain.

In the **one-group pretest-posttest design,** a group of subjects is selected and then measured on some pretest. After the pretest has been administered, all of the same subjects receive the treatment that is (supposedly) being tested. Finally, their behavior is measured again, and the scores on pretest and posttest are compared to each other. Figure 8.2 presents a diagram of the one-group pretest-posttest design.

If you compare Figure 8.2 to Figure 8.1, you'll see that the only difference between the one-group pretest-posttest design and the one-shot case study is the addition of a pretest. The problems connected to testing only one group of subjects haven't disappeared.

An Example: Treating Headaches with Biofeedback

The use of biofeedback in reducing headache pain might make an interesting example here. To refresh your memory, biofeedback occurs when subjects are hooked up to an apparatus that monitors some physiological activity such as electrical brain waves, blood pressure, heart rate, or muscle contraction. The apparatus provides feedback to the subject concerning these biological activities. That feedback allows subjects to attempt to alter whatever activity is being monitored. For example, it is not difficult to raise your body temperature by conjuring up a feeling of rage or to slow your heart rate by imagining that you are lying on a soft warm expanse of white sand with the sound of quiet waves lapping up onto the beach nearby. (Feels good already, doesn't it?)

Biofeedback is used to teach people to control their physiological arousal so that states of relaxation and pain reduction can occur. People can learn through biofeedback to lower their blood pressure, relax their muscles, slow their heart rate, and achieve a certain type of brain wave. All these changes add up to a feeling of deep relaxation that is beneficial to their physical and mental health.

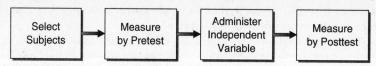

Figure 8.2
One-Group Pretest-Posttest Design

Biofeedback has been used to treat problems such as arthritic pain, anxiety, tension headaches, fear, sexual dysfunction, and epilepsy (Wickramasekera, 1976).

Tension headaches are linked to prolonged contraction of the muscles in the scalp and neck. Early researchers believed that biofeedback might be useful in teaching subjects to relax those muscles so that tension headaches could be relieved. Suppose that we were to test this hypothesis by providing biofeedback to a group of subjects who had experienced tension headaches regularly for a number of years. In the pretest phase, subjects are asked to keep track of the intensity and frequency of their headaches over a period of 3 weeks. This information will be used as a baseline for comparison with later posttest measurements. In the treatment phase, the contraction of each subject's neck and scalp muscles is monitored by the biofeedback apparatus. When those muscles are tense, a high tone can be heard by the subject, but each time the muscles become relaxed, a low tone is presented. The subject's task is to keep the tone low by attempting to relax neck and scalp muscles. This procedure might be used in six sessions of 30 minutes each over a second 3-week period. Finally, in the posttest phase, subjects would be asked to record the intensity and frequency of their headaches during a third 3-week period.

The results of this one-group pretest-posttest might show that headache intensity and frequency were much lower after biofeedback training than they were before such training. But was it really the biofeedback that caused a change in the headaches? What do you think? Are there other factors that might have played a role in reducing headache pain? Try to make a quick list of those other factors before reading further. Scribble a few ideas in the margin, if nothing else.

Undoubtedly, you were able to see that factors other than biofeedback could have caused the change in headache pain. For example, just thinking about headaches all the time might cause one to occur. Events that happened in subjects' lives during the 9-week study, like changing jobs or buying a new car, might alter the number of headaches experienced. I'm sure your list contains several other plausible factors as well.

COMMON SOURCES OF CONFOUNDING VARIABLES

The designs of one-shot case studies and one-group pretest-posttests are especially susceptible to certain problems. These problems can be viewed as sources of potential confounding variables, and they should be avoided in all types of scientific research (Campbell & Stanley, 1966). After discussing each one in relation to the study of headache relief through biofeedback, I'll introduce three types of experimental designs that help us to overcome these common flaws.

History

The problem known as **history** occurs whenever some historical event causes subjects' behavior to change. For example, the one-group pretest-posttest design is based on the assumption that only one thing happened to subjects during the weeks between pretest and posttest: the administration of the experimental treatment. But, of course, this isn't true at all. Over the course of a 9-week study, hundreds of events could occur that might affect tension headaches. Perhaps a well-known celebrity raved about the wonders of biofeedback in a prime-time televison interview while the subjects were participating in the biofeedback study. Such an event might encourage them to practice relaxation more seriously. On the other hand, it's possible that a series of earthquakes occurred suddenly in the location where subjects were being tested. Undoubtedly, these quakes would increase stress and tension, causing headaches to increase. In either case, changes in headache frequency or intensity would be caused by the confounding historical event rather than by the biofeedback.

Maturation

A second source of confounding is known as **maturation.** People change over time even when no particular event occurs that would cause this change. The longer the duration of the research, the more serious becomes the problem of maturation. Scientists who study human development through infancy, childhood, and adolescence must be especially careful to account for the effects of rapid maturation. However, even when adults are tested over relatively short intervals (e.g., a few weeks), their attitudes may develop in subtle ways that can influence behavior.

To apply this principle to our example, consider the effect of gradually acquired knowledge on tension headaches. Even before hearing of the biofeedback study, subjects who experience severe headaches are likely to read magazine articles on the topic and talk to friends about it. As time goes by, the subject's understanding of the problem increases gradually. This increasing knowledge about headache pain may be considered a form of maturation that might eventually alter the subject's experience with headaches. What we have then is a situation in which headache behavior changes slowly over time according to factors that have nothing to do with biofeedback.

Testing

Subjects' behavior in a one-group pretest-posttest design may change simply because they took the pretest. This problem is called **testing,** and it occurs whenever the test itself (rather than the administration of the treatment) causes a change to occur. In the biofeedback study, the very act of recording headaches during the pretest phase could cause subjects to realize that their headaches are actually less frequent than they had imagined. This encouraging discovery alone might lead subjects to worry less about their plight, and that reduced worry (not the biofeedback) could lead to a decrease in the number of tension headaches over time.

Instrumentation

Instrumentation, or **instrument decay,** is a fourth problem that crops up in bad designs. Here, accurate measurement of behavior begins to decay over time. This decay can be caused by a variety of reasons: Sometimes observers become lazy or tired and forget to mark down each incident that occurs; other times observers become more skilled with practice so that their records become more accurate. Either way, the inconsistency in measurement can become a confounding variable.

After several weeks of recording headaches in the biofeedback study, either of these two patterns could occur in subjects. Some people might become more attuned to their headaches, while others will begin to pay less attention than they did when the pretest phase began. Furthermore, instrumentation is a more likely problem when the subjects record their own behavior than it is when objective outsiders record the subjects' behavior. The biofeedback study that I have described is open to a strong effect of instrumentation, which could alter the results in a way that had nothing to do with the biofeedback treatment.

Statistical Regression

A fifth problem is called **statistical regression,** or sometimes **regression to the mean.** It's a little difficult to understand at first, so bear with me. Basically, regression means that extreme scores will become less extreme as they are measured again and again. Let's return to the basketball court of Chapter 3 for a moment. Suppose that you were expected to stand at center court and shoot as many baskets as you could. Now, most of you would probably agree that this is a pretty difficult task. (In fact, to some of us, it makes counterbalancing look easy!)

Let's suppose that one fine day, you were in fabulous shooting form, and actually hit 10 of the 20 baskets that you threw. This might be your absolute best score, an *extreme* score that you would probably not be able to reproduce again tomorrow or the next day. Chances are that today's extremely high score will not be achieved again for a long time. It simply is not the kind of behavior that is typical over the long run.

That's statistical regression in a nutshell: An extreme score usually cannot be reproduced again. That's why it is extreme in the first place. Therefore, if you start with a very high or very low score, your future performance is likely to drop or rise slightly to meet the typical, or average, performance that you are normally capable of producing.

Statistical regression can be troublesome whenever a set of extreme scores occurs in the pretest. For example, suppose we had selected for our biofeedback study only those subjects who reported the most severe and frequent tension headaches. This kind of decision might well be made in reality, because it doesn't do much good to test the effectiveness of biofeedback on people who don't experience many tension headaches in the first place. After selecting only those subjects who experience headaches most frequently, the mean number of headaches is likely to decrease regardless of whether we provide biofeedback or not. In other words, extreme scores, like extreme headaches, simply cannot be sustained over the long haul.

Because of statistical regression, any result showing that very frequent headaches had decreased after the biofeedback treatment phase would be flawed by the fact that extremely high scores tend naturally to drop over time. Likewise, extremely low scores tend naturally to rise.

A More General Look at Design Flaws

History, maturation, testing, instrumentation, and statistical regression are among the most common design flaws. You will hear other researchers discuss them, and you will need to learn how to spot them quickly in research reports that you read. Although I have applied each source of confounding to the one-group pretest-posttest design, it is important to understand that these problems are just as likely to occur in the one-shot case study. For that matter, they are also prevalent in several types of nonexperimental and quasi-experimental research. Any design that lacks an equivalent comparison group of subjects is prone to the five weaknesses we have discussed.

Since we did use biofeedback as a primary example, however, you may be interested to know that some of these weaknesses were corrected in a biofeedback study that did include a group of control subjects for comparison. Wickramesekera (1976) compared the reduction in tension headaches among subjects who received real biofeedback to the reduction among subjects who received phony biofeedback. The control group participated in the same number of biofeedback sessions as did the experimental group, but the control subjects received biofeedback that was relevant to someone else's body rather than to their own. Results showed that real biofeedback reduced the intensity and frequency of tension headaches, whereas phony biofeedback did not.

It's only fair to add that studies of both biofeedback and hypnosis are highly susceptible to placebo effects and demand characteristics. Because of this, it is not always possible to know whether positive effects were caused by the biofeedback and hypnosis or whether they were caused by the placebo effects and demand characteristics. Placebo effects can be measured and separated from treatment effects by the use of a placebo control group, but demand characteristics are very difficult to remove without destroying the very techniques of hypnosis or biofeedback. After all, we cannot expect to teach our subjects how to use biofeedback for pain reduction without giving them clues as to the results we expect. Even the researchers who specialize in hypnosis and biofeedback (e.g., Wadden & Anderton, 1982; Wickramasekera, 1976) agree that more rigorous science is needed in these areas.

Despite the bad science of one-shot case studies and one-group pretest-posttest designs, they are used commonly in consumer research. Many of the studies you hear advertised on television or in magazines are modeled after these bad designs. Think carefully about the claims you hear every day evaluating toothpastes, soda pop, diet aids, cosmetics, and a variety of other products for sale. Many of the claims that are allegedly based on scientific research studies are actually based on very bad designs that prevent any solid conclusions from being drawn. Once you know which problems to look for, you'll begin seeing them frequently.

MULTIPLE-GROUP DESIGNS

By now it should be very apparent that good experimentation demands a design with at least two equivalent groups. This way, it is possible to administer the treatment to only one group of subjects, but still compare their results with those of another group of subjects who did not receive the same treatment. Of course, the two equivalent groups could be composed of the same subjects (a within-subjects design) or different subjects assigned randomly to conditions (a between-subjects design).

Introducing an equivalent comparison group reduces the impact of the five common sources of confounding that we have discussed. If a historical event affected both groups of subjects but a treatment was administered to only one group, any difference in results could be attributed to the treatment rather than to the historical event. If subjects in one group mature over time, so will subjects in a comparison group. Only the treatment varies. The same logic can be used to address the problems of testing, instrumentation, and statistical regression. Whenever a potential problem affects both groups of subjects, results should remain consistent across the two groups. If a difference in results does occur, it must have been caused by the independent variable because that is the only factor that differed between the two groups.

In contrast to poor designs like the one-shot case study and one-group pretest-posttest design, there are three general types of good experimental designs. These include the multiple-group posttest design, the matched-group design, and the multiple-group pretest-posttest design. Although these designs are certainly not immune to every confounding variable, they are less susceptible to the common sources of confounding that have been introduced in this chapter.

The Multiple-Group Posttest Design

We've already discussed several experiments that fall into the general category of multiple-group posttest designs. Loftus and Palmer's (1974) study of eyewitness memory and Mishkin and Forgays' (1952) research on brain hemispheres are both good examples of the multiple-group posttest design.*

Because it is the most common type of experiment, let's quickly review the basic building blocks of the multiple-group posttest design. In Figure 8.3, you can

---

*The general category of multiple-group designs includes experiments with two or more conditions.

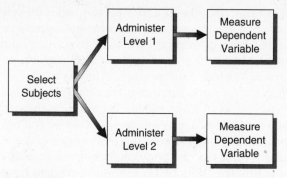

Figure 8.3
Multiple-Group Posttest Design

see that the first step is selecting subjects who will either be assigned to one of two groups or expected to participate in both groups. The independent variable is often manipulated by administering a treatment to one group (often called the **experimental group**) and no treatment to another group (called the control group). Sometimes, as we have seen, no control group is necessary. This certainly does not mean that we can design the experiment with only one condition! Instead, it means that we sometimes use a comparison group rather than a control group. The comparison group receives some treatment, but that treatment must be different from the one administered to the first group of subjects. As you can see from the diagram in Figure 8.3, after treatment has been administered, we measure the performance of all subjects in both groups, or conditions, and compare the results. If any significant difference in scores is obtained, and if all confounding variables have been controlled, we can be fairly certain that the difference in performance was caused by the treatment that was given to the subjects.

The Matched-Group Design

You learned in Chapter 7 that matching is a control technique used to equate stimuli. It can also be used to equate subjects across different experimental conditions. By the term *equate*, I do not mean to imply that we can create groups of subjects who are clones of each other. The small random differences that all individuals exhibit are not of concern here; instead, we use matching when strong differences between subject groups seem troublesome.

The **matched-group design** is a between-subjects experiment in which important features such as age, income, or IQ are matched across subjects. In other words, two groups of subjects are selected by virtue of their having similar characteristics. For example, we might select 50 people randomly to participate in one condition of a study on spending behavior and then select 50 others who have similar incomes to participate in a comparison condition of the same study. Income would thus be matched across the two groups of subjects, so that any obtained difference in spending behavior could not be attributed to pre-experimental differences in the amount of money that various subjects earned. Once the subjects are matched in this way, the design continues, with differing treatments being administered to each group and behavior being measured in a posttest.

Except for the matching of subjects on one or two crucial dimensions, the matched-group design is identical in form to the multiple-group posttest design. For that reason, I have not included a separate diagram of it.

There is one risk that we run when using a matched-group design. To match a feature like income across two groups of subjects, we have to be rather selective in choosing subjects from the population of interest. Carried too far, this selectivity can violate the principle of random selection, leaving us with a subject sample that does not accurately represent the population. For this reason, several scientists (e.g., Rosenthal & Rosnow, 1991; Seitz, 1984) have warned researchers to use the matched-group design only when it is absolutely necessary.

The Multiple-Group Pretest-Posttest Design

The **multiple-group pretest-posttest** is another good design; in fact, it has several advantages over the multiple-group posttest design that we concentrated on in Chapter 6. These advantages are made possible by adding a pretest to the experiment. The diagram in Figure 8.4 shows how a multiple-group pretest-posttest experiment would be designed.

Let's consider the simplest form of the multiple-group pretest-posttest design, in which only two conditions are used. First, two equivalent groups of subjects are selected and pretested. Again, the two groups could be composed of one set of subjects (within-subjects design) or they could be composed of two sets of subjects assigned randomly to conditions (between-subjects design). Once the pretest behavior has been measured, two levels of the independent variable are administered, one to each group of subjects. After this has been accomplished, the performance of both groups of subjects is measured again through a posttest. Results are obtained by comparing pretest performance to posttest performance.

The multiple-group pretest-posttest design is often used in evaluating the effectiveness of new programs. We need to know whether our prison systems are working, which method of teaching children to read is best, and how we can train athletes most effectively. The addition of a pretest to research studies of such topics is helpful because it allows a direct comparison of performance before and after the program has been used.

An Example: Learning to Read

Let's see how the principles of this design have been applied in a real research study. Reading is a skill that has received a lot of attention in the United States over several decades. Widespread studies were conducted during the 1960s and 1970s (e.g., Bond & Dykstra, 1967; Stebbins, St. Pierre, Proper, Anderson, & Cerva, 1977) to settle a scathing debate among educators (e.g., Flesch, 1955, 1985) as to which method of teaching reading was best.

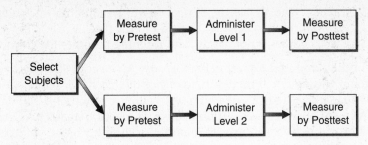

Figure 8.4
Multiple-Group Pretest-Posttest Design

One of the most thorough studies that evaluated various methods of teaching first-graders to read was conducted from 1964 to 1967. Over 3 years, 27 coordinated experiments were conducted on thousands of first-graders at various schools throughout the United States, and their data were analyzed and interpreted in a combined report by Bond and Dykstra (1967). Many of you were probably taught to read by a method that was advocated on the basis of this research program. A few of you older college students might even have served as subjects in the study. The multiple-group pretest-posttest design was used in each of the 27 studies. The actual research program was much more complicated than my description implies; those of you who are interested in the topic of reading may want to refer to the original report for further details.

At the beginning of the school year, a primary battery of the Stanford Achievement Test was administered to first-grade school children. This pretest assessed the children's abilities to recognize individual words, understand the meaning of a spoken paragraph, use spoken vocabulary, spell simple words, discriminate between different speech sounds, and combine the sounds of various letters together. After the pretest results were recorded, the children were taught to read by one of six methods over a period of 140 school days. To simplify the example, we'll consider only three of the methods that were tested:

1. *Basal.* The basal method was the time-worn tradition at the time, so it was considered a control condition. It requires a series of basic books (like *Dick and Jane*) that children use while they practice repeating vocabulary words aloud, recognizing whole words by sight rather than sound, comprehending overall meaning, and reading silently.

2. *Basal plus phonics.* In this condition, the basic texts of the basal program were used along with materials that would teach children the sounds that were combined to make words. Phonics is a generic term that is used (and misused) widely; in general, it refers to learning to read by sounding out the letters of a word from left to right, combining the sounds, then recognizing the word's meaning by its sound.

3. *Language experience.* Children learn to read through writing in this method of instruction. They begin by dictating their own stories to their

teacher, who writes the stories down. Eventually, the student learns to write stories and read them aloud to the teacher. Basic books are seldom used, phonics is not taught, and teaching becomes highly individualized.

In the Bond and Dykstra (1967) study, each set of students within a given classroom was assigned randomly to one of the teaching methods. After the children had participated in one of these teaching methods for 140 days, Stanford Achievement posttests were administered. Teachers were not given the tests until the night before posttesting was to occur, and both pretests and posttests were scored by the researchers, not by the teachers.

Can you identify the vital features of this design quickly? What was manipulated? What was measured? What was controlled? By now, you should be able to answer these questions easily. The researchers used one independent variable (method of teaching reading) with six levels, of which we have considered only three (basal, basal plus phonics, and language experience). Because each child was taught to read by only one of the randomly assigned methods, the independent variable must have been manipulated between subjects. The researchers measured a variety of abilities related to reading, using the Stanford Achievement Test as a pretest and posttest. They also controlled extraneous variables such as the teacher's knowledge of test questions and potential biases in scoring.

When the pretest is added to an experiment, **difference scores** are usually calculated. These scores simply reflect the difference in performance between a subject's pretest score and that same subject's posttest score. For example, let's suppose that Johnny received a score of 97 on one aspect of the Stanford Achievement pretest. After the 140 days of learning to read by a particular method, he received a score of 106 on the posttest. Thus, a difference score of +9 on a particular test would indicate that Johnny's reading ability improved by 9 points, whereas a difference score of, say, −7 would have indicated that his reading had become worse. A statistical test appropriate to the features of the design (one-way ANOVA in this example) would then be conducted, using the difference scores rather than the raw data. This analysis of the difference scores would allow us to determine whether there is a significant difference in the amount of improvement between one group of subjects and another.

The reason that a pretest is so important in research that explores the teaching of children is that children always develop over time regardless of what they might be taught. You probably recall that this is known as a maturation effect. Because of maturation, we would expect any child's reading ability to improve during the first grade. By using the multiple-group pretest-posttest design, we can compare relative amounts of improvement instead of absolute reading ability. This process allows us to draw more solid conclusions than the posttest-only design would.

Bond and Dykstra found that difference scores in the basal plus phonics program showed the most reading improvement over the school year. The basal and language experience programs produced about the same amount of improvement in reading over the school year, but language experience yielded more variability in students' scores. This greater variability was explained by the fact that highly intelligent students tended to blossom in the language experience program, whereas less intelligent students were lost. Overall, the researchers concluded that the basal plus phonics program was the best method of the three for teaching most first-graders to read. Consequently, in the late 1960s, the teaching of many American children was changed to include phonics.

An interesting by-product of this research could not have been discovered without the existence of a pretest in the design. It seems that first-grade girls showed significantly better reading ability than boys did, regardless of which method was used to teach them. By including the pretest, Bond and Dykstra determined that this effect was probably caused by the girls' greater readiness to learn to read before the programs began, not by greater learning among girls during their first-grade instruction. In other words, girls' difference scores were not significantly different from boys', but their absolute scores at both pretest and posttest were higher than boys'. Thus, girls' superior reading ability existed at the time of pretest and was merely maintained throughout the 140 days of reading instruction. This fact has been used many times since 1967 to speculate that female brains are better prepared to read than are male brains at typical first-grade age. Without the pretest, readers of the Bond and Dykstra report might have assumed incorrectly that the difference was caused by greater motivation to improve or greater ability to learn among young girls.

Aftermath of the Reading Research

Despite Bond and Dykstra's careful research reported in 1967, about 60 million adult Americans were considered to be either functionally or marginally illiterate in 1985. Kozol (1985) argues that this number is reached "by even the most conservative calculations" (p. 10), and it represents one third of the adult population in the United States. This means that one out of every three adults in America can not read well enough to understand a newspaper. One fifth of the adult population cannot even decipher the words on a street sign! One of the saddest statistics indicates that 18% (nearly one in every five) of all the high school graduates in the United States can not read their diplomas (Perry, 1988).

You might wonder why one out of three Americans is marginally illiterate 20 years after Bond and Dykstra's research provided clear directions to follow. There are several reasons: First, there are many factors other than teaching methods that may doom even the best reading program. For example, children from poor families may have no access to public libraries or privately purchased books. In addition, cultural encouragement to watch television instead of reading seeps into many American homes, regardless of social class. Second, although the research program coordinated by Bond and Dykstra was well designed and tightly controlled, some of the research on reading has been "shoddy" (Adams, 1991, p. 38). Too often, bad designs are used and confounding variables are left uncontrolled by people who do not know enough about basic research methods to design a rigorous study. Finally, reading research is a good example of scientific study that has not been applied because of its political and social consequences.

Flesch (1955, 1985) and Adams (1991) provide clear explanations of these issues, for those of you who are interested in learning more about illiteracy in America.

ADVANTAGES AND DISADVANTAGES OF PRETESTING

We have seen that the multiple-group pretest-posttest design can be very effective in certain contexts, especially when the effectiveness of some training program is being evaluated. Do not think, however, that each study you design or evaluate should include a pretest. The multiple-group posttest design is perfectly acceptable for many research topics.

Incidentally, to clarify a common confusion, a pretest is not the same as a pilot study. As we discussed in Chapter 7, experimenters often try out their tasks on people who will not act as subjects in the real study. These pilot studies are very effective at allowing researchers to find errors in their experimental procedures before real subjects are tested. However, they are pilot studies, not pretests! The pilot study is conducted on people who will not participate as subjects in the real experiment, and their performance will not be used in analyzing the results of the final experiment. A pretest is conducted on real subjects, whose performance before the treatment is measured and recorded, then compared with performance after the treatment.

Aside from their use as a design feature that allows us to compare performance, pretests help us to select subjects with certain characteristics and to measure the effects of a problem we call mortality. We'll consider each of these uses so that you can add the pretest to the warehouse of tools that will help you to explore human and animal behavior.

Selecting High or Low Scorers

Suppose that you were prepared to test the effectiveness of a new program that was intended to reduce racial prejudice. As always, it would be important to ensure that the subject groups were equivalent by assigning them randomly to conditions or using a within-subjects design. But would you also need to select subjects on the basis of any particular characteristic for this study? If not, why not? If so, what would a likely selection characteristic be?

Well, it seems to me that a study of prejudice reduction would be doomed from the start if you selected subjects who exhibited very little racial prejudice. How could we reduce something that barely exists? Therefore, it would be important to select subjects who do show some degree of racial prejudice before we immerse them in the reduction program.

One way of finding such subjects would be to give all the randomly selected subjects in your sample a pretest concerning racial prejudice. Those who received very low scores, indicating that they show little prejudice toward people of other races, would be excluded from the remainder of the experiment. Their pretest data would be discarded, and the results of the experiment would be based strictly on data from subjects who received high scores on the prejudice pretest.

"Rigging" the selection process in this way is perfectly acceptable, as long as the procedure is stated clearly and honestly in your experimental report. Other researchers need to know that the results of your study are limited to subjects with specific characteristics before they can design follow-up studies to learn more. Furthermore, researchers who use pretests for selection must be aware that the process may lead to the problem of statistical regression, and that it definitely will narrow the generality of their results.

Measuring Mortality Effects

Mortality occurs when large numbers of subjects drop out of an experiment before it is completed. The problem becomes especially serious when the dropout (or mortality) rate is significantly greater in one condition than in another.

Let's turn once again to our example concerning racial prejudice. Suppose that we selected 48 subjects from our random sample whose pretest scores indicated a high degree of prejudice. Twenty-four of the subjects were assigned randomly to a condition in which no training program was given, though the subjects did meet as a group twice a week for 1 month. The other 24 subjects were assigned randomly to the training program condition, with the prejudice reduction training being administered to the group twice a week for 1 month. All subjects were paid $5.00 per hour for their time. Let's say that the plan was to compare the pretest prejudice scores to the posttest prejudice scores for each subject in both groups. We could go even further and imagine that a *t*-test (using difference scores) showed that the training program really was effective in reducing people's prejudices toward other races. This would be the same as saying that there was significantly greater improvement in prejudice scores from the experimental condition than from the control condition.

Sounds fine so far, but let's introduce a twist. How would the interpretation of results be influenced by a high mortality rate in the experimental condition? To state that more simply, what would the results mean if many of the subjects who experienced the training program dropped out of the study halfway through? If you said they wouldn't mean much, you're absolutely right.

Suppose that the mortality rate in the experimental condition was 50%. This means that half of the subjects in that condition quit before the experiment was finished. The crucial question is this: Who are the subjects that dropped out? Chances are high that they are the people who resented the training program in the first place. For whatever reason, they disliked the program so much that they refused to continue even though they were being paid for their participation. These people may be exactly the ones who need prejudice reduction training the most.

On the other hand, the mortality rate in the control condition might have been 10%, indicating that only one tenth of the subjects in that condition quit the experiment. This isn't too hard to explain, either. Most of these subjects found it pleasant, or at least tolerable, to chat with other group members twice a week while being paid for participating in an experiment. Yes, a few people found it a waste of time and quit, but the majority stuck it out and received their pay.

Two problems crop up immediately when a mortality effect is present. First, some researchers are not aware that data from unbalanced designs must be analyzed with special statistical tests, especially if ANOVA is used (Keppel, 1982). An **unbalanced design** is one in which the number of subjects in each condition is not equal. In our example, the 50% mortality rate would leave only 12 subjects in the experimental condition, but the 10% mortality rate would leave about 22 subjects in the control condition. Whenever you run across a study in which conditions with differing numbers of subjects were compared to each other, check to be sure the researchers accounted for the lack of balance in their choice of statistical tests.

The second problem is much more serious. Even if the correct statistical test were applied, the subjects who remained in each condition are very different from the subjects who decided to drop out. Those who remained in the experimental condition probably found the prejudice reduction program to be interesting or helpful. If so, they were motivated by internal forces to try to recognize and reduce their own prejudices. Perhaps it was this motivation, rather than the training program, that caused these subjects to receive lower prejudice scores on the posttest than they had received on the pretest. This possibility makes the results of the experiment meaningless—effects of the independent variable have been contaminated by individual differences that now pertain to an entire group of subjects.

We can measure the effects of mortality through the use of a pretest. In this example of prejudice reduction, it would be possible to go back to the original pretests and determine the prejudice scores of those subjects who dropped out. This process would allow us to check our suppositions about the subjects who quit rather than merely assuming those suppositions were true.

A Disadvantage of the Pretest

Until now, I have implied that pretests are good for nearly everything—they help us to make more direct comparisons among subjects, they help us to select high- and low-scoring subjects, and they help us to measure mortality effects. However, the pretest isn't always good. The most likely negative effect of administering a pretest is demand characteristics.

Recall what most subjects do in the context of an experiment: They try to figure out what the researcher wants to know, right? Well, then, if we provide them with a pretest that is relevant to the topic of the experiment, we are giving them more clues to the puzzle. The danger is that soon they will have the puzzle solved. For example, subjects who received a pretest asking lots of questions about their behavior toward people of other races will figure out quickly that the experimenter is concerned with racial prejudice. As we saw in Chapter 7, this knowledge can change natural behavior, leaving us with results that do not reflect reality.

Consider the pretest a tool, then—one that is useful in some circumstances but not in others. It is up to you, as Sherlock the principal investigator, to decide when and how to use the tools of basic research. Each tool, such as a pretest or a balanced Latin Square, should be selected for a specific purpose. Moreover, when you read studies done by other researchers, remember to ask yourself whether a certain design feature (such as a pretest) was really needed. Don't blindly accept the idea that published scientists always make the right decisions in designing their research. Sometimes we don't!

EXPERIMENTAL VALIDITY

Over the past two chapters, we have considered a number of potential flaws in research, from the tiniest extraneous variable to the most fundamental problem in overall design. The thought of controlling all these potential flaws must seem overwhelming to the beginning researcher, but with time and practice, you will find it easier to design tight experiments of your own and to spot the loose ends in other people's work.

It is now time to introduce more formally the concept of validity in experimental design. You probably remember that we already discussed the idea of validity in dependent variables, but held off on overall validity of research. Now that you are familiar with the many things that can go wrong in a research study, we can consider the internal validity, external validity, and ecological validity of scientific research.

Internal Validity

In order to draw meaningful conclusions from the results of a research study, the study must have **internal validity.** A study that is internally valid is not flawed by any confounding variables or bad design features. Another way of looking at this concept is to say that an internally valid experiment truly tests the hypothesis that we had intended to test. Any difference in performance between groups is caused by manipulation of the independent variable, not by uncontrolled factors. In other words, an internally valid study is one that was designed properly and controlled tightly.

Any of the problems we have discussed over the past two chapters can damage the internal validity of an experiment. A study that is plagued by demand characteristics is not internally valid; a study in which order effects have not been controlled is not internally valid; a study without at least two groups for comparison is not internally valid.

To say that an experiment is not internally valid is a very stern criticism because a study that lacks internal validity cannot possibly answer its research question conclusively. Thus, internal validity is an absolute requirement of good scientific research. If there is one simple rule in all of research methods, it is this: *Never trust the results of an experiment that is not internally valid.*

External Validity

A research study that has **external validity** is one whose results apply to a wide and general population of subjects in a variety of settings. This is a desirable feature of good research, but not a mandatory obligation. In the best of all worlds, we would hope that our research results can be applied to many different people regardless of age or sex or cultural background. After all, we are engaged in the search for an understanding of *general* human behavior! However, in actual practice, external validity is difficult to achieve. Factors such as age, sex, and cultural background do alter people's behavior, and researchers who try to test a variety of subjects from all these groups often find that true effects are masked by random error from strong individual differences.

A study whose results are true for divorced leopard trainers younger than 23.5 years of age may be internally valid, but it is not externally valid. The subject sample is so narrow that the results say very little about the behavior of the typical human. Likewise, if you have to reproduce identical stimuli and test subjects in identical surroundings to replicate the results of a study, that research is not externally valid. An externally valid study is one whose results can be generalized beyond specific subjects, stimuli, and settings.

Although external validity is desirable, sometimes scientists do conduct and publish research studies that are not externally valid. In exploring new topics, for instance, it is useful to gather any relevant information at all. Once glimmers of knowledge begin to appear, we can then widen the scope of a research question to see whether the results of a narrow study will generalize to broader populations. Therefore, even very narrow studies can contribute in important ways to the general state of knowledge in a new research field. Of course, researchers who have conducted a study that is not externally valid must take responsibility for publishing that fact clearly.

Ecological Validity

A study that has **ecological validity** is one that reflects people's true behavior in real life, not merely in the laboratory. It is perfectly possible to conduct a study that has internal and external validity, but no ecological validity.

Neisser (1982) provided a sharp critique of research on human memory when he argued that it says nothing about the kind of remembering that people do every day. One of the earliest studies of human memory, for example, was conducted by Hermann Ebbinghaus, who memorized long lists of nonsense syllables like "gev" and "rab." Through a tightly controlled series of studies, Ebbinghaus (1885/1913) discovered the classic forgetting curve, which indicated that many syllables were forgotten shortly after being learned, whereas fewer syllables were forgotten after that.

Ebbinghaus's research on forgetting was internally valid: He did indeed take care to control extraneous variables that could have diluted the results. In addition, his research was later found to be externally valid: Hundreds of studies have been done over the years on thousands of subjects, and the forgetting curve appears consistently each time.

But was Ebbinghaus's research ecologically valid? Many researchers, including Neisser (1982), would say that it isn't. How often, in everyday life, do you memorize nonsense syllables? It isn't something I spend a lot of time doing! Memory for nonsense syllables does not reflect the use of human memory in real life, so it lacks ecological validity. Neisser argued that other abilities were much more important to study: abilities such as retaining the information we read and hear, recalling people's names, learning a new language, and remembering where the car is parked.

SUMMARY OF MAIN POINTS

- This chapter introduces five types of common designs. One-shot case studies and one-group pretest-posttest designs are bad choices because they allow no comparison between conditions. Matched-group designs are effective for certain research questions but should be used sparingly. Multiple-group posttest designs and multiple-group pretest-posttest designs are good choices for experimental research because they include equivalent groups of subjects for statistical comparison.

- Five common sources of confounding are especially likely to occur in one-shot case studies and one-group pretest-posttest designs. They are history, maturation, testing, instrumentation, and statistical regression. These problems must be avoided in scientific research.

- Good experimentation requires the use of equivalent groups for comparison. Equivalence is achieved by using within-subjects designs or by assigning subjects randomly to the conditions of between-subjects designs.

- Pretests have the advantage of showing relative amounts of improvement or impairment in various subjects. They are also useful in selecting subjects on the basis of certain characteristics and in measuring the effects of mortality. However, pretests have the disadvantage of increasing demand characteristics.

- An experiment is internally valid if obtained differences are caused by the independent variable, not by confounding variables or by other flaws in design.

- A research study is externally valid if its results generalize to other subjects, stimuli, and settings.

- A research study is ecologically valid if it explores behaviors that occur commonly in real life.

CHAPTER EXERCISES

1. Use your own words to define these key terms.

one-shot case study	regression to the mean
demonstration	experimental group
equivalent groups	matched-group design
one-group pretest-posttest design	multiple-group pretest-posttest design
history	difference scores

maturation	mortality
testing	unbalanced design
instrumentation	internal validity
instrument decay	external validity
statistical regression	ecological validity

2. In this chapter, the five common sources of confounding are applied to a sample study concerning the treatment of tension headaches. To solidify your knowledge of these sources of confounding, apply each of them to either the Kline (1970) study of hypnotherapy or the Key (1973) study of subliminal advertising.

3. Head Start is an educational program that is sometimes offered to children who achieve very low scores on preschool achievement tests. Once these children have been identified through testing, they are given special educational training to help them succeed in school. Given this information, what problem would you expect to see in studies that evaluate the effectiveness of the Head Start program? Why?

4. Suppose that you design an experiment in which the effectiveness of high-carbohydrate drinks is tested on long-distance mountain bike racers. Unfortunately, the race course assigned to subjects in your high-carb drink condition turns out to be much more demanding than the race course assigned to subjects in your low-carb drink condition. Is this study internally valid? Why or why not? Is it ecologically valid? Why or why not?

5. A frequent television advertisement for diet pills during the early 1990s claimed that "clinical studies show four out of five people lose weight with Dexatrim." Describe how this conclusion might have been reached using
   a) a one-shot case study
   b) a one-group pretest-posttest design
   c) a multiple-group posttest design
   d) a matched-group design
   e) a multiple-group pretest-posttest design

After describing each hypothetical study, select the one that would provide the most trustworthy results. Be prepared to defend your selection.

9

Factorial Designs

In what ways does appearance affect people's perception of your work performance?

By now, you've learned how to design, conduct, interpret, and evaluate simple experiments, which have only one independent variable. The same principles of research are applied to complex experiments, which have more than one independent variable. The most popular type of complex experiment is the factorial design. We'll start with a real-life example of this type of complex experiment, then double back later to pick up the necessary vocabulary.

FACTORIAL DESIGN BY EXAMPLE

Conjure up a mental image of some of the people you know, perhaps family members or friends. Some are more physically attractive than others, right? Do you think their appearances affect other people's perceptions of them very much? You might be surprised at some of the research findings that psychologists have obtained concerning this question. Here are just a few of the advantages that attractive people have over unattractive people:

1. Attractive job candidates are considered to be more highly qualified; therefore, they are more likely to be hired (Dipboye, Arvey, & Tepstra, 1977).
2. Attractive burglars are less likely to be sentenced harshly in a court of law (Sigall & Ostrove, 1975).
3. Attractive hospital patients are believed to have greater chances of regaining their health (Nordholm, 1980).
4. Attractive students are perceived as earning better grades in school, whether they really do or not (Rich, 1975). In addition, the academic work of attractive students tends to be evaluated more positively, so they often do receive higher grades (Landy & Sigall, 1974; Felson, 1980).
5. Attractive professors are viewed by students as better teachers. Students are more likely to recommend attractive professors to other students and are less likely to blame attractive professors for failing grades (Romano & Bordieri, 1989).
6. In general, attractive people are considered to be more intelligent (Clifford & Walster, 1973) and more successful (Dion, Berscheid, & Walster, 1972) than unattractive people.

Are you convinced? Physical appearance really does affect our perceptions of other people. It would be easy to verify this finding by conducting a simple experiment, in which subjects were asked to rate some attribute such as health, intelligence, or success of people who appeared to be either attractive or unattractive. Only one independent variable would be used: appearance.

The trouble with using only one independent variable is that it might limit our knowledge of the human complexities concerning attractiveness. Is it really true that we consistently prefer attractive people *under any circumstances?* Put yourself into an imaginary situation: Suppose you have a terrible case of the flu and need to visit a physician. Do you want to be examined by a female physician who is extremely beautiful, or would you prefer someone whose looks are more typical? Would your answer to this question depend partly on whether you are male or female yourself? Would it depend on how sick you felt at the time? What if you suspected a terminal illness such as cancer instead of the flu? Would your answer depend on whether the physician displayed a quiet form of natural beauty or a heavily made-up face with tight knit clothes stretched over a full figure?

My own feelings about seeing the physician would depend on all these factors, or variables. When we explore the effects of only one variable, we are ignoring many others that may be equally important. Complex experiments, such as factorial designs, allow us to consider the combined effects of several variables at once. This way, we see a more realistic picture of complex human behavior.

An Example: Physical Appearance and Occupation

Heilman and Stopeck (1985) reviewed the literature of attractiveness in the workplace and wondered whether the traditional effect of physical attractiveness depended partly on people's occupations. Does being beautiful benefit female executives in the same way that it benefits female secretaries? What about men in differing occupations? What's your opinion?

In an effort to answer these research questions, Heilman and Stopeck designed a complex experiment with several independent and dependent variables. We shall consider only one aspect of their study, but those of you who are especially interested in physical appearance may want to read their research report for further details. To find out whether people's perceptions of employees were affected by appearance and occupation, Heilman and Stopeck (1985) had to manipulate both of these independent variables within the same experiment.

Subjects in the experiment were asked to read the annual performance reviews of employees who supposedly worked for a manufacturing firm. The subjects were not aware that the level of all employees' skills was held constant (on paper) by the experimenters. Occupation was manipulated on the cover page of each performance review. According to the cover page, half of the reviews pertained to female clerks who earned approximately $10,000 per year. The other half of the reviews presented female managers who earned about $15,000 per year. Appearance was manipulated by including an employee photograph with each performance review. Half of the photos presented attractive women; the other half presented unattractive women. (We all know that "beauty lies in the eye of the beholder," so you may be wondering how Heilman and Stopeck decided who was attractive and who was not. The decisions were made according to ratings from a group of people who did not participate in the experiment.)

After subjects read these reviews carefully, they rated each employee's overall work performance on a nine-point scale. Several other measures were also recorded, such as recommendations for promotion, potential for advancement in the company, and the amount of money subjects believed each employee deserved for a merit pay raise. We shall ignore all dependent variables except employee performance, but you may want to scan the original study to find out more.

Table 9.1 MEAN RATINGS OF EMPLOYEE PERFORMANCE

	Occupation	
	Clerk	Manager
Attractive	7.35	5.65
Unattractive	6.19	7.71

Appearance (row label between Attractive and Unattractive)

From "Being Attractive, Advantage or Disadvantage? Performance Based Evaluations and Recommended Personnel Actions as a Function of Appearance, Sex, and Job Type" by M. E. Heilman and M. H. Stopeck, 1985, *Organizational Behavior and Human Decision Processes, 35*, pp. 202–215. Copyright 1985 by Academic Press, Inc. Adapted by permission.

Table 9.1 shows the mean ratings of employee performance, averaged across all subjects and employee reviews. Each employee review was set up either for an attractive clerk, an unattractive clerk, an attractive manager, or an unattractive manager. These four conditions are represented in Table 9.1, with higher mean ratings reflecting more favorable responses. As you can see, the best performance evaluations were given to attractive clerks and unattractive managers. Take a good look at these four means, because we will refer to them repeatedly throughout this chapter. Before we get into the analysis and interpretation of Heilman and Stopeck's experiment, however, you need to learn the vocabulary of factorial designs.

FACTORIAL DESIGN BY DEFINITION

Once you understand the basic concept of a factorial design, which is to determine the combined effect of two or more independent variables, you must also learn the vocabulary of complex experiments. The terms we have studied so far still retain their original meanings; factorial designs have independent variables that are manipulated, dependent variables that are measured, and extraneous variables that must be controlled. The independent variables can be manipulated within subjects or between subjects, just as before. However, there are some new terms that are used only for complex experiments.

Crossed, or Factorial, Designs

First, by definition, a **factorial design** is an experiment in which two or more independent variables are manipulated simultaneously. In addition, the factorial design requires that all independent variables are **crossed** with each other. This means that every level of one independent variable is combined with every level of the other independent variable. Heilman and Stopeck's independent variables of appearance and occupation were crossed: attractive was combined with clerk, unattractive was combined with clerk, attractive was combined with manager, and unattractive was combined with manager.

Conditions, Levels, and Cells

The crossing of independent variables yields a certain number of **conditions.** You've heard the term *conditions* before, but it was used interchangeably with *levels*. In the factorial design, conditions and levels do not have the same meaning. A level refers to one aspect of one independent variable, such as *clerk* or *unattractive*. A condition refers to the crossed combination of two levels, such as *attractive clerk* or *unattractive manager*. To test your understanding of the distinction, how many levels does each independent variable have in the Heilman and Stopeck experiment? (Your answer should be two.) And how many conditions occurred? (Four.)

Another term is sometimes used to refer to conditions in a factorial design. When we are discussing the statistical analysis of a factorial design, it is common to use the term **cell** to refer to a condition of the experiment. When we talk about the number of subjects in each cell or the mean response per cell, we are talking about the number of subjects who participated in each condition and the mean of all scores within each condition.

Between-Subjects, Within-Subjects, and Mixed Designs

As I mentioned previously, a complex experiment may employ a between-subjects design or a within-subjects design. In the between-subjects factorial design, each subject participates in only one condition. Thus, with four conditions, Heilman and Stopeck would have needed four distinct sets of subjects to conduct a between-subjects experiment. In the within-subjects factorial design, each subject participates in all conditions. For that reason, a within-subjects experiment with four conditions would need only one set of subjects.

In a factorial experiment, it is also possible to conduct a **mixed design.** This means that one independent variable is manipulated within subjects, while another is manipulated between subjects. Heilman and Stopeck (1985) used a mixed factorial design in their experiment on appearance and occupation. Appearance was manipulated within subjects, so that each subject reviewed performance evaluations for both attractive and unattractive employees. However, occupation was manipulated between subjects, so that each subject was assigned randomly to either the clerk level or the manager level. If you had been a subject in that experiment, you would have participated in a total of two conditions (either attractive clerk and unattractive clerk, or attractive manager and unattractive manager).

Sometimes, the mixed design is called a **split-plot design.** Having interchangeable terms like this is confusing, I know, but there is no way to avoid it. People do use both terms, so you should be familiar with them. Finally, in factorial designs, as with simple experiments, it is usually desirable to manipulate independent variables within subjects. This reduces the number of necessary subjects, increases statistical power, and eliminates the need for random assignment to conditions.

Common Jargon Like "Two-by-Two"

Sounds like we're boarding Noah's ark, doesn't it? Often, you will hear seasoned scientists refer to factorial designs with phrases like "two-by-two," "three-by-three," or even something like "four-by-two-by-three-by-six." This terminology comes from the number of levels of each independent variable as well as the number of independent variables in the experiment. For example, a "three-by-two" (usually written as 3×2) experiment has two independent variables; one variable has three levels, and the other has two levels. The 2×2, like Heilman and Stopeck's experiment, has two independent variables, each having two levels. How many independent variables would a $4 \times 2 \times 3 \times 6$ factorial design contain? Four is the correct answer. And how many levels would each of those independent variables have? The first independent variable would have four levels, the second would have two levels, the third would have three levels, and the fourth would have six levels.

This casual way of referring to factorial designs provides even more information about the experiment than just the number of independent variables and levels it contains. In addition, it allows us to determine the number of conditions that occurred. A 2×2 factorial design has a total of 4 conditions; a 3×3 has 9 conditions. The $4 \times 2 \times 3 \times 6$ factorial that I mentioned would have a whopping 144 separate conditions!

Theoretically, any number of independent variables with any number of levels can be crossed in a factorial design. However, in practice, wise researchers limit the number of independent variables and levels to avoid problems of interpretation after the data are gathered. A $4 \times 2 \times 3 \times 6$ factorial design is so complex that many researchers would have trouble interpreting its results, and few readers would understand the interpretation anyway. We shall see why this is so as we begin to consider how the results of even a basic 2×2 factorial design are interpreted.

EYEBALLING THE DATA

Once the data of an experiment have been collected, some people feel an irrepressible urge to race out and analyze the data statistically. (I'll bet you never thought that would happen!) In complex experiments, however, it is especially important to tally up condition means and consider them carefully before starting the statistical program on your computer. In the long run, eyeballing the data for general patterns will save you time.

Let's consider the simplest possible factorial design: an experiment with two independent variables, each having two levels, and only one dependent variable.

In this most basic case, there are three possible results that must be explored. First, we search for a combined effect of the two independent variables considered jointly. Next, we look for an effect of one independent variable alone. Third, we see whether there is an effect of the other independent variable alone. A 2×2 factorial design can produce any combination of these three effects, with each one having its own size and significance.

Interactions

The combined effect of two independent variables is called an **interaction:** The effects of one independent variable combine, or "interact," with the effects of the other independent variable. In practical terms, this means that the two factors act together to alter subjects' scores on the dependent variable. In Heilman and Stopeck's experiment, an interaction between the two independent variables would occur if appearance and occupation acted together to make us view an employee's performance positively or negatively. To say the same thing in yet another way, if the effect of appearance *depends on* the effect of occupation, then we have an interaction.

To look for an interaction, we draw a graph of the cell means. The cell means for Heilman and Stopeck's experiment were shown in Table 9.1, remember? It is standard practice to use line graphs when searching for an interaction, even if your independent variables do not fall along a continuum. When preparing figures for a research report, you will need to decide whether the independent variables warrant a bar graph or a line graph, but for the purpose of eyeballing data in the privacy of their own labs, most researchers use a line graph. It's easier to see the interaction that way.

Figure 9.1 takes you, step by step, through the process of graphing the cell means of a 2×2 factorial design, using the data from Heilman and Stopeck's experiment. As in Figure 9.1A, begin by drawing the axes of a standard line graph. The ordinate always represents the dependent variable. The abscissa may represent either of the independent variables—it doesn't matter which one you choose. I decided to place "appearance" along the horizontal axis.

The panel in Figure 9.1B takes you a step further. Here you plot cell means by drawing a mark at the point corresponding to the value of that mean. The cell mean for attractive clerks was 7.35, so I drew a circle at that point on the graph. The cell mean for unattractive clerks was 6.19, which is represented by a circle higher on the ordinate and farther to the right on the abscissa. We simply connect these two circles with a solid line, which will represent the effect of appearance on the performance ratings of female clerks.

The panel in Figure 9.1C shows you our next step. We must do the same for the two cell means concerning managers as we did for the cell means concerning clerks. The data points for managers should look different than those for clerks, so instead of circles, I used squares. You can use any kind of geometric shape, as long as the data points and connecting lines for the two independent variables remain distinct. This time, we simply draw the two squares in proper position and connect them with a dotted line. Finally, we add a legend to the upper right cor-

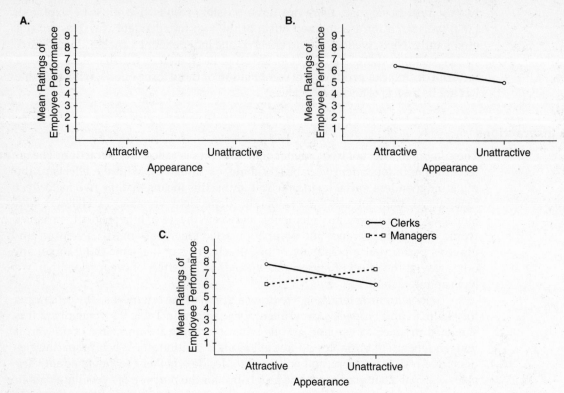

Figure 9.1
How to Plot Cell Means
A, Step One; B, Step Two (Clerks); C, Step Three (Clerks and Managers).
Source: Based on Heilman and Stopeck, 1985.

ner of the graph so that people can see easily which line signifies clerks and which signifies managers.

The resulting line graph illustrates Heilman and Stopeck's results. The easiest way to determine whether there is a possible interaction is to look at the two lines on the graph. If those two lines are parallel to each other, the two variables do not interact. If the two lines are not parallel to each other, however, you may have obtained an interaction. Of course, we can't know whether the interaction is significant until the statistical tests have been done. Heilman and Stopeck's data appear to produce an interaction, whose size and significance we will assess later in this chapter.

One of the most common mistakes students make in searching a line graph for interaction is thinking that the two lines must cross before any interaction could be possible. This is not true. The two lines must not be parallel to each other, but there is no need for them to cross. Sometimes they do cross, as in Figure 9.1, but often they don't. Either way, if they're not parallel, you have obtained a

Table 9.2 CELL AND MARGINAL MEANS
FOR RATINGS OF EMPLOYEE PERFORMANCE

Occupation

	Clerk	Manager	
Attractive	7.35	5.65	6.50
Unattractive	6.19	7.71	6.95
	6.77	6.68	

Appearance (label at left, between Attractive and Unattractive rows)

From "Being Attractive, Advantage or Disadvantage? Performance Based Evaluations and Recommended Personnel Actions as a Function of Appearance, Sex, and Job Type" by M. E. Heilman and M. H. Stopeck, 1985, *Organizational Behavior and Human Decision Processes, 35,* pp. 202–215. Copyright 1985 by Academic Press, Inc. Adapted by permission.

possible interaction. Incidentally, supposing that the lines must cross is a flaw of interpretation that sometimes appears in popular magazines or newspapers, so keep an eye out for it.

Main Effects

After searching for an interaction, we must see whether there is a main effect of either independent variable alone. A **main effect** is a difference between the two levels of one independent variable when the other independent variable is ignored momentarily. We can use Heilman and Stopeck's cell means to determine whether either of the independent variables had a main effect. Refer to Table 9.2 as we go through the process of searching for main effects.

To determine the main effect of appearance alone, we must average across the cell means for occupation. Thus, as shown in Table 9.2, the mean of 7.35 and 5.65 is 6.50. This number, 6.50, represents the mean performance rating for employees who are attractive, regardless of what occupation they hold. We will compare this number to the mean performance rating for employees who are unattractive, regardless of occupation. To get this rating, we calculate the mean of 6.19 and 7.71, which is 6.95. These two numbers, 6.50 and 6.95, are different from each other, so there is a possibility of a main effect of appearance. From eyeballing the data, it looks like unattractive people may receive slightly more favorable performance ratings than attractive people do. To determine whether this possible main effect is significant, we will conduct the proper statistical analysis. However, it is important to get as much information from your data as possible before you begin to run statistical tests.

The numbers that we just calculated to determine whether a main effect exists are called **marginal means.** You can see by Table 9.2 that they are aptly named—they are simply means that appear in the margins of the table. The marginal means that allow us to explore the main effect of appearance are on the right-hand side of this table, because we had to average across both levels of occupation for each level of appearance.

The same process can be used to explore the possibility of a main effect of occupation. Before reading further, try to calculate the proper marginal means by yourself. Do the marginal means suggest that there is a possible main effect of occupation? If so, how would you describe that possible main effect in words? Really trying to answer these questions on your own will mean less studying later on.

What were your conclusions? You should have compared the two marginal means on the bottom of Table 9.2, 6.77 and 6.68. The first marginal mean was obtained by averaging 7.35 and 6.19; the second marginal mean was obtained by averaging 5.65 and 7.71. Comparing these two numbers allows you to ignore the effect of appearance momentarily and look only at occupation. Because the performance rating for clerks was a little higher than that for managers, regardless of appearance, you can conclude that there was a possible main effect of occupation. (It's *possible*; you're correct to note that the difference between 6.77 and 6.68 is very small.) Again, whether that possible main effect is significant remains to be determined by a statistical analysis.

In general, when eyeballing the data of a 2×2 factorial design, search for all three possible effects. Main effects are explored by calculating marginal means and checking to see whether they differ. Even very small differences between marginal means suggest that a main effect is possible. The interaction is investigated by plotting cell means on a line graph and checking to see whether the lines are parallel to each other.

STATISTICAL ANALYSIS: THE TWO-WAY ANOVA

By calculating marginal means and graphing cell means, scientists are able to determine quickly whether a factorial design has produced possible main effects or an interaction. That process also helps us to truly understand the results, which is vital if we are to explain them accurately. Researchers who move directly from data collection to statistical analysis without this intervening process are making final interpretation much harder for themselves. They skip one simple step in the middle only to find themselves faced with twice as much work at the end.

If the marginal and cell means suggest that there is a possibility of main effects or an interaction, the next step is to assess the statistical significance of these effects. According to Table C.1 (on page 312), the appropriate statistical test for a 2×2 factorial design is a two-way ANOVA. More specifically, because the design was mixed, we select a two-way mixed ANOVA. Verify this decision for yourself by consulting Table C.1. Whenever a design contains two independent variables and the dependent variable is measured on an interval or ratio scale, the two-way ANOVA is used.

In principle, the two-way ANOVA works just like the one-way ANOVA does. It compares the amount of variability in data between groups to the amount of variability in data within each group. If the data vary more between groups than they do within groups, a significant effect is likely to be found. The main difference between the one-way ANOVA and the two-way ANOVA is that the latter performs this process of comparison three times over: once for the main effect of one independent variable, once for the main effect of the other independent variable, and once for the interaction.

Because the process is performed three times in a two-way ANOVA, you end up with three separate F values, each with its own pair of degrees of freedom. Each F value refers to one of the three possible effects that we considered in the previous section of this chapter.

Assessing the Significance of *F*

Each obtained F value must be compared to the critical value on a standard statistical table for F, like Table C.6 on page 317. The same method that was used for assessing the significance of F in a one-way ANOVA is used for a two-way ANOVA as well.

Here are the three F values that Heilman and Stopeck obtained in their experiment:

1. For the main effect of appearance, $F(1, 32) = .37$.
2. For the main effect of occupation, $F(1, 32) = .01$.
3. For the interaction between appearance and occupation, $F(1, 32) = 13.28$.

Using the critical value table on page 317, determine the significance of each F value for yourself. If you've forgotten how to use two values for degrees of freedom, review page 149, where the process is explained thoroughly.

Are any of the three effects significant? You should have decided, as Heilman and Stopeck did, that the interaction between appearance and occupation was significant. The main effect of appearance and the main effect of occupation were not statistically significant.

The size of each significant effect may also be determined for a factorial experiment. As with the measurement of effect size for F in a one-way ANOVA, omega-squared can be used to determine effect size in a two-way ANOVA. However, the formula for calculating omega-squared becomes rather complicated for the two-way ANOVA, so we will not deal with it in this book. If you go on to more advanced research methods or statistics courses, the calculation of omega-squared for a two-way ANOVA will probably be taught.

The Need for Post-hoc Tests

There's one remaining statistical glitch that we need to discuss before turning to the interpretation of results. You probably remember that a one-way ANOVA is conducted when there are more than two levels of one independent variable. Because of this, post-hoc tests must be done to find out exactly which of several possible comparisons between means is significant.

The same principle must be applied to the two-way ANOVA. Whenever a significant effect is based on comparing more than two means with each other, the F value alone can not tell us the exact location of the significance. In a 2×2 factorial design, do any of the three effects require a comparison between more than two means?

Well, the main effect of appearance, in our example, is based on only two marginal means (corresponding to attractive and unattractive levels). Therefore, a significant F value indicates that any existing difference must occur between those two means. Where else could it be? The same reasoning is true of the main effect of occupation. There are only two levels of occupation in the experiment (clerk and manager), so if the difference is significant, it has to appear between those two marginal means. Neither of the main effects would require post-hoc analysis, then.

The hitch comes into play when we get to the interaction. Which means are used to determine the significance of an interaction? You should know the answer to that question: It's the cell means. And how many cell means are there in a 2×2 factorial? Yes, there must be four. With four cell means, several possible comparisons could be made. The exact differences leading to the significance of this interaction might occur between unattractive managers and attractive clerks, or between attractive managers and unattractive clerks, for example.

A significant F value for the interaction means only that there is a consistent difference somewhere among those four means. It doesn't tell us where. One of the various types of post-hoc tests (e.g., Scheffé, Tukey, Newman-Keuls) must be used to discover the exact location of the significance.

INTERPRETING FACTORIAL RESULTS

Different people have their own favorite methods for interpreting the results of a factorial experiment. As you become more experienced in designing and evaluating scientific research, you too may devise a method that suits your working style best.

For now, however, I will offer three suggestions for accurate interpretation of factorial results. First, describe the results in plain English. Second, try to explain what the results mean; that is, why they occurred. Separating the process of interpretation into these two steps is usually helpful for beginners. Finally, throughout the interpretation process, focus on the interaction if it is significant. In other words, when a factorial experiment produces a significant interaction, the main effects should be interpreted in light of that interaction. Attempts to interpret the three effects separately usually fail when the interaction is significant.

Describing the Results in Words

Many times, beginning scientists understand the principles of factorial design but don't know how to apply them. When first asked to describe the results of a complex experiment, my students often say, "Well, the main effects of appearance and occupation were not significant, but there was a significant interaction." This statement is accurate, but it does not *describe* the results at all; it merely states the outcome of a statistical test.

To describe the results, you must use plain English that any intelligent person can comprehend. With the Heilman and Stopeck experiment, we could start by describing the interaction shown in Figure 9.1C, on page 212. Look at that figure for a moment and try to describe what it shows. Aim for a description that anyone can understand without first taking a class in statistics. This is what a good description should achieve.

Here's how I might describe the interaction between appearance and occupation:

> People who work as clerks receive more favorable performance ratings if they are attractive than if they are unattractive. However, for managers this effect is reversed: Unattractive managers are perceived as better performers than are attractive managers.

Of course, you don't have to come up with those exact words in order to describe the results clearly. Be sure that you understand the general principle, though: Results must be described in plain English at some point in a report or presentation. Furthermore, the ability to describe results plainly usually aids researchers in interpretation.

Let's try describing that same interaction in more practical terms. Imagine that a female friend who just got a job in the world of business asks you, "What sort of physical appearance should I try to achieve to be perceived as a good employee?" Think about how you might answer that question.

The answer would have to be, "Well, it depends." According to Figure 9.1C, if your friend works as a manager, her work performance will be rated most favorably if she dresses in a way that minimizes her attractiveness. On the other hand, if she works as a clerk, her work performance will be rated most favorably if she dresses to maximize her natural attractiveness.

Of course, we must remember that in this experiment, actual work performance was controlled. In the real world of business, your friend's best bet at getting good performance reviews will come from hard work, perfect attendance, positive attitude, and consistent competence. Still, Heilman and Stopeck have shown that her appearance will also have an effect.

Now, what about the main effects? In Heilman and Stopeck's experiment, a special type of interaction was obtained, called a **crossover interaction.** A crossover interaction occurs whenever the cell means plotted on a graph form lines that make a fairly balanced **X**. This pattern signifies that the two independent variables depend on each other to similar extents in altering scores on the dependent variable.

Let's make that more concrete. Looking at the right-hand side of Figure 9.1C, you can see that the unattractiveness of a female manager raises her performance rating by about two points on the rating scale. At the same time, the unattractiveness of a clerk *lowers* her ratings by about the same amount. The main effect of attractiveness alone, then, is completely dependent upon occupation. In other words, the results of this experiment do not allow us to say that attractiveness enhances or reduces job performance ratings across the board. Instead, attractiveness enhances performance ratings for clerks, but it reduces performance ratings for managers.

The same logic can be applied to the main effect of occupation, which in this case depends completely on attractiveness. That is, the results do not suggest that managers receive performance ratings that are inherently higher or lower than those received by clerks. Rather, managers who are unattractive receive higher ratings than clerks, but managers who are attractive receive lower ratings than clerks. In effect, then, the significant crossover interaction cancels out both main effects. In keeping with this fact, neither main effect was significant in the Heilman and Stopeck experiment.

Of course, some factorial experiments do produce significant interactions that are not of the crossover variety. Many also produce main effects that are significant and can be interpreted meaningfully on their own. We shall consider an example of such a main effect later in this chapter.

Before we go on, let me reassure those of you who feel rather confused by the last few paragraphs. The relationship between interactions and main effects is probably one of the most difficult concepts to be found in this book. Don't be dismayed if it isn't perfectly clear to you yet. Nobody, not even Einstein, grasps everything the first time around.

Explaining the Results

We have already discussed how to analyze the data of a factorial design. That analysis can be stated in the statistical terms of "main effects," "interactions," and "significance." We then discussed how to describe those results in plain English. Now, we need to explain why our results occurred. In other words, what do they mean? Why did they turn out the way they did?

Ask yourself these questions in relation to Heilman and Stopeck's experiment on physical appearance. Why do clerks get higher performance ratings if they are attractive, while managers get higher performance ratings if they are unattractive? To put it another way, why is beauty an asset to a clerk but a liability to a manager? Can you think of any possible reasons for this departure from the standard "beauty-is-best" effect? Sometimes it helps to consider such questions by imagining yourself in a relevant situation: If you were the supervisor of a beautiful manager, why might you perceive her work performance to be relatively poor? Another way of looking at the same issue is to ask what your underlying feelings might be if you perceived an unattractive manager to be exceptionally good at her work.

We probably all can think of different answers to those questions. Some of these possible answers can be put to an empirical test, which is exactly how researchers design follow-up studies that extend published work. Heilman and Stopeck believed that attractiveness causes people to perceive a female employee as more feminine. This heightened femininity would be beneficial in a stereotypically feminine job, such as a clerk or secretary. However, the same increase in femininity would detract from women who were employed in stereotypically masculine positions, such as a manager.

To test this interpretation further, Heilman and Stopeck asked subjects to rate each stimulus employee on a femininity-masculinity scale. Those ratings verified that the unattractive women were perceived as being more masculine, whereas the attractive women were perceived as feminine. Employees whose job titles didn't fit these perceptions were rated as poor performers.

INCREASING THE COMPLEXITY OF FACTORIAL DESIGNS

Throughout this chapter, we have considered only the most basic form of factorial design—one with only two independent variables, each having only two levels. However, as I mentioned briefly, it is possible to increase the complexity of such an experiment by adding independent variables to the design or by adding more levels to each independent variable.

After reading about the Heilman and Stopeck experiment, for example, you might wonder how job titles that are neither stereotypically masculine nor feminine might affect the performance ratings of beautiful women. To explore this research question, it would be fairly simple to add an intermediate level to the independent variable of occupation. You might end up with three levels, such as "clerk," "salesperson," and "manager." If you could show that sales positions really are not perceived as particularly feminine or masculine and that attractiveness accordingly has little effect on performance ratings, then your results might strengthen Heilman and Stopeck's interpretation of their research. On the other hand, your results might show that sales positions are viewed as extremely masculine or feminine, but that this stereotype has little effect on the performance ratings of attractive or unatttractive employees. In that case, you will have shown that Heilman and Stopeck's interpretation is likely to be wrong. Just adding one level to the design allows you to consider new research questions or, at least, to verify the answers to old ones.

Sometimes there is also good reason to add an extra independent variable to a factorial design. Heilman and Stopeck, for example, thought it was important to determine whether the effect we have discussed for women also holds true for men. Therefore, they set up a $2 \times 2 \times 2$ factorial, with three independent variables: applicant appearance (attractive or unattractive), applicant occupation (clerk or manager), and applicant sex (male or female). Results showed that attractiveness had no bearing on people's perceptions of a man's work performance, regardless of whether he worked as a clerk or as a manager.

Some research questions can only be answered adequately by manipulating more than two independent variables at one time. Let me caution you once again, however: It can be very difficult, even for experienced researchers, to interpret the results of factorial designs with many independent variables. As you know, a design with two independent variables produces the possibility of three effects (two main effects plus one interaction). A design with three independent variables produces six possible effects: three main effects, two 2-way interactions, and one 3-way interaction. Figuring out how the various effects of all these variables fit together is tough to do. Imagine the headache that a design with four or five independent variables can generate!

REVIEWING THE FACTORIAL DESIGN

In many beginning research methods courses, factorial designs cause more confusion than any other type of research. There may be two reasons for this. One is that an understanding of the factorial experiment depends on a solid grasp of the most basic methods and vocabulary. Students who still aren't sure how to distinguish an independent variable from a dependent variable, for instance, are sure to find factorial designs bewildering. A second reason is that complex experiments are indeed difficult to understand at first. Few people can digest the factorial design all at once by reading a chapter such as this, without applying the principles to concrete studies that they conduct in the laboratory. For these reasons, I offer another, much briefer, example of the factorial experiment. As we work through it, try to anticipate each step for yourself.

An Example: Enhancing Creativity in Children

Traditionally, elementary and secondary school systems in the United States have emphasized rational logic to the point of sacrificing some of the natural creativity that most children possess. You might remember, as I do, being taught as a child to stay inside the lines when coloring pictures, to solve a math problem by the same dreary method that our teacher followed, or to play only the musical notes that were written on the sheet. Rarely were we encouraged to apply our creativity to these tasks.

Over the last decade or two, educators have been encouraged to give creativity a more favored seat in the education of American school children (Gowan, Khatena, & Torrance, 1981). This desire to enhance children's creativity has inspired scientific research on the topic. Educators need to know exactly how they can encourage creative thinking in children, and scientists have begun to conduct research to address their needs.

Berretta and Privette (1990) conducted a 2×3 factorial experiment investigating the effects of play on creative thinking in fourth-grade children. These researchers manipulated two independent variables: play experience (flexible or structured) and play activity (art, drama, or playground). Both independent variables were manipulated between subjects. Thus, each child was assigned randomly to one of six conditions in which the researchers provided some combination of play experience and play activity. For instance, children who had been assigned to the "flexible art" condition might have been encouraged to draw or paint anything they wished as a form of playing. After the play, subjects' creativity was measured on a standard test of creative thinking.

Table 9.3   CELL MEANS FOR CREATIVITY SCORES

Play Activity

		Art	Drama	Playground
	Flexible	83.31	89.36	89.67
Play Experience				
	Structured	78.41	84.00	78.27

From "Influence of Play on Creative Thinking" by S. Berretta and G. Privette, 1990, *Perceptual and Motor Skills*, *71*, pp. 659–666. Copyright 1990 by *Perceptual and Motor Skills*. Adapted by permission.

Berretta and Privette predicted that flexible play experiences would encourage creative thinking, but they weren't sure how the three play activities would influence creativity. Teachers who tend to scoff at the importance of playground activities might expect that art and drama would produce greater creativity. The researchers also left open the possibility of an interaction between play experiences and activities. Perhaps flexible play would generate more creativity when combined with certain activities than with others.

The cell and marginal means from Berretta and Privette's study are shown in Table 9.3. From the cell means, Figure 9.2 was drawn to see whether an interaction would appear. In a 2×3 factorial, an interaction is possible if any portions of the two lines connecting data points are not parallel to each other. Thus, you can see that no apparent interaction was produced by the type of play experience used in artistic and dramatic activities. (The left-hand portions of both lines are parallel.) However, because the right-hand portions of both lines are not parallel to each other, an interaction is possible based on that aspect of the data.

If we go back to Table 9.3 for a moment, you can see that each independent variable produced differences in the marginal means. This suggests that main effects of play experiences and play activities may have occurred.

A two-way between-subjects ANOVA was conducted to assess the significance of the main effects and interaction. The interaction between play experience and play activity was not significant, $F (2, 178) = .34$, $p > .05$. The main effect of play activity was also not significant, $F (2, 178) = .90$, $p > .05$. However, the main effect of play experience was significant, $F (1, 178) = 4.08$, $p < .05$.

What do all these fancy statistical sentences mean? Well, it appears that children's creativity is not affected by the type of play activity they engage in before taking creative thinking tests. However, the type of play experience does make a difference: Children tend to exhibit more creativity after flexible play experiences than they do after structured play experiences. The moral of the story? If you are a teacher who wishes to encourage creative thinking, avoid structured play. In-

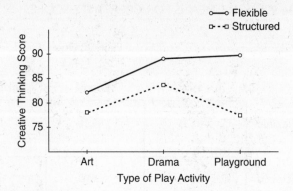

Figure 9.2
The Effects of Play Experience and Activity on Creative Thinking
Source: From Berretta and Privette, 1990.

stead, give your students the opportunity to play as they wish, with a minimum of adult direction.

You may have noticed that the previous paragraph, in which Berretta and Privette's study is interpreted, focuses entirely on the main effects. This focus is quite different from the one we used when interpreting Heilman and Stopeck's experiment on physical appearance. There, a significant interaction was obtained, so each main effect had to be considered with regard to that interaction. However, in the creative thinking experiment, the interaction was not significant. Therefore, we were able to focus on each of the main effects alone.

Let's summarize the interpretation of factorial designs once again at this point. If an interaction is significant, both main effects must be interpreted with respect to that interaction. This is especially important when the significant interaction takes on the shape of a crossover. However, if an interaction is not significant, then the main effects may be interpreted directly, without concern for any action that one independent variable may exert on the other.

Berretta and Privette (1990) reported some interesting practical applications of their research. First, they pointed out that children's games can be made more flexible by encouraging and praising imaginative behavior during the games. Second, children's schedules can be planned so that creativity is enhanced. For example, school work like creative writing might be scheduled for times immediately after flexible play experiences in art or drama or on the playground. Both of these applications can enhance creative thinking in school children, and they stem directly from the results of a factorial experiment.

THE IMPORTANCE OF FACTORIAL DESIGNS

We often start out with simple experiments when we learn basic research methods. However, quickly it becomes apparent that simple experiments are not as powerful as we would like. They can answer very simple questions, looking at one factor at a time, but human behavior is not simple. In real life, many factors combine to cause us to behave in the ways we do. It's vital that psychology has some method of exploring the combined effects of such factors. A complex experiment allows us to investigate the complicated effects that everyday living represents.

For these reasons, complex experiments receive far more attention than do simple experiments. In fact, nearly all of the research reported in psychological journals nowadays explores the effects of multiple variables. Furthermore, within a complex experiment, an interaction always gets top billing. Main effects are considered more meager contributions to the state of knowledge in science. Since causal interactions can be detected only through the use of complex experiments, factorial designs are very popular.

To gain maximum advantage from your new knowledge of factorial designs, consider the possibilities of combined effects when specifying your own research questions. As you read the literature on a chosen topic, ask yourself what other variables might interact with the published effect to change the results in some way. And finally, be skeptical when you read the interpretation of a factorial design that was written by a newspaper reporter with no scientific training.

SUMMARY OF MAIN POINTS

- The most common type of complex experiment is the factorial design, in which the levels of two or more independent variables are crossed to create multiple conditions.

- Factorial designs have the advantage of allowing us to explore the combined effects of several factors simultaneously. For this reason, they provide a more realistic picture of complex human and animal behavior than simple experiments can provide.

- Before analyzing the data of a factorial experiment, we search for general patterns in the form of main effects and interactions. Main effects are explored by calculating marginal means and comparing them with each other. Interactions are explored by plotting cell means on a graph and checking to see whether the resulting lines are parallel.

- An interaction between two independent variables means that both variables act together to cause changes in subjects' behavior. When an interaction occurs, the effect of one independent variable depends on the level of the other independent variable.

- Statistical analysis of a factorial design produces separate inferential values (such as F) for each possible effect. Each of these values must be assessed in order to determine whether the effect it represents is significant.

- To locate the particular comparisons that are significant within an interaction, post-hoc tests must be conducted. Any main effect with more than two levels also requires post-hoc analysis for the same reason.

- The interpretation of factorial results can be simplified by separating the process into two steps: First, describe the results in plain English, then try to explain why they occurred.

- A significant interaction always takes precedence as the highlight of a factorial study. Therefore, main effects must be interpreted with respect to the significant interaction.

CHAPTER EXERCISES

1. Use your own words to define these key terms:

factorial design	split-plot design
crossed	interaction
conditions	main effect
cell	marginal means
mixed design	crossover interaction

2. What is the minimum number of total subjects needed in a $2 \times 3 \times 2$ within-subjects factorial design? What is the minimum number needed in a $2 \times 3 \times 2$ between-subjects design? How many subjects are needed if the design is mixed so that the first variable is manipulated within subjects but the other two are manipulated between subjects?

3. Research on voting behavior has shown that fear campaigns are effective in certain instances. A fear campaign is used when the candidate urges voters to be afraid of future events that may happen if the candidate does not win. The hypothetical data below show mean voting preferences on a nine-point scale, on which higher numbers indicate greater preference.

   Plot the cell means on a graph and calculate marginal means, then answer the following questions:
   a) Does an interaction appear to be present? If so, describe it in plain English.
   b) Does a main effect of campaign appear to be present? If so, describe it in plain English.
   c) Does a main effect of candidate appear to be present? If so, describe it in plain English.

	Type of Campaign	
	Fear	No-fear
Type of Candidate — President	5.2	5.3
Senator	8.4	5.3

4. Suppose you were drawing the graph in exercise number 3 for publication. If you plotted type of campaign along the abscissa, would a bar graph or a line graph be most appropriate? Why? If you plotted type of candidate along the abscissa, which graph would be most appropriate? Why? (Information on page 281 of Appendix A may help you to answer this question.)

5. Write a two-page research proposal in which a factorial design is used to answer some research question of your own choosing. In this proposal, include statements of your research question and predictions, and specify the independent variables, dependent variables, and experimental task that would be used. Feel free to be creative and have some fun with this assignment, but take care to design the proposed study rigorously.

TYSON, BOXING AND RAPE
By Joyce Carol Oates

Newsweek

February 24, 1992 : $2.95

Is This Child Gay?

Born or Bred: The Origins of Homosexuality

10

Quasi-Experimental Research

One of many popular interpretations
of quasi-experimental research.

y this time, two of the knowledge trees growing on your garden trellis should be healthy and strong: the ones that stand for nonexperimental and experimental research. The third, quasi-experimental research, is easy to nurture once the first two are established. With an understanding of these three major types of scientific research, you will be ready to design and conduct studies that can answer all sorts of research questions. More importantly, you will be able to evaluate most of the research that is presented on television and in newspapers or magazines, coming to your own conclusions about the validity of each study.

QUASI-EXPERIMENTS

The word *quasi* means "like" or "resembling," so a **quasi-experiment** is simply a research study that resembles a between-subjects experiment. It is not a true experiment because the subjects are not assigned randomly to conditions. Because assignment is not random, we cannot determine cause as conclusively in a quasi-experiment as we can in a true experiment.

Nonrandom assignment to conditions is probably the easiest way for you to identify a quasi-experimental design. First, rule out the possibility that a design is nonexperimental by looking for the identifying clues of surveys, case studies, archival research, natural observations, and correlations. Next, try to decide whether the design is a within-subjects experiment. Once you have excluded the possibility of nonexperimental research and are certain that the design is not a within-subjects experiment, look for random subject assignment to conditions. If the subjects were assigned randomly to conditions, the design you are evaluating is probably a between-subjects experiment. If not, it is probably a quasi-experiment.

You might wonder why any self-respecting researcher would design a study in which random condition assignment was not used. After all, you learned way back in Chapter 6 that random assignment is a critical method of control in every between-subjects experiment. The answer is that some research questions do not permit us to assign subjects randomly to various conditions. Those questions are still important enough, however, that we must find a way to investigate them.

For example, suppose you were interested in sex differences or maybe certain aspects of personal appearance like height. It just isn't possible for even the most clever scientist to assign normal human subjects to the conditions "male" and "female" in a random manner. The sex variable is not under the experimenter's control; it can not be manipulated. A subject is either male or female to begin with, and must be assigned to one of those two categories in a nonrandom manner. Similarly, we can not assign subjects randomly to height conditions like "short" or "tall." A woman who is 6 feet tall can not possibly be assigned to a "short" condition, just as a man can not possibly be assigned to a "female" condition.

These inherent characteristics of human and animal subjects are known as **subject variables.** Such variables include sex, height, intelligence, and age, just to mention a few examples. We used to include factors like hair and eye color, but they can now be manipulated in humans through artificial hair coloring and contact lenses. True subject variables are not under the researcher's control. For that reason, quasi-experimental research is often used to determine the effects of subject variables.

WHEN TO USE QUASI-EXPERIMENTAL RESEARCH

There are three general situations in which quasi-experimental research is very useful. They are:

1. When subject variables are being investigated,
2. When the effects of natural disasters are being investigated, and
3. When true manipulation of a variable would be unethical.

We have already considered the first of these three situations. A study that explores the effects of age or intelligence or height must resort to either the nonexperimental or quasi-experimental design, because it is not possible to manipulate these subject variables in humans or animals.

The same is true for investigating the effects of natural disasters. No scientist has control over the occurrence of an earthquake or a forest fire. However, these disasters may still produce important effects on behavior. Children who grow up in earthquake-prone areas like southern California may be affected by the constant stress of wondering when The Big One is going to come. Likewise, animals who have survived forest fires may exhibit unusual patterns of behavior that tell us something about evolution or adaptation. These research questions are important, but they cannot be answered through experimentation.

Finally, some manipulations are possible but unethical. Smoking is a good example. Scientists have tried to demonstrate with certainty for years that smoking cigarettes is dangerous, but we have been held back by an inability to conduct experimental smoking studies on humans.

Think of how an experiment on smoking effects would have to be designed. In the simplest possible plan, a randomly assigned group of subjects would have to be forced to smoke cigarettes on a regular basis for a long time. Some other randomly assigned group would be required not to smoke. Obviously, this can't be done! It would be unethical to randomly assign anyone to either a "smoking" or "nonsmoking" condition, so we can not conduct a true experiment in exploring this vital question. This is exactly why scientists have had to rely on correlational studies and animal experiments to demonstrate the hazardous effects of tobacco.

We can, however, design a quasi-experiment. Here, we would sample two groups of subjects. One group would include people who have smoked for a long time and are still smoking. We would assign them to the "smoking" condition. The other group would be made up of people who had never smoked. We would assign them to the "nonsmoking" condition. Assignment to conditions is not random, which makes this a quasi-experiment.

Although a quasi-experiment that explored the effect of cigarette smoking on human health would be an ethical alternative to nonexperimental forms of research, it still suffers from a major disadvantage: Any conclusions we draw from its results are tainted by the fact that smokers and nonsmokers differ from each other in many ways. An effect of tobacco use is likely to be confounded with all these other systematic differences between smokers and nonsmokers.

THE SIMPLE QUASI-EXPERIMENT

Until now, I have implied that all quasi-experiments are alike. In fact, several different designs are used in this category of scientific research. These include the simple quasi-experiment, the complex quasi-experiment, and the interrupted time series design. The distinction between simple and complex quasi-experiments is based on the number of variables in the study. Let's consider first the **simple quasi-experiment,** which has only one quasi-independent variable.

A simple experiment, as you know, has only one independent variable. Any simple experiment may be altered to become quasi-experimental. If the independent variable can not truly be manipulated, for whatever reason, we sacrifice the control of random assignment in return for the chance to explore our research question quasi-experimentally. The smoking study that we made up in the previous section illustrates the simple quasi-experiment. Results from a group of smokers are compared to those from a group of nonsmokers. Any significant differences in health must be caused either by the smoking behavior or by other systematic variations between the two groups of subjects.

An Example: Homosexuality

Let's work through a simple quasi-experiment conducted in 1991 that had tremendous social and political impact. We're all probably familiar with the nature/nurture debate that has been applied to sexuality: Are sexual orientations determined biologically, or are they learned as we grow up? LeVay (1991) investigated this question by comparing the brains of people with differing sexual orientations. One group of subjects was composed of men who were known to be homosexuals, and a second group was composed of men who were thought to be heterosexuals.* You should be able to identify immediately from the previous sentence that LeVay's study was quasi-experimental. It would be impossible to randomly assign homosexuals to the "heterosexual" condition or heterosexuals to the "homosexual" condition, right? If that doesn't make sense, stop now and re-read. There's no sense in waiting until you're thoroughly confused.

LeVay explored the brains of these men by surgical means. The men had died, but their brains were intact, so LeVay was able to locate in each brain the hypothalamus, which is thought to regulate human motives such as hunger, thirst, and sex. A certain part of the hypothalamus of every brain was measured, then LeVay compared hypothalamus size between the two groups of subjects.

As usual, it will help to identify quasi-independent variables, levels, and dependent variables in this study before going further. What were they? It should

---

*LeVay's original research included a third group of subjects: women who were presumed to be heterosexual.

Box 10.1 COMPARING INTERPRETATIONS—HOMOSEXUALITY

In the article he published in *Science,* LeVay interpreted his results carefully. The difference in hypothalamus size between homosexuals and heterosexuals, he said, merely "suggests that sexual orientation has a biological substrate" (1991, p. 1034.) Furthermore, LeVay readily admitted that all 19 of the homosexual men in his study had died of AIDS, whereas only 6 of the 16 heterosexual men had met the same fate. Because of this, LeVay noted that "there is the possibility that the small size of [the hypothalamus] in the homosexual men is the result of AIDS or its complications and is not related to the men's sexual orientation" (p. 1036). Finally, he argued that "Further interpretation of the results of this study must be considered speculative. In particular, the results do not allow one to decide if the size of [the hypothalamus] in an individual is the cause or consequence of that individual's sexual orientation" (p. 1036). What this means, of course, is that instead of being born smaller, the hypothalamus might have *become* smaller during a homosexual's lifetime because of his sexual experiences.

Now, keeping LeVay's own words in mind, let's read what *Woman's Day* had to say about the same results: "He found a distinct difference in the size of the brain area that's believed to control sexual activity, which lends support to the idea that genes influence sexual orientation" (Bartocci, 1992, p. 78). *Newsweek* went even further: "It was perhaps the first direct evidence . . . that whether or not [homosexuals] choose to be different, they are born different" (Gelman, Foote, Barrett, & Talbot, 1992, p. 46). Research with such political and emotional impact as LeVay's deserves more accurate reporting than this.

---

be easy for you to determine that the quasi-independent variable was sexual orientation, that the two levels were "homosexual" and "heterosexual," and that the dependent variable was hypothalamus size. Because subjects were not assigned randomly to the two conditions, we know the research was quasi-experimental. Similarly, because sexual orientation can not be controlled by an experimenter, we know the variable of interest was not truly independent, but only quasi-independent.

What LeVay found was that, on average, the hypothalami of homosexual men were less than half the size of the hypothalami of heterosexual men. When the work was published in a reputable refereed journal, *Science* (1991), LeVay interpreted this result very cautiously. However, popular magazines pounced on the study immediately as a hot cover story that would sell many copies. LeVay was also interviewed on talk shows (e.g., *Donahue*) and became something of an instant celebrity after spending much of his life as a quiet, respected scientist. If you're not sure why you need to know about quasi-experimental research, just take a look at Box 10.1. It compares LeVay's own interpretation of his results with the interpretations that most Americans read in popular magazines and newspapers.

The most important thing to remember about quasi-experimental research is that it must be interpreted with great care. Many uncontrolled differences exist between quasi-experimental conditions, aside from the variable of interest. As LeVay pointed out, subjects in his study varied between conditions not only in sexual orientation but also in cause of death and perhaps in number of sexual partners. Many factors other than strict sexual orientation could have been at least partly responsible for the observed difference in hypothalamus size.

Statistical Analysis: Simple Quasi-Experiments

The statistical analysis that is appropriate for simple quasi-experiments may be selected by using the same flowchart (shown in Table C.1 on page 312) that we have used throughout this course. As always, the first step is to identify the scale of measurement that was used in collecting the data. LeVay used millimeters in measuring the size of the hypothalamus, so his scale of measurement was ratio. Second, we decide how many independent or quasi-independent variables were used in the research. LeVay had only one quasi-independent variable (sexual orientation). When we choose a statistical analysis, the distinction between truly independent and quasi-independent variables does not matter. It becomes crucial during interpretation, however. The third question asks how many levels of each variable were used. We considered only a subset of LeVay's research, in which two levels were compared (homosexual men and heterosexual men). And finally, we must decide whether a between-subjects or a within-subjects design was used. LeVay certainly could not have assigned subjects to both homosexual and heterosexual conditions, so the design was between subjects.

Given the answers to these four questions, refer to Table C.1 and see which statistical analysis would be appropriate for LeVay's research. To compare the hypothalamus sizes of homosexual and heterosexual men, you should have selected the independent *t*-test.

THE COMPLEX QUASI-EXPERIMENT

Simple experiments and quasi-experiments are similar in having only one independent or quasi-independent variable. Likewise, a **complex quasi-experiment** resembles a complex experiment in its use of several independent or quasi-independent variables. A complex quasi-experiment must contain at least two factors of interest, and at least one of those factors must be quasi-independent. The other variables may also be quasi-independent, or they may be truly independent. Either combination is acceptable.

To illustrate the complex quasi-experiment, I have selected a study that investigates gender differences in mathematical ability across three cultures. This study, as you will see, combines two quasi-independent variables to create a factorial design. It is quasi-experimental because subjects could not be assigned randomly to all conditions.

Stereotypes of Female Inferiority in Math

For decades, perhaps centuries, women have suffered from the stereotype of being poor at math. And, in fact, during the 1960s and early 1970s, some simple quasi-experiments showed that males did produce significantly higher scores on math tests than females did (Hyde, Fennema, & Lamon, 1990). Such results were often interpreted as evidence that mathematical superiority is biological in males.

For example, Stafford (1972) believed that a recessive gene carried on the X chromosome is responsible for decreased math ability. This means that females, who by definition have two X chromosomes on each gene, may be poor in math no matter how hard they try to do well. In addition, it means that males, who by definition can have only one X chromosome, might fail in math by laziness or lack of schooling, but never by inborn genetics. In other words, according to Stafford, being a woman is what prevents most females from excelling mathematically; being a man is what allows most males to succeed mathematically.

You know enough about quasi-experiments already to be suspicious of the notion that gender differences are purely biological. Many variables are left uncontrolled in quasi-experimental research, and any of them could be responsible for the difference in math performance that was seen between males and females.

What kinds of nonbiological factors could cause such differences in mathematical ability? Your own personal experiences with math in school may help you to generate some answers to this question. Before reading further, scribble your ideas down in the margin or on a piece of scratch paper.

There are all kinds of cultural and social factors that vary between men and women in addition to their biological differences. For example, your list might include the fact that males usually take more math courses in school than females do. In addition, males receive more encouragement to pursue math from their parents, counselors, and teachers. During the 1960s and 1970s, when the gender difference in math was stronger than it is now, most math teachers were men, and most math textbooks contained examples and applications that were biased toward male occupations such as carpentry and engineering. The point here is not that biological interpretations are wrong and cultural interpretations are correct; rather, it is that quasi-experimental research is not capable of distinguishing conclusively between the two possible interpretations.

Over the years, some of the cultural factors related to gender differences in math have changed. Some math texts now include examples and applications that appeal to both males and females. The ratio of male to female math teachers in grade school is more evenly balanced in the 1990s, and girls are encouraged a little more frequently these days to pursue traditionally masculine interests.

As these aspects of culture have changed, the size of the gender effect in math performance has decreased (Hyde, Fennema, & Lamon, 1990). The old stereotype of female inferiority in math is not entirely false in the 1990s, but it is much more narrow than most people realize. Hyde, Fennema, and Lamon (1990) reviewed 100 studies of gender differences in math, with data from more than three million subjects in total. They found that the difference between male and female math performance is small and nonsignificant in the general population.

When subjects are selected from narrower populations, a different picture emerges. In grade school, males and females perform equally well on tests of mathematical ability. In high school, however, a small but significant difference begins to appear, with males outperforming females. This difference grows larger in size through college and early adulthood (Hyde, Fennema, & Lamon, 1990). The gap tends to be largest among students who achieve the very top scores in mathematics (Benbow & Stanley, 1980).

Because the stereotype of general female inferiority in math is still strong, regardless of the evidence, the topic still receives a great deal of research attention. In an effort to determine the external validity and cultural underpinning of gender differences in math, Lummis and Stevenson (1990) conducted a cross-cultural study that provides a good example of the complex quasi-experiment.

An Example: Cross-Cultural Gender Effects in Math

The research question that Lummis and Stevenson (1990) explored was whether the gender effect in math would occur in Oriental cultures to the same extent that it occurs in American culture. Another way of saying this is that they wanted to find out whether gender interacts with culture when mathematical ability is measured. Because traditional Oriental societies usually favored boys, and because such favoritism often results in enhanced academic opportunities and parental encouragement, Lummis and Stevenson hypothesized that an interaction would occur. Specifically, they predicted that the gender effect in math would be stronger among Japanese and Chinese children than it is among American children.

To test this prediction, Lummis and Stevenson crossed two quasi-independent variables factorially to make a complex quasi-experiment. The variables they explored were gender (male or female) and culture (Chinese, Japanese, or American). Thus, Lummis and Stevenson's quasi-experiment was a 2×3 factorial, with six conditions. Obviously, neither quasi-independent variable allows random assignment of subjects to conditions, so the design meets that vital requirement of quasi-experimental research. The dependent variable that we will concentrate on was mathematical ability. In all, more than 2,000 subjects were tested in this study, but we will focus our attention on the 720 fifth-graders who participated in the mathematical portion of the research.

The battery of mathematics tests given to each child in the study contained nine subsections. Each subsection was devoted to a different aspect of the general topic that we call "mathematics," including word problems, mathematical computation, ability to read graphs, estimation, and speeded addition, just to name a few. One of the most interesting results in this study concerned mathematical word problems, so we will focus on that subsection of the dependent variable.

As in a factorial experiment, cell means are needed before we can eyeball the data, perform statistical analyses, and interpret the results. The cell means for word problem performance among boys and girls of the United States, Taiwan, and Japan, are presented in Table 10.1. As usual, higher numbers reflect better performance.

Several interesting patterns appear in Table 10.1, if you know how to find them. In general, follow the same procedure that I suggested in Chapter 9. First, plot the six cell means on a graph and look for an interaction between gender and culture. Next, calculate marginal means and assess the possibility that a main effect of either gender or culture has occurred. Go ahead, give it a try on your own.

Table 10.1 CELL MEANS SHOWING SCORES
FOR SOLVING MATH WORD PROBLEMS

		Culture		
		American	Chinese	Japanese
Gender	Male	13.1	18.2	19.0
	Female	12.4	16.1	18.1

From "Gender Differences in Beliefs and Achievement: A Cross-Cultural Study" by M. Lummis and H. W. Stevenson, 1990, *Developmental Psychology*, 26(2), pp. 254–263. Copyright 1990 by American Psychological Association, Inc. Adapted by permission.

Plotting the cell means should produce a graph similar to the one shown in Figure 10.1. Because both lines are almost perfectly parallel to each other, I would guess that Lummis and Stevenson (1990) did not obtain an interaction between gender and culture. (We'll check that guess in a later section of this chapter.) It looks like the gender effect occurred in each culture to about the same extent and in the same direction: Males were better at word problems than females were in American, Chinese, and Japanese cultures.

Now, let's consider the main effects. The marginal means for the main effect of gender are 16.77 points (for males) and 15.53 points (for females). You should have obtained the same numbers as I did. Comparing the two numbers shows that there is a difference between them, so a main effect of gender is possible. Try to describe this main effect in plain English. I'd say that fifth-grade boys achieved higher scores than girls did in solving mathematical word problems.

The marginal means for the main effect of culture were 12.75 points (for Americans), 17.15 points (for Chinese), and 18.55 points (for Japanese). These three numbers also reflect a chance of significant differences, so we know that a main effect of culture is also possible. How would you describe it? It looks to me like Chinese and Japanese children perform better on word problems than do American children, regardless of their gender.

Statistical Analysis: Complex Quasi-Experiments

To determine whether the interaction or main effects were significant, Lummis and Stevenson (1990) performed a two-way between-subjects ANOVA. As with simple quasi-experiments, statistical tests are chosen on the basis of scale of measurement, number of quasi-independent variables, and number of levels. Table C.1 (on page 312) will guide you to the correct test when you conduct or evaluate quasi-experiments yourself.

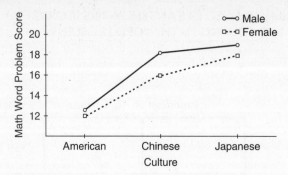

Figure 10.1
Effects of Gender and Culture on Math Word Problem Scores
Source: From Lummis and Stevenson, 1990.

After performing the two-way ANOVA, Lummis and Stevenson found that the interaction between gender and culture was not significant, as we suspected. However, the main effects of gender and culture were significant for performance on word problems. Because it contained more than two levels, the main effect of culture was analyzed further using post-hoc tests to determine the exact location of significant differences. These post-hoc tests showed significant differences in word problem ability among all three cultures: Japanese children were significantly better at solving math word problems than were American or Chinese children, and Chinese children were significantly better at solving math word problems than were American children.

Incidentally, analyses of other aspects of the study showed that boys and girls from all three cultures did not differ significantly in their performance on most subsections of the mathematics battery. Word problems were one of the only math subtests to produce a significant gender difference. Despite evidence that most math tests yield no gender effect, the old stereotype that females are inferior in general mathematical ability was alive and well in all three cultures: Most first-grade children and their mothers in Japan, Taiwan, and America said they believed that boys were better at math than girls.

Interpreting Results of the Complex Quasi-Experiment

The design and statistical analysis of the complex quasi-experiment should remind you of an experimental factorial design up to this point. In general, design and analysis are not altered much by the distinction between a truly independent variable and a quasi-independent variable. The most important difference between the two types of designs appears when we begin to interpret significant effects.

At the risk of being repetitive, let me say once again that every quasi-independent variable is linked to many confounding variables. For that reason, quasi-experimental research is never conclusive in determining cause. Gender, for example, is confounded with all kinds of factors: Genes, hormones, stereotypes, upbringing, schooling, encouragement, occupation, income, and expectations are only a few possibilities. Matching is often used to reduce the number of confounding variables in quasi-experimental research. For example, subjects in a gender study could be matched across conditions for educational level or income. Other differences would remain uncontrolled, however. Any differences in results such as math scores, then, could be caused by any or all of the remaining confounding variables.

With this caution in mind, interpreting a quasi-experiment becomes more an exercise in description than in explanation. The Lummis and Stevenson results can be described fairly easily. There were no differences between American, Chinese, and Japanese boys and girls in most tests of mathematical ability. However, in all three cultures, boys were better than girls at solving math word problems. Furthermore, Chinese and Japanese children of both sexes were superior to American children in their math performance.

Explaining these results is a much more difficult matter. Let's consider just one aspect of the main effect of culture as an example. This result showed that American children received low math scores in relation to their Chinese counterparts. Why might this be so? A few people might argue that inherent racial differences between Orientals and Caucasians are the underlying cause of this main effect. Of course, to entertain this interpretation at all, we would have to show that most of the American children in this study were Caucasian. Others would say that the cultural emphasis on education in Chinese society causes such differences to occur. Several additional interpretations are also possible.

From Lummis and Stevenson's quasi-experiment alone, we cannot determine which of these two opposing interpretations is correct. We can, however, use knowledge gathered in other scientific studies, bringing it to bear on the question at hand. Most psychologists agree, for example, that purely biological differences between races are negligible, especially for attributes like intelligence. This does not fit with the biological interpretation of math performance.

On the other hand, we also know that educational differences between Oriental and American cultures are huge, a fact that favors the cultural interpretation. For example, Stevenson (1984) found that Chinese first-graders attend school 240 days per year, whereas their American counterparts attend only 178 days per year. The mothers of Chinese first-graders estimate that their children spend an average of 493 minutes per week doing homework, while American first-graders spend an average of 77 minutes per week doing homework. By considering related results like these, we can develop tentative conclusions that are likely, but not certain, to be correct.

Math and Gender in the 1990s

The stereotype of female inferiority in math is still with us today, even though the size of the actual effect has dropped considerably over the years. Causes of the effect are still debated heatedly among scholars. Some of them, like Stafford did back in 1972, still argue that females are innately inferior to males when it comes to math (e.g., Benbow, 1988; Levin, 1987). Although many psychologists disagree with this biological interpretation, Box 10.2 shows how popular it seems to be among magazine writers.

When we combine related facts with quasi-experimental evidence, the cultural interpretation of math ability seems fairly strong:

1. In studies done during the 1980s, both male and female students stated explicitly that they believe math skills are more important for men than for women (Leder, 1990).
2. Mothers believe that their sons are better at mathematics than their daughters, despite conflicting evidence from test scores and school grades (Lummis & Stevenson, 1990).
3. In the United States, United Kingdom, and Australia, significantly fewer females than males enroll in trigonometry, precalculus, and calculus courses (Leder, 1990).
4. In the classroom, males usually receive more praise, less criticism, more interaction, and more help from their teachers than females do (Fennema, 1990). Sadly enough, these results are not limited to the mathematics classroom but seem to extend throughout most of the American educational system.
5. Some teachers still perpetuate the old math stereotype in their classrooms. For example, Koehler (1990) tells the anecdote of a high school algebra teacher in the late 1980s who "chastised the boys in the class for 'letting' a *girl* get the highest grade on an exam." (p. 129).
6. Teachers tend to attribute success in math to different causes, depending on gender. Most math teachers believe that males who succeed in math do so by ability, whereas females who succeed in math do so by effort. In addition, when males fail in math, their teachers tend to blame themselves for not providing enough help (Leder & Fennema, 1990).

Given these obstacles, it is remarkable that females manage so often to perform as well as males on tests of mathematical ability. After all, it seems that an inherent biological inferiority would be fueled by these cultural factors to the point that grown women would be nearly incapable of simple addition! Instead, we find that the gender effect has diminished over the years as our social climate has changed, and that females in the general population today do as well as their male counterparts on math tests. To me, after studying the literature on gender effects, the combined results favor a cultural interpretation. However, you critical readers will note that the results I have presented do not rule out a biological interpretation. You now have the tools to find, read, and evaluate the literature, then come to your own conclusions.

THE INTERRUPTED TIME SERIES DESIGN

A third type of quasi-experimental design is used to study the effects of uncontrolled events over a period of time. Such events might include natural disasters

Box 10.2 COMPARING INTERPRETATIONS—MATH AND GENDER

Benbow and Stanley have conducted several studies of math ability among unusually bright junior high and high school students (e.g., Benbow & Stanley, 1980, 1983; Benbow, 1988; Lubinski & Benbow, 1992). Consistently, they find that in this special population, boys tend to outperform girls by a large and statistically significant margin. Although Benbow and Stanley are among the strongest scientific proponents of the idea that gender differences may be biological, they have been cautious in interpreting results from quasi-experimental research.

For example, Benbow and Stanley concluded one of their most widely publicized journal articles with the following statement:

> We favor the hypothesis that sex differences in achievement in and attitude toward mathematics result from superior male mathematical ability. . . . This male superiority is probably an expression of a combination of both endogenous and exogenous* variables. We recognize, however, that our data are consistent with numerous alternative hypotheses. (Benbow & Stanley, 1980, p. 1264)

Furthermore, these researchers admitted openly that "only selected mathematically able, highly motivated students were tested" (p. 1264) and that "it is hard to dissect out the influences of societal expectations and attitudes on mathematical reasoning ability" (p. 1264).

Now, let's see how the popular press presented Benbow and Stanley's research to an unsuspecting American public. Here's what we were told about the study by *Time* magazine: "According to its authors, Doctoral Candidate Camilla Persson Benbow and Psychologist Julian C. Stanley of Johns Hopkins University, males inherently have more mathematical ability than females" ("The Gender", 1980, p. 57).

Newsweek quoted the scientists directly, a process that should have been pretty safe. "The authors' conclusion: 'Sex differences in achievement in and attitude toward mathematics result from superior male mathematical ability'" (Williams, 1980, p. 73). Sounds pretty definite, doesn't it? Except, of course, that Benbow and Stanley prefaced that sentence with five crucial words that *Newsweek* chose to ignore: "We favor the hypothesis that. . . " (Benbow & Stanley, 1980, p. 1264). *Newsweek's* quote doesn't sound like a hypothesis at all.

A glance through some publications that are popular among American educators is also revealing. *The Chronicle of Higher Education* told college professors what to expect from their students: "Are boys born superior to girls in mathematical ability? The answer is probably Yes, say Camilla Persson Benbow and Julian C. Stanley" ("Male", 1980, p. 14).

And, finally, let's look at *Education USA*, a periodical published for teachers in elementary and secondary schools around the nation. The first sentence of their article proclaimed that "Boys are inherently better at math than girls, according to an eight-year study of 10,000 gifted students" ("Boys", 1980, p. 122). This kind of rampant misinterpretation, especially when directed toward the very people who teach math to young boys and girls, is inexcusable.

---

*"Endogenous" means having an internal origin and refers to biological causes. "Exogenous" means having an external origin and refers to environmental causes.

like floods or fires, new laws that require citizens to change some aspect of their behavior, or even programs designed to educate people about a dangerous behavior like drinking and driving. The clue that will allow you to identify an **interrupted time series design** is that data are collected over a long period of time, with some important event interrupting that time period. The purpose of the interrupted time series design is to see whether that important event is linked to changes in people's behavior. As with other types of quasi-experimental research, the interrupted time series design does not allow us to determine conclusively whether the event caused the change.

An Example: Child Car Seat Laws

Guerin and MacKinnon (1985) conducted an interrupted time series study that tested the effectiveness of a new law that was enacted in the state of California in 1983. This law required children under the age of 4 years to be secured in car seats whenever they were taken somewhere by car. The purpose of the law was to reduce the number of children who were injured in car accidents. To find out whether the law really served that purpose, Guerin and MacKinnon compared the number of injured children before the law went into effect with the number of injured children after the law went into effect.

Why did Guerin and MacKinnon have to resort to quasi-experimental research to find out whether the law was worthwhile? Try to answer this question yourself before reading further. The reason is that it would have been extremely unethical for the researchers to place children in situations that would endanger their lives. We certainly couldn't take a random sample of children, place only half of them in protective car seats, and then take them all out joy-riding on the freeway to get into a bad accident where the toddlers might be hurt or killed! In addition, Guerin and MacKinnon had no say in whether or when the child seat law would go into effect. That decision was made partly by the voters of California and partly by their legislature. The researchers did not have control of the law, and they did not have control of which children were going to be placed in car seats or involved in accidents.

As I mentioned earlier, in the interrupted time series design, scientists track the incidence of some behavior or occurrence over a long period. At some point, that period is interrupted by an event that the researchers believe might cause some change in the observed behavior. To evaluate the car seat law, Guerin and MacKinnon recorded the number of children injured during each month from January 1979 through December 1983. Then, they compared the number of injuries that occurred before January 1983 (when the law went into effect) with the number that occurred after January 1983. This comparison was made for children 0 to 3 years of age, who had to be placed in car seats according to the law, and for children 4 to 7 years of age, who were unaffected by the law.

Figure 10.2 shows the standard graph of results that usually accompanies an interrupted time series design. You can see that injuries did appear to be reduced for 0- to 3-year-old children after the car seat law went into effect at the beginning of 1983.

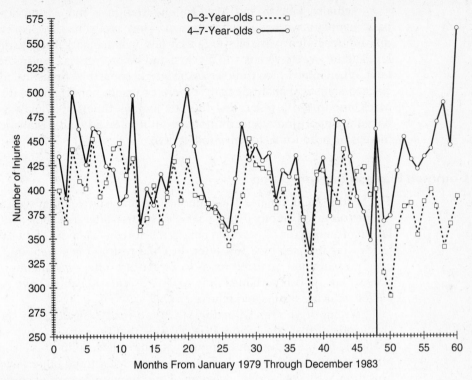

Figure 10.2

Data From an Interrupted Time Series Design
Source: From Guerin and MacKinnon, 1985.

Statistical Analysis: Interrupted Time Series Designs

The data from interrupted time series designs can be analyzed in a number of ways, depending on the precise research question that is being asked. For the most general question (e.g., does behavior change after an event?), the design can be visualized as having two levels of only one quasi-independent variable. For example, we could imagine a simplified version of Guerin and MacKinnon's study, in which only the injuries of 0- to 3-year olds were compared before and after the law went into effect. In this case, the quasi-independent variable would be instatement of the 1983 California car seat law, and the two groups to be compared could be defined as "before the law" and "after the law." Injuries have an absolute zero point and equal numerical intervals, so we would categorize the scale of measurement as ratio.

Using this information, we would determine from Table C.1 (on page 312) that the *t*-test is an appropriate statistical test for this simplified version of Guerin and MacKinnon's research question. The *t*-test would need to take into account all data before the interruption and compare them to all data after the interruption. As Campbell and Stanley (1966) point out, there are instances in which such an analysis by simple *t*-test would be incorrect for even the most basic interrupted time series design, but in this case it would be adequate.

Actually, Guerin and MacKinnon's design is more complicated than the basic template we have just imagined. They really had the equivalent of two quasi-independent variables (age and law instatement). Each variable had two levels (0 to 3 years versus 4 to 7 years, and before versus after instatement of the law). When interrupted time series designs become this sophisticated, we use specialized statistical analyses that you are probably not familiar with. Guerin and MacKinnon used a test called the Box-Jenkins time series analysis. You might have the opportunity to learn more about it in an advanced statistics course, but there is no need for us to delve into it here.

Common Flaws in Interpretation

The results of Guerin and MacKinnon's research showed that significantly fewer injuries occurred among 0- to 3-year-old children after instatement of the restraint law than among 0- to 3-year-old children before instatement of the law. In fact, injuries were reduced by 8.36% after the child restraint law went into effect. However, no reduction occurred for 4- to 7-year-olds after enactment of the law. The car seat law, which pertained only to 0- to 3-year-olds, must have been responsible for reducing deaths and injuries, right?

Wrong. If you're evaluating what you read critically, you should be very suspicious of that conclusion. It is possible that the car seat law was indeed responsible for the reduction in injuries among children, but it is also possible that other factors played a role. Let's think about what these other factors might be. This time, we'll concentrate on some of the common sources of confounds, which were presented in Chapter 8.

Instrumentation. One potential problem is instrumentation. You may remember that instrumentation refers to the possibility that some decay in the measurement of behavior is responsible for the obtained results. The measurement used in Guerin and MacKinnon's quasi-experiment was based on police reports of car accidents involving children. After the law went into effect in 1983, parents who did not place their children in car seats were fined.

What does this mean? Think about it. Before 1983, there was no penalty for parents who reported that their children had been injured in an accident. However, after January of 1983, parents who didn't use car seats might have been reluctant to report minor accidents in which their children were injured slightly. After all, they had broken the law by not confining the child to a car seat, and human nature prevents most of us from calling the police to volunteer information for which we will be penalized. Thus, the number of injured children might have decreased after January 1983 simply because fewer parents were willing to report the accidents.

Guerin and MacKinnon attempted to rule out this explanation by comparing the number of deaths among children who had been in car accidents before or after instatement of the law. Deaths must be reported one way or another, and very few bereaved parents will worry about a fine when their beloved child has died. Therefore, although injury reports might have decreased because of the fine that parents had to pay, death reports would not have been affected. In other words, deaths are not subject to the same problem of instrumentation that occurs when only injuries are recorded. Thus, if the law is really effective, deaths should also have been reduced after January 1983.

Upon testing this prediction, Guerin and MacKinnon found that children's deaths were not reduced significantly after enactment of the law. They argue that the small number of automobile deaths among young children (about four per month) prevented detection of the effect. Whether this argument is true or not, the possibility of a confound by instrumentation is still open for the injury data.

History. Another problem of interpretation might show up in potential history effects. We have been assuming that only one change occurred in 1983 that was relevant to the safety of children in cars. But there is plenty of reason to believe that this assumption is wrong. Few states invoke new laws without drawing attention first to some social problem that the law is intended to correct. In other words, it is likely that television shows and popular articles were delivered to Californians before 1983, informing them of the large numbers of toddlers who were hurt each month in traffic accidents.

Now, if you were a caring, responsible parent, would you wait for a law to be instated before taking charge of the children in your car? Probably not. No, as soon as you heard of the problem and realized that car seats could save the life of your child, you would probably place the child in a car seat long before the law required you to do so. This means that the media attention, not the state law, could have been responsible for the change in parental behavior.

How would a clever researcher rule out this alternate explanation? If this was your study, what would you do? Well, one solution would be to find some other state in which media attention to the car seat issue occurred, but no law was in effect. Guerin and MacKinnon chose the state of Texas because it is about the same size as California. If it was the law, and not the media attention, that caused the change in car seat behavior, then no significant reduction in injuries to children should have occurred in Texas after 1983. The results showed exactly that, suggesting that the California car seat law did contribute to reduced deaths and injuries.

Nonequivalent Control Groups

The use of Texas and older children as comparison conditions in this interrupted time series design are examples of **nonequivalent control groups.** Although the two states are similar in size, a lot of Texans will tell you that Texas is not completely equivalent to California, and most Californians will agree! Likewise, 0- to 3-year old children are not equivalent to 4- to 7-year-old children—along with the quasi-independent variable of age, they also differ in size, education, use of language, ability to understand instructions that might prevent minor injuries, and physical ability to withstand major impacts.

If it is possible to do so, we use an equivalent control group for comparison. In quasi-experimental research, however, this is almost never possible. In such cases, using a nonequivalent control group is better than using no control group at all. In the car seat example, the comparisons between states and between ages do not rule out every possible alternate explanation, but they do help to weaken some explanations.

ADVANTAGES AND DISADVANTAGES OF QUASI-EXPERIMENTAL DESIGNS

We have now considered three basic types of quasi-experimental research, including simple and complex quasi-experiments and interrupted time series designs. The most important general principle to remember about quasi-experimental designs is that they are never as conclusive as a true experiment. Quasi-experimental subject groups vary in systematic ways that the researcher can not possibly control. Because of this systematic and uncontrolled variation, the causes of any obtained behavior can not be determined with certainty. Another way of saying this is that every quasi-independent variable is by nature confounded with other factors. We can not know which of those factors actually caused a certain behavior to occur.

Because quasi-experimental research necessarily produces weak conclusions, it is especially important to be wary of it. Television news reporters and magazine writers often fail to specify whether the results of a study came from an experiment or a quasi-experiment. Sadly enough, many of them do not know the difference. However, you do, so whenever you see that the effects of subject variables, natural disasters, or unethical manipulations have been investigated in an "experiment," you will know that it was probably a quasi-experiment. If so, the published conclusions may be much weaker than your newspaper, magazine, talk show host, or friendly newscaster implies.

Given the weakness of their conclusions, it is ironic that quasi-experiments are often used to explore the very behaviors that are most critical to society. Violent crime, drug abuse, gang warfare, alcoholism, and racism are all good examples. They are among the most pressing problems in America today, yet we are forced to investigate them with a relatively weak type of design. Unfortunately, the alternatives are worse: Nonexperimental research will provide weaker conclusions still, and the only other choice is not to study these important behaviors scientifically at all.

SUMMARY OF MAIN POINTS

- Quasi-experimental research assesses the effects of quasi-independent variables, which cannot truly be manipulated, on dependent variables.

- Because subjects are not assigned randomly to conditions in quasi-experimental research, inherent differences between subject groups are automatically confounded with the factor of interest. Therefore, we cannot know whether an effect was caused by the factor of interest or by one of the many confounding variables.

- Quasi-experimental research is used to test the effects of subject variables, natural disasters, and manipulations that would otherwise be unethical.

- The simple quasi-experiment contains one quasi-independent variable, and subjects are not assigned randomly to conditions.

- The complex quasi-experiment contains at least one quasi-independent variable, plus at least one other variable that is either quasi-independent or truly independent. Subjects are not assigned randomly to all conditions.

- The interrupted time series design is used when we want to compare behavior before and after a certain event occurred. The nonequivalent control group is a useful addition to interrupted time series designs.

- The results of quasi-experimental research must be interpreted with care. Confounding variables are almost always linked to quasi-independent variables, so we cannot know for sure which factors are causing the behavior we have observed.

CHAPTER EXERCISES

1. Use your own words to define these key terms:
   quasi-experiment   complex quasi-experiment
   subject variables   interrupted time series design
   simple quasi-experiment   nonequivalent control group

2. When discussing Lummis and Stevenson's (1990) study of gender and culture, I used the main effect of culture for a sample interpretation. Re-read my description of the study carefully (on pages 234–237), then make a list of possible interpretations of the nonsignificant interaction between gender and culture. In other words, why did the gender effect in mathematics occur to similar extents in all three cultures? Be sure to identify alternate interpretations.

3. I'll bet you're familiar with the Muller-Lyer illusion pictured below, even if you didn't know its name. Many people perceive the line on the left as being longer than the one on the right, even though both lines are actually identical in length. Some psychologists (e.g., Gregory, 1977) have theorized that this illusion is caused by our lifelong experience perceiving angles and corners. To test

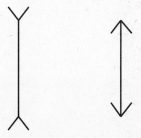

that theory, Pederson and Wheeler (1983) measured the degree to which the Muller-Lyer illusion occurred in two groups of subjects. One group of subjects were Navajos who had lived in traditional Navajo houses that are round. The other subjects were Navajos who had lived in rectangular houses, where they perceived corners and angles frequently. The results showed that the people who had lived in angular houses reported seeing the illusion to a significantly greater extent than did people who had lived in round houses.

` What type of research and which specific design does this study represent? What variables and levels were used? What was the dependent variable? Which statistical test is appropriate for this design, and why?

4. In the last section of this chapter, I said that "violent crime, drug abuse, gang warfare, alcoholism, and racism are all good examples" of research that is critical to society but cannot be explored through experimental research. Select one of these examples and design a hypothetical quasi-experimental study related to it. Be specific in describing your proposal.

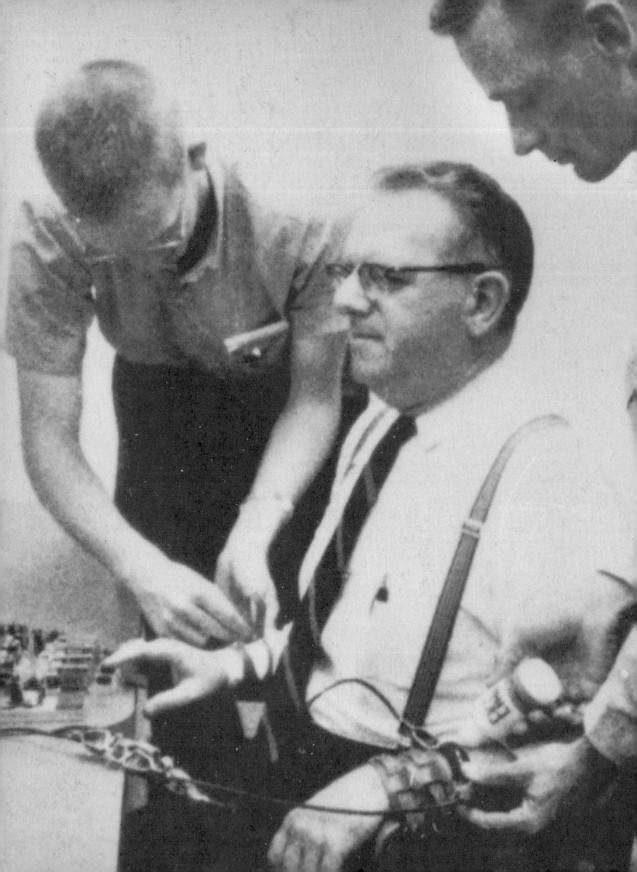

11

Ethics in Scientific Research

Wiring the learner in Milgram's obedience studies, c. 1965.

Sometimes researchers dwell so deeply on design issues like stimulus matching and interrater reliability that we forget to step back and view the more general aspects of our work. We tend to remain stooped over the microscope, so to speak, without taking a broad look at the panoramic movie screen once in a while. Ethics is probably the most important aspect of scientific research that appears in that larger picture. Every scientist, whether professional or amateur, must accept the responsibility of research and protect the rights of human and animal subjects.

SCIENTIFIC RESPONSIBILITY

Research scientists have tremendous power over their subjects. Many human subjects, especially those used in psychological research, are young college students who may be uncertain of their own rights and impressed by the vision of A Real Scientist (white lab coat and all). Many of these subjects are willing to try nearly anything that the researcher suggests, even if it seems unhealthy or immoral. If you doubt that this is true, read on: You may find Milgram's obedience experiments very interesting.

Along with the power that a researcher wields comes the responsibility to protect subjects from potential danger. This responsibility becomes especially important when the subjects are children or animals, who may not be able to express their concerns or leave the experimental laboratory. But the responsibility should never be disregarded with adult human subjects, either. Adults may be capable of making intelligent, healthy decisions concerning risk, but only if they are aware of the details of a research plan. Often, especially in psychological science, the details of a research program are kept secret from subjects who agree to participate.

In general, the ethics of subject treatment in most scientific research is assessed by considering a trade-off: *Is the potential benefit to society strong enough to warrant the potential risk to an individual?* Studies that do have the capacity to produce results with societal importance are sometimes performed at mild risk to the subjects participating in them. On the other hand, studies that are unlikely to benefit society substantially are usually forbidden unless the risk to individual subjects approaches zero.

Consider the word "potential" in my statement of the ethical trade-off, though. How do we know for sure that any study will produce a benefit to society? Simply stated, we don't know. One highly promising study may in the end produce nothing of use to society. Another, perhaps one that was considered trivial, may have consequences far more powerful than were ever imagined. Furthermore, because scientific research is a journey into the unknown, we can't be sure of the potential risks to subjects. Because of such uncertainty, guidelines for ethical research have been developed.

A BRIEF HISTORY OF ETHICS IN TESTING HUMAN SUBJECTS

Both human and animal subjects are used in psychological research, as you know. We'll consider the ethical guidelines for each of these two sets of subjects. Let's begin with a brief history of ethical concerns in testing human subjects.

The Nuremberg Code

The roots of today's ethical guidelines are found in the **Nuremberg code.** This code is a list of 10 principles that were developed in 1948, when the Nazi war crime trials were conducted at the end of World War II. These war crimes involved many horrifying atrocities, which led to the deaths of more than six million innocent men, women, and children. Although most of the tortured captives were Jews, the Nazis also "exterminated" Communists, Polish intellectuals, Gypsies, homosexuals, alcoholics, prostitutes, drug addicts, and people who were mentally retarded, physically handicapped, or emotionally disturbed (Lerner, 1992; Proctor, 1988).

Let me give you a brief idea of the sorts of abuse that occurred during the Nazi war crimes in the name of "research." The innocent captives were sterilized surgically without anesthesia, were tortured slowly to see how long they would survive, were frozen to death gradually in large tanks of ice water, and had their bones broken repeatedly so that medical doctors could learn more about the healing process. Many others were deliberately infected with diseases such as typhus, epidemic jaundice, and malaria (Katz, 1972).

The Tuskegee Experiment

Although they may have conducted the most horrifying modern-day "experiments," the Nazis weren't the only people performing unethical studies. Beginning in 1932, right here in the United States, a highly unethical program of research known as the **Tuskegee experiment** was continued for a period of 40 years (J. H. Jones, 1981). The study was conducted by the United States Public Health Service in an effort to explore the most serious effects of syphilis. To determine the disease's long-term effects, researchers denied treatment to about 400 black subjects who were known to have syphilis. A control group of about 200 healthy black men was also used in the study. Most of the subjects were poor, illiterate residents of Tuskegee, Alabama.

Subjects were enticed to participate in the Tuskegee experiment by offers of free meals, free physical examinations, free rides to town, and money for their burial. However, they were never told that they were not being treated for the disease, which many of them did not realize they had. Of course, some of the subjects suspected wrongdoing and went to other doctors in the area for advice. Those subjects who accepted any form of treatment were dropped from the study (thereby losing their free meals and other benefits). Worse yet, medical doctors in the Tuskegee area were told explicitly by officials of the United States Public

Figure 11.1
The Tuskegee Experiment
Source: Reprinted with permission from *The Atlanta Journal* and *The Atlanta Constitution.*

Health Service not to treat these patients for syphilis. Figure 11.1 provides a sad picture of the subjects' situation.

When the Tuskegee experiment began in 1932, cures for syphilis were available but not trustworthy. However, by the 1940s, penicillin was known to be a safe and effective treatment. Nevertheless, the research continued until 1972, while subjects in the study developed the symptoms of late-stage syphilis: heart palpitations, tumors, bone deterioration, paralysis, blindness, deafness, and slow destruction of the brain. To make matters worse, the Tuskegee experiment was known and accepted within the American medical community, through reports published in medical journals and presentations given at professional conferences. In his enlightening book on the topic, J. H. Jones (1981) points out that the 40 years of experimentation provided little new knowledge even though 400 men were sacrificed for it. The cause, development, symptoms, and complications of untreated syphilis were all known before 1932.

The Tuskegee experiment began before the Nuremberg code was in place, but continued long after it had been developed. The code provided scientists with clear guidelines for conducting ethical research, emphasizing subjects' voluntary consent based on a clear understanding of the procedures and risks of the research to be done. As we have seen by the continuation of the Tuskegee experiment for 24 years after the Nuremberg code was implemented in 1948, it was not enforced adequately. Other unethical studies also slipped past, such as the one in 1963 in which 22 American patients were injected with live cancer cells. This procedure was carried out despite the Nuremberg code, without the patients' knowledge, and with full approval of the hospital's director of medicine (Katz, 1972).

In addition to its lack of enforcement, the Nuremberg code was limited to medical research. But by the late 1940s, members of the American Psychological Association (APA) were claiming that ethics were also an important issue in psychological studies. After all, physical harm is not the only dangerous consequence of research; a subject might also be damaged by mental or emotional conflict. For this reason, the APA published its first set of ethical guidelines for human subjects in 1953. Like the Nuremberg code, it also required voluntary consent based on knowledge of research procedures and risks.

Milgram's Obedience Experiments

Ten years after those APA guidelines were first published, a series of experiments by Milgram (1963) stirred up the ethical controversy once again. Milgram wanted to know just how far people would go in obeying the instructions of authority figures. His research developed partly out of concern for the Nazi holocaust during World War II: Why did normal Germans obey military authority to the degree that they would torture innocent civilians to death? Could the same thing happen elsewhere?

To answer these research questions, Milgram set up a situation in which subjects were asked to deliver electric shocks to other people. In fact, no electric shocks were actually given, but the subjects didn't know that. Let's walk through the experiment step by step, as a subject would have.

You arrive at the appointed time and are met by an important-looking man who ushers you into an experimental laboratory. He explains, as you listen attentively, that the experiment investigates the effects of punishment on the human learning process. Pairs of subjects are arranged, so that you will be a teacher and your partner (another subject whom you have just met) will be a learner. The learner's job is to memorize a list of word pairs (like *cat-tree*) that you read aloud. Later, when you present the first word ("cat") as a cue, the learner selects the correct response ("tree") from four choices.

Well, this seems simple enough, right? However, the researcher then tells you that your job as teacher will include punishing the learner by electric shock whenever an error is made. Your eyes grow wide as you question the researcher about this. "Although the shocks can be extremely painful," he says, "they cause no permanent tissue damage."

The experiment begins and, sure enough, the learner makes a few mistakes. Each time, you deliver a shock, beginning with 15 volts and increasing the level by 15 added volts each time, as you've been told to do. As the study proceeds, you find the learner continuing to make mistakes. Although you hesitate, the researcher tells you it is necessary to increase the shock voltage further in order to continue the learning experiment. The voltage meter is labeled clearly; you scan from left to right, and as the voltage increases, you read labels beginning with "slight shock" and progressing finally to "Danger: Severe Shock."

As the experiment goes on, the researcher continues urging you to increase the voltage. You protest several times: "Isn't this dangerous? Am I hurting the learner?" But the authoritative researcher is calm: "The experiment requires that you continue," he says.

As the voltage increases beyond average levels, the learner begins to yelp audibly whenever you deliver a shock. Now you are truly worried; sweat is getting in your eyes and your hands tremble as you pull the shock switch. As the voltage nears the "Danger" zone, the learner's yelps turn into screams and pleas: "OW! Please stop!" Meanwhile, the experimenter reminds you, "You have no other choice, you *must* go on."

OK, you get the idea. Now here's the big question: How strong a shock would subjects deliver before absolutely refusing to go on? What results would you expect? If you really had been a subject, how far up the scale would you have gone before refusing to follow the researcher's instructions? Do you suppose that any subjects actually delivered the strongest shock possible, the one up in the "Danger" zone, while the learner was screaming?

The answer is that nearly two thirds (65%) of Milgram's subjects did deliver the maximum shock, labeled at 450 volts, even when learners screamed in pain. In fact, no one was physically harmed in this experiment: The learners were **confederates** (people who work for the experimenter to deceive subjects), and they didn't really experience any shocks. However, the crucial fact is that Milgram's subjects did not know this! They believed that the learners really received each electric shock they administered, yet the majority of them continued to deliver dangerous shocks despite the learners' cries.

CURRENT GUIDELINES FOR TESTING HUMAN SUBJECTS

Milgram's obedience studies would not be allowed today. Even though the subjects were debriefed after participating in the experiment, Milgram was scolded by his colleagues (e.g., Baumrind, 1964) for putting subjects through undue psychological stress, for teaching them things about themselves that they may have preferred not to know, and for failing to stop the experiment when subjects displayed extreme concern. Milgram (1964) argued that he did not deserve such harsh criticism, providing the results of a post-experimental survey in which 84% of his subjects said they were glad that they had participated. In general, though, the study pointed out a fundamental problem: On the one hand, Milgram's results were extremely valuable to society; on the other hand, obtaining those results caused individuals emotional pain.

Today, guidelines for psychological research are enforced by professional organizations and the federal government. The APA has strengthened its ethical principles for research several times since 1953, culminating in the most recent (1992) version. In addition, the United States government developed a set of Federal Protection Regulations in 1982, which are enforced by Institutional Review Boards (IRBs) that oversee all federally funded research involving human subjects. Any institution in America that receives government funding for research must comply with the Federal Protection Regulations.

The most recent professional guidelines for testing human subjects are published in the APA's (1992) booklet entitled *Ethical principles of psychologists and code of conduct*. A similar code of principles is published by the federal government's Department of Health and Human Services (HHS). Although the two codes are too lengthy to be reprinted here, we will consider the major ethical constraints set forth by both the APA and the HHS. These policies are followed regularly by psychological scientists.

Designing an Ethical Study

Before testing any human subjects in studies that present a risk, researchers must submit their plans to the IRB associated with their college or university. The IRB consists of several people who have no personal interest in the research being conducted, so that they can view the proposal with an unbiased eye. It is their task to ensure that researchers follow the HHS regulations. After considering the research proposal carefully, they will either approve or deny it. Only after approval has been given may the researcher begin testing subjects.

The researcher always holds ultimate responsibility for potential harm to subjects. This means that you are fully liable for the effects of your research, even if other people (like research assistants) conducted the actual testing. Assistants are also liable for harmful effects of research, even if they did not design the study and were merely following orders in subject testing. Harmful effects can include obvious examples like physical pain or extreme stress, but they can also include embarrassment or breach of privacy. At a bare minimum, researchers who test human subjects must protect those subjects against risks by obtaining informed consent, allowing subjects to withdraw from the research at any time without penalty, keeping individual data confidential, and debriefing all subjects. Let's consider each of these procedures in turn.

Obtaining Informed Consent. Before participating in any study that presents a degree of risk, each subject must sign a consent form that describes the nature of the research being conducted. On the surface, **informed consent** is a simple matter of explaining the basic research plan to subjects, then asking them to sign a standard form.

The idea of informed consent seems simple, but the internal validity of a research study may be weakened by demand characteristics if subjects know too much about the experimenter's plans. To avoid this problem, consent forms are usually written in a manner similar to walking a tightrope: Subjects are given just enough, but not too much, information about the study in which they are participating. APA guidelines require psychologists to explain any aspect of a study that could alter a subject's desire to participate. We must also answer honestly any questions the subjects ask about the research. Doing this will ensure that you have met the ethical principles of informed consent, but it may harm the internal validity of your carefully planned design.

Occasionally, an important study is done in which it is impossible to follow the guidelines of fully informed consent without destroying internal validity. In such cases, where subject deception is needed, special guidelines must be followed. These guidelines are specified in the APA's (1992) booklet of ethical principles.

Allowing Subjects to Withdraw. Even after subjects have signed a consent form and started to participate in a research study, they may refuse to continue at any time. In other words, subjects have the right to change their minds and leave the laboratory freely, without being pestered by the researcher to stay.

Keeping Data Confidential. Although the overall results of a study may be published at any time, individual scores must remain confidential. For example, it is fine to report that the mean IQ of subjects in a particular condition was 95, but it is unethical to report that the IQ of the subject named Mary Smith was 95. This is personal information that may be known to you and the subject, but to no one else.

To maintain confidentiality, most researchers devise a numbering system so that each score corresponds to a subject number rather than a name. This way, all individual data are preserved for later use, but names are not associated with them. Such subject numbering systems also have the advantage of allowing us to see condition categories at a glance: All subjects in Condition 1, for example, might be assigned a number beginning with a 1 (e.g., 1001, 1002, 1003), whereas subjects in Condition 2 might be assigned a number beginning with a 2 (e.g., 2004, 2005, 2006).

Debriefing All Subjects. Most subjects agree to participate in research partly out of curiosity. They want to know how research works, what kinds of questions experimenters explore, and how their performance compares to the norm. In a sense, then, participation in research is educational; subjects can learn something from being involved in the study. Because of this, every subject must be **debriefed,** or told the purpose and hypothesis of the study, after they have participated in it.

Some subjects are embarrassed to show their natural curiosity about the research process. This embarrassment causes them to pretend to be uninterested in the study when in fact they often are eager to know what it was all about. I see both sides of this behavior by virtue of being both a scientist and a professor. As a scientist, I see subjects who act as if they are in a big rush to leave the laboratory and who seem bored if I ask them to stay for debriefing. However, as a professor, most of my students complain bitterly when they participate in someone's experiment only to be told nothing about the study after it is over. They feel cheated—and rightfully so. Be certain that you debrief every person who does you the favor of participating as a subject. In addition, when you act as a subject for someone else, insist that you be told what the experiment was about after it is finished.

The guidelines that we have covered in this section cover only the main points of the entire code of ethics for testing human subjects. Research that involves deceiving subjects or testing children, for example, is governed by stricter regulations than we have considered. The complete professional and federal codes for such research may be obtained from the APA and from the United States Department of Health and Human Services, should you ever need them.

ETHICS OF TESTING ANIMAL SUBJECTS

You might imagine that the regulations governing the use of animals as subjects would be less strict than those governing the use of humans. In fact, the opposite is true: Animals are protected by law to a greater extent than are humans, presumably because animals do not have the same capacity to protect themselves from unethical scientists.

The care and use of animals in research is governed by the APA, the federal government's HHS, the United States Department of Agriculture's Animal Welfare Act, state laws, and local laws. Animal research laboratories are inspected regularly by committees that must include a research scientist, a veterinarian, and someone who is completely unaffiliated with the institution. This mix is intended to provide an informed and objective inspection of each laboratory based on medical, practical, and scientific considerations. These committees, known as Animal Research Committees or ARCs, are regulated by the United States Department of Health and Human Services. In addition to the legal need to follow HHS laws closely, animal researchers also take ARCs seriously because the best journals in the field (e.g., *Animal Behavior* and *Journal of Comparative Psychology*) refuse to publish any research from laboratories that have not been fully approved.

When an ARC visits an animal research laboratory, it makes sure that HHS regulations are met. These regulations are more extensive than you might suppose. For example, animals of different types must be housed separately from one another so that noisy animals do not bother quiet animals, temperature and ventilation must be kept comfortable and constant, veterinary care must be provided to prevent disease and perform surgery, and personnel must be qualified according to specific criteria set forth by the HHS.

Additional regulations are provided by the United States Department of Agriculture's (USDA) Animal Welfare Act, which was revised in 1985. These laws require animal researchers to provide runs for daily exercise and to provide special cages that promote psychological well-being, in addition to many other regulations. The cost of these restrictions, which went into effect in 1991, is estimated at $876 million for initial improvements to laboratory facilities plus $207 million per year for maintenance (Rowan, 1989). The USDA also requires that each animal research facility be governed by an Institutional Animal Care and Use Committee (IACUC). Thus, researchers must abide by regulations enforced by both the ARCs and the IACUCs.

In general, many scientists believe that the regulations governing the use of animals in research have become unnecessarily strict. They argue that the trade-off between social benefits and individual risk has tipped too strongly to one side.

The Animal Rights Controversy

Most of you are probably familiar with the controversy over whether animals should be used in research at all. Certainly, there have been cases in which individual animals were mistreated needlessly with little potential benefit to society. Since the early 1980s, animal rights activists have been quite vocal in their desires to stop all use of animals in medical and psychological research, educational training, and product testing. You have probably seen some of their advertisements, which include photographs designed to grab our emotions.

It is true that some abuse has occurred. It is also true that the tightening of professional and federal regulations during the 1980s has alleviated most of that abuse. Within any field, however, no matter how strict the rules, there will always be a few people who continue to operate in an unethical fashion. Let's consider the facts that scientists believe the public should know before making an informed decision about the use of animals in medical and psychological research.

1. *The number of abuse cases in the research community is low.* After performing surprise inspections across the nation, the National Institute of Health reported only six cases of animal abuse from 1981 until 1988 (White, 1988). With more than 800 animal research laboratories in the United States during that time, and with each one conducting many different studies, six cases of abuse is a remarkably low number. How nice it would be if the murder rate in any one of our cities were so low!

   The six cases of abuse that were reported involved animals that were medicated inadequately for pain or left without care over a long weekend. Private individuals have been found guilty of criminal abuse that far exceeds these mistakes. For example, in 1992, a couple in Colorado abandoned their 36 horses in an open pasture without food for several weeks during an exceptionally bitter winter. Twenty-four of the animals starved to death before the remaining twelve were rescued ("Prosecutor," 1992). At least the lives of those research animals that must be sacrificed are lost in return for some benefit to society.

   The animal rights activists themselves have damaged animals by releasing them into the wild when they are no longer capable of surviving. The Animal Liberation Front, for example, turned loose 467 research animals at the University of California, Riverside, after destroying equipment and laboratory records worth more than half a million of your tax dollars. In a 2-year period alone, animal rights activists carried out 26 similar crimes at research laboratories across the country (White, 1988).

2. *The animals used in research are not family pets.* Many people imagine that research facilities are filled with puppies and kittens that are being tor-

tured for no reason at all. This simply is not true. In fact, 90% of the animals used in scientific research are rodents, and fewer than 1% are dogs or cats (White, 1988). Most of these dogs and cats are bred for research purposes, but some of them come from city pounds, where they were abandoned and doomed to die by their owners.

3. *Animal research has been extremely valuable to human life.* Without animal research, millions of people in the world today would die of diabetes, polio, smallpox, and leukemia. There would be no vaccines against mumps, measles, rubella, or diphtheria. Open-heart surgery, organ transplants, and brain tumor removal would not be possible. Currently, researchers use animal subjects to fight the battle against fatal diseases like AIDS and cancer, with the potential for tremendous benefit to society.

Moreover, these medical advances are not restricted to saving human lives—they are also used to save animals' lives. Your dog, for example, can now have cataract surgery to cure blindness because dogs bred for research were used to perfect the necessary surgical techniques.

The value of animal research is not limited to the medical profession, either. Psychologists now know much more about human blindness, for instance, from studying the visual systems of monkeys and cats. Although Seligman's (1975) studies of learned helplessness have been criticized severely by animal rights activists, the results have been applied to a variety of human problems. We now know the importance of internal personal control in increasing the morale and lowering the stress of elderly people who are confined to nursing homes, for example. In addition, Seligman's research led to advances in the rehabilitation of prisoners as well as treatment for battered wives and abused children. Neurological research on the human brain has been boosted tremendously by the use of animals as subjects, so that we now know much more about how neurotransmitters alter human moods, for example. This new knowledge may seem frivolous at first glance, but it allows psychiatrists to treat hundreds of thousands of people who suffer from schizophrenia or manic-depressive disorder.

Most Americans, even those who protest the use of animals in scientific research, have enjoyed the benefits of that research for many years now. Indeed, many of my students point out the hypocrisy of a society that denies the importance of animals in life-saving research, while wearing leather shoes and eating hamburgers. Of course, you may disagree with my opinion that it is ethical to use protected, well-kept animals as subjects in research that truly has the potential for improving society. At least, however, you have listened to a scientist's side of the story and have developed the powers of critical evaluation to decide for yourself. Those of you who wish to know more about the animal activists' view will have no trouble finding relevant material in your local or college library. Just be sure that you are getting current information that takes into account recent legal guidelines.

SCIENTIFIC FRAUD

Aside from the ethics of testing human and animal subjects, researchers must also maintain professional ethics. **Scientific fraud** can take various forms, from changing a few numbers in a set of raw data to making up all of the data, from plagiarizing a few paragraphs of someone's unpublished manuscript to reprinting every word of a previously published article as your own. Some forms of fraud are less clear: If a study is flawed by strong experimenter bias, for example, it is difficult to know whether the bias was caused by incompetence or by intent.

The extent of scientific fraud in the United States is hard to estimate. By 1991, the National Institute of Health was receiving about 150 allegations of fraud each year, many of which concern medical research (Sise, 1991). In one study of 400 medical students, 88% admitted cheating, a practice that may lead to especially high rates of fraud once the M.D. is obtained (Barrett, 1985). Walter Stewart, a biomedical scientist at the National Institute of Health who investigates cases of fraud, estimates that "as much as one-fourth of all scientific data published each year may be fraudulent or otherwise tainted" (as quoted by Henderson, 1990, p. 58). However, Cozby (1989) argues that fraud is rare within the discipline of psychology.

Whether fraud is truly rare or just seldom detected remains to be seen, but there are reasons for a rise in the incidence of fraud. First of all, the pressure on scientists to publish meaningful research results has reached all-time highs in recent years. According to the American Psychological Society, the most productive psychology department in the United States is located at the University of California, Los Angeles, where 728 publications were produced from 1986 through 1990 (Garfield, 1992). Extremely productive scientists today might publish as many as 6 or 8 articles a year; Broad and Wade (1982) point out that until the 1970s, top scientists published only two dozen articles in an entire lifetime! Second, because so many articles are published and so few are read, it is becoming easier to falsify data without getting caught. One million scientific articles are now published each year in some 40,000 journals (Henderson, 1990); how can we wade through them carefully enough to verify each piece of raw data? Third, 90% of all scientists throughout history are alive today (Broad & Wade, 1982), so competition is keen, and counting publications is an easy way to assess a scientist's qualifications. When the number of publications determines whether you will land a good job, the temptation to cut corners might be difficult for an unethical person to resist.

A Historical Example: Sir Cyril Burt

The most famous example of scientific fraud within psychology was perpetrated by Sir Cyril Burt, a British researcher whose work showed that human intelligence was largely inherited. To support this conclusion, Burt tested the intelligence of identical twins who had been raised in separate environments. From 1912 until his death in 1971, Burt maintained that he had solid evidence showing that intelligence was largely inherited. For example, he reported statistical correlations showing that the intelligence of one genetically identical twin was very similar to the intelligence of the other twin.

Burt's reported correlations were extremely strong in many cases, and occasionally coefficients were identical across various studies. Other scientists began to worry that the numbers were flawed in some way. Because such suspicions arose while he was writing Burt's biography, Hearnshaw (1979) investigated the records completely and uncovered 30 years' worth of intentional fraud. Not only had Burt falsified his data, he had also published completely fictional articles supporting his work. These articles were supposedly authored by people who did not exist or by students who did not write them. Unfortunately, Burt's tainted work concerning intelligence set the stage for many of the problems with IQ testing and racial bias that we suffer today.

A Modern Example: Stephen Breuning

Scientific fraud in psychology is not limited to historical times. During the 1980s, Stephen Breuning published a series of landmark studies showing that IQ doubled when mentally retarded patients were taken off a particular type of tranquilizer. This research led to fame and respect for Breuning, and in response to his research, psychiatrists began to take their patients off the drug in record numbers. Because the drug alleviated symptoms of physical violence seen in some mentally retarded patients, canceling the medication was potentially dangerous to both the patients and their caretakers.

Breuning's problems started when his colleagues became suspicious of the amount of work he was allegedly doing. From 1980 to 1983, while in his late twenties and only at the very beginning of his career, Breuning published 24 scientific articles. Roman (1988) notes that this number represented a full third of all the literature in existence on that topic. In addition, Breuning was involved in several other projects and was supposed to have tested many of the subjects in these 24 research studies personally. How could one mortal human be that productive? One of Breuning's colleagues, Robert Sprague, was suspicious enough to begin a thorough investigation.

Sprague uncovered a number of interesting discrepancies aside from Breuning's unbelievable productivity (Roman, 1988). First, he noticed that several of the studies had allegedly been conducted by Breuning in one city at a time when he was known to be visiting some other city. Second, the data showed very little variability across different observers; in other words, the interrater reliability was almost perfect—too perfect to be real. Third, Breuning was not able to furnish much of his raw data when asked to provide it. Somehow, it had been "lost."

After years of investigating Breuning's conduct and nagging the government institute that had funded Breuning's research, Sprague finally had the satisfaction of hearing a full confession. As a result of his unethical practices, Breuning resigned from his university position and was barred from receiving any government grants for 10 years. In addition, he was convicted in 1988 by the federal government on two criminal counts of false grant statements (Sise, 1991).

Safeguards Against Scientific Fraud

The majority of scientists are honest and ethical, but given the pressures to cheat, you might wonder why. In fact, there are several safeguards that prevent fraud, aside from fear of the penalties that might ensue. They include honor, replication, refereed journals, professional guidelines, and federal guidelines.

The Scientist's Code of Honor. In its most general sense, the purpose of science is to discover new knowledge. That is, science is conducted so that we may learn about the world—so that we may find out what makes a pine tree develop special cone seeds that open only after the intense heat of a forest fire, what makes the human brain produce endorphins that relieve pain, what makes you and me able to use language so rapidly and effectively every day. Because of this foundation in the discovery of new knowledge, scientists are extremely concerned that results are presented honestly. Without honest presentation, science would ultimately come to a standstill, unable to proceed in any direction at all. Thus, most scientists operate with a deep belief in the importance of honestly tested knowledge, and they react swiftly and sternly to people who mock that belief.

Replication of Results. Replication is a common activity in science, even though it isn't usually published in scientific journals. When a new result comes out, other researchers in the field scurry to follow it up with testable ideas of their own. To begin testing those new ideas, they must first verify that the original result is trustworthy. Results that cannot be replicated are brought to the attention of the original researcher, who must supply the raw data to be analyzed again by someone else. Replication may be the ultimate safeguard against fraud because scientists know that their work will be investigated carefully if other scientists cannot replicate their findings. If the lack of replication is found to be caused by fraudulent research, their careers and personal reputations will be ruined.

Refereed Journals. Most scientific journals are refereed, so that each published article has gone through an intensive process of review before appearing in the journal. You probably remember from Chapter 2 that when a new manuscript arrives, the editor of a refereed journal usually sends copies of it to several expert reviewers. After reading such manuscripts carefully, these referees recommend acceptance or rejection of the article. This process ensures that scientific results are assessed carefully before being published. Obvious flaws, whether intentional or not, would cause a manuscript to be rejected.

Now, it is true that not every scientific journal is refereed. Thus, researchers whose manuscripts had been rejected by several refereed journal editors might well submit their work to a nonrefereed journal. However, even there, most editors will look over the research carefully and make a prudent decision regarding publication. A few bad manuscripts do slip past, which is why it's so important to evaluate the validity of research studies for yourself instead of merely accepting the work because it is published in a journal. In general, though, nonrefereed journals are much less prestigious than refereed journals, and researchers within the scientific community know why.

Professional Guidelines. As with the testing of human and animal subjects, the APA also serves as a watchdog for scientific fraud. Well-founded suspicions of fraud may be reported to the APA, which will appoint a peer-review committee to investigate.

Federal Guidelines. The federal government doles out huge chunks of money for scientific research and training in the United States. For example, the National Institute of Health alone funds the research of about 50,000 health-related scientists each year. In 1991, this funding produced a staggering annual tab of about $8,340,609,000 (United States Office of Management and Budget, 1992). The money is used for a variety of purposes: to find cures for fatal or debilitating diseases, to train students in scientific and clinical methods, to develop crucial technology like brain scans, to implement treatment programs for people who desperately need help.

Because of increasing concern with scientific fraud, the government has begun to hire researchers whose primary task is to sniff out violations of professional ethics (Henderson, 1990). The competition for grants is strong, so scientists who submit proposals for research funding make certain that their reputations are squeaky clean.

PENALTIES FOR VIOLATING ETHICAL GUIDELINES

We've talked a lot about guidelines and safeguards and regulations, but maybe you're still a bit skeptical. Sure, it's fine to have rules and regulations about testing subjects and reporting data, but who's enforcing them? Isn't it possible to get around those rules and safeguards, just like Stephen Breuning did? Well, yes, it is possible; after all, every profession has its quacks just as every population has its criminals. Let's see what happens, then, to people who violate the ethical principles of scientific research.

Loss of Government Funding

A tremendous amount of university research is funded by our government. The National Institute of Health is the largest research-funding organization in this country and, as I mentioned, spends billions of dollars each year to keep scientific research, training, and health-related treatment afloat. If a scientist violates ethical principles (by bypassing an IRB, harming animal subjects, or falsifying data, for example), the government can take back every cent of the grant that was awarded. If a multi-million dollar grant is rescinded, a lot of scientists, research assistants, students, and support staff are going to find themselves out of work, and they're not going to be happy about it.

In addition to losing the funding for a particular project, the unethical scientist will not be given government funds again in the future. Although Breuning was prevented from receiving government grants by law for only a period of 10 years, it is unlikely that he will receive any grants even after that 10-year period is over. Without funding, much of the research needed to maintain a professional scientific career is impossible to perform.

Loss of Professional Credentials

When the APA appoints a committee of peers to review potentially unethical research, the ethics of the accused scientist are immediately called into question. This is one reason that allegations of unethical behavior are not made lightly. If the APA peer review committee finds that the accused psychologist did indeed perform unethical research, penalties include public loss of membership in the professional organization. This penalty itself is sometimes less severe than the implications it carries for the psychologist's professional future, which we will consider next.

Loss of Career

It takes a long time for a scientist to build a reputable career. In psychology, graduate education alone takes an average of 7 challenging years to complete (Berger, 1989). Yes, that's 7 years beyond completion of the bachelor's degree from college. Once the Ph.D. is finally acquired, the young scientist is able to begin building a career, by working long, hard hours for many more years and by producing a body of meaningful, statistically significant results.

This scientist's hard-won reputation can be ruined by just one study in which subjects were treated unethically or data were fabricated. Because of the publicity associated with losing government funding and professional credentials, unethical scientists do not remain in business for long. The scientific community is small enough that unethical behavior becomes widely known very soon.

Legal Liability

Along with losing their research funding, professional credentials, career, and personal integrity, unethical scientists can also be penalized legally. Subjects who have been mistreated may sue the researcher for negligence, malpractice, or invasion of privacy. Damages are not limited to physical harm but could also include mental cruelty and psychological stress. Lawsuits of this kind can be directed at the institution for which the scientist works. However, researchers may also be sued personally, in which case a subject's legal victory could mean loss of the researcher's personal possessions.

In addition, any fraudulent scientist whose research is federally funded can be prosecuted by the government on criminal charges. Stephen Breuning, for example, was found guilty of submitting false data to get a federal grant in the amount of $200,000. The money was repaid to the government by the university that insisted on Breuning's resignation.

ALLEGATIONS OF UNETHICAL PRACTICES

By now, you should be aware that scientists consider unethical practices to be a very serious crime. Such practices erode the public's faith in science, and they can harm many individuals beyond the subjects who participated in an unethical study. Breuning's research, for example, led to dramatic changes in the treatment of mental retardation—changes that could have caused serious harm to both patients and caretakers.

Because of the severity of these scientific crimes, it is vital that allegations never be made lightly. To suggest, jokingly or in an offhand remark, that a study you read recently was probably fraudulent is a serious breach of ethics in itself unless you have hard, cold evidence of fraud. Similarly, never accuse someone of mistreating their research animals or placing their human subjects under undue stress unless you are certain that you have the necessary facts. People within the scientific profession do not take such accusations lightly.

It is also important, however, to begin careful steps of investigation if you honestly believe that ethical guidelines have been violated. Ignoring the problem won't make it disappear, and you have a responsibility as an informed researcher to watch for unethical practices. Consider all the facts available to you, then discuss your suspicions privately with someone who is knowledgeable in the area, perhaps a professor. Most important of all, make sure your own science meets the guidelines of ethical research.

SUMMARY OF MAIN POINTS

- Every scientist is responsible for protecting the rights of human and animal subjects and for reporting scientific information honestly.

- The ethics of subject testing depend on a trade-off: Is the potential benefit to society strong enough to warrant the potential risk to an individual?

- The horrors of "research" conducted by the Nazis during the 1930s and 1940s led to development of the Nuremberg code, from which today's ethical guidelines have developed. Despite the Nuremberg code's implementation in 1948, unethical medical research was still conducted, such as the Tuskegee experiment.

- Milgram's study of obedience led scientists to strengthen guidelines for ethical research in psychology, with special attention to psychological stress in subjects.

- Today, human subjects are protected by professional guidelines and by federal regulations that are overseen by Institutional Review Boards. Every federally funded study that presents a risk to subjects must be approved by an Institutional Review Board before the research may begin.

- Ethical guidelines for testing human subjects include obtaining informed consent, allowing subjects to withdraw at any time, maintaining confidentiality of data, and debriefing subjects.

- Today, animal subjects used in psychological research are protected by five governing agencies: the American Psychological Association, the United States Department of Health and Human Services, the United States Department of Agriculture's Animal Welfare Act, state laws, and local laws.

- Animal research laboratories are governed by Institutional Animal Care and Use Committees. They are also inspected by Animal Research Committees that visit research institutions throughout the United States.

- Scientific fraud is safeguarded by the scientist's code of honor, replication of results, refereed journals, professional guidelines, and federal laws.

- Penalties for scientific fraud include loss of research funding, loss of professional credentials, loss of career, and legal liability in both civil and criminal lawsuits.

- Allegations of scientific fraud and subject abuse are extremely serious. Such accusations should never be made casually, and accusers should be certain of their facts before bringing the matter to public attention.

CHAPTER EXERCISES

1. Use your own words to define these key terms:

   Nuremberg code   informed consent
   Tuskegee experiment   debriefing
   confederates   scientific fraud

2. As a class exercise, select a panel of classmates to act as an Institutional Review Board, and appoint someone to play the role of Stanley Milgram. Have "Milgram" present his obedience study to the "IRB" as if he were requesting approval to conduct it. The "IRB" should provide a thorough consideration of "Milgram's" intended research, according to the guidelines that are used today by the APA.

3. Regardless of your own opinion, write a one-page argument against the use of animals in medical and psychological research. Provide at least two recent pieces of evidence in support of your argument.

4. This chapter ignored the ethics of using animals for educational training. Do you believe that animals should be used for dissection in high school biology courses, for example? What about in medical school? Write a one-page statement concerning the use of animals in educational training. State your opinion clearly, but be sure to provide evidence that supports it.

5. Because this book is devoted to methods of research, and not to methods of clinical treatment, I have ignored the ethical guidelines by which psychological clients are treated. Research the topic in your library, then write a one-page summary of these guidelines. Helpful sources include *Ethical principles of psychologists and code of conduct*, published by the APA (1992), and *Ethics in psychology*, by Keith-Spiegel and Koocher (1985).

A Final Message to Students

This book has introduced you to the basics of design and evaluation in scientific research. You now have the knowledge you need to answer many research questions, questions that may be vital to you or your family and friends in the coming years. In addition, you have learned how to evaluate those brief research reports that bombard us through the popular media every day. With this knowledge, you can make intelligent decisions about the validity of such reports instead of relying on others to make decisions for you. I hope you have also developed both the ability and the desire to read more critically than you have in the past, so that you do not blindly swallow each tidbit of information that a published author places before you.

Reaching the end of this book may mean that you never perform another analysis of variance again. But that's OK; the book was written with a much different purpose in mind than to teach the meaning of F. Too many people in our country fail to take the time and devote the energy needed to develop a full understanding of the problems that face us. With the future approaching at a rapid rate, it will not be enough for us to merely read and listen and think. Instead, all of us need to read critically, listen carefully, and think responsibly. If this book has helped you, even a little bit, to develop those abilities, then I have done my job.

Thank you for your patience and effort in working through the principles of basic research methods with me. They are not always easy; they are sometimes not much fun; they often require hard work and careful reading. However, I believe sincerely that your effort will be repaid again and again, no matter what path you choose in future years.

Writing Research Reports

A

Y ou may recall from Chapter 2 that scientists write reports of their own research rather than relying on professional authors to do the job for them. Writing a good research report is not easy, even for people who write well. Because the process is lengthy and challenging, there may come a time when you wonder why you are required to do it. Exactly how will you benefit from learning to write scientific research reports? Let's consider this question in more detail.

THE VALUE OF WRITING RESEARCH REPORTS

Designing and conducting good research is a valuable skill, but being able to explain that research to others is equally important. Without the ability to explain clearly what you have done and why, even the best research is limited in worth. If no one can understand your study, what good is it?

In addition to the need to explain your research clearly so that readers will understand it, learning to write research reports will also help you to understand and evaluate the scientific studies that you read. Just as novelists understand the construction of a novel more thoroughly than the average reader does, scientists understand the construction of someone else's research report because they have written so many reports themselves.

Those are two reasons for learning to write a good research report: to explain your research to others and to understand the research studies you read. But, wait a minute. We've forgotten the most important reason of all: Good writing skills are one of the most valuable assets that people can have, regardless of whether they plan to become scientists.

Good writing skills can be developed by writing all kinds of documents—letters to Mom and Dad let us create a personal voice, poems require that we choose words precisely, essays make us think about the relationship between opinion and evidence, pleas to the electric company develop our powers of persuasion, and even a simple grocery list can teach us organization. What's so special about a research report?

Research reports explain difficult concepts, concepts that many people never really considered before. This means that the content must be mastered at the same time the writing is done. Using writing as a tool to help you think is something that grocery lists and pleas to the electric company seldom require. The difficulty of the concepts to be explained is the single most likely cause of complaints from good students about their grades on scientific research reports. "I never got less than an A minus on my English papers," they say heatedly, after receiving another C on a research report. And when professors ask, "What were those English papers about?", students produce a list of topics that often require little mastery of difficult new knowledge. It is usually easier to write an essay that supports your personal feelings concerning abortion, for instance, than it is to write a report of a complicated experiment that you barely understood.

Writing scientific research reports will teach you how to explain difficult concepts clearly, it will teach you to write concisely with an eye toward the precise meaning of each word you select, and it will help you to organize your thoughts in a logical, step-by-step manner. These are qualities that will enhance any kind of writing. No matter what your future occupation, the ability to write well will help you. Those of you who go into business organizations will be required to write reports and memos frequently. In fact, many business positions require more writing than you are expected to do in college. If you work as a teacher, you'll be writing notes to parents, memos to administrators, and exams for students. Most importantly, you'll be responsible for teaching others to write! Plumbers, electricians, and bricklayers all have to submit written bids and bills for their work, in addition to writing letters to suppliers and contractors. Even if your ultimate career goal is to flip burgers at McDonald's, you'll likely have to write letters to distant family members, explanations to your children's teachers, and written arguments to the telephone company when it overcharges you.

Think of writing research reports, then, as practice for everyday life. It's good for communicating and understanding scientific research, too, but that may not be your ultimate aim.

GOALS OF SCIENTIFIC COMMUNICATION

The immediate purpose of writing a research report is to tell other scientists about your work, about the new knowledge you have discovered. This is easier said than done because psychological experiments are complex, and it is difficult to explain them clearly. The research report should be clear enough that any scientist could replicate your study without telephoning you to ask for details. In addition, the research must be explained clearly enough that a scientist could evaluate its merits and flaws, solely on the basis of the written word on the page. After all, this is what you do each time you read someone else's published report.

To allow for replication and evaluation, *the ultimate goal of scientific communication must be clarity*, not creativity. An elegant turn of phrase may be beautiful in a novel or poem, but often it is only ambiguous in a scientific report. For that reason, it is best at this stage to save your creative powers for research design. Eventually, you will learn to write research reports clearly enough to risk adding beauty to the sentences, but first you must master clarity. Remember that when you read a journal article, you are looking for information. Your readers are seeking the same thing.

Scientific writing usually requires a formal style. This, again, is because its purpose is to convey information clearly and directly. The personal, informal style used in this textbook would not be appropriate for a scientific journal article. Appendix B contains a sample research report that will give you a good idea of the writing style that is expected of budding scientists.

APA STYLE

The American Psychological Association (APA) has strict guidelines for the editorial style and organizational format of written research reports. By **editorial style,** I simply mean the accepted conventions for the mechanics of writing. For example, when you reach the end of a line, should a long word be hyphenated or allowed to stretch out into the right margin? How large should the margins be?

What should be listed first in a source reference—the author's name or the title of the book? The APA answers these questions for us so that every psychologist uses the same standard conventions.

APA style also specifies an organizational format that helps us to meet the scientific goals of clear communication. The method of categorizing information into sections of introduction, method, results, and discussion is one way that communication is made clearer. It helps readers to find certain types of information quickly.

This appendix introduces you to the basics of APA style. Every rule presented here follows APA guidelines, so you will not be learning bad habits that may need to be changed later. However, you will not find each detail of APA style listed here—that would require a full-length book in itself. I prefer to concentrate on clear scientific writing, instead of on details like whether to use "14" or "fourteen" in text. Therefore, we'll start with only the basic rules of APA style. When you have mastered the basics thoroughly and are ready to advance toward the sophisticated nuances of flawless APA style, you will need to acquire a copy of the *Publication Manual of the American Psychological Association* (1994). It contains all the guidelines that you need to know in order to write a research report in perfect APA style.

Finally, before we begin discussing the nuts and bolts of writing a research report, let me provide one caution: Learning to write research reports is like learning to ride a bike. No one really learns the process by reading about it. Instead, we have to get on the bike, and we also have to fall off. The experience of learning to write research reports will be more pleasant if you expect from the beginning to make mistakes. You will soon see that the process is complicated enough that no one could possibly tell you everything you need to know to write an outstanding report the first time around. Instead, plan to make mistakes and to learn from them as you go. With that attitude, you'll soon be writing like a pro!

WRITING SECTION BY SECTION

Before getting into various tips and techniques for writing well, let's consider the type of information that belongs in each section of an APA-style report. In Chapter 2, we considered four of the sections, but now we will add the remaining three. A full APA-style report should contain the following sections in this order:

- Title page
- Abstract
- Introduction
- Method
- Results
- Discussion
- References

As we go through the information to be presented in each section, we'll also consider the editorial style to be used in presenting that information. Refer to the sample paper in Appendix B whenever you need a concrete example of exactly what to do.

Title Page

Select your title carefully. Too many students slap any old title on their papers, without realizing that the title often determines whether a potential reader will ignore the article or read it with interest. The title should refer to the major variables or findings of the study. It should be centered in the top half of the page, followed by your name and the name of your college. All lines of an APA-style report should be doublespaced, and margins should be set at a minimum of 1 inch on all four sides of every page. The page number 1 should be located in the top righthand corner of the title page. Every subsequent page of the paper should be numbered in the same place.

Abstract

We talked about abstracts in Chapter 2, and by now, you should have read several of them in the literature. Therefore, you already know that the abstract is a one-paragraph summary of your research. It should contain no more than 120 words, focusing only on the highlights of your study. Begin by centering the word *Abstract* at the top of page 2. In your abstract, briefly describe

1. the question under investigation,
2. the method used to explore that research question,
3. the main results of the study, and
4. your conclusions.

Because the abstract presents a general overview of the entire study, many authors leave it as their final task even though it appears on the second page of the manuscript. Remember that the purpose of an abstract is to allow potential readers to determine whether your article is likely to contain the information they need.

Introduction

The introduction begins on page 3 of your manuscript, with the title of the paper centered at the top of the page. Its purpose is to introduce the topic, present relevant background literature, explain the purpose and hypothesis of your study, and state predictions. The introduction should begin at a general level and become more specific as it continues.

The first paragraph of the introduction is usually a general explanation of the topic, in terms that an intelligent person can understand without knowing much about psychology. Subsequent paragraphs are devoted to a more specialized explanation of theories or past discoveries that are relevant to your study.

This explanation usually leads into a statement of the purpose of the study, although the statement of purpose may come before the description of background literature if you prefer. The statement of purpose often looks like a general hypothesis. For example, it might say, *"The purpose of this study was to explore the relationship between people's personalities and the degree to which they suffer from coronary heart disease (CHD)."*

Once your purpose is clear, you will need to explain the method briefly, just enough so that readers will understand your predictions. A complete explanation of the method appears in the next section, so don't say too much about it here. Predictions should be specific, detailed statements of the results you expect to obtain (such as, *"Subjects who often became angry were expected to experience greater degrees of CHD than subjects who seldom became angry"*). Be sure the predictions are linked to the earlier content of your introduction, so that readers can see why you expected one pattern of results and not another.

Method

Do not begin the method section on a new page. Instead, double-space once vertically at the end of your introduction and start the method section there, by centering the word *Method*. The purpose of this section is to describe your experimental method in enough detail that another researcher could replicate the study. To achieve this, it helps to subdivide the method into four smaller subsections: *Subjects, Design, Materials and Apparatus,* and *Procedure.* Each of these four subheadings should be underlined and typed at the left margin with no indentation.

As you would imagine, information about subjects should be presented in the subjects subsection. Describe how many subjects participated in the study, what their minimum and maximum ages were, what the mean or median age was, how many were males and how many were females, why they participated in the study, and where they were recruited from. Other scientists will need to know all of these details in order to evaluate or replicate your work.

The design subsection is optional, but my students say that it helps them to organize material clearly in their reports. It should define the independent variable(s) and levels, the dependent variable(s), and the type of design (e.g., within-subjects, between-subjects, factorial, mixed). These terms are described in detail in Chapters 6 and 9. Variables and levels can be operationally defined in this subsection as well. If the research you are describing is nonexperimental, you might decide to omit or revise the design subsection. Check with your professor for guidance.

In the materials and apparatus subsection, you should describe in detail all of the stimuli and equipment that were used when you conducted the study. **Stimuli** are items such as objects, drawings, or words to which a subject responds. Experimental controls that were achieved by designing these stimuli in a certain way are often described in this subsection, along with the reasons for including those controls.

The procedure subsection is a chronological explanation of the events that occurred during the experiment. Describe exactly what the subjects did, from beginning to end, as they participated in the experiment. Explain what they were required to do and how they were given instructions about the task.

There are two common sources of confusion in writing method sections. The first one is deciding whether a certain detail should be included or left out. This can usually be answered by asking yourself a question: Could that detail possibly have affected the results that were obtained? If so, include it. For example, the use of a number 1 pencil on a hand-scored questionnaire would probably not alter the results in any way. Therefore, you wouldn't need to include that information in the method section of your report. However, the use of a number 1 pencil on a machine-scored questionnaire might alter the results, especially if the machine could only decipher the marks of a number 2 pencil. In this case, you would include the information regarding the type of pencil that was used.

The second common source of confusion in writing a method section is deciding whether a certain piece of information belongs in the material and apparatus or in the procedure subsection. It is easiest to make this decision by separating in your mind the physical items needed to conduct the study from the events that occurred while conducting the study. Imagine a table covered with the items that you needed to conduct your experiment. Perhaps the table holds a couple of stopwatches, some white cards with words written on them, and some blank response sheets for subjects to fill out. When you go to the room in which you are conducting the experiment, you must take everything on the table with you. Those items on the table are materials and apparatus, so they should be described in that subsection.

When you arrive in the research room, you will set those items down and begin to do things, such as assigning subjects to conditions and giving them instructions to read. These things that you do are procedural events, so they should be explained in the procedure subsection. When in doubt, ask yourself: Is this a description of some object that I used during the research (materials and apparatus), or is it an event that happened after the subject arrived (procedure)?

Results

The purpose of the results section is to present, not to interpret, the results of your statistical analysis. Raw data themselves should never be presented in a research report. No reader wants to paw through page after page of individual scores that haven't even been summarized! However, after analysis, the raw data should be saved in case others ask to see them.

Like the method section, the results section does not begin on a new page. Simply doublespace once vertically after the method section ends, then center the word *Results*. Begin presenting your results with a general statement of the main finding. This statement should be written in English, not in "statistese" or "scientificitis." In other words, any intelligent layperson should be able to understand this statement easily. An example of the general opening statement might be: *"Subjects who reported feeling angry often were most likely to suffer from severe CHD."*

You can then go into the details: Report means and standard deviations for each condition, identify the statistical analysis that was used, and report the results of that analysis. In this example, let's suppose that the severity of CHD that each subject experienced was rated by a physician on a scale from 0 (no symptoms of CHD) to 20 (very strong symptoms of CHD). Means and standard deviations would be reported like this:

> High hostility subjects received higher ratings on the CHD scale ($\underline{M} = 16.42$, $\underline{SD} = .73$) than low hostility subjects received ($\underline{M} = 6.71$, $\underline{SD} = .55$).

The statistical format used to report significant differences includes the value of the statistic (like t or F), the degrees of freedom, and the probability level.

> For a t-test: $\underline{t}\ (17) = 4.57$, $\underline{p} < .05$

> For an ANOVA: $\underline{F}\ (3, 14) = 21.05$, $\underline{p} < .05$

If you used a computer program that provides the exact value of p it can be reported in this fashion: $\underline{t}\ (17) = 4.57$, $\underline{p} = .03$. Either usage is acceptable. These statistical values are usually presented at the end of a sentence, like this:

> With an alpha level of .05, an independent $\underline{t}$-test showed that this difference in CHD ratings was significant, $\underline{t}\ (17) = 4.57$, $\underline{p} < .05$.

If the difference between means was not statistically significant, this format is changed slightly but it is still used. To indicate a lack of significance, we state that the probability of error (p) was greater than .05 instead of less than .05. The resulting sentence would look something like this:

> With an alpha level of .05, an independent $\underline{t}$-test showed that the difference in CHD ratings was not significant, $\underline{t}\ (17) = .72$, $\underline{p} > .05$.

Throughout the results section, remember to underline abbreviations such as $\underline{M}$, $\underline{SD}$, $\underline{p}$, $\underline{t}$, and $\underline{F}$. These underlines tell the printer of a manuscript that the letters should be presented in italics when the final article is produced.

A table or figure may also help readers to understand the results. A **table** is a listing of words or numbers, such as means per condition, whereas a **figure** is a graph or picture that illustrates the results. These visual aids are used sparingly because they are expensive to reproduce, but there's nothing wrong with including just one or two of them to help readers understand complex results. If you do use a table or figure, it should appear at the end of the research report (after the references), and an insertion cue should be placed within the text of the results section, like this:

Insert Table 1 about here

TABLE A.1 EXAMPLE OF APA-STYLE TABLE

Table 1

Percentage Incidence of Coronary Heart Disease

	Age (in years)	
Personality Type	45–64	65–74
Type A	26.4	22.2
Type B	9.1	7.7

From "The Relationship of Psychosocial Factors to Coronary Heart Disease in the Framingham Study: III. Eight-year Incidence of Coronary Heart Disease" by S. G. Haynes, M. Feinleib, and W. B. Kannel, 1980, *American Journal of Epidemiology, III*, pp. 37–58. Copyright 1980 by American Journal of Epidemiology. Adapted by permission.

This cue will tell the printer where your table or figure should appear within the text of the finished article.

In the text of your results section, bring every table or figure to your readers' attention by describing it briefly. For example, you might say, *"Table 1 shows the severity of CHD for subjects with varying levels of hostility."* This tells readers that a relevant table has been provided and reminds them to look for it.

Making Tables. A table presents numbers (or sometimes words) arranged in a row-and-column format that makes the patterns within the results easy to see. Table A.1 provides an example of APA style to use in designing your own tables. It presents some simple frequency counts from a real study of personality type and CHD (Haynes, Feinleib, & Kannel, 1980). In general, the table shows that people with Type A personalities (who tend to be impatient, rushed, and sometimes hostile) experience more CHD than do people with Type B personalities (who are usually calm and relaxed). You may also recognize the Type Z personality shown in Figure A.1.

You can see from the example that tables should be titled and set off with horizontal lines. As you become more familiar with the use of tables, you may want to check the *APA Publication Manual* for further details. For now, though, just try to imitate the format you see in Table A.1.

Drawing Figures. A figure usually illustrates the main highlights of data that have been collected in a research study. By presenting descriptive statistics in the form of figures, you can often help readers to understand exactly what your data were like. In addition to being easy to understand, cognitive psychologists have discovered that pictures are easier than words for most people to remember (Shepard, 1967). The most common types of figures in published psychological research are bar graphs and line graphs.

The **bar graph** usually presents frequencies or means in the form of vertical bars so that readers can see overall patterns easily. Figure A.2 provides you with

Figure A.1
Type Z Behavior
Source: Drawing by D. Reilly; © The New Yorker Magazine, Inc.

an example of a bar graph. This sample figure shows the same data that were presented in Table A.1, so that you can compare the table and figure formats directly.

Several conventions set forth by the *APA Publication Manual* help us to standardize figures so that we can understand them easily. Graphs are drawn with two lines, or **axes,** one horizontal and the other vertical. Common names for these two axes, on which data are represented, are the abscissa and the ordinate. The **abscissa** is the horizontal line, which always represents the independent variable or factor of interest. The **ordinate** is the vertical line, which always represents measurements of the dependent variable. You can see in Figure A.2 that the abscissa represents personality types and the ordinate represents the percentage of subjects who had CHD (Haynes et al., 1980). Once the axes are in place, a bar is drawn to represent the descriptive statistic of interest. In Figure A.2, you can see that four bars are drawn, each one standing for the percentage of subjects with a certain personality type and a certain age who had experienced CHD. By looking at the bar graph, we can see that subjects with Type A personalities in both age ranges are more likely to have heart trouble than are subjects with Type B personalities.

It is vital to label each axis and the points along it very clearly. This is one of the most common errors seen among beginning research methods students and professional authors who have little training in scientific research. A poorly labeled figure is almost impossible to understand—instead of clarifying and illus-

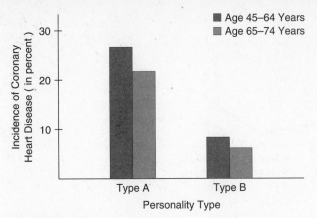

Figure A.2
Example of an APA-Style Bar Graph
Source: Adapted from Haynes, Feinleib, and Kannel, 1980.

trating results, it only confuses everyone. Note the labeling that is used in Figure A.2. It's accurate and easy to understand. It is also thorough—on the abscissa, both the axis and each bar are labeled. Similarly, the ordinate includes an axis label as well as labels for each measurement point.

Line Graphs. Sometimes bar graphs aren't appropriate for the type of results being presented. The use of a bar graph to illustrate results implies that the independent variable is **discrete,** or capable of being broken up into separable units. Sometimes this is true, as when we consider personality types that are very different from each other. For example, Type A and Type B personalities are discrete—there is not much continuity between them. Therefore, data concerning the two personality types should be represented by a bar graph because it accurately suggests a discrete separation between conditions.

However, other types of independent variables do have some continuity. In these cases, we use **line graphs,** in which data are represented by one continuous line instead of by separated bars. Figure A.3 is a good example of a line graph, showing the actual effects of hostility on incidence of CHD (Barefoot, Dahlstrom, & Williams, 1983). Hostility is a continuous variable in the sense that people can feel (and psychologists can measure) many slightly varying degrees of it, from just a tiny bit of hostility, to a medium amount, and on to extreme feelings of hostility. Because the purpose of Figure A.3 is to illustrate the effects of a continuous variable, a line graph was used.

Whenever you have to decide whether to use a line graph or a bar graph, consider the variable represented along the abscissa carefully. If it seems to represent something that could be stretched out over a continuing period of time (e.g., seconds, days, years) or amount (e.g., milligrams of drug dosage), use a line graph. On the other hand, if the variable represented along the abscissa signifies a discrete factor with completely separable qualities (e.g., type of drug, type of personality), use a bar graph.

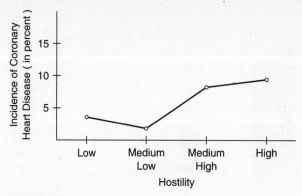

Figure A.3
Example of an APA-style Line Graph
Source: From Barefoot, Dahlstrom, and Williams, 1983.

Discussion

The discussion section is the place to interpret and evaluate the results of your study. Use this section to show readers how your study has helped to answer the research question that you investigated. Did the expected results occur or not? What do the results mean? Good discussions start at a specific level and move toward general conclusions.

Begin by doublespacing once after the results section ends and centering the heading *Discussion*. The first sentence of your discussion should state explicitly whether the results supported the predictions. Then compare your findings with those from past research studies that were presented in the introduction. Explain how your results do or do not support relevant theories that were mentioned in the introduction. If the results do not support your predictions, speculate about why this happened. Discuss any serious problems with your method, and explain how they might be solved in future research.

End your discussion on a positive note by pointing out the importance of your findings. Explain the implications your results have for relevant theories and future research. Discuss ways in which your results might be applied to practical situations. Finally, try to achieve a general and optimistic tone at the end of your discussion.

Citations

APA style has specific rules for **citing,** or referring to, original sources in the text of your paper. Most journal articles and books in psychology use that style, so there are plenty of examples available to you. Using a standard format makes it easier for readers to locate reference sources in their own libraries.

Let's stick with our example concerning the effects of hostile emotions on physical health. That program of research began when two medical doctors, Friedman and Rosenman, noticed that women were less likely to have heart attacks than men, even though the women ate the same amounts of cholesterol and fat. Friedman and Rosenman suspected that the difference might be caused by stress. To test this hypothesis, they conducted a classic 10-year study using about 3,500 healthy men. The men were classified as Type A or Type B according to their personalities. You may recall that Type A people are impatient, competitive, aggressive, and angry—in short, they are likely to feel great stress. Type B people are relaxed and easy-going. To make a long story short, Friedman and Rosenman found that middle-aged Type A men were nearly three times more likely to suffer heart attacks than were middle-aged Type B men. The same pattern is now known to occur in women as well.

Now, if we were writing a research report about the effects of mental stress on physical health, the Friedman and Rosenman study certainly would be relevant background material. We would describe it in our introduction section and cite the source so that other researchers could check our interpretation or find out more about the original study. An APA-style citation requires that we list the authors' last names and the date of the study we are referring to, like this:

> Friedman and Rosenman (1974) found that men with Type A personalities were significantly more likely to suffer heart attacks than were men with Type B personalities.

Another APA-style citation technique that is sometimes used places the authors' names and date at the end of the sentence, like this:

> Two cardiologists studied the effects of personality types on physical health (Friedman & Rosenman, 1974).

Notice that either of these two methods may be used whenever you write about someone else's work. There is a third technique for citation, too: If you use the exact words of another author in your paper, you must place the words in quotation marks and cite the author's name, date of the publication, and page number, like this:

> "The most significant trait of the Type A man is his habitual sense of time urgency" (Friedman & Rosenman, 1974, p. 70).

Failure to place another author's words in quotation marks means that you have plagiarized that author's work. (Inset blocked paragraphs may be used instead of quotation marks for very long quotes.) We'll follow up on the topic of plagiarism later in this chapter.

References

With the exception of direct quotes, only the author's last name and the source's date of publication are cited in the text of a research report. However, this information alone is not enough to allow a reader to locate the source easily. The library might contains lots of studies that were done by somebody named Friedman in 1974! Readers need to know which Friedman and which of that Friedman's studies you're talking about. In an APA-style research report, we provide the full reference for each source on a separate page that follows the discussion section.

Be sure you understand the difference between a reference section, which is used in APA-style documents, and a bibliography, which is not. A **references section** lists only those sources that you actually cited in your paper. On the other hand, a **bibliography** is a complete listing of all relevant sources that you read in preparing the report, regardless of whether they were actually cited. What you want to include in an APA-style research report is a references section, not a bibliography.

To add the references section to your report, begin the section on a new page just after the discussion, with the word *References* centered at the top of the page. Every source that is cited in the text of your paper must be listed here. Do not list sources that you read while preparing the research study but did not mention in the paper.

APA style provides a special format for source references. To simplify matters, we'll only consider the format for referring to authored books, edited books, book chapters, journal articles, and magazine articles because they are the most common references used. The proper reference formats for these five types of publications are listed in Table A.2.

Writing references correctly is a little like winning at your favorite sport: It's important to pay attention to detail. Note the spacing between each element of the references, the capitalization of certain words, and the underlining of certain titles. These details are not arbitrary—in fact, they are quite meaningful to people who are accustomed to APA style. For example, Table A.2 shows that book titles are underlined but only the first letter of the title is capitalized, whereas journal titles are underlined and all first letters are capitalized. This tiny distinction in capitalization saves us time in the library by showing us immediately whether to search for a book or a journal.

I can sympathize with your dismay at being required to follow the tedium of a new referencing format. The only consolation to offer is that your future psychology courses will require the same kind of referencing. Therefore, once you learn APA style reference formats, you will be able to use them again and again. The formats must seem confusing at first, but remember that it could be worse: We're only dealing with 5 reference formats here; the *APA Publication Manual* contains 77!

The Big Picture

When you finish writing all sections of your report, look at the paper as a whole. Readers should be able to see the connection between the research question you set forth in the introduction, the method you used to investigate this research question, the results you obtained, and your conclusions regarding the entire project. Furthermore, the introduction and discussion sections should be written so that they flow smoothly even if the reader ignores the more detailed information found in the method and results sections of the report. If these connections are not apparent, you need to revise your paper until they are.

TABLE A.2 APA-STYLE REFERENCE FORMATS

For an authored book:
    Friedman, M., & Rosenman, R. H. (1974). Type A behavior and your heart. New York: Knopf.

For an edited book:
    Chesney, M.A., & Rosenman, R. H. (Eds.). (1985). Anger and hostility in cardiovascular and be-havioral disorders. New York: Hemisphere.

For one chapter from an edited book:
    Spielberger, C. D., Johnston, E. H., Russell, S. F., Crane, R. J., Jacobs, G. A., & Worden, T. J. (1985). The experience and expression of anger: Construction and validation of an anger expression scale. In M. A. Chesney & R. H. Rosenman (Eds.), Anger and hostility in cardiovascular and behavioral disorders (pp. 5-30). New York: Hemisphere.

For a journal article:
    Friedman, M., Rosenman, R. H., Straus, R., Wurm, M., & Kositcheck, R. (1968). The relation-ship of behavior pattern A to the state of coronary vasculature. American Journal of Medicine, 44, 525-537.

For a magazine article:
    Sandroff, R. (1992, February). Do you have a heart disease personality? McCall's, 119, 32-40.

GENERAL TIPS FOR WRITING

Research reports do not just fall out of the typewriter or computer printer per-fectly written. They require multiple revisions and a lot of hard work. Even the very best writers revise their work again and again before it's ready to be seen by anyone outside their families. You may be familiar with James Michener's novels of exotic places, like *The Covenant, Poland*, or *Alaska*. He says:

> Nothing I write is good enough to be used in first draft, not even personal letters, so I am required to write everything at least twice. Important work, like a novel, must be written over and over again, up to six or seven times. (Michener, as quoted by Daigh, 1977, p. 148)

And how about Ernest Hemingway? Surely you've all heard of him! Consider this short excerpt from an interview of Hemingway:

> Hemingway: "I rewrote the ending of *Farewell to Arms*, the last page of it, thirty-nine times before I was satisfied."
> Interviewer: "Was there some technical problem there? What was it that had stumped you?"
> Hemingway: "Getting the words right." (Hemingway, 1965, as quoted by Trim-ble, 1975, p. 95)

Indeed, simply getting the words right can be a difficult task for all of us. Don't feel bad if the words you want don't come to you immediately. After all, if two of the world's most famous authors have to revise this much, you should ex-pect to also. There are several things you can do to make the writing process eas-ier and more successful.

Start Early

Perhaps the single best tip I can give you is to allow yourself enough time to turn out a top-quality project. Because the content of a typical research report is difficult, allow thinking time as well as writing time. Don't wait until every piece of the research is finished to start writing. For example, you can write the introduction and method sections before your data have even been gathered or analyzed. My own students agree that starting early is vital. No one, not even the most experienced scientist, can write a good research report by beginning the night before it is due.

Make an Outline

Now, don't panic. It doesn't have to be a fancy outline with all those Roman numerals and capital letters. Just scribble down the various points you want to present and then try to organize them by section. If you have a rough list of points that need to be presented in the introduction section, for example, it will be much easier to start writing that section. You may want to try organizing those points in a logical order, also. That way, you'll know exactly what points to start with and which ones to leave for later. This will save you time when the actual writing begins.

Plan to Revise

Whenever an author attempts to explain difficult concepts clearly, the task is going to require revision. Even the most experienced scientific writers plan to revise everything they write, so how can you, as a beginner, expect to dash off a first draft that is adequate? *Revising is absolutely mandatory.* Trust Michener and Hemingway on this.

Use the Tools of the Trade

Carpenters wouldn't dream of arriving at the construction site without their tools, and neither would a writer begin to write without a dictionary, thesaurus, grammar or style handbook, and typewriter or computer. The advantages of using a computer instead of a typewriter are endless, especially when multiple revisions are needed. Once you learn basic computer skills, writing by computer will save you time, allow you to produce more work, increase the quality of your work by making revision easy, and provide on-line dictionaries and automatic spell-checkers. Some computer programs will also check your grammar and provide you with an on-line thesaurus.

The disadvantage of computers, of course, is cost. However, you might be surprised at the large discounts available to students through their college bookstores. In addition, even the smallest colleges nowadays provide students with computers to use for fairly low fees. Take the time to learn word processing by computer—it will help you a hundred times over in the future, and "computer skills" won't look bad on your resume, either.

One computer caution, though: *Always make back-up copies of your work on a disk of your own.* In addition, print out a copy of your work on paper every now and then. You don't want to spend a week getting each word just right, only to find that the computer file is lost when you need to print out the final paper. I'm not kidding here; this really happens! Don't make the mistake of thinking that it can't happen to you.

Proofread

You must proofread each draft of your paper to revise it intelligently. There are several tips that make the process of proofreading easier and more effective:

1. Wait till you're fresh. It is useless to proofread a paper just after you've spent 10 hours writing it. You're tired then. Allow enough time so that you can let the paper sit for a day while you rest or work on other projects. When you come back to the draft, errors and ambiguities will be much easier to see.

2. Don't try to proofread for everything at once. There are many aspects to consider in writing a good paper: content, accuracy, clarity, logical organization, spelling, and grammar, to name a few. It will be impossible to consider all of these items carefully if you try to proofread the paper only once. Instead, divide up the labor. For example, you might proofread the first time for accuracy of content only. Ignore the other aspects of the paper, and ask yourself if the information you have presented is correct. The second time around, proofread for clarity. The information is correct, but is it clear? The third time, you may want to look at general organization or grammar. You may decide to ignore spelling and punctuation until your last proofreading check. The point is to concentrate on only one aspect of the paper during each separate proofreading.

3. Many students have trouble with correct grammar and don't even know it. If you suspect that you might fall into this category, read your paper aloud to yourself. This suggestion sounds a bit weird, I know, but it is effective. Because grammar is learned mostly through speech and less by reading, you will hear errors that you may never have seen. If you feel silly reading your work out loud, lock yourself in the closet with a flashlight or hike out into the boondocks to do it. It's well worth the effort.

4. Recognize your current position as someone who is only beginning to learn how to write research reports. If you were only beginning to ride a bike, you wouldn't enter the Tour de France for your first expedition. Similarly, when you write a research report, don't try to use the kind of complex language that you read in journal articles. Be sure you know exactly what your words mean. This advice may seem obvious, but many people use words that they can't even pronounce, in an effort to "sound scientific." Instead, try to sound clear.

5. Seek help when you need it. Because the concepts of research can be difficult, don't be afraid to ask your professor for help. If you can not write a clear explanation of some concept in your report, despite hard work, perhaps you simply do not understand the concept. Go to your professor, or perhaps a classmate, and try to work out a clear understanding of the topic you're writing about.

MECHANICS COUNT

The mechanics of writing, such as spelling, grammar, and punctuation, are important for several reasons. First, poor mechanics can make a sentence difficult or impossible to comprehend. All it takes is one misplaced comma or one misspelled word to turn the meaning of your sentence into mishmash.

Second, poor mechanics sometimes change the meaning of the sentence. This is especially dangerous because the sentence now has a comprehensible and obvious meaning, but not the one you intended.

Third, poor mechanics distract your readers. The purpose of your report is to present difficult research clearly and accurately, remember? Every time readers are stopped in their tracks by a mechanical error, their train of thought is lost. This is annoying enough when reading something simple, but readers can get downright angry when you force them to slog through silly errors in difficult material.

Finally, the remaining reason that accurate mechanics are important is that they present an image of you, a first impression. Would you show up at a job interview in an old dirty tee shirt and sandals? Would you invite special guests to your home if the house was filthy? Would you write your child's teacher a note full of bad grammar? If you did, do you suppose your child would be treated differently by that teacher in the future? These kinds of judgments may not be fair, but they certainly are realistic.

Mechanical errors in your writing imply a lack of interest and a tendency to be sloppy. Misspelled words weaken your credibility as a writer and a researcher. Readers will assume that you don't care much about your ideas if you don't even bother to set them down in clear, correct language. They'll wonder if you were as sloppy in designing and conducting your research as you were in reporting it. Right or wrong, they'll conclude that you don't take much pride in yourself or your work. As unfair as that may be, readers are judging your personal character, your professional ability, your intelligence, and your integrity partly by the number of mechanical errors you allow in final versions of your writing. To put it bluntly, mechanical mistakes make you look stupid even when you're not.

Common Errors in Spelling

All right, so mechanics count. But what are we going to do to avoid mechanical errors? There are a few common mistakes that you can correct easily with a little guidance.

BOX A.1 PITFALLS OF THE SPELLING CHECKER

We have a spelling checker.
It came with the PC.
It plainly marks four hour revue
Mistakes wee cannot sea.
Weave run this poem threw it,
Were sure your pleased too no.
Its letter perfect in it's weigh,
Hour checker tolled us sew.

From "Spelling Checker Poem" by P. Mowery, *National Association of Secretarial Services Newsletter,* May 1992. Copyright 1992 by National Association of Secretarial Services. Adapted by permission.

Use a Spelling Guide. It might be an old-fashioned dictionary, or a high-tech computer, or one of those hand-held spelling checkers, but unless you are the one in a million college students who can spell every word you use, get help.

Watch out for Homonyms. Homonyms are words that sound alike but have different spellings and different meanings. For example, *to, too,* and *two* are homonyms, as are *there, their,* and *they're.* Be sure you are using the word you really want, or the meaning of your own sentences could surprise you. I once received a paper containing this sentence:

Theories have been disguarded because of knew findings.

Apparently, the author didn't know the difference between *discard* (which means *throw away*) and *disguard* (which isn't in my dictionary but seems to mean *stop guarding*). The distinction between *new* and *knew* obviously wasn't too clear to this author either. What the author meant was this:

Theories have been thrown away because of new findings that refuted them.

What the author actually said was something like this:

People have stopped guarding theories because of findings they knew about.

Incidentally, homonym errors are most common when authors rely completely on computer spell-checkers. The computer knows that both *knew* and *new* are correctly spelled words, but it doesn't know which of the two words you want to use. That decision is yours. Perhaps the poem in Box A.1 will help you to understand the problem more clearly. Can you locate the 17 misspellings it contains?

Stimuli/Stimulus and Affect/Effect. Learn the spelling of words that are commonly used in psychological research. Two typical errors occur with the words *stimuli/stimulus* and *affect/effect.* Recall that stimuli are test materials used in research. If you present words written on cards to subjects during an experiment, those words are stimuli. Now, notice that *stimuli* is plural—it refers to more than one of a certain item. *Stimulus* is singular—it refers to only one word or one card, in our example.

The distinction between *affect* and *effect* is more complex because each of these words has several meanings. Select the right spelling according to the particular meaning you want.

affect: 1.   (noun) a mood or emotion
                  He shows hostile affect.

            2.   (verb) to influence something
                  His hostile mood affected me.
                  Mental stress affects physical health.

effect: 1.   (noun) an influence
                  His hostile mood had an effect on me.
                  Mental stress has an effect on physical health.

            2.   (verb) to cause something to happen
                  This treatment should effect a change in his mood.

Common Errors in Grammar

Certain mistakes in English grammar occur frequently, too. The most popular grammatical errors among college students are problems with noun-verb agreement and possessives. If you tend to have problems with other aspects of grammar, get a good grammar or writing handbook from your library or bookstore. Then, most importantly, use it!

Noun-Verb Agreement. Noun-verb agreement may sound complicated, but it's not. If we start with a ridiculous example, you'll see what I mean. Which of the following sentences are grammatically correct and which are incorrect?

1. *The cats are black.*
2. *The cat is black.*
3. *The cats is black.*
4. *The cat are black.*

Well, that's obvious—you undoubtedly knew at a glance that Sentences 1 and 2 are right and Sentences 3 and 4 are wrong. What's wrong with Sentences 3 and 4? Their nouns don't agree with their verbs. Whenever a plural noun (like *cats*) is used, it requires a plural verb (like *are*). Likewise, singular nouns (*cat*) require singular verbs (*is*). The principle should be very plain in this foolish example.

As simple as noun-verb agreement may seem to you, I would estimate that 50% of college students make this error regularly in their writing. What happens is that the sentence gets a little more complicated, like this:

The order of the words were determined by random shuffling.

This sentence is grammatically incorrect, just like Sentences 3 and 4 about the cats. I'll bet you didn't see the error so quickly this time, though. Perhaps it will help to consider this example in a little more detail. Was it the words that were determined by random shuffling? No, it was their order. Then, shouldn't we say *"the order was determined"* rather than *"the order were determined"*? Yes, we should.

As sentences become longer and more complicated, noun-verb agreement becomes more difficult to determine. When in doubt, ask yourself which noun is being operated on by the verb. In this example, something was being determined. Was it the first noun (the *order*), or was it the second noun (the *words*)? Choose the verb that goes with whichever noun was intended.

Possessives. You already know that we use apostrophes to signify ownership or possession of something. If your brother owns a football, then it is *your brother's football*. That's easy enough. But if you have several brothers and they all own the football jointly, then it will be *your brothers' football*. Life becomes more difficult here, not only because most brothers will fight over joint ownership of one football, but also because the switch from singular (*one brother*) to plural (*several brothers*) requires moving the apostrophe.

Let's consider another example that's more in keeping with psychological research reports:

1. *The subject's personality was classified as Type A or B.* (Only one subject is being discussed here, so the apostrophe precedes the final *s*.)
2. *The subjects' personalities were classified as Type A or B.* (This refers to several subjects, so the apostrophe follows the final *s*.)
3. *The subjects were classified according to personality.* (There's no apostrophe here because we aren't signifying possession of anything.)

This section will probably annoy some of you who learned the proper placement of apostrophes way back in the fifth grade. Unfortunately, you are in the minority. Many of the papers I read are full of errors with possessives. These errors appear frequently in the work of college seniors and college sophomores, from the most selective colleges and from indiscriminate colleges. It seems that a lot of people were out sick on the day that their fifth-grade teachers explained apostrophes.

It's and Its. The word *it* is a difficult exception to the standard rules of possession. *Its* does signify possession even though there is no apostrophe in the word. Thus, we are correct to say *The tree lost its leaves*. On the other hand, the word *it's* is not a possessive. Instead, this word is a contraction: *it's* means *it is*. Read the next few examples and make sure you know which are grammatically correct and which are not.

1. *It's a flawless research study.*
2. *Its a flawless research study.*
3. *The research study was flawed by its lack of control.*
4. *The research study was flawed by it's lack of control.*
5. *The research study was flawed by its' lack of control.*

Table A.3 SUMMARY OF COMMON MECHANICAL ERRORS

Stimulus/Stimuli. The word *stimulus* is singular; the word *stimuli* is plural. Examples:
1. *"One stimulus was shown to the subjects."*
2. *"Fourteen stimuli were shown to the subjects."*

Affect/Effect. Usually, in psychological research, the word *affect* is a verb meaning "to influence," and the word *effect* is a noun meaning "an influence." Examples:
1. *"Mental stress affects physical health."*
2. *"Mental stress has an effect on physical health."*

Noun-Verb Agreement. When a plural noun is used, plural verbs like *are* and *were* must also be used. Examples:
1. *"The order of the words was determined by random shuffling."*
2. *"The orders of the conditions were determined by counterbalancing."*

Possessives. To signify possession, the apostrophe usually precedes "s" for a singular noun but follows "s" for a plural noun. Examples:
1. *"One subject's personality was classified as Type A."*
2. *"All of the subjects' personalities were classified as Type A."*

Its/It's. The possessive form of the word "it" is *its* without an apostrophe. The word *it's* means "it is." Examples:
1. *"The research study was flawed by its lack of control."*
2. *"It's a flawless research study."*

Sentences 1 and 3 are correct; Sentences 2, 4, and 5 are wrong. If you don't understand why, now is the time to learn. Don't wait until you lose a job over your inability to write standard English.

Table A.3 is a quick reference guide that summarizes the common mechanical errors we have considered so far. You may find it helpful when writing, proofreading, and revising your research reports.

Avoiding Sexist Language

Before scientific research was conducted on the effects of sexist language, it was customary in English to use the pronoun *he* to refer to any male or female person. Other words, like *man* and *mankind*, were also used to refer to all humans.

Thanks to many psychologists and linguists who have studied the effects of this usage, we now know that English-speaking Americans consider words like *he*, *man*, and *mankind* to refer strictly to men. Such words completely exclude women. Perhaps a brief example will help. Consider this sentence:

The typical surgeon always washes his hands.

Many studies have shown that both children and adults believe that sentences like this refer to men and only men. According to this sentence, female surgeons either do not wash their hands or do not exist. The problem becomes even more apparent by simply reversing the usual gender-bound use of *he*, as in

The typical midwife always washes his hands.

A few English grammar teachers may still try to tell us that *he* refers to everyone, but we all know that it doesn't.

Political correctness is not the issue here. Instead, because our ultimate goal in scientific writing is to communicate clearly, we must say exactly what we mean. Suppose that you read the following sentence in a scientific research report:

Every subject was classified according to his age.

This sentence means that all of the subjects in the study were male. If this is true, then the use of the word *his* is correct. However, if any of the subjects were female, the sentence is incorrect and will confuse careful readers. The problem with sexist language in scientific writing, then, is primarily a problem of clarity, not politics.

Some writers try to avoid the pronoun problem by using cute combinations like *he/she* or *s/he* (or, most laughably, *s/h/it*). These terms sound horrible, and when strung together in a sentence, clarity fades rapidly:

The subject was told to place his/her hands on the table in front of him/her and twiddle his/her thumbs until the experimenter told him/her to stop.

I'm sure you've been frustrated by this so-called solution in your own reading. Other writers try to substitute a plural pronoun, like *their* for the awkward *him/her*. However, a plural pronoun cannot refer to a singular noun and still be grammatically correct. Therefore, this "solution" only substitutes an error in grammar for an error in style.

The best solutions are to change the noun to plural form so that it matches a plural pronoun, to omit the pronoun, or to revise the entire sentence. Table A.4 provides examples of bad solutions and good solutions to sexist language. It may be aggravating to correct old habits of pronoun usage at first, but with a little practice you'll find it's easy. This textbook can act as a model for you; never once in all of these pages has it been necessary to use the bad choices listed in Table A.4.

PLAGIARISM

Hardly a college student exists who hasn't heard the word *plagiarism*, but many don't know exactly what it means. **Plagiarism** is stealing someone else's words or ideas and presenting them as your own, without giving credit to the original author. It should be obvious to you that this practice is immoral and irresponsible. You may not realize that it is also against the law.

Some cases of plagiarism are more transparent than others. Students who buy papers from mail-order research mills and submit those papers as their own are obviously guilty of plagiarism, as are students who photocopy a friend's paper from last term and change the name. However, the person who truly writes part of a paper, but includes the exact words of other authors and fails to put quotation marks around those words is also guilty of plagiarism.

The penalties for plagiarism among students differ from one college to another. Probably the very least that a plagiarist can expect is to receive a zero score on the plagiarized assignment. Most colleges add to that an F for a final course

Table A.4 USING PRONOUNS

Bad Choice #1: Use "he" or "his" as if it refers to anyone, even though it really refers only to men.
Example: *"Every subject was classified according to his age."*

Bad Choice #2: Use "he/she" and "him/her," even though they're distracting and awkward.
Example: *"Every subject was classified according to his/her age."*

Bad Choice #3: Add the word "or" to "he/she" and "him/her," as if that makes the sentence less clumsy.
Example: *"Every subject was classified according to his or her age."*

Bad Choice #4: Use plural pronouns like "they" or "their," thereby making the sentence ungrammatical.
Example: *"Every subject was classified according to their age."*

****

Good Choice #1: Revise the noun to plural form so that it matches the pronoun.
Example: *"All subjects were classified according to their ages."*

Good Choice #2: Omit the pronoun entirely.
Example: *"Every subject was classified according to age."*

Good Choice #3: Revise the entire sentence.
Example: *"Age was the classification used for all subjects."*

grade, even if all of that student's other work in the course was A-plus quality and clearly original. Many colleges go further: Common penalties include being placed on probation by an academic standards committee, being suspended for one or more school terms, or being expelled from college entirely. The moral of the story? Don't try it.

At the same time, however, don't be frightened of inadvertent plagiarism. Science does progress only by building on the research work of previous scientists. You certainly aren't required to think of every new idea by yourself, nor would we ask you to ignore the body of important background research that has already been done. The key is simply to know and use the rules of citation and referencing, so that you always give proper credit where credit is due. In addition, it helps to either avoid taking notes word-for-word from articles or to specify clearly that your notes are really quotations so that you won't be tempted to use them verbatim later. Finally, try not to paraphrase what other people have written by merely substituting a different word here and there. Instead, present *your* thoughts, while referring and giving credit to other authors whose ideas helped you along the way.

Sample
Research Report

The sample research report is based on a simple experiment that was designed and conducted by a beginning research methods student, Tammy McKelvey. The design is much more basic than what you would typically find in a scientific journal. It is presented here so that you can concentrate on learning how to write scientific reports without trying to decipher a difficult research design at the same time. I wrote this report of Tammy's research so that you could see a strong example of scientific writing applied to the kind of experiment that you might design as a preliminary project.

The results of Tammy's experiment were not significant, an occurrence that is common in early stages of scientific research. The sample paper presents fictitious data that reflect this lack of statistical significance, so that you can see how to describe such findings in writing. It is followed by a second set of abstract, results, and discussion sections, in which the same experiment is described but significant (and fictitious) findings are presented.

1

Do Expectations of Difficulty
Influence Performance?
Janet L. Jones and Tammy K. McKelvey
Fort Lewis College

Note: In an actual research report, every line should be double spaced.

Abstract 2

This experiment was conducted to determine whether perceived expectations of difficulty would impede human performance. Subjects were timed while completing a puzzle task that was characterized as either "difficult" or "easy." The difference between completion times for the two groups was not significant. Factors contributing to these results were small sample size and inadequate emphasis on instructions.

3

Do Expectations of Difficulty
Influence Performance?

People respond differently to the news that a
particular task is considered difficult. Some may feel challenged
by that information; others may feel discouraged. In either
case, the perception that a task is difficult may alter our
abilities to perform it, regardless of whether the task
really is difficult.

Psychologists have investigated human expectations
across a wide variety of applications. Rosenthal and
Jacobson (1968), for example, have demonstrated that the
academic ability of school children is enhanced when their
teachers perceive them as intelligent. Orne (1969) has
explained the dangers of an experimenter's expectations about
subject performance in psychological research studies.
Merton (1948) was the first to describe self-fulfilling
prophecies, in which people behave in ways that will
fulfill their positive or negative expectations. Certainly, a
body of solid evidence suggests that humans are influenced
not only by the reality of a task, but also by their
expectations about that task.

The foundations laid by these classic studies continue
to yield fruitful research findings today. For example,
Horn and Downey (1990) recently explored people's attitudes
toward perceived expectations. Their subjects believed that
positive expectations were quite likely to enhance their
performance. However, these same subjects assumed that
negative expectations would be relatively unlikely to hamper
them.

Bandura's (1977) social learning theory suggests that
our responses to perceived expectations may be driven by
motivational forces. Human performance is motivated by

4

factors such as the likelihood of failure or success, the standards produced by our goals, and our beliefs regarding personal competence. In other words, being told that a task is difficult may cause subjects to question the likelihood of their success, to set goals that accommodate lower standards, and to doubt their own competence.

If perceived expectations of difficulty do cause subjects to experience these feelings, then their task performance might well be hampered. The purpose of this experiment was to determine whether perceived difficulty really does influence human performance in a negative manner. Furthermore, the experiment was designed so that the manipulation of subject expectations would be quite subtle, involving the substitution of only one word in a set of instructions. Resulting alterations in task performance would be compatible with Loftus and Palmer's (1974) research, in which subjects' beliefs about the severity of an automobile accident depended solely upon whether they were told that the cars "smashed into" each other or merely "hit."

In this experiment, subjects completed a picture arrangement puzzle that was characterized as either "difficult" or "easy." Subjects who were told that the puzzle was difficult were expected to take more time to complete it than subjects who were told that the puzzle was easy. Such results would demonstrate that human performance may be altered significantly by a subtle manipulation of expectations.

Method

Subjects

The subjects were comprised of 8 female and 12 male college students, all of whom were enrolled in an introductory psychology course at Fort Lewis College in Durango,

5

Colorado. Their ages ranged from 18 to 29 years, with a mean
age of 21.73 years. All subjects received extra course
credit in return for their participation.

Design

    To alter subjects' expectations about the puzzle task,
the wording of written instructions was manipulated as the
independent variable. Two levels of this independent
variable allowed the portrayal of the same task as either
"easy" or "difficult," in a between-subjects manipulation.
The time needed for each subject to complete the puzzle
task was measured in seconds.

Materials and Apparatus

    The materials and apparatus employed in this experiment
included a puzzle task, written instructions, a poster
board, and a stopwatch. The picture arrangement puzzle was
taken from a simulated sample of the Wechsler Intelligence
Scale for Children (Psychological Corporation, 1994). It
consisted of three 3-in. squares of paper, each showing a
drawing that represented part of a complete story. The
drawings are reproduced in Figure 1.

Insert Figure 1 about here

    Each set of instructions was typed on one sheet of
8 1/2-in. by 11-in. paper. The instructions indicated that
subjects would be timed while arranging three drawings into
an order that represented a meaningful story. They also
clarified that subjects would be given up to three trials
in which to complete the picture arrangement puzzle
accurately. Both sets of instructions were identical, with

6

the exception that one set of instructions characterized
the task as "easy," whereas the other set characterized it
as "difficult."

One piece of 8 1/2-in. by 11-in. blue poster board was
used to cover the puzzle upon task completion. Each
subject's completion time was measured with a standard
stopwatch.

Procedure

Subjects were tested individually in a small laboratory
room. Upon entering the room, subjects were assigned
randomly to one of the two experimental conditions and given
a set of written instructions corresponding to their assigned
condition. After subjects read these instructions silently,
they were asked if they understood the instructions. An
affirmative response caused the experiment to begin.

Subjects were seated at a table on which the three
drawings, in random order, were stacked underneath the
poster board. The stopwatch was started when the subject
first uncovered the drawings, and it was stopped when the
subject used the poster board to cover the drawings again.
The experimenter then inspected the order of drawings. If
the three drawings had been arranged in incorrect order,
the subject was asked to try again.

Subjects were allowed three trials to complete the
puzzle accurately. Each trial was timed independently, then
summed to provide a total completion time per subject.
After completing the puzzle correctly or making three
unsuccessful attempts, subjects were debriefed and thanked
for participating in the study.

Results

Subjects in both experimental conditions completed the
picture arrangement puzzle in about the same amount of

7

time. Instructions that portrayed the task as "easy"
produced a mean completion time of 11.40 seconds ($\underline{SD}=1.17$).
Instructions that portrayed the task as "difficult"
yielded a mean completion time of 10.10 seconds ($\underline{SD}=1.66$).
An independent $\underline{t}$-test based on an alpha level of .05
showed that the difference in completion time between these
two conditions was not significant, $\underline{t}$ (18) = .115,
$\underline{p}$ > .05.

Discussion

The prediction that perceived difficulty would slow
completion times was not supported by the results. Despite
the fact that previous research has produced strong
expectancy effects, the subjects in this experiment were
not influenced by instructions that characterized an upcoming
task as either "easy" or "difficult." These results are not
compatible with basic tenets of social learning theory
(Bandura, 1977) regarding motivational factors that should
be influenced by human expectations.

In reviewing the experimental method, two problems
became apparent. First, only 10 subjects participated in each
experimental condition. Although this number fulfills
minimum requirements for statistical validity, it remains
quite small. Perhaps a greater number of subjects would
have reduced the high variability among completion times
that may obscure any real effect.

Second, and most importantly, it was obvious during the
experiment that most subjects did not read the instructions
carefully. Instead, many participants glanced quickly at
the instructions, asked a few questions to clarify the
task, reported that they understood it, then began
completing the puzzle. With such careless reading, the
subtle one-word manipulation may never have been seen by the

8

majority of participants. This problem could be solved by requiring each subject to read the instructions aloud.

Because a large body of evidence in the psychological literature demonstrates the existence of expectancy effects, the failure of this experiment to support its prediction was probably caused by some combination of small sample size and inadequate emphasis on instructions. If these problems were corrected, future research should demonstrate that completion time is lengthened when subjects expect a task to be difficult.

Expectation is a general phenomenon that affects all of us to some degree, often more than we wish to concede. By developing a deeper understanding of the effects of positive and negative expectation, we may learn to motivate employees, encourage children, and improve our own performance.

9

References

Bandura, A. (1977). <u>Social learning theory.</u> Englewood Cliffs, NJ: Prentice-Hall.

Horn, G., & Downey, J. (1990). Perception and expectancy effects. <u>Psychological Reports, 67,</u> 651-655.

Loftus, E. F., & Palmer, J. C. (1974). Reconstruction of automobile destruction: An example of the interaction between language and memory. <u>Journal of Verbal Learning and Verbal Behavior, 13,</u> 585-589.

Merton, R. (1948). The self-fulfilling prophecy. <u>Antioch Review, 8,</u> 193-210.

Orne, M. (1969). Demand characteristics and the concept of quasi-controls. In R. Rosenthal & R. Rosnow (Eds.), <u>Artifact in behavior research</u> (pp. 143-179). New York: Academic Press.

Psychological Corporation.(1994). Simulated test item from the Wechsler Intelligence Scale for children. San Antonio, TX: The Psychological Corporation.

Rosenthal, R., & Jacobson, L. (1968). <u>Pygmalion in the classroom.</u> New York: Holt, Rinehart, & Winston.

In this second run through a sample paper, let's suppose that the results of this experiment had been statistically significant. Under these circumstances, only three sections of the report would need to be revised: the abstract, the results, and the discussion sections. All other sections would remain the same.

The following portions of a sample paper are included to show you how a good report might present significant findings. The results presented in it are fictitious.

2

Abstract

This experiment was conducted to determine whether perceived expectations of difficulty would impede human performance. Subjects were timed while completing a puzzle task that was characterized as either "difficult" or "easy." As predicted, subjects who expected the task to be "difficult" took more time to complete it than did subjects who expected the task to be "easy." These results demonstrate that expectations alter normal performance, even when they are based on the manipulation of only one word.

7

Results

Subjects who expected a "difficult" puzzle required significantly more time to complete it than did subjects who expected an "easy" puzzle. Instructions that portrayed the task as "easy" produced a mean completion time of 11.40 seconds ($\underline{SD} = 1.17$). By comparison, instructions that portrayed the task as "difficult" yielded a mean completion time of 15.22 seconds ($\underline{SD} = 1.73$). Using an alpha level of .05, an independent $\underline{t}$-test showed that this difference in completion time was significant, $\underline{t}(18) = 4.13$, $\underline{p} < .05$. Effect size was very large ($\omega^2 = .45$), indicating that 45% of the variability in completion times was accounted for by instructions.

Discussion

The prediction that perceived difficulty would slow completion times was supported by the results. In keeping with previous research that has produced strong expectancy effects, the subjects in this experiment were influenced by instructions that characterized an upcoming task as either "easy" or "difficult." The lengthened completion times that were observed among subjects who expected the picture arrangement puzzle to be difficult are also compatible with Bandura's (1977) motivational explanation.

One minor problem that occurred in this experiment should be corrected in the future. Several subjects did not appear to read the instructions carefully. Instead, they glanced quickly at the instructions, asked a few questions to clarify the task, reported that they understood it, then began completing the puzzle. In future studies, subjects could be required to read instructions aloud to ensure that they are reading each word carefully.

8

    The results of this experiment corroborate past research demonstrating the existence of expectancy effects. In addition, they show that the alteration of only one word in a set of instructions influences speed of performance significantly. Whether such subtle manipulation will also alter the accuracy of untimed performances remains to be explored in future studies.

    Expectation is a general phenomenon that affects all of us to some degree, often more than we wish to concede. By developing a deeper understanding of the effects of positive and negative expectation, we may learn to motivate employees, encourage children, and improve our own performance.

Statistical Tables
of Critical Values

C

Table C.1 SELECTING A STATISTICAL TEST*

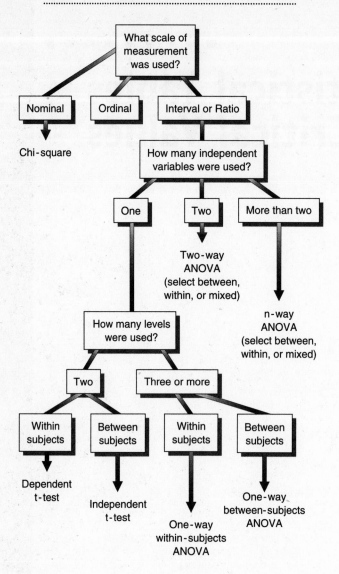

*This flowchart includes only those statistical tests that are presented in this book. The flowchart is adapted from an unpublished document developed by E. L. Bjork.

Table C.2 RANDOM NUMBERS TABLE

12	13	98	21	39	36	74	39	83	77	79	37	89	4	20	21	91	98	90
39	31	69	14	22	50	40	54	12	71	98	25	26	20	61	52	93	90	76
53	10	28	46	41	29	74	46	64	39	4	47	55	98	22	69	9	15	34
29	95	79	80	35	0	9	65	42	99	69	90	22	16	34	81	44	3	24
20	59	12	35	63	52	35	2	56	40	85	2	85	2	58	26	94	48	0
2	19	26	78	95	1	4	72	81	80	60	49	67	32	10	28	90	72	25
37	40	96	68	6	95	55	82	16	36	58	68	68	69	7	11	31	17	39
1	0	13	31	19	63	90	75	17	33	49	13	54	32	26	66	38	1	7
63	88	20	20	75	16	70	26	75	22	48	6	1	89	99	21	48	6	9
64	93	100	50	95	76	94	84	25	67	98	94	23	75	40	33	86	87	76
95	13	66	49	11	48	20	54	51	65	63	33	98	80	13	84	70	85	93
18	35	10	64	79	70	5	55	92	41	92	14	63	52	94	56	5	40	55
40	62	28	72	82	81	51	7	45	9	26	47	34	47	47	95	45	38	82
33	7	97	68	76	44	73	73	0	80	55	84	77	74	27	5	17	57	75
15	60	83	28	56	78	9	27	52	79	68	90	48	12	51	55	77	48	10
58	1	28	1	64	50	28	8	69	70	96	26	100	6	31	89	0	31	91
71	94	59	17	43	50	34	12	14	45	30	79	63	76	72	18	67	87	47
73	24	19	13	98	0	64	44	90	20	13	66	81	97	81	11	38	7	37
97	82	87	98	29	97	69	24	62	100	12	28	84	86	10	69	25	66	93
2	23	76	42	76	87	64	99	5	7	13	33	19	18	37	96	73	95	91
17	85	42	29	80	53	92	6	44	100	18	24	31	5	6	37	63	93	42
83	42	53	54	93	63	19	59	30	80	75	8	91	48	79	2	40	6	56
30	3	41	73	63	76	18	82	8	13	30	78	45	43	77	77	99	98	40
64	7	19	80	64	4	34	30	65	63	11	72	20	15	22	30	82	77	51
90	24	25	98	38	79	45	84	30	49	64	98	48	25	14	0	12	63	67
20	40	25	87	45	88	52	19	33	17	63	60	62	46	12	59	99	5	88
87	62	78	25	71	57	6	98	59	79	34	20	77	87	83	12	74	29	12
54	10	53	29	37	82	5	77	54	4	69	7	40	18	32	85	37	73	42
45	35	11	73	30	16	3	75	56	58	98	46	93	58	96	29	73	6	71
69	17	54	7	86	29	18	86	98	5	56	78	0	78	24	34	73	95	11
72	60	78	88	27	45	80	66	25	37	73	7	67	29	27	12	90	60	97
93	9	58	84	88	90	73	47	49	53	95	62	28	11	61	0	91	49	32
74	75	27	81	28	48	4	65	87	69	32	14	46	52	52	36	21	13	70
36	42	53	92	96	19	52	38	2	22	47	26	94	34	57	81	28	49	74
5	28	80	31	99	77	39	23	69	0	15	49	100	2	22	64	73	92	53
29	71	48	4	87	32	17	90	89	9	99	34	58	8	61	73	98	48	89
90	94	19	80	70	36	2	17	48	63	82	39	85	26	65	27	81	69	83
62	66	48	74	86	6	66	41	15	65	6	41	85	57	84	64	70	39	64
67	54	3	54	23	40	25	95	93	55	59	46	77	55	49	82	26	8	87
75	27	62	15	81	36	22	26	69	42	44	91	55	0	84	48	68	65	5
70	19	7	100	94	53	81	76	73	40	22	58	49	42	96	18	66	89	8
75	7	9	20	58	92	41	42	79	26	91	44	63	87	45	21	23	15	6
55	70	10	23	25	73	91	72	29	47	93	58	21	75	80	52	9	12	36
83	42	62	53	55	12	11	54	19	2	45	43	67	13	5	74	30	93	11
94	20	76	23	65	72	55	27	44	19	10	72	50	67	83	18	67	22	49
51	10	72	9	59	47	66	32	17	6	75	8	54	22	37	3	46	83	95
99	50	22	2	92	9	98	9	40	23	34	8	63	58	49	31	70	39	83
9	12	3	23	2	0	82	75	36	63	71	19	78	26	66	63	16	75	7
20	40	50	29	51	82	81	47	73	69	74	100	80	37	14	67	1	90	92
90	92	54	52	74	0	88	71	45	49	38	54	80	2	85	42	75	47	20
25	6	92	30	19	31	22	41	0	22	79	87	84	61	6	19	67	97	60
13	12	94	76	29	61	50	67	29	76	27	70	97	16	83	88	100	22	48
91	77	51	3	92	85	46	22	0	58	84	64	87	93	94	94	13	98	41

Table C.3 CRITICAL VALUES OF χ^2

Probability level for two-tailed test

df	.10	.05	.01
1	2.70554	3.84146	6.63490
2	4.60517	5.99147	9.21034
3	6.25139	7.81473	11.3449
4	7.77944	9.48773	13.2767
5	9.23635	11.0705	15.0863
6	10.6446	12.5916	16.8119
7	12.0170	14.0671	18.4753
8	13.3616	15.5073	20.0902
9	14.6837	16.9190	21.6660
10	15.9871	18.3070	23.2093
11	17.2750	19.6751	24.7250
12	18.5494	21.0261	26.2170
13	19.8119	22.3621	27.6883
14	21.0642	23.6848	29.1413
15	22.3072	24.9958	30.5779
16	23.5418	26.2962	31.9999
17	24.7690	27.5871	33.4087
18	25.9894	28.8693	34.8053
19	27.2036	30.1435	36.1908
20	28.4120	31.4104	37.5662
21	29.6151	32.6705	38.9321
22	30.8133	33.9244	40.2894
23	32.0069	35.1725	41.6384
24	33.1963	36.4151	42.9798
25	34.3816	37.6525	44.3141
26	35.5631	38.8852	45.6417
27	36.7412	40.1133	46.9630
28	37.9159	41.3372	48.2782
29	39.0875	42.5569	49.5879
30	40.2560	43.7729	50.8922
40	51.8050	55.7585	63.6907
50	63.1671	67.5048	76.1539
60	74.3970	79.0819	88.3794
70	85.5271	90.5312	100.425
80	96.5782	101.879	112.329
90	107.565	113.145	124.116
100	118.498	124.342	135.807

df = (r − 1)(c − 1)
r = number of rows
c = number of columns in contingency table

Table C.4 CRITICAL VALUES OF r

Probability level for two-tailed test

df	.10	.05	.01
1	.988	.997	.9999
2	.900	.950	.990
3	.805	.878	.959
4	.729	.811	.917
5	.669	.754	.874
6	.622	.707	.834
7	.582	.666	.798
8	.549	.632	.765
9	.521	.602	.735
10	.497	.576	.708
11	.476	.553	.684
12	.458	.532	.661
13	.441	.514	.641
14	.426	.497	.623
15	.412	.482	.606
16	.400	.468	.590
17	.389	.456	.575
18	.378	.444	.561
19	.369	.433	.549
20	.360	.423	.537
25	.323	.381	.487
30	.296	.349	.449
35	.275	.325	.418
40	.257	.304	.393
45	.243	.288	.372
50	.231	.273	.354
60	.211	.250	.325
70	.195	.232	.303
80	.183	.217	.283
90	.173	.205	.267
100	.164	.195	.254

$df = N - 2$
N = number of subjects

This table is adapted from Table 8 of the *Biometrika Tables for Statisticians* (Vol. I, 3rd ed.) by E. S. Pearson and H. O. Hartley, (Eds.), 1970, New York: Cambridge University Press. Used with the kind permission of the Biometrika trustees.

Table C.5 CRITICAL VALUES OF t

Probability level for two-tailed test

df	.10	.05	.01
1	6.314	12.706	63.657
2	2.920	4.303	9.925
3	2.353	3.182	5.841
4	2.132	2.776	4.604
5	2.015	2.571	4.032
6	1.943	2.447	3.707
7	1.895	2.365	3.499
8	1.860	2.306	3.355
9	1.833	2.262	3.250
10	1.812	2.228	3.169
11	1.796	2.201	3.106
12	1.782	2.179	3.055
13	1.771	2.160	3.012
14	1.761	2.145	2.977
15	1.753	2.131	2.947
16	1.746	2.120	2.921
17	1.740	2.110	2.898
18	1.734	2.101	2.878
19	1.729	2.093	2.861
20	1.725	2.086	2.845
21	1.721	2.080	2.831
22	1.717	2.074	2.819
23	1.714	2.069	2.807
24	1.711	2.064	2.797
25	1.708	2.060	2.787
26	1.706	2.056	2.779
27	1.703	2.052	2.771
28	1.701	2.048	2.763
29	1.699	2.045	2.756
30	1.697	2.042	2.750
40	1.684	2.021	2.704
60	1.671	2.000	2.660
120	1.658	1.980	2.617
∞	1.645	1.960	2.576

df for independent t-test = $N_1 + N_2 - 2$
df for dependent t-test = $N - 1$
N = total number of subjects
N_1 = number of subjects in group 1
N_2 = number of subjects in group 2

Table C.6 CRITICAL VALUES OF *F* AT *p* < .05

	1st *df*														
2nd *df*	1	2	3	4	5	6	7	8	9	10	12	15	20	24	30
1	161.4	199.5	215.7	224.6	230.2	234.0	236.8	238.9	240.5	241.9	243.9	245.9	248.0	249.1	250.1
2	18.51	19.00	19.16	19.25	19.30	19.33	19.35	19.37	19.38	19.40	19.41	19.43	19.45	19.45	19.46
3	10.13	9.55	9.28	9.12	9.01	8.94	8.89	8.85	8.81	8.79	8.74	8.70	8.66	8.64	8.62
4	7.71	6.94	6.59	6.39	6.26	6.16	6.09	6.04	6.00	5.96	5.91	5.86	5.80	5.77	5.75
5	6.61	5.79	5.41	5.19	5.05	4.95	4.88	4.82	4.77	4.74	4.68	4.62	4.56	4.53	4.50
6	5.99	5.14	4.76	4.53	4.39	4.28	4.21	4.15	4.10	4.06	4.00	3.94	3.87	3.84	3.81
7	5.59	4.74	4.35	4.12	3.97	3.87	3.79	3.73	3.68	3.64	3.57	3.51	3.44	3.41	3.38
8	5.32	4.46	4.07	3.84	3.69	3.58	3.50	3.44	3.39	3.35	3.28	3.22	3.15	3.12	3.08
9	5.12	4.26	3.86	3.63	3.48	3.37	3.29	3.23	3.18	3.14	3.07	3.01	2.94	2.90	2.86
10	4.96	4.10	3.71	3.48	3.33	3.22	3.14	3.07	3.02	2.98	2.91	2.85	2.77	2.74	2.70
11	4.84	3.98	3.59	3.36	3.20	3.09	3.01	2.95	2.90	2.85	2.79	2.72	2.65	2.61	2.57
12	4.75	3.89	3.49	3.26	3.11	3.00	2.91	2.85	2.80	2.75	2.69	2.62	2.54	2.51	2.47
13	4.67	3.81	3.41	3.18	3.03	2.92	2.83	2.77	2.71	2.67	2.60	2.53	2.46	2.42	2.38
14	4.60	3.74	3.34	3.11	2.96	2.85	2.76	2.70	2.65	2.60	2.53	2.46	2.39	2.35	2.31
15	4.54	3.68	3.29	3.06	2.90	2.79	2.71	2.64	2.59	2.54	2.48	2.40	2.33	2.29	2.25
16	4.49	3.63	3.24	3.01	2.85	2.74	2.66	2.59	2.54	2.49	2.42	2.35	2.28	2.24	2.19
17	4.45	3.59	3.20	2.96	2.81	2.70	2.61	2.55	2.49	2.45	2.38	2.31	2.23	2.19	2.15
18	4.41	3.55	3.16	2.93	2.77	2.66	2.58	2.51	2.46	2.41	2.34	2.27	2.19	2.15	2.11
19	4.38	3.52	3.13	2.90	2.74	2.63	2.54	2.48	2.42	2.38	2.31	2.23	2.16	2.11	2.07
20	4.35	3.49	3.10	2.87	2.71	2.60	2.51	2.45	2.39	2.35	2.28	2.20	2.12	2.08	2.04
21	4.32	3.47	3.07	2.84	2.68	2.57	2.49	2.42	2.37	2.32	2.25	2.18	2.10	2.05	2.01
22	4.30	3.44	3.05	2.82	2.66	2.55	2.46	2.40	2.34	2.30	2.23	2.15	2.07	2.03	1.98
23	4.28	3.42	3.03	2.80	2.64	2.53	2.44	2.37	2.32	2.27	2.20	2.13	2.05	2.01	1.96
24	4.26	3.40	3.01	2.78	2.62	2.51	2.42	2.36	2.30	2.25	2.18	2.11	2.03	1.98	1.94
25	4.24	3.39	2.99	2.76	2.60	2.49	2.40	2.34	2.28	2.24	2.16	2.09	2.01	1.96	1.92
26	4.23	3.37	2.98	2.74	2.59	2.47	2.39	2.32	2.27	2.22	2.15	2.07	1.99	1.95	1.90
27	4.21	3.35	2.96	2.73	2.57	2.46	2.37	2.31	2.25	2.20	2.13	2.06	1.97	1.93	1.88
28	4.20	3.34	2.95	2.71	2.56	2.45	2.36	2.29	2.24	2.19	2.12	2.04	1.96	1.91	1.87
29	4.18	3.33	2.93	2.70	2.55	2.43	2.35	2.28	2.22	2.18	2.10	2.03	1.94	1.90	1.85
30	4.17	3.32	2.92	2.69	2.53	2.42	2.33	2.27	2.21	2.16	2.09	2.01	1.93	1.89	1.84
40	4.08	3.23	2.84	2.61	2.45	2.34	2.25	2.18	2.12	2.08	2.00	1.92	1.84	1.79	1.74
60	4.00	3.15	2.76	2.53	2.37	2.25	2.17	2.10	2.04	1.99	1.92	1.84	1.75	1.70	1.65
120	3.92	3.07	2.68	2.45	2.29	2.17	2.09	2.02	1.96	1.91	1.83	1.75	1.66	1.61	1.55
∞	3.84	3.00	2.60	2.37	2.21	2.10	2.01	1.94	1.88	1.83	1.75	1.67	1.57	1.52	1.46

One-Way Within-Subjects ANOVA: first df (between-groups variability) = a – 1
second df (within-groups variability) = (a – 1)(s – 1)
One-Way Between-Subjects ANOVA: first df (between-groups variability) = a – 1
second df (within-groups variability) = a (s – 1)
Two-Way ANOVA: source A df = a – 1
source B df = b – 1
source A × B df = (a – 1)(b – 1)
second df (within-groups variability) = (a)(b)(s – 1)
a = number of levels in independent variable A
b = number of levels in independent variable B
s = number of subjects in each condition

This table is adapted from Table 18 of the *Biometrika Tables for Statisticians* (Vol. 1, 3rd ed.) by E. S. Pearson and H. O. Hartley, (Eds.), 1970, New York: Cambridge University Press. Used with the kind permission of the Biometrika trustees.

Table C.7 CALCULATING EFFECT SIZE*

Statistical Test	Inferential Statistic	Formula for Effect Size	"Small" Effect	"Medium" Effect	"Large" Effect
Chi-square with 2×2 contingency	χ^2	$\phi^2 = \dfrac{\chi^2}{N}$	.01	.09	.25
Pearson's product-moment correlation	r	r^2	.01	.09	.25
Independent t-test	t	$\omega^2 = \dfrac{\lvert t \rvert^2 - 1}{\lvert t \rvert^2 + N_1 + N_2 - 1}$	.01	.06	.14
Dependent t-test	t	$\omega^2 = \dfrac{\lvert t \rvert^2}{\lvert t \rvert^2 + N - 1}$	.01	.06	.14
One-Way ANOVA	F	$\omega^2 = \dfrac{(a-1)(F-1)}{(a-1)(F-1) + as}$	.01	.06	.14

*The information presented in this table has been gathered and adapted from Cohen (1977), Hays (1981), and Keppel (1982). Guidelines for small, medium, and large effects are controversial when taken out of context and should be treated only as very general rules of thumb.

Glossary

The number following each definition specifies the page on which it is discussed.

Abscissa: The horizontal axis of a bar graph, line graph, or scatterplot. (107, 280)

Abstract: A short summary stating the purpose, method, results, and conclusion of a research study. (35)

Alpha: A measurement of the likelihood that a decision to reject the null hypothesis will be wrong. (65)

Alternate hypothesis: The statistical assumption that there will be some difference in data gathered from two or more conditions. (60)

Alternative-form reliability: A correlational assessment of the extent to which alternate forms of a test will produce similar results. (122)

Anthology: A book that contains several previously published articles written by various authors. (30)

Applied science: An area of science in which knowledge gained through pure research is applied to practical problems. Can also refer to the discovery of new knowledge in applied settings. (15)

Archival research: The study of existing data such as birth, death, marriage, and divorce records. (77)

Authority: A way of gaining knowledge by accepting the word of a famous or respected person without skepticism. (10)

Automation: A control technique in which automatic devices, such as tape recorders or computers, remove unintended variation in research studies. (161)

Average: A general reference to all three measures of central tendency (mean, median, and mode). (54)

Axes: The two lines, abscissa and ordinate, of any bar graph, line graph, or scatterplot. (280)

Balanced Latin Square: A special technique that allows us to distribute order effects evenly while maintaining a small number of condition orders. (172)

Bar graph: A figure that presents data in the form of vertical bars so that readers can see overall patterns easily. (279)

Between-groups variability: Differences between scores that are caused by the manipulation of an independent variable or by inadequate control of a confounding variable. (134)

Between-subjects design: A research design in which each subject is assigned to only one condition. (Also called independent groups design.) (131)

Bibliography: A list of all sources used by an author in preparing a publication. (284)

Carryover effect: An undesirable effect that occurs whenever the treatment that is given in one experimental condition alters behavior in later conditions. (167)

Case study: A detailed look at one individual who usually shows some rare form of behavior. (76)

Ceiling effect: An undesirable effect that occurs when most data scores approach the top, or ceiling, of the possible range of scores. (164)

Cell: A statistical term referring to each condition for which data were collected. (209)

Central tendency: The descriptive statistic that describes the average or center point of a set of raw data. (54)

Chi-square: An inferential statistic that is used on nominal data to assess a relationship between differing sets of frequencies. (94)

Citing: Referring to another author's work by mentioning the author's last name and date of source publication. (282)

Coefficient of determination: A value (equal to r^2) that assesses effect size for a correlation. (112)

Common sense: A way of knowing by unspecialized individual judgment. (11)

Complete counterbalancing: A control technique in which a group of subjects completes every possible order of conditions. (171)

Complex experiments: Experiments that have more than one independent variable. (128)

Complex quasi-experiment: A quasi-experiment in which at least one quasi-independent variable is manipulated along with some other quasi-independent or independent variable. (232)

Concurrent validity: The ability of a new dependent variable to produce the same consistent results that a standard measure of the same behavior has produced in the past. (137)

Condition: A particular situation or level of the independent variable during a research study. (131, 209)

Confederates: People who work with the experimenter to deceive subjects. (254)

Confounding variable: An extraneous variable that is left uncontrolled and varies systematically with the levels of the independent variable. (129)

Construct validity: An assessment of how well a dependent variable measures the theoretical construct that it is supposed to measure. (137)

Contingency table: A table that displays observed frequencies in a chi-square analysis. (95)

Control group: A group of subjects to whom no treatment is given. (130)

Convenience sampling: An undesirable method of selecting subjects from a population according to availability and willingness to participate. (91)

Correlation: A type of statistic that measures the relationship between two dependent variables. (Can also refer to correlational research.) (104)

Correlation coefficient: The value (usually r) that is calculated to assess the significance of a correlation. (110)

Correlational research: A nonexperimental type of research in which the relationship between at least two sets of measurements is assessed and sometimes used for prediction. (104)

Counterbalancing: A control technique that distributes undesirable order effects across all conditions evenly in a within-subjects design. (168)

Criterion variable: In correlational research, the set of future measurement scores that are to be predicted. (120)

Crossed: A factorial design in which every level of one independent variable is combined with every level of the other independent variable. (209)

Cross-lagged correlation: A correlational technique in which a set of measurements gathered at one time are related to a set of measurements gathered at some other time. (114)

Crossover interaction: A special type of interaction that occurs when each independent variable exerts an equal but opposite effect on the other independent variable. (217)

Curvilinear relationship: A pattern of correlation in which one dependent variable increases or decreases with another dependent variable only up to a point, at which time the direction of the relationship changes. (109)

Debriefing: The act of telling subjects the purpose and hypothesis of a study after they have participated in it. (256)

Deception: A method of controlling demand characteristics in which the researcher hides important facts from the subjects until after they have participated in the study. (157)

Demand characteristics: Subtle cues in a research study that provide information to subjects about expected behavior. (156)

Demographic questions: Questions that request information such as age, sex, race, education level, and annual income. (88)

Demonstration: A bad design in which only one group of subjects is tested (also known as the one-shot case study). (182)

Dependent variable: The variable that is measured by the researcher as subjects carry out the research task. (19, 128)

Descriptive statistics: Numbers, such as means and standard deviations, that describe key characteristics of a large data set. (52)

Difference scores: Numbers that reflect the difference in performance between a subject's pretest score and that same subject's posttest score. (194)

Discrete: The separable, discontinuous nature of levels of certain types of independent variables. (281)

Double-barreled question: A survey question that really asks for two potentially different responses, but only allows the subject to make one response. (85)

Double-blind testing: A control technique in which neither the subject nor the experimenter knows which condition the subject is in. (162)

E-mail: An abbreviation for electronic mail, which allows scientists to communicate with each other by computer. (45)

Ecological validity: The extent to which a research study investigates people's true behavior in everyday life. (200)

Edited book: A book that contains several previously unpublished articles written by different authors. (30)

Editorial style: A set of standard writing conventions used by all authors in a certain discipline. (273)

Emotion: A way of knowing based on feelings. (11)

Empirical evidence: Knowledge gathered by observing real events. (12)

Empiricism: A philosophy based on gathering information by observing events and organisms in the real world. (12)

Empty control group: A group of subjects who receive no treatment at all. (159)

Equivalent groups: A requirement of good experimental research, in which subjects in comparable groups do not differ from each other in systematic ways. (183)

Evaluation research: A special type of applied science in which social programs are evaluated by researchers to find out whether they are effective. (15)

Expectancy effect: The undesirable effect that occurs when a researcher's expectations of subjects alters their natural behavior. (160)

Experimental group: The group of subjects who receive the treatment in an experiment. (191)

Experimental research or **experimentation:** A type of scientific research in which the manipulation of an independent variable allows scientists to determine cause. (14, 21)

Experimenter bias: The undesirable effect that occurs whenever a researcher's actions, words, or appearance lead subjects to behave in a certain way. (160)

External validity: The extent to which a study's results apply to a general population of subjects in a variety of settings. (199)

Extraneous variable: An extra factor that was left uncontrolled in an experiment, adding random error or a confound to the design. (129)

Face validity: The extent to which a dependent variable seems to measure what it's supposed to measure. (137)

Factorial design: An experiment in which two or more independent variables are manipulated simultaneously. (208)

Fatigue effect: An undesirable effect in which subjects become tired with participation in successive conditions, so that performance worsens over time. (167)

Field observation: A type of scientific research in which subjects are observed in their natural settings. (Also known as natural observation.) (80)

Figure: Usually a graph that illustrates the main pattern of results in a set of data. Can also refer to photographs, diagrams, or drawings. (278)

Floor effect: An undesirable effect that occurs when most data scores remain near the bottom, or floor, of the possible range of scores. (165)

Frequency: A number that shows how many times a particular event occurred in a given category. (53)

Hawthorne effect: An undesirable effect in which subject behavior is altered by attention received during a research study. (163)

History: A common source of confounding in which unexpected events occur between pretest and posttest and may influence subjects' behavior. (187)

Hypothesis: An educated guess about the general relationship between variables under scientific investigation. (14)

Independent groups design: A research design in which each subject is assigned to only one condition. (Also called between-subjects design.) (131)

Independent variable: The variable that is manipulated by the researcher in order to alter observed behavior. (19, 128)

Indexes: Large sets of books listing journal and magazine articles that have been published in a given discipline. (31)

Inferential statistics: Numbers that are used to determine whether the results of a small sample of subjects are also representative of a larger population. (58)

Informed consent: The ethical requirement that subjects sign their consent to participate in a research study that presents risk. (255)

Instrument decay: A problem that results from the decay of accurate measurement of behavior over time. (Also called instrumentation.) (188)

Instrumentation: A problem that results from the decay of accurate measurement of behavior over time. (Also called instrument decay.) (188)

Interaction: The combination of the effects of one independent variable with the effects of another independent variable on subjects' performance. (211)

Interlibrary loan: A procedure that allows libraries to share books and periodical articles with each other. (39)

Internal validity: The extent to which a research study produces effects that are caused by manipulation of an independent variable, and not by confounding variables or bad design features. (199)

Interrater reliability: A correlational value that represents the amount of agreement between two or more people observing similar behaviors. (121)

Interrupted time series design: A quasi-experimental design in which data are collected over a long period of time, with some important event interrupting that period. (240)

Interval: A scale of measurement in which the data are measured in units that differ from each other by an equal amount above and below zero. (52)

Intuition: A way of knowing in which solutions seem to occur without conscious effort. (12)

Inverse relationship: A relationship between two sets of measurements in which an increase in one variable is accompanied by a decrease in the other variable. (Also known as negative correlation.) (109)

Levels: The different values of an independent variable that are used in an experiment. (130)

Library research: A type of research in which known, published information is obtained from the library. (2)

Likert rating scale: A five-, seven-, or nine-point scale on which subjects express the extent to which they agree with some statement. (87)

Line graph: A figure in which patterns of results are depicted by continuous lines instead of by separated bars. (281)

Line of best fit: The line that represents the central tendency of the relationship between dependent variables in a correlational scatterplot. (Also called a regression line.) (110)

Literature: The body of published knowledge about a certain topic in a particular discipline. (26)

Literature review: The process of learning about a certain topic by reading and evaluating pertinent journal articles and books. (26)

Logic: A way of knowing by making conclusions based on premises. (13)

Main effect: The effect of only one of the independent variables in a factorial design. (213)

Marginal means: The numbers that are calculated from cell means in order to determine whether a main effect exists in a factorial design. (214)

Matched-group design: A between-subjects experiment in which important features such as age, income, or IQ are matched across subjects. (191)

Maturation: A common source of confounding in which normal change over time may interfere with results. (187)

Mean: The central point of a data set when all its values are added, then divided by the number of values in the set. (54)

Median: The number that falls in the center of a data set when all of its numbers have been placed in order by value. (54)

Mixed design: A factorial design in which one independent variable is manipulated between subjects, while another is manipulated within subjects (also called a split-plot design). (209)

Mode: The number that appears most often in a data set. (55)

Monograph: Any book containing specialized information on a particular topic. (30)

Mortality: A threat to internal validity that occurs when large numbers of subjects drop out of a particular condition. (197)

Multiple correlation: A correlational technique in which the relationship between more than two factors is assessed. (120)

Multiple-group pretest-posttest design: An experiment in which two or more groups of subjects are given a pretest and a posttest with differing treatments administered between the tests. (192)

Natural observation: A type of nonexperimental research in which human or animal behavior is observed in natural settings. (Also called field observation.) (80)

Negative correlation: A relationship between two sets of measurements in which an increase in one variable is accompanied by a decrease in the other variable. (Also known as an inverse relationship.) (109)

Negative skew: A distribution of obtained data in which there is a large number of high scores. (56)

Nominal: A scale of measurement in which the numbers represent named categories with no inherent numerical value. (51)

Nonequivalent control group: A control group of subjects that differs in systematic ways from the experimental group. (243)

Nonexperimental research: A type of research that describes behavior but does not include the manipulation of independent variables. (21)

Nonparametric statistics: Inferential tests that are designed for data sets that do not meet the requirements of normal distribution. (70)

Nonparticipant observation: A type of natural observation in which the researcher is not considered a member of the group that is being studied. (80)

Normal distribution: The way in which raw data usually congregate around the mean, with few scores occurring at either extreme. (55)

Null hypothesis: The statistical assumption that there will be no difference between scores from various conditions. (60)

Nuremberg code: A list of 10 principles that were developed in 1948 as a guide to ethical research. (251)

Objective: Unbiased. (13)

Omega-squared: A value (ω^2) that assesses effect size, based on t or F. (142)

One-group pretest-posttest design: A bad design in which one group of subjects is given a pretest, a treatment, and a posttest. (185)

One-shot case study: A bad design in which only one group of subjects is tested (also known as a demonstration). (182)

Open-ended question: A survey question in which no particular means of response is suggested. (86)

Operational definitions: Very precise ways of defining certain concepts or behaviors in procedural terms. (81)

Order effect: An undesirable effect that occurs whenever the order of participating in multiple conditions changes normal behavior. (166)

Ordinal: A scale of measurement in which the numbers stand for categories that can be ranked in a clear order but do not vary by equal amounts. (51)

Ordinate: The vertical axis of a bar graph, line graph, or scatterplot. The ordinate represents increments of a dependent variable. (107, 280)

Paradigm shift: A dramatic change in the traditional way of thinking about and studying a certain scientific topic. (14)

Parametric statistics: Inferential tests that are designed for data sets that have a normal distribution. (70)

Partial correlation: A statistical technique in which the effects of a potential third variable are removed from a correlation. (115)

Partially open-ended question: A survey question that is followed by a selection of possible answers plus a choice termed "other" for which subjects can write a response. (86)

Participant observation: A type of natural observation in which the researcher becomes a member of the group being studied. (80)

Periodicals: Publications that are issued repeatedly at regular intervals, like newspapers, magazines, and journals. (31)

Phi-squared: A value (ϕ^2) that measures effect size, based on a chi-square test. (97)

Physical sciences: Disciplines in which science is used to explore aspects of the universe that are primarily determined by natural physical forces. (16)

Pilot study: A trial run of a research study, conducted on people whose data will not be included in the real study. (157)

Placebo: Originally, a pill that contains no active substance. Now, this refers to any situation in which subjects believe they are receiving some treatment, when really they are not. (159)

Placebo control group: A group of subjects who receive what they believe is a treatment, when actually it is not. (159)

Placebo effect: A type of subject bias in which a subject's belief that some treatment will have an effect actually causes the effect to occur. (159)

Plagiarism: The act of presenting another author's words or ideas without giving proper credit, as if they were your own. (293)

Popular press: Type of published knowledge including books, magazines, and newspapers that are readily available to anyone. (26)

Population: The entire set of every potential subject that falls into our category of interest. (59)

Positive correlation: A relationship between two sets of measurements in which an increase in one variable is accompanied by an increase in the other variable. (108)

Positive skew: A distribution of obtained data in which there is a large number of low scores. (56)

Poster session: A public event in which the highlights of research studies are presented on posters. (46)

Post-hoc test: A statistical test that is performed after a significant F value is obtained in order to determine which of the differences between means are significant. (150)

Power: The ability of a statistical test to detect a significant difference between means if it exists. (68)

Practice effect: An undesirable effect in which subjects perform increasingly well in successive conditions. (166)

Prediction: A specific statement of the results that a researcher expects to obtain in a given study. (18)

Predictive validity: The extent to which one set of scores may be used to predict performance that will be measured by some other set of scores. (120, 137)

Predictor variable: In correlational research, the variable that is known at the present time and used to predict future behavior. (120)

Probability: The likelihood that a particular statistical hypothesis is true in the population. (65)

Probability level (p): The likelihood of rejecting the null hypothesis by mistake when inferring that the results of a sample apply to a population. (65)

Proportionate random sampling: A method of selecting subjects so that the sample contains the same proportions of different types of people as the population contains. (90)

Publication lag: The long period of time between submitting a manuscript for publication and actually seeing it in print. (44)

Pure science: The scientific discovery of new facts without concern for their practical use. (14)

Quasi-experiment or **Quasi-experimental research:** A type of research in which the main variable of interest cannot be manipulated, leading to nonrandom assignment of subjects to conditions. (21, 228)

Random sampling: An ideal method of subject selection in which every member of a population has an equal chance of being selected as a member of the sample. (89)

Range: A measure of variability representing the difference between smallest and largest values in a set of numbers. (58)

Ratio: A scale of measurement in which the data represent equal amounts of change at each value but can not drop below zero. (52)

Rationalism: A philosophy in which logical reasoning is used to gather and evaluate new knowledge. (13)

Raw data: Numbers that have been generated by subjects in a research study. (50)

Reactivity: The change in behavior that occurs when subjects react to the process of being measured. (138)

Referees: Experts who critique manuscripts before they are published in scientific journals. (27)

References: A listing of full information for all sources that are cited in a publication. (284)

Regression line: The line that represents the central tendency of the relationship between dependent variables in a correlational scatterplot. (Also called the line of best fit.) (110)

Regression to the mean: The process by which extreme scores become less extreme as they are measured again and again. (Also called statistical regression.) (188)

Reliable: Consistent in producing the same outcome repeatedly. (81)

Repeated measures design: A research design in which each subject participates in all conditions. (Also called a within-subjects design.) (132)

Replication: The act of obtaining results that are similar to those another scientist has obtained, after observing similar events. (13)

Research hypothesis: A statement of the general relationship that is expected to occur between variables, based on past research, theory, and/or logical reasoning. (60)

Response rate: The percentage of subjects who responded to a survey. (91)

Restricted question: A survey question that is followed by a selection of possible answers. (86)

Sample: A small group of people who participate in a research study. (59)

Scattergram: A graph that illustrates data obtained through correlational research. (Also called scatterplot.) (106)

Scatterplot: A graph that illustrates data obtained through correlational research. (Also called scattergram.) (106)

Science: A way of knowing that combines observation by sense experience plus reasoning by deductive logic. (13)

Scientific fraud: Unethical actions that taint research results, such as changing raw data or lying about a study's outcome. (260)

Scientific research: A method of discovering new knowledge based on the principles of observation, replication, and logical reasoning. (2)

Sense experience: A way of knowing based on human observation of events. (12)

Simple experiment: An experiment with only one independent variable. (128)

Simple quasi-experiment: A quasi-experiment in which only one quasi-independent variable is investigated. (230)

Simple random sampling: A method of selecting subjects in which every member of the population has an equal chance of being selected for the sample. (89)

Skewed: A description of data that are not distributed in a symmetrical fashion. (56)

Social desirability bias: The tendency for subjects to behave in ways that they believe are desired by others. (158)

Social sciences: Disciplines in which science is used to explore aspects of civilization that are primarily determined by social forces. (16)

Split-plot design: A factorial design in which one independent variable is manipulated between subjects while another independent variable is manipulated within subjects. (Also called a mixed design.) (209)

Spurious relationship: A false correlation in which two dependent variables are related to each other significantly but only by accident or by virtue of an unidentified third variable. (113)

Standard deviation: A number that represents the average amount by which each score in a data set varies from the mean, in units of measurement that match the data. (58)

Statistical hypothesis: A statement of alternate outcomes used in inferential statistics. (59)

Statistical regression: The process by which extreme scores become less extreme as they are measured again and again. (Also called regression to the mean.) (188)

Stimuli: Items to which a subject responds during a research study, such as words, pictures, or objects. (276)

Stratified random sampling: A method of selecting subjects in which the sample takes into account different types of people within a population. (90)

Subject bias: Hopes and beliefs that cause subjects to respond to the research environment in ways that alter natural behavior. (157)

Subject variables: Inherent characteristics of human and animal subjects such as height and age. (228)

Survey research: A form of nonexperimental research in which questionnaires are administered to many subjects to determine their opinions and beliefs. (82)

Syllogism: A form of logical reasoning in which a series of premises leads to a conclusion. (13)

Table: A visual aid arranged in a row-and-column format that makes information easy to understand. (278)

Tachistoscope: A device that presents stimuli visually for very brief durations of time. (143)

Technology: Technical inventions, developed through science, that serve people in their homes and workplaces. (15)

Tenacity: A way of knowing in which the believer holds stubbornly to repeated notions without skepticism. (10)

Testing: A threat to internal validity that occurs whenever the test, rather than the treatment, causes a change in behavior. (187)

Test-retest reliability: A correlational technique for assessing the consistency of scores produced by a test that is given repeatedly. (122)

Theoretical construct: An abstract concept that plays a central role in a theory but may not exist in real life. (137)

Theory: A series of basic principles that explain various types of complex behavior. (18)

Third variable: A variable that was not measured but is responsible for a correlation between two or more other variables. (115)

Treatment: Some action that is imposed on a subject, usually as a level of an independent variable. (130)

Tuskegee experiment: An experiment conducted near Tuskegee, Alabama, from 1932 until 1972, in which subjects were allowed to die slowly and painfully from a disease that could have been treated. (251)

Type I error: The mistake we make when we reject the null hypothesis even though it was really true, measured by the value called p for probability level. (65)

Type II error: The mistake we make when we decide to accept the null hypothesis even though it was really false. (68)

Unbalanced design: A design in which the numbers of subjects in each condition are not equal. (198)

Validity: The extent to which a dependent variable really measures what it was intended to measure. Also, the extent to which an experiment's results may be trusted. (137, 199)

Variability: The amount by which a set of scores varies from its central tendency. (57)

Variance: A measure of variability that tells us how much each score in a data set differs on average from the mean. (58)

Virtual communities: Groups of scientists at different locations working together by computer. (45)

Within-groups variability: Fluctuations between scores within the same condition that are caused by individual differences and random error. (134)

Within-subjects design: An experimental design in which each subject participates in every condition. (Also called repeated measures design.) (131)

References

Abrams, D. B., & Wilson, G. T. (1983). Alcohol, sexual arousal, and self-control. *Journal of Personality and Social Psychology, 45,* 188–198.

Adams, M. J. (1991). *Beginning to read: Thinking and learning about print.* Cambridge: The MIT Press.

American Psychological Association. (1994). *Publication manual of the American Psychological Association.* Washington, DC: American Psychological Association.

American Psychological Association. (1992). *Ethical principles of psychologists and code of conduct.* Washington, DC: American Psychological Association.

American Psychological Society Steering Committee. (1992, February). Human capital initiative: Report of the National Behavioral Science Research Agenda Committee. *The APS Observer,* pp. 1–33.

Anastasi, A. (1972). Reminiscences of a differential psychologist. In T. S. Krawiec (Ed.), *The psychologists* (pp. 3–37). London: Oxford University Press.

Anderson, J. (1992, May 12). Riot. *The Durango Herald,* pp. 1, 10.

Andreasen, N. C. (1988). Brain imaging: Applications in psychiatry. *Science, 239,* 1381–1388.

Atkinson, R. L., Atkinson, R. C., Smith, E. E., & Bem, D. J. (1990). *Introduction to psychology.* New York: Harcourt Brace Jovanovich.

Baars, B. J. (1986). *The cognitive revolution in psychology.* New York: Guilford.

Barefoot, J. C., Dahlstrom, W. G., & Williams, R. B., Jr. (1983). Hostility, CHD incidence, and total mortality: A 25-year follow-up study of 255 physicians. *Psychosomatic Medicine, 45* (1), 59–63.

Barrett, L. (1985, May). The premed machine. *Washington Monthly,* pp. 41, 43.

Bartocci, B. (1992, November 3). Mom, I'm gay. *Woman's Day,* pp. 76–81.

Baumrind, D. (1964). Some thoughts on ethics of research: After reading Milgram's "Behavioral study of obedience." *American Psychologist, 19,* 421–423.

Bem, S. L. (1974). A measure of psychological androgyny. *Journal of Consulting and Clinical Psychology, 42,* 155–162.

Benbow, C. P. (1988). Sex differences in mathematical reasoning ability in intellectually talented preadolescents: Their nature, effects, and possible causes. *Behavior and Brain Sciences, 11,* 169–183, 217–232.

Benbow, C. P., & Stanley, J. C. (1980). Sex differences in mathematical ability: Fact or artifact? *Science, 210,* 1262–1264.

Benbow, C. P., & Stanley, J. C. (1983). Endogenous influences are probably responsible. Sex differences in mathematical reasoning ability: More facts. *Science, 222,* 1029–1031.

Berger, J. (1989, May 3). Slow pace toward doctorates prompts fear of unfilled jobs. *The New York Times,* pp. A1, B7.

Berretta, S., & Privette, G. (1990). Influence of play on creative thinking. *Perceptual and Motor Skills, 71,* 659–666.

Bond, G. L., & Dykstra, R. (1967). The cooperative research program in first-grade reading instruction. *Reading Research Quarterly, 2,* 5–142.

Bordens, K. S., & Abbott, B. B. (1991). *Research design and methods: A process approach.* Mountview, CA: Mayfield Publishing Company.

Bower, G. H. (1972). Mental imagery and associative learning. In L. Gregg (Ed.), *Cognition in learning and memory.* New York: Wiley.

Bowles, J. (1992, May 10). Gates: Deadly force needed to control riots. *The Durango Herald,* p. 9A.

Boys have superior math ability, study says. (1980, December 15). *Education USA,* p. 122.

Bransford, J. D., Barclay, J. R., & Franks, J. J. (1972). Sentence memory: A constructive versus interpretive approach. *Cognitive Psychology, 3,* 193–209.

Broad, W., & Wade, N. (1982). *Betrayers of the truth.* New York: Simon and Schuster.

Campbell, D. T., & Stanley, J. C. (1966). *Experimental and quasi-experimental designs for research.* Chicago: Rand McNally.

Cannon, W. B. (1927). The James-Lange theory of emotions: A critical examination and an alternative theory. *American Journal of Psychology, 39,* 106–124.

Clifford, M. M., & Walster, E. (1973). The effect of physical attractiveness on teacher expectations. *Sociological Education, 46,* 248–258.

Cohen, J. (1977). *Statistical power analysis for the behavioral sciences.* New York: Academic Press.

Collins, E. (1988). Exonerating sodium. *Scientific American, 258,* 32.

Committee of the Institute of Medicine. (1982). *Marijuana and health.* Washington, DC: National Academy Press.

Cozby, P. C. (1989). *Methods in behavioral research.* Palo Alto, CA: Mayfield Publishing Company.

Daigh, R. (1977). *Maybe you should write a book.* Englewood Cliffs, NJ: Prentice-Hall.

Descartes, R. (1952). Discourse on the method of rightly conducting the reason and seeking for truth in the sciences. In R. M. Hutchins (Ed.), *Great books of the western world: Rene Descartes* (Vol. 31, pp. 41–67). Chicago: Encyclopaedia Britannica, Inc. (Original work published 1637)

Dillman, D. A. (1978). *Mail and telephone surveys: The total design method.* New York: Wiley.

Dion, K. K., Berscheid, E., & Walster, E. (1972). What is beautiful is good. *International Journal of Personality and Social Psychology, 24,* 285–290.

Dipboye, R. L., Arvey, R. D., & Tepstra, D. E. (1977). Sex and physical attractiveness of raters and applicants as determinants of resume evaluations. *Journal of Applied Psychology, 60,* 39–43.

Ebbinghaus, H. (1913). *Memory: A contribution to experimental psychology* (H. A. Roger & C. E. Bussenius, Trans.). New York: Columbia University Press. (Original work published 1885)

Ekman, P., Levenson, R. W., & Friesen, W. V. (1983). Autonomic nervous system activity distinguishes among emotions. *Science, 221,* 1208–1210.

Ellis, A. W. (1984). *Reading, writing, and dyslexia: A cognitive analysis.* Hillsdale, NJ: Lawrence Erlbaum Associates.

Eron, L. D., Huesmann, L. R., Lefkowitz, M. M., & Walder, L.D. (1972). Does television violence cause aggression? *American Psychologist, 27,* 253–263.

Faludi, S. (1991). *Backlash: The undeclared war against American women.* New York: Crown Publishers.

Felson, R. B. (1980). Physical attractiveness, grades, and teachers' attributions of ability. *Representative Research in Social Psychology, 11,* 64–71.

Fennema, E. (1990). Justice, equity, and mathematics education. In E. Fennema & G. C. Leder (Eds.), *Mathematics and gender* (pp. 1–9). New York: Teachers College Press.

Fischbach, G. D. (1992). Mind and brain. *Scientific American, 267* (3), 48–57.

Flesch, R. (1955). *Why Johnny can't read.* New York: Harper and Row.

Flesch, R. (1985). *Why Johnny can't read* (2nd ed.). New York: Harper and Row.

Fossey, D. (1983). *Gorillas in the mist.* Boston: Houghton Mifflin Company.

Freedman, D., Pisani, R., & Purves, R. (1980). *Statistics.* New York: W. W. Norton & Company.

Friedman, M., & Rosenman, R. H. (1974). *Type A behavior and your heart.* New York: Knopf.

Freud, S. (1952). A general introduction to psychoanalysis. In R. M. Hutchins (Ed.), *Great books of the western world: Major works of Sigmund Freud* (Vol. 54, pp. 449–638). Chicago: Encyclopaedia Britannica. (Original work published 1917)

Garfield, E. (1992, November). A citationist perspective on psychology. *APS Observer,* 8–13.

Gelman, D., Foote, D., Barrett, T., & Talbot, M. (1992, February 24). Born or bred? *Newsweek,* pp. 46–53.

The gender factor in math. (1980, December 15). *Time,* p. 57.

George, C., & Main, M. (1979). Social interactions of young abused children: Approach, avoidance, and aggression. *Child Development, 50,* 306–318.

Gerbner, G., Gross, L., Signorielli, N., & Morgan, M. (1986). Television's mean world: Violence profile No. 14–15. Philadelphia: Annenberg School of Communications, University of Pennsylvania.

Gillespie, R. (1991). *Manufacturing knowledge: A history of the Hawthorne experiments.* New York: Cambridge University Press.

Godden, D. R., & Baddeley, A. D. (1975). Context-dependent memory in two natural environments: On land and underwater. *British Journal of Psychology, 66,* 325–331.

Goodwin, D. W., Powell, B., Bremer, D., Hoine, H., & Stern, J. (1969). Alcohol and recall: State dependent effects in man. *Science, 163,* 1358.

Gowan, J. C., Khatena, J., & Torrance, E. P. (1981). *Creativity and its educational implications.* Dubuque, IA: Kendall/Hunt.

Gregory, R. L. (1977). *Eye and brain.* New York: McGraw-Hill.

Guerin, D., & MacKinnon, D. P. (1985). An assessment of the California child passenger restraint requirement. *American Journal of Public Health, 75*(2), 142–144.

Hardy, J. D., Wolff, H. G., & Goodell, H. (1952). *Pain reactions and sensations.* Baltimore: Williams & Wilkins.

Haynes, S. G., Feinleib, M., & Kannel, W. B. (1980). The relationship of psychosocial factors to coronary heart disease in the Framingham study: III. Eight-year incidence of coronary heart disease. *American Journal of Epidemiology, 111,* 37–58.

Hays, W. L. (1981). *Statistics.* New York: Holt, Rinehart and Winston.

Hearnshaw, L. S. (1979). *Cyril Burt, psychologist.* Ithaca, NY: Cornell University Press.

Heilman, M. E., & Stopeck, M. H. (1985). Being attractive, advantage or disadvantage? Performance based evaluations and recommended personnel actions as a function of appearance, sex, and job type. *Organizational Behavior and Human Decision Processes, 35,* 202–215.

Henderson, J. (1990, March 1). When scientists fake it. *American Way,* pp. 56–62, 100–101.

Herzberg, F. (1966). *Work and the nature of man.* Cleveland: World Publishing.

Hite, S. (1987). *Women and love: A cultural revolution in progress.* New York: Knopf.

Humphreys, L. (1970). *Tearoom trade.* Chicago: Aldine.

Hyde, J. S., Fennema, E., & Lamon, S. J. (1990). Gender differences in mathematics performance: A meta-analysis. *Psychological Bulletin, 107*(2), 139–155.

Intersalt Cooperative Research Group. (1988). Intersalt: An international study of electrolyte excretion and blood pressure. *British Medical Journal, 297,* 319–328.

James, W. (1952). The principles of psychology. In R. M. Hutchins (Ed.), *Great books of the western world: William James* (Vol. 53). Chicago: Encyclopaedia Britannica, Inc. (Original work published 1891)

Johnston, L. D., O'Malley, P. M., & Bachman, J. G. (1989). *Drug use, drinking, and smoking: National survey results from high school, college, and young adult populations 1975–1988.* Washington, DC: United States Department of Health and Human Services.

Jones, J. H. (1981). *Bad blood: The Tuskegee syphilis experiment.* New York: Free Press.

Jones, M. C. (1924). A laboratory study of fear: The case of Peter. *Pedagogical Seminary, 31,* 308–315.

Judd, C. M., Smith, E. R., & Kidder, L. H. (1991). *Research methods in social relations.* Fort Worth, TX: Holt, Rinehart and Winston.

Kaplan, R. M., & Saccuzzo, D. P. (1989). *Psychological testing.* Pacific Grove, CA: Brooks/Cole.

Katz, J. (1972). *Experimentation with human beings: The authority of the investigator, subject, professions, state in the human experimentation process.* New York: Russell Sage Foundation.

Keith-Spiegel, P. (1990). *The complete guide to graduate school admission: Psychology and related fields.* Hillsdale, NJ: Lawrence Erlbaum Associates.

Keith-Spiegel, P., & Koocher, G. P. (1985). *Ethics in psychology.* New York: Random House.

Keppel, G. (1982). *Design and analysis: A researcher's handbook.* Englewood Cliffs, NJ: Prentice-Hall.

Key, W. B. (1973). *Subliminal seduction: The ad media's manipulation of a not so innocent America.* Englewood Cliffs, NJ: Prentice-Hall.

Kleinmuntz, B., & Szucko, J. J. (1984). A field study of the fallibility of polygraph lie detection. *Nature, 308,* 449–450.

Kline, M. (1970). The use of extended group hypnotherapy sessions in controlling cigarette habituation. *International Journal of Clinical and Experimental Hypnosis, 18,* 270–282.

Koehler, M. S. (1990). Classrooms, teachers, and gender differences in mathematics. In E. Fennema & G. C. Leder (Eds.), *Mathematics and gender* (pp. 128–148). New York: Teachers College Press.

Kozol, J. (1985). *Illiterate America.* New York: New American Library.

Kramer, J. J., & Conoley, J. C. (Eds.) (1992). *The eleventh mental measurements yearbook.* Lincoln, NE: University of Nebraska Press.

Kuhn, T. S. (1962). *The structure of scientific revolutions.* Chicago: University of Chicago Press.

Landy, D., & Sigall, H. (1974). Beauty is talent: Task evaluation as a function of the performer's physical attractiveness. *Journal of Personality and Social Psychology, 29,* 299–304.

Landy, F. J. (1985). *Psychology of work behavior.* Homewood, IL: Dorsey Press.

Latané, B. (1981). The psychology of social impact. *American Psychologist, 36,* 343–356.

Latané, B., & Darley, J. M. (1968). Group inhibition of bystander intervention in emergencies. *Journal of Personality and Social Psychology, 10,* 215–221.

Latané, B., & Darley, J. M. (1970). *The unresponsive bystander: Why doesn't he help?* New York: Appleton-Century-Crofts.

Lawler, E. E. (1973). *Motivation in work organizations.* Monterey, CA: Brooks/Cole.

Leder, G. C. (1990). Gender differences in mathematics. In E. Fennema & G. C. Leder (Eds.), *Mathematics and gender.* New York: Teachers College Press.

Leder, G. C., & Fennema, E. (1990). Gender differences in mathematics: A synthesis. In E. Fennema & G. C. Leder (Eds.), *Mathematics and gender* (pp. 188–200). New York: Teachers College Press.

Lerner, R. M. (1992). *Final solutions.* University Park, PA: The Pennsylvania State University Press.

LeVay, S. (1991). A difference in hypothalamic structure between heterosexual and homosexual men. *Science, 253,* 1034–1036.

Levin, M. (1987). *Feminism and freedom.* New Brunswick, NJ: Transaction.

Levy, L. (Ed.). (1965). *Space: Its impact on man and society.* New York: W. W. Norton.

Lewis, H. (1990). *A question of values.* San Francisco: Harper and Row.

Likert, R. (1932). A technique for the measurement of attitudes. *Archives of Psychology, 140.*

Locke, M. (1992, May 27). Firm yet tasty tomatoes readied for consumers. *The Durango Herald,* p. 3B.

Loftus, E. F., & Palmer, J. C. (1974). Reconstruction of automobile destruction: An example of the interaction between language and memory. *Journal of Verbal Learning and Verbal Behavior, 13,* 585–589.

Lowinger, P., & Dobie, S. (1969). What makes the placebo work? A study of placebo response rate. *Archives of General Psychiatry, 20,* 84–88.

Loye, D. (1983). *The sphinx and the rainbow.* Boston: Shambhala.

Lubinski, D., & Benbow, C. P. (1992). Gender differences in abilities and preferences among the gifted: Implications for the math-science pipeline. *Current Directions in Psychological Science, 1*(2), 61–66.

Lummis, M., & Stevenson, H. W. (1990). Gender differences in beliefs and achievement: A cross-cultural study. *Developmental Psychology, 26*(2), 254–263.

Madigan, C. O., & Elwood, A. (1983). *Brainstorms and thunderbolts: How creative genius works.* New York: Macmillan.

Male superiority. (1980, December 15). *The Chronicle of Higher Education,* p. 14.

Matlin, M. (1988). *Sensation and perception.* Boston: Allyn and Bacon.

Milgram, S. (1963). Behavioral study of obedience. *Journal of Abnormal Social Psychology, 67,* 371–378.

Milgram, S. (1964). Issues in the study of obedience: A reply to Baumrind. *American Psychologist, 21,* 848–852.

Mishkin, M., & Forgays, D. G. (1952). Word recognition as a function of retinal locus. *Journal of Experimental Psychology, 43,* 43–48.

Monen, C. T. W., Van Zijl, P. C. M., Frank, J. A., Lebihan, D., & Becker, E. D. (1990). Functional magnetic resonance imaging in medicine and physiology. *Science, 250,* 53–61.

Moorman, J. E. (1986). The history and the future of the relationship between education and marriage. United States Bureau of the Census.

Morton, J., & Patterson, K. (1980). A new attempt at an interpretation, or, an attempt at a new interpretation. In M. Coltheart, K. Patterson, & J. C. Marshall (Eds.), *Deep dyslexia* (pp. 91–118). London: Routledge & Kegan Paul.

Myers, D. G. (1990). *Exploring psychology.* New York: Worth.

Naisbitt, J. (1984). *Megatrends.* New York: Warner.

Neisser, U. (1982). *Memory observed: Remembering in natural contexts.* San Francisco: W. H. Freeman and Company.

Nordholm, L. A. (1980). Beautiful patients are good patients: Evidence for the physical attractiveness stereotype in first impressions of patients. *Social Science and Medicine, 14A,* 81–83.

O'Neal, E. C. (1991). Violence and aggression. In R. M. Baron, W. G. Graziano, & C. Stangor (Eds.), *Social psychology.* Fort Worth, TX: Holt, Rinehart and Winston.

Orne, M. T. (1962). On the social psychology of the psychological experiment with particular reference to demand characteristics and their implications. *American Psychologist, 17,* 776–783.

Ornstein, R., & Swencionis, C. (1990). *The healing brain.* New York: Guilford Press.

Passmore, J. (1978). *Science and its critics.* New Brunswick, NJ: Rutgers University Press.

Pederson, D. M., & Wheeler, J. (1983). The Muller-Lyer illusion among Navajos. *Journal of Social Psychology, 121,* 3–6.

Perry, N. J. (1988). Saving the schools: How business can help. *Fortune,* 42–56.

Proctor, R. N. (1988). *Racial hygiene.* Cambridge, MA: Harvard University Press.

Prosecutor: Horses were so starved they ate the bark off trees. (1992, October 7). *The Durango Herald,* p. 7.

Radecki, T. (1989). On picking good television and film entertainment. *NCTV News, 10,* 5–7.

Random House (1987). *The Random House dictionary of the English language.* New York: Random House.

Rayner, K., & Pollatsek, A. (1989). *The psychology of reading.* Englewood Cliffs, NJ: Prentice-Hall.

Revkin, A. C. (1989, September). Crack in the cradle. *Discover,* pp. 62–69.

Rich, J. (1975). Effects of children's physical attractiveness on teacher's evaluations. *Journal of Educational Psychology, 67,* 599–609.

Roman, M. B. (1988, April). When good scientists turn bad. *Discover,* pp. 50–58.

Romano, S. T., & Bordieri, J. E. (1989). Physical attractiveness stereotypes and students' perceptions of college professors. *Psychological Reports, 64,* (3, Pt. 2), 1099–1102.

Rosenthal, R. (1986). Media violence, antisocial behavior, and the social consequences of small effects. *Journal of Social Issues, 42*(3), 141–154.

Rosenthal, R., & Jacobson, L. (1968). *Pygmalion in the classroom.* New York: Winston.

Rosenthal, R., & Rosnow, R. L. (1991). *Essentials of behavioral research.* New York: McGraw-Hill.

Rowan, A. (1989, November 29). Scientists must help find ways to give the public a significant role in overseeing animal research. *The Chronicle of Higher Education,* pp. B1–3.

Salholz, E. (1986, June 2). Too late for Prince Charming. *Newsweek,* pp. 54–57, 61.

Schein, J. (1987). The sodium-hypertension connection. *Consumer's Research, 70,* 11–14.

Schreiber, F. R. (1973). *Sybil.* New York: Warner.

Schultz, D. P., & Schultz, S. E. (1987). *A history of modern psychology.* San Diego: Harcourt Brace Jovanovich.

Seitz, V. (1984). Methodology. In M. H. Bornstein & M. E. Lamb (Eds.), *Developmental psychology: An advanced textbook.* Hillsdale, NJ: Lawrence Erlbaum Associates.

Seligman, M. E. P. (1975). *Helplessness: On depression, development, and death.* San Francisco: Freeman.

Shapiro, R. (1991). *The human blueprint: The race to unlock the secrets of our genetic script.* New York: St. Martin's.

Shepard, R. N. (1967). Recognition memory for words, sentences, and pictures. *Journal of Verbal Learning and Verbal Behavior, 6,* 156–163.

Sigall, H., & Ostrove, N. (1975). Beautiful but dangerous: Effects of offender attractiveness and nature of crime on juridic judgment. *Journal of Personality and Social Psychology, 31,* 410–414.

Singer, J. L. (1984). *The human personality.* San Diego, CA: Harcourt Brace Jovanovich.

Singer, J. L., & Singer, D. G. (1986). Family experiences and television viewing as predictors of children's imagination, restlessness, and aggression. *Journal of Social Issues, 42*(3), 107–124.

Sise, C. B. (1991). Scientific misconduct in academia: A survey and analysis of applicable law. *San Diego Law Review, 28,* 401–428.

Smith, P. (1990). *Killing the spirit.* New York: Viking.

Squires, S. (1987, October 27). Modern couples say they're happy together. *Washington Post,* p. 8.

Stafford, R. E. (1972). Hereditary and environmental components of quantitative reasoning. *Review of Educational Research, 42,* 183–201.

Stebbins, L. B., St. Pierre, R. G., Proper, E. C., Anderson, R. B., & Cerva, T. R. (1977). *Education as experimentation: A planned variation model (Vol. IV-A). An evaluation of Project Follow Through.* Cambridge, MA: Abt Associates.

Stern, L. (1992, June 2). Keeping day care healthy. *Woman's Day,* p. 22.

Stevenson, H. W. (1984). Learning to read Chinese. In *Issues in cognition: Proceedings of a joint conference in psychology.* Washington, DC: American Psychological Association.

Strauss, J. B., & Margolis, C. G. (1986). Hypnosis with substance abusers. In E. T. Dowd & J. M. Healy (Eds.), *Case studies in hypnotherapy.* New York: The Guilford Press.

Tavris, C. (1992). *The mismeasure of woman.* New York: Simon and Schuster.

Trimble, J. R. (1975). *Writing with style: Conversations on the art of writing.* Englewood Cliffs, NJ: Prentice-Hall.

United States Bureau of the Census. (1989). *Statistical abstract of the United States* (109th ed.). Washington, DC: United States Department of Commerce.

United States Bureau of the Census. (1992). *Statistical abstract of the United States* (112th ed.). Washington, DC: United States Department of Commerce.

United States Office of Management and Budget. (1992). *Budget of the United States government.* Washington, DC: United States Government Printing Office.

Vallery-Radot, R. (1928). *The life of Pasteur.* New York: Doubleday, Doran, & Company.

Wadden, T. A., & Anderton, C. H. (1982). The clinical use of hypnosis. *Psychological Bulletin, 91,* 215–243.

Wallis, C. (1987, October 12). Back off, buddy. *Time,* pp. 68–73.

Weaver, C. N. (1980). Job satisfaction in the United States in the 1970s. *Journal of Applied Psychology, 65,* 364–367.

White, R. J. (1988, March). The facts about animal research. *Reader's Digest*, pp. 127–132.

Whitehead, A. N. (1925). *Science and the modern world*. New York: Free Press.

Whitman, D. (1993, May 31). The untold story of the LA riot. *U. S. News & World Report*, pp. 35–59.

Wickramasekera, I. (1976). *Biofeedback, behavior therapy, and hypnosis: Potentiating the verbal control of behavior for clinicians*. Chicago: Nelson-Hall.

Wiley, R. (1987, December 14). Which way will you go, Bo? *Sports Illustrated*, p. 26.

Williams, D. A. (1980, December 15). Do males have a math gene? *Newsweek*, p. 73.

Yesavage, J. A., Leirer, V. O., Denari, M., & Hollister, L. E. (1985). Carry-over effects of marijuana intoxication on aircraft pilot performance: A preliminary report. *American Journal of Psychiatry, 142,* 1325–1329.

Yerkes, R. M., & Dodson, J. D. (1908). The relation of strength of stimulus to rapidity of habit formation. *Journal of Comparative and Neurological Psychology, 18,* 459–482.

Acknowledgments

CHAPTER 2

Table 2.3: Reprinted with permission from *Thesaurus of Psychological Index Terms*, 7th ed., 1994. American Psychological Association, all rights reserved.

Table 2.4: Reprinted with permission from *Thesaurus of Psychological Index Terms*, 7th ed., 1994. American Psychological Association, all rights reserved.

Table 2.5: This material is reprinted with the permission of the American Psychological Association, publisher of *Psychological Abstracts*, all rights reserved.

Table 2.6: This material is reprinted with the permission of the American Psychological Association, publisher of *Psychological Abstracts*, all rights reserved.

CHAPTER 3

"Carry Over Effects of Marijuana Intoxication." *American Journal of Psychiatry*, 142:11, 1325-1329, 1985. Copyright 1985, The American Psychiatric Association. Reprinted with permission.

CHAPTER 4

"Keep up the good work, whatever it is, whoever you are." Drawing by Stevenson; © 1988 The New Yorker Magazine, Inc.

CHAPTER 5

"I Like It!" by Chris Britt reprinted with permission of Chris Britt and Copley News Services.

CHAPTER 6

Table 6.2 from E. F. Loftus and J. C. Palmer, "Reconstruction of Automobile Destruction," *Journal of Verbal Learning and Verbal Behavior* 13 (1974): 585–589. Reprinted with permission.

Figure 6.1 from *Psychology of Language* by D. W. Carroll. Copyright © 1986 by Wadsworth, Inc. Original source *Left Brain, Right Brain* by S. P. Springer & G. Deutsch (Freeman, 1981). Reprinted by permission of Brooks/Cole Publishing Company.

Figure 6.2 from Ekman, Levenson, & Friesen 1983, copyright Paul Ekman, 1983. Reprinted with permission from *Science*, Vol. 221, 1983, Page 1209, Ekman et. al.

CHAPTER 7

"It was more of a triple-blind test . . ." reprinted with permission of Sidney Harris.

CHAPTER 10

Figure 10.2 from D. Guerin and D. P. MacKinnon, "An Assessment of the California Child Passenger Restraint Requirement," *American Journal of Public Health*, 1985, Vol. 75, No. 2, p. 143. Reprinted with permission.

CHAPTER 11

"Tuskegee Study" by Lou Erickson reprinted with permission from *The Atlanta Journal* and *The Atlanta Constitution*.

APPENDIX A

"Type Z behavior." Drawing by D. Reilly; © 1987 The New Yorker Magazine, Inc.

"Hostility, Coronary Heart Disease Incidence, and Total Mortality" by Barefoot, Dahlstrom, and Williams in *Psychosomatic Medicine*, Vol. 45, No. 1, 1983, p. 60. Reprinted with permission.

Box A.1 from "Spelling Checker Poem" by P. Mowery, National Association of Secretarial Services. Adapted by permission.

APPENDIX B

Simulated items from the *Wechsler Intelligence Scale for Children* reprinted with permission of The Psychological Corporation.

Name Index

Subject Index